THE ANTHROPOMETRY OF THE AMERICAN NEGRO

THE ANTHROPOMETRY
OF THE AMERICAN NEGRO

BY

MELVILLE J. HERSKOVITS

HASKELL HOUSE PUBLISHERS Ltd.
Publishers of Scarce Scholarly Books
NEW YORK, N. Y. 10012
1970

First Published 1930

HASKELL HOUSE PUBLISHERS LTD.
Publishers of Scarce Scholarly Books
280 LAFAYETTE STREET
NEW YORK, N. Y. 10012

Library of Congress Catalog Card Number: **73-121370**

Standard Book Number 8383-1116-4

Printed in the United States of America

TABLE OF CONTENTS.

Preface	xiii
Corrections and Additions	xv
Chapter I	1
The sample and its composition.	
Chapter II	19
Measurements and Observational Errors.	
1. Stature	21
2. Height Sitting	22
3. Width of Shoulders	22
4. Width of Hips	23
5. Length of Head	23
6. Width of Head	23
7. Cephalic Index	24
8. Height of Head	24
9. Minimum Forehead Width	25
10. Distance Between Inner Corners of Eyes	26
11. Distance Between Outer Corners of Eyes	26
12. Interpupillary Distance	26
13. Height of Nose	26
14. Width of Nose	28
15. Depth of Nose	28
16. Distance from Crease to Tip of Nose, Right Side	28
17. Upper Facial Height	29
18. Total Facial Height	30
19. Bizygomatic Width	31
20. Width of Mouth	32
21. Thickness of Lips (Center)	32
22. Thickness of Lips (Right Side)	32
23. Physiognomic Height of Ear (Ear Length)	33
24. Width of Ear	33
25. Width of Right Hand	34
26. Length of Middle Finger, Right Hand	34
27. Pigmentation, Black (N) Element, Upper Outer Arm	34
28. Pigmentation, Red (R) Element, Upper Outer Arm	37
29. Pigmentation, Yellow (Y) Element, Upper Outer Arm	38
30. Pigmentation, White (W) Element, Upper Outer Arm	38
Chapter III	40
A Description of the American Negro Type.	
1. Stature	43
2. Height Sitting	44
3. Width of Shoulders	46
4. Width of Hips	47
5. Length of Head	49
6. Width of Head	50
7. Cephalic Index	51
8. Height of Head	52
9. Minimum Forehead Width	53
10. Distance Between Inner Corners of Eyes	55
11. Distance Between Outer Corners of Eyes	55
12. Interpupillary Distance	56
13. Height of Nose	57
14. Width of Nose	58

15. Depth of Nose.. 58
  16. Distance from Crease to Tip of Nose, Right Side 59
  17. Upper Facial Height 59
  18. Total Facial Height 61
  19. Bizygomatic Width 62
  20. Width of Mouth... 63
  21. Thickness of Lips, (Center) 64
  22. Thickness of Lips, (Right Side)............................. 64
  23. Physiognomic Height of Ear, (Ear Length) 65
  24. Physiognomic Width of Ear 67
  25. Width of Right Hand 67
  26. Length of Middle Finger Right Hand 68
  27. Pigmentation, Black (N) Element, Upper Outer Arm 69
  28. Pigmentation, Red (R) Element, Upper Outer Arm 71
  29. Pigmentation, Yellow (Y) Element, Upper Outer Arm 72
  30. Pigmentation, White (W) Element, Upper Outer Arm 73

Chapter IV 76
  DIFFERENCES WITHIN THE SERIES.
  1. Stature 80
  2. Height Sitting 81
  3. Length of Head 82
  4. Width of Head... 83
  5. Cephalic Index 83
  6. Height of Head 84
  7. Height of Nose 84
  8. Width of Nose 85
  9. Upper Facial Height 86
  10. Total Facial Height 87
  11. Bizygomatic Width 88
  12. Thickness of Lips 89
  13. Height of Ear.. 89
  14. Width of Ear 90
  15. Pigmentation, Black (N) Element, Upper Outer Arm 90
  16. Pigmentation, Red (R) Element, Upper Outer Arm 92
  17. Pigmentation, Yellow (Y) Element, Upper Outer Arm 93
  18. Pigmentation, White (W) Element, Upper Outer Arm 93

Chapter V 96
  GROWTH CURVES AND SEX DIFFERENCES.

Chapter VI 177
  THE VALIDITY OF THE GENEALOGIES.
  1. Stature 179
  2. Height Sitting 182
  3. Width of Shoulders 184
  4. Width of Hips 185
  5. Length of Head 187
  6. Width of Head.. 187
  7. Cephalic Index 190
  8. Height of Head 192
  9. Minimum Frontal Width 193
  10. Distance Between Inner Corners of Eyes 195
  11. Distance Between Outer Corners of Eyes 196
  12. Interpupillary Distance 198
  13. Height of Nose 198
  14. Width of Nose... 200
  15,-16. Depth of Nose 202
  17. Upper Facial Height 204

Table of Contents

18. Total Facial Height 205
19. Bizygomatic Width 207
20. Width of Mouth.. 209
21. Thickness of Lips, (Center) 211
22. Thickness of Lips, (Right Side) 212
23. Physiognomic Height of Ear, (Ear Length) 214
24. Physiognomic Width of Ear 215
25. Width of Right Hand 216
26. Length of Middle Finger, Right Hand 218
27. Pigmentation, Black (N) Element, Upper Outer Arm 219
28. Pigmentation, Red (R) Element, Upper Outer Arm 222
29. Pigmentation, Yellow (Y) Element, Upper Outer Arm ... 223
30. Pigmentation, White (W) Element, Upper Outer Arm ... 225

Chapter VII 228
   CORRELATION OF TRAITS.

Chapter VIII 234
   RESULTS OF THIS STUDY.

REFERENCES... 281

LIST OF TABLES

I. Number of American Negroes. By Age-Groups for the Several Series of This Study 6
II. Birthplaces of American Negroes, Adult Males and Females ... 7
III. Birthplaces of those Having Indian Ancestry in the Howard University Sample of American Negroes............... 16
IV. Width of Shoulders, Howard University Series 48
V. Width of Hips, Howard University Series 48
VI. Minimum Forehead Width, Howard University Series .. 54
VII. Distance Between Inner Corners of Eyes, Howard University Series 54
VIII. Distance Between Outer Corners of Eyes, Howard University Series 54
IX. Interpupillary Distance, Howard University Series 54
X. Nasal Depth, (sn-tip), Howard University Series 60
XI. Nasal Depth, (cr-tip), Howard University Series....... 60
XII. Upper Facial Height, Howard University Series....... 60
XIII. Total Facial Height, Howard University Series........ 60
XIV. Width of Mouth, Howard University Series........... 66
XV. Thickness of Lips (Right Side), Howard University Series 66
XVI. Width of Hand (Met. lat.-Met. med.), Howard University Series 66
XVII. Length of Middle Finger (Phal. III — Dak. III), Howard University Series 66
XVIII. Stature. Age Norms for Males and Females........... 101
XIX. Distribution of Stature in Age Groups, Males 101
XX. Distribution of Stature in Age Groups, Females 103
XXI. Height Sitting. Age Norms for Males and Females 106
XXII. Distribution of Height Sitting in Age Groups, Males 108
XXIII. Distribution of Height Sitting in Age Groups, Females .. 110
XXIV. Ratio Between Height Sitting and Stature. Age Norms for Males and Females............................. 112
XXV. Length of Head. Age Norms for Males and Females..... 113
XXVI. Distribution of Length of Head in Age Groups, Males... 114
XXVII. Distribution of Length of Head in Age Groups, Females 116
XXVIII. Width of Head. Age Norms for Males and Females 118
XXIX. Distribution of Width of Head in Age Groups, Males.... 120
XXX. Distribution of Width of Head in Age Groups, Females.. 122

XXXI.	Cephalic Index. Age Norms for Males and Females	124
XXXIa.	Cephalic Index. Norms Derived from Three-Year Running Averages, Males and Females	125
XXXII.	Distribution of Cephalic Index in Age Groups, Males	126
XXXIII.	Distribution of Cephalic Index in Age Groups, Females	128
XXXIV.	Distribution of Height of Head, in Age Groups, Males	130
XXXV.	Distribution of Height of Head in Age Groups, Females	132
XXXVI.	Height of Head. Age Norms for Males and Females	134
XXXVII.	Height of Nose. Age Norms for Males and Females	135
XXXVIII.	Distribution of Height of Nose in Age Groups, Males	136
XXXIX.	Distribution of Height of Nose in Age Groups, Females	138
XL.	Distribution of Width of Nose in Age Groups, Males	140
XLI.	Distribution of Width of Nose in Age Groups, Females	142
XLII.	Width of Nose. Age Norms for Males and Females	144
XLIII.	Bizygomatic Width. Age Norms for Males and Females	145
XLIV.	Distribution of Bizygomatic Width in Age Groups, Males	146
XLV.	Distribution of Bizygomatic Width in Age Groups, Females	148
XLVI.	Distribution of Thickness of Lips, in Age Groups, Males	150
XLVII.	Distribution of Thickness of Lips in Age Groups, Females	152
XLVIII.	Thickness of Lips. Age Norms for Males and Females	154
XLIX.	Height of Ear. Age Norms for Males and Females	155
L.	Distribution of Height of Ear in Age Groups, Males	156
LI.	Distribution of Height of Ear in Age Groups, Females	158
LII.	Distribution of Width of Ear in Age Groups, Males	160
LIII.	Distribution of Width of Ear in Age Groups, Females	160
LIV.	Width of Ear. Age Norms for Males and Females	162
LV.	Pigmentation, (Upper Outer Arm) % N. Age Norms for Males and Females	163
LVI.	Distribution of Pigmentation (Upper Outer Arm, Black [N] Element) in Age Groups, Males	164
LVII.	Distribution of Pigmentation (Upper Outer Arm, Black [N] Element) in Age Groups, Females	164
LVIII.	Pigmentation, (Upper Outer Arm) % R. Age Norms for Males and Females	166
LIX.	Pigmentation, (Upper Outer Arm) % Y. Age Norms for Males and Females	167
LX.	Distribution of Pigmentation (Upper Outer Arm, Red [R] Element) in Age Groups, Males	168
LXI.	Distribution of Pigmentation (Upper Outer Arm, Red [R] Element) in Age Groups, Females	168
LXII.	Distribution of Pigmentation (Upper Outer Arm, Yellow [Y] Element) In Age Groups, Males	170
LXIII.	Distribution of Pigmentation (Upper Outer Arm, Yellow [Y] Element) In Age Groups, Females	170
LXIV.	Distribution of Pigmentation, (Upper Outer Arm, White [W] Element) In Age Groups, Males	172
LXV.	Distribution of Pigmentation, (Upper Outer Arm, White [W] Element) in Age Groups, Females	174
LXVI.	Pigmentation, (Upper Outer Arm) % W. Age Norms for Males and Females	176
LXVII.	Distribution of Stature in the Genealogical Classes, Howard University Series	181
LXVIII.	Distribution of Height Sitting in the Genealogical Classes	183
LXIX.	Distribution of Width of Shoulders in the Genealogical Classes	185
LXX.	Distribution of Width of Hips in the Genealogical Classes	186
LXXI.	Distribution of Length of Head in the Genealogical Classes	188
LXXII.	Distribution of Width of Head in the Genealogical Classes	189
LXXIII.	Distribution of Cephalic Index in the Genealogical Classes	191

Table of Contents

LXXIV. Distribution of Height of Head in the Genealogical Classes 192
LXXV. Distribution of Minimum Frontal Width in the Genealogical Classes 194
LXXVI. Distribution of Distance Between Inner Corners of Eyes in the Genealogical Classes........................ 196
LXXVII. Distribution of Distance Between Outer Corners of Eyes in the Genealogical Classes........................ 197
LXXVIII. Distribution of Interpupillary Distance in the Genealogical Classes 199
LXXIX. Distribution of Height of Nose in the Genealogical Classes 200
LXXX. Distribution of Nasal Width (al-al), in the Genealogical Classes 201
LXXXI. Distribution of Nasal Depth (sn-tip), in the Genealogical Classes 203
LXXXII. Distribution of Nasal Depth (cr-tip), in the Genealogical Classes 203
LXXXIII. Distribution of Upper Facial Height in the Genealogical Classes 204
LXXXIV. Distribution of Total Facial Height in the Genealogical Classes 206
LXXXV. Distribution of Bizygomatic Width in the Genealogical Classes 208
LXXXVI. Distribution of Width of Mouth in the Genealogical Classes 210
LXXXVII. Distribution of Thickness of Lips, (center), in the Genealogical Classes 212
LXXXVIII. Distribution of Thickness of Lips, (right), in the Genealogical Classes 213
LXXXIX. Distribution of Physiognomic Height of Ear in the Genealogical Classes 214
XC. Distribution of Physiognomic Width of Ear in the Genealogical Classes 216
XCI. Distribution of Width of Hand (Met. lat. — Met. med.) in the Genealogical Classes 217
XCII. Distribution of Length of Middle Finger (Phal. III — Dak. III) in the Genealogical Classes 218
XCIII. Distribution of Pigmentation, (Upper Outer Arm, Black Element [N]) in the Genealogical Classes 221
XCIV. Distribution of Pigmentation, (Upper Outer Arm, Red Element [R]) in the Genealogical Classes 223
XCV. Distribution of Pigmentation, (Upper Outer Arm, Yellow Element[Y]) in the Genealogical Classes 224
XCVI. Distribution of Pigmentation, (Upper Outer Arm, White Element [W]) in the Genealogical Classes 226
XCVII. Averages and Standard Deviations for Traits Measured in Male and Female American Negro Adults.......... 235
XCVIII. Skin-Color of Husbands and Wives, New York Negroes 246
XCIX. Proportion of Persons in Howard University Series Reporting All or Part of Their Ancestry in the First and Second Ascending Generations. 270
C. Averages and Variabilities of Howard University Genealogical Groups for those of Completely and Incompletely Reported Grandparental Ancestry............ 271
CI. Variabilities of Traits Measured in Adult Male American Negroes, by Classes of Various Degrees of Mixture According to Genealogical Statements.................... 272
CII. Variabilities of Genealogical Classes in Traits Given in Table CI, Reduced to Percentage of Average Weighted Variability of All Classes in Each Trait 274

LIST OF FIGURES

Fig. 1. Forms Used for Collecting Anthropometric Data 11
Fig. 2. Form Used for Collecting Genealogical Information.......... 12
Fig. 2a. Form Used for Collecting Anthropometric and Genealogical Data 13
Fig. 3. Growth in Stature....................................... 105
Fig. 4. Growth in Height Sitting................................ 107
Fig. 5. Growth in the Ratio Between Height Sitting and Stature. 112
Fig. 6. Growth in Length of Head 113
Fig. 7. Growth in Width of Head................................ 119
Fig. 8. Age-Changes in Cephalic Index 124
Fig. 9. Age-Changes in Cephalic Index, Smoothed................. 125
Fig. 10. Growth in Height of Head............................... 134
Fig. 11. Growth in Height of Nose............................... 135
Fig. 12. Growth in Width of Nose................................ 144
Fig. 13. Growth in Bizygomatic Width 145
Fig. 14. Growth in Thickness of Lips............................. 154
Fig. 15. Growth in Height of Ear................................. 155
Fig. 16. Growth in Width of Ear 162
Fig. 17. Age-Charges in Pigmentation, Black (N) Element, Upper Outer Arm... 163
Fig. 18. Age-Changes in Pigmentation, Red (R) Element Upper Outer Arm 166
Fig. 19. Age-Changes in Pigmentation, Yellow (Y) Element, Upper Outer Arm 167
Fig. 20. Age-Changes in Pigmentation, White (W) Element, Upper Outer 176
Fig. 21. Average Skin-Color of Wives (% black) for Increasingly Dark Husbands 245
Fig. 22. Average Skin-Color of Husbands (% black) for Increasingly Dark Wives 248
Fig. 23. Change in Average Values in Height Sitting and Stature, with Various Degrees of Mixed Negro-White Ancestry, Howard University Sample 253
Fig. 24. Change in Average Value in Acromion Width, with Various Degrees of Mixed Negro-White Ancestry, Howard University Sample 254
Fig. 25. Change in Average Values of Width of Hip and Height of Head, with Varying Degrees of Mixed Negro-White Ancestry, Howard University Series 255
Fig. 26. Change in Average Values of Head Length, Head Width, and Cephalic Index, with Varying Degrees of Mixed Negro-White Ancestry, Howard University Series 256
Fig. 27. Change in Average Values of Distance Between Inner and Outer Corners of the Eyes and Interpupillary Distance, with Varying Degrees of Mixed Negro-White Ancestry, Howard University Series 257
Fig. 28. Change in Average Values of Nasal Height and Width and Nasal Depth (sn.-tip), with Varying Degrees of Mixed Negro-White Ancestry, Howard University Series 258
Fig. 29. Change in Average Values of Nasal Depth (cr.-tip) and Height and Width of Ear, with Varying Degrees of Mixed Negro-White Ancestry, Howard University Series 259
Fig. 30. Change in Average Values of Upper and Total Facial Height and Bizygomatic Width, with Varying Degrees of Mixed Negro-White Ancestry, Howard University Series 260
Fig. 31. Change in Average Values of Lip Thickness, Center and Right, and Width of Mouth, with Varying Degrees of Mixed Negro-White Ancestry, Howard University Series 261

Fig. 32. Change in Average Values of Width of Hand, Length of Middle Finger, and Minimum Forehead Width, with Varying Degrees of Mixed Negro-White Ancestry, Howard University Series .. 262
Fig. 33. Change in Average Values of Pigmentation, Black (N), and Red (R) Values, with Varying Degrees of Mixed Negro-White Ancestry, Howard University Series 263
Fig. 34. Change in Average Values of Pigmentation, Yellow (Y) and White (W) Values, with Varying Degrees of Mixed Negro-White Ancestry, Howard University Series 264

PREFACE.

The research on which this work is based was carried on principally by means of assistance granted by two agencies, the National Research Council and the Columbia University Council for Research in the Social Sciences. As Fellow of the former body, I was privileged to spend the period from 1923 to 1926 in gathering the data for this study of racial crossing, and it is a pleasure in this place to express my gratitude to the members of the Board of Fellowships in the Biological Sciences, whose appointments made possible the employment of all my time to this end. At the completion of my term as Fellow, the Columbia University Council, at the instance of Professor Franz Boas, allowed me yet another year's research on the problem, and this period was utilized for working up the material which had been collected. I am indebted both to Dr. Boas and the Council for having given me the opportunity to complete the study on which I had embarked. The Committee on Human Migrations of the National Research Council, at the suggestion of Dr. Clark Wissler, granted funds which assisted me in carrying on research at Howard University, and I wish to thank them for this aid.

The manuscript of this study was completed in August, 1927. Although inevitable delays have prevented its earlier publication nothing has since appeared that would invalidate the conclusions reached in this study. Several studies have been published since that date, the latest, that of Davenport and Steggerda on the Jamaican Negroes, having become available while this work was in press. The latest publications of the Laboratory of Anatomy, Western Reserve University, which are of such great significance for the study of the problem with which I am here concerned, are included in the references, and their publication has made available data which were already in my possession. These had been given to me by Professor T. Wingate Todd, to whom, in addition to thanks for these favors, I owe so great a measure of appreciation for the penetrating advice and criticism which he so readily accorded me.

In the interval between the completion of this study and the publication of the present full report, I availed myself of an opportunity to make generally accessible the results of my research in the form of an abridged statement, published in 1928.[1] The criticisms which were made of the abridged account of this work are answered, I hope, in this complete presentation; such deficiencies as lack of a

---

[1] "The American Negro, a Study in Racial Crossing", A. A. Knopf, Inc., New York.

detailed account of the manner in which the measurements were taken, distribution tables for the various series and for all the traits studied, and detailed comparative tables, were unavoidable in an account intended for the general reader. With the objection raised by several reviewers, that a sample gathered in the main in northern cities is one which cannot be accepted as conclusively representing the character of the entire American Negro population, I am in complete accord. Only further measurements, taken in rural and urban communities in the south, will finally tell whether the sample of this study represents the American Negroes in general, or not. In the text I have indicated why I hold the series of this study to be representative.

There are many persons who have contributed toward the completion of this research, and toward whom I feel deeply indebted. Frau von Luschan and Miss Beatrice Blackwood have both been more than generous in allowing the use of measurements of American Negro series which proved of the greatest value. The cooperation of Dr. Jacob M. Ross, Principal of Public School 89, New York City, and later Principal of Junior High School 139, made possible the measuring of children in these schools; and, when the measuring of entire families was undertaken, his endorsement gave me entrée to their homes. The faculty of Howard University, especially Professors Ernest E. Just and Alain Leroy Locke, placed every facility of their institution at my disposal and by lending the sanction of their approval helped me to measure the students. The aid given me by Mr. Louis E. King, Professor Abram L. Harris, and Miss Zora Hurston, my assistants, in measuring our subjects and in working over the data was of the greatest help to me. I am grateful to Professor E. L. Thorndike, one of the advisors in my research during the term of my Fellowship, for the counsel he gave me. My greatest debt, however, is to Professor Franz Boas. His deep interest in this study, and his numerous suggestions, which enabled me to clear my way at many perplexing points, were a constant stimulus to me in this work. Further, it was he who, when the work was completed, made possible the publication of the manuscript, and who, as editor of the series in which it appears, has given it his time and care.

To the many unnamed subjects who gave their time that I might measure them and obtain their genealogies, I can only repeat what I have written before: "Without the graciousness of the people whose measurements go to make up this study, without their cooperation when they would have been entirely justified in withholding it, my research could not have proceeded."

Evanston, Illinois, MELVILLE J. HERSKOVITS
December 23, 1929.

CORRECTIONS AND ADDITIONS.

p. 15, in text table, column (3), line 4, for 9.3 read 10.0; in column (6), line 2, for 6.9, read 6.7, and line 4, for 5.5 read 4.8.
p. 20, line 14: for "members;", read "members,"
p. 22, line 2 of Section 3: delete the comma following "that"
p. 38, line 4 of Section 30; insert "for" before "the W"
p. 43, The text table should follow the sentence, "Comparison may be made with the following populations;", and the portion which precedes Section 1 should be placed before the portion which now comes after the sentence quoted.
p. 45, line 11 of the text; change "percents" to "percentages"
p. 182, in text table, read NW (I), 45 89.1 ±3.35
p. 183, last line, for "fourth" read "third"
p. 192, in text table, Section 8, read; N (I) 33 132.2 ± 4.67
         NNW 113 134.0 ± 4.65
p. 195, in text table, Section 10, read; N (I) 36 34.2 ± 2.78
         NNW 129 33,4 ± 3.04
line 16 below table, for "third" read "second"
line 17 below table, end sentence at "lowest" and delete the phrase "and between them lies the NNW."
p. 199, in text table, Section 13, read; NW 95 53.7 ± 3.24
p. 201, in text table, Section 14, read; NW(I) 57 39.7 ± 3.75
p. 202, line 4, insert comma after the word "nose"
p. 207, in text table, Section 19, read; NW (I) 57 138.5 ± 5.60
p. 215, in text table, Section 24, read; NW (I) 57 34.0 ± 2.74
         NWW(I) 31 33.4 ± 2.97
p. 224, in text table, Section 29, read; NW 94 12.98 ± 4.07
p. 225, in text table, Section 30, read; NW 94 12.90 ± 8.21
         NWW 30 23.0 ± 10.37
p. 229, line 14, for "absolute" read "average".
p. 240, last line of footnote, for "(XIV)" read "(XIII)"
p. 242, line 25, insert "working" before "wives"
line 27, for "is" read "his"
p. 246, at bottom of Table XCVIII, read; "Wives 67.7 ± 13.56
p. 256, in table for Head Length, read; (W 727 197.3 ± 6.0)
p. 270, Table XCIX, in column headed "Genealogical Class", the phrase "% of total H. U. series" should be changed to "%"
p. 276, line 5 of text, delete the comma at the end of the line.
p. 281, insert as first title under "References" the following: Barnes, Irene (I). The Inheritance of Pigmentation in the American Negro. Human Biology, i (1929), pp. 321—381.
p. 283, line 10, for "Ashant" read "Ashanti".

CHAPTER I.
THE SAMPLE AND ITS COMPOSITION.

1.

The American Negro has long been recognised as constituting one of the major social and economic problems of the United States. Although there have been numerous studies resulting from this recognition, most of these deal with the more imperative phases of the problems of the association of Negroes and Whites. Nor is this strange, for the presence of a considerable body of individuals among a large population from whom they differ in physical type, and particularly in such an easily recognized trait as skin color, must inevitably bring on a body of taboos, repressions, conflicts, and social and economic complications of more or less grave import.

That the scientific world, however, has given little attention to the significance of this population for the study of some of the problems involved in the biological phenomenon of racial mixture, is strange. For in the American Negro population there exists what practically amounts to a laboratory condition for the study of race crossing. Historically, we know of large amounts of mixture which occurred during the period of slavery, between the dominant Whites and their Negro slaves. There is the contact with the aboriginal Indian inhabitants of eastern North America as well, although this, at best, is an uncertain quantity, and is almost invariably completely overlooked in any discussion of the American Negro. To make these potential data even more attractive for the study of such a problem, we have these crossed individuals present in millions, not small numbers such as Professor Eugen Fischer found when he travelled to South Africa, seeking to study just this phenomenon of racial mixture among the Bastards of that country. The crossing in this country has been on such a vast scale that the resulting offspring may be studied with the assurance of sufficient numbers to validate such statistical results as may be obtained from the data, once they have been collected.

In the light of these well known facts, it is surprising, as I have said, that the physical aspect of the effects of the presence of the Negro in the dominant White population, and the crossing that has occurred between them, has been so much neglected. Some minor studies have been made, of course,[1] but aside from these there is only the work of Todd and his associates on the cadavera and

---

[1] Hrdlička's bibliography (V), which is quite complete, makes the point admirably.

skeletal material available in the Hamann Museum of Western Reserve University, although the Civil and World Wars occasioned the collection of data through measurements made on soldiers and recruits, Negro as well as White.

These studies suffer in two ways. Either the samples which have been utilized have been too small to allow of our being sure that the results are other than chance ones, caused by the utilisation of material however unconsciously selected, or the number of measurements which have been taken have been too few for adequate description. Thus, the work of Todd and his associates is remarkable for its thoroughness, and is of the highest importance where comparison between American Negroes and American Whites is concerned.[1] But the number of cases is relatively small, about 100, and therefore, unless confirmatory evidence is available, such a sample cannot be considered as representative of the American Negro. The army series measured during the World War, on the other hand, was very large. It contained over 6000 Negroes, who were measured by Davenport and Love and their assistants. However, in this case the measurements were primarily made for other than scientific purposes, those necessary to construct clothing sizes. This was the imperative need of the moment, and therefore relatively few measurements were obtained.

Similarly, in these studies the amount of racial mixture represented by the individuals who were measured was unknown. Thus, in the army, it was obviously impossible to inquire into the amount of crossing which had occurred in the ancestry of each man measured, while the fact that Todd's data are from cadavera or consist of skeletal measurements speaks for itself on this point. Yet the statement that the American Negro represents vast amounts of crossing does not have to be proved to the generality of the people living in this country. Indeed, the use of the word "Negro" to describe him is without justification from a biological point of view. It is this very fact of mixture, particularly the amount of mixture represented in the American Negro population and various portions of it, that has constituted a stumbling-block in the study of this group from other than sociological and economic points of view. And to all this there is added another difficulty, not generally recognized, that not only is there considerable variation in the traits of the Europeans who compose the ancestry on the White side, but that there are as great differences between the various types of African Negroes who were brought to this country, and who became the forefathers of the present colored population.

In the present study the attempt has been made to investigate the physical form of the American Negro with the points mentioned

---

[1] Professor Todd has recently made keen and extended comment on "the influence of numbers," defending the representativeness of his sample. Todd and Lindala (I), pp. 46—49.

above in mind. In the first place, I have tried to consider the problem from the general point of view of the variability of this population as representing a vast experiment in racial crossing; to see whether or not the demands made by current theories as to the results of racial crossing, in terms of variability, may or may not be met by this mixed group. With this, and bearing on the second problem involved, I have tried to inquire into the extent to which the groups to be studied actually represent mixture, whether this crossing is continuing today, and the forms which the physical development of the sub-groups of varying degrees of mixture within the Negro population have taken. As this discussion progresses it will be seen that such measurements were taken as seemed to promise enlightenment in the consideration of the particular problem in hand, the study of Negro-White crossing. That is, I have attempted to study the behavior of such traits as seemed, from comparison of series of measurements already available, to be significantly different between Europeans and Negroes. Such traits would naturally include skin-color, nose width and lip thickness, but they also include others such as the width of the face, height sitting and stature, the length of the fingers, ear measurements, and the like. The outstanding omission in this list is the form of the hair, which could not be considered in this study mainly because the generous use of ointments and other devices to straighten the hair is exceedingly widespread, and would vitiate any observations of this nature which might have been made.

The other problem to be attacked is the one concerning which there are the fewest data available (if there be any at all), — that of the genealogical background of the American Negro population. That we are almost in complete ignorance with regard to this is not surprising. There is, in the first place, the current belief which is very strong even in scientific circles,[1] that the value of genealogical statements on the part of Negroes is very small; that, in short, the American Negro knows very little about his ancestry and cares less. It cannot be denied that genealogical material, whether given by Negroes or Whites, is of uncertain value and must be handled with the greatest care. Yet there is no other kind of information available concerning descent, as far as the American Negro is concerned. In times of slavery, there were no official statistical records kept of the births of the Negro slaves, very naturally, while the situation is little better in this regard at the present time in those States in which most American Negroes live. In the second place, even though the desirability of gathering such data be

---

[1] As, for example, Professor Bean's statement regarding this point in his review of my book "The American Negro", (Bean III, p. 219) in which he states that "a life of over fifty years in close association with the southern Negro... lead(s) me to doubt that much can be gained from genealogies of Negroes".

admitted, and the current supposition as to their value be disregarded until proved, the difficulties in the way of obtaining such information from American Negroes are enormous. There is a natural suspicion directed toward the White inquirer who seeks intimate personal information of this sort, and unless a technique is perfected whereby the confidence of the persons whose genealogies are desired can be obtained, the information may be wholly withheld, or, what is worse, the inquiries may be falsely answered. I attempted to guard against this in several ways. First, during the earlier part of this research, no person was approached with the request that he permit himself to be measured (the genealogies were obtained from the persons measured, and at the time of measurement) to whom I was not vouched for by some Negro whom he knew and of whose integrity he could have no doubt. Later, when measurements of families in Harlem were taken, there was the advantage of having measured the children in the schools with the resulting confidence that went with their recognition of me when I approached their parents. In other cases, my assistants were known personally to the families whose measurements they took. There was, further, no element of compulsion. Any question the subject might ask regarding the objects and the desirability of the study were met as fully as possible, and there was no undue urging in the event of continued objections. Finally, every subject was assured that, as far as individual genealogies were concerned, there would be the most complete confidence maintained, and that publication of the results would be by number only, thus effectively preventing any identification of the individuals measured.

2.

The sample which is employed in this study is composed of American Negroes of both sexes and of all ages, from one year to adulthood. This last I have arbitrarily set, for the purpose in hand, as being 20 years of age and upwards, for both sexes. In number, the series totals 5,659 individuals, of whom 3,378 are males and 2,281 are females. It is composed of a number of series, which were measured by different individuals and at different times. These, in chronological order, are as follows. First, there is a series measured by Professor Felix von Luschan, in 1915, in St. Louis, Mo., Greenville, Miss., New Orleans, La., Memphis, Tenn., Tuskegee, Ala., and Hampton, Va. Next is one composed of school children, measured by myself in Harlem (New York City) during the winter of 1923—1924; and this is followed by a third series, also measured by myself, composed in the main of adult males, a few of whom were measured in Harlem, but most of whom were measured at Howard University, in Washington, D. C. This series will be referred to as the "Howard University series". It was studied during the winter and spring of 1925. and, since I myself gathered genealogies from the individuals who comprise it, and exercised particular care in doing so, it is the one which has been selected for intensive genealogical analysis to investigate the validity of Negro genealogies by checking them with anthropometric data gathered at the same time.[1]

The fourth series is composed of three sub-series, which were all measured by Miss Beatrice Blackwood at Fisk University and the Tennessee Agricultural and Industrial State Normal College, both at Nashville, Tenn., and at Tuskegee Institute, Tuskegee, Ala., during the spring and early summer of 1925. Next was measured a series in New York City during the winter of 1925—1926, using a different school than the one which served as a base of operations in 1923—1924, although both schools represent, in the main, the same Harlem population. The work was done by an assistant, Mr. Louis King, and myself, and we measured a large number of families, parents and children, from the adult members of which genealogies were obtained. This series comprises males and females of all ages, and the families were those of the children who had been measured in school. The sixth series was measured by Mr. King in the rural districts of West Virginia. Like the one measured in Harlem, it comprises individuals of both sexes and all ages, in family groups, the genealogical data being obtained from the adults. It was measured during the summer of 1926. In the same summer the final series was measured by another assistant, Miss Zora Hurston, among the well-to-do and professional portion of the population of the Harlem district of New York City. Here again, families were sought and obtained, and therefore this series, like the others immediately preceding it, includes both sexes and all ages. The ages of the persons composing the several series, as well as the number of cases for each age-sex group for the series as a whole, may be seen in Table I.

Numerically the series is a large one, but the element of possible selection in a series even the size of this must be considered before its validity as representing the general American Negro population may be assumed. I have, therefore, tabulated the places of birth of the adults (persons of 20 years of age and upwards) for these series, with the exception of the three measured by Miss Blackwood, for which these data were not available when the tabulation was made. Such a distribution should give an excellent idea of the extent to which this series may be called representative. The details are given in Table II. Considering the totals, it will be seen that not only the states where Negroes would be expected to have been born are heavily represented, but that there is an adequate series from the West Indian islands as well. This is not really surprising, as there has been a considerable migration to the United States, particularly to New York City, from these islands of the Carribean Sea during

---
[1] See Chapter VI.

Table I
Number of American Negroes, by Age-Groups for the Several Series of this Study

3,378 Males

Age	Von Luschan (1915)	Harlem 1923—4 (MJH)	Howard Univ. 1925	Harlem 1926 (MJH)	Harlem 1926 (King)	Harlem Selec. (Hurston)	West Va. (King)	Total
1	—	—	—	4	—	4	3	11
2	1	—	—	9	3	6	5	24
3	1	—	—	5	8	4	13	31
4	3	—	—	15	9	8	19	54
5	5	22	—	9	7	3	7	53
6	8	55	—	50	16	4	7	140
7	1	108	—	49	11	3	7	179
8	5	127	—	23	12	3	9	179
9	2	131	—	17	7	—	10	167
10	4	137	—	7	14	1	8	171
11	3	141	—	16	33	1	13	207
12	2	127	—	30	61	1	13	234
13	4	141	—	45	94	—	18	302
14	9	117	—	27	88	2	15	258
15	2	81	—	18	86	2	3	192
16	5	30	1	6	18	5	3	68
17	8	12	4	5	8	4	6	47
18	6	3	19	3	22	3	2	38
19	5	—	40	—	5	8	3	61
Adult	54	—	475	125	105	106	97	962

2,281 Females

Age	Von Luschan (1915)	Harlem 1923—4 (MJH)	Howard Univ. 1925	Harlem 1926 (MJH)	Harlem 1926 (King)	Harlem Selec. (Hurston)	West Va. (King)	Total
1	1	—	—[1]	1	—	2	1	5
2	1	—	—	7	1	4	8	21
3	5	—	—	10	9	2	10	36
4	—	—	—	8	3	3	9	23
5	2	22	—	10	7	6	15	62
6	3	14	—	29	9	5	18	78
7	2	36	—	27	10	3	19	97
8	2	26	—	24	13	—	14	79
9	4	6	—	11	9	2	23	55
10	8	8	—	9	11	2	16	54
11	3	5	—	10	7	4	23	52
12	7	1	1	15	12	2	26	64
13	11	—	5	4	7	6	11	44
14	5	—	15	5	7	1	17	50
15	12	—	29	6	7	3	12	69
16	11	—	67	7	7	6	6	104
17	11	—	88	5	7	7	7	125
18	11	—	148	4	4	3	6	176
19	14	—	133	1	3	2	3	156
Adult	108	—	170	197	131	131	133	931

[1] Blackwood, 1925.

The Sample and Its Composition

Table II
Birthplaces of American Negroes
Adult Males and Females

Birthplace	Harlem '26	Harlem Selected	West Va.	Howard Univ.	Von Luschan	Total
Alabama	3	4	—	18	5	30
Arkansas	—	—	—	9	1	10
California	—	—	—	1	—	1
Connecticut	4	—	—	8	—	12
Delaware	2	—	—	2	—	4
Dist. of Columbia	9	12	—	47	—	68
Florida	14	8	—	12	1	35
Georgia	42	17	2	29	—	90
Illinois	1	3	—	3	1	8
Indiana	—	—	—	4	—	4
Kansas	—	—	—	6	—	6
Kentucky	1	3	—	9	4	17
Louisiana	—	2	—	17	13	32
Maryland	9	15	4	33	4	65
Massachusetts	2	2	—	7	—	11
Michigan	—	2	—	2	—	4
Mississippi	2	—	—	10	28	40
Missouri	—	1	—	3	11	15
Nebraska	—	—	—	1	—	1
New Jersey	4	1	—	20	—	25
New York	39	45	1	18	—	103
North Carolina	30	17	1	47	1	96
North Dakota	—	—	—	1	—	1
Ohio	—	3	—	12	3	18
Oklahoma	—	—	—	2	—	2
Pennsylvania	9	14	1	29	3	56
Rhode Island	—	1	—	6	—	7
South Carolina	54	25	2	25	1	107
Tennessee	2	7	1	9	18	37
Texas	2	1	—	23	3	29
Virginia	83	26	61	63	26	259
Washington	—	—	—	1	—	1
West Virginia	5	—	158	4	—	167
Wisconsin	—	1	—	—	—	1
British West Indies	235	15	1	37	—	288
French W. I.	4	—	—	—	—	4
Dutch W. I.	1	—	—	—	—	1
Virgin Islands	26	—	—	—	—	26
Porto Rico	2	—	—	—	—	2
Haiti	1	—	—	—	—	1
Cuba	—	4	—	—	1	5
British Guiana	10	1	—	9	—	20
Bahama Islands	6	—	—	—	—	6
Panama	5	—	—	—	—	5
Bermuda	4	—	—	—	—	4
Others	—	4	—	11	—	15

the past few years, and it was actually found that about fifty per cent of the persons measured in New York were West Indians. As far as adults are concerned, this gives us a series of West Indian Negroes that is comparable to the American-born Negro series from Harlem. The children of these West Indians have been included, age for age, with the American-born children of the same series, whether or not they were born in the United States.

It will be seen that the states which are drawn on most heavily are Georgia, Maryland, New York, North Carolina, South Carolina, Virginia, and West Virginia. The preponderance of the last state is explained by the fact that the second series measured by King was a rural community centering mainly on the northwestern border of West Virginia, although it overlapped into Virginia, which has by far the greatest numbers of individuals represented for any one state. A part of those from Virginia are accounted for by King's series mentioned. Another portion is due to the location of Howard University, which is in the District of Columbia in close proximity to Virginia. But the Harlem series also draws heavily from that state, as well as from all the eastern group of the southern states. This seems to throw an interesting light on one aspect of the phenomenon of Negro migration which has already been observed; namely, that the lines of migration tend to go north and south, and that there is comparatively little movement from the western group of southern states to the eastern ones of the north. It is not strange then that we find few persons who were born in Texas living in New York City, as there would probably be found relatively few Georgians in the Chicago Negro community. At the same time, the sample seems to be an adequate geographical one which may be said to represent the American Negro population. And it must be noted that I include in this term, and shall include when "American Negro" is used in the rest of this work, the West Indian Negroes who have migrated to this country.

At the same time, tests other than geographical ones may be made as to the extent to which this sample may be regarded as representative of the American Negro population in general. During the World War, Davenport and Love[1] made an anthropometric study of recruits for the purpose of ascertaining and standardizing clothing measurements. In the course of this work, data from some 6,000 Negroes were obtained. These men were measured mainly in cantonments in the south, and, therefore, certainly number among them a majority of men who had come from all parts of the south. These would not be of the same type as the Negroes who had migrated to the north, or who had been born there, if there is any difference in type present. This series is the largest one of American Negroes from which anthropometric

---

[1] Davenport and Love, (I).

data have been reported, and it is of interest to see to what extent differences between the three measurements common to the two series are significant. For it is of importance to ascertain whether the average differences between these series of Davenport and Love and mine are real ones or whether statistical comparison indicates that they result from the fact that both series are samples of the larger population of which they form parts.

In this comparison the total number of adult males are used to represent the series obtained in the course of this study; though for hip width, the third trait for which comparison may be made, the Howard University series alone is employed.

Trait	Negro Troops Davenport and Love			Male Adults of Present Series		
	No.	Average	Sigma	No.	Average	Sigma
Stature (cm.)	6,454	172.0	± 6.9	887	170.5	± 6.4
Ht. Sitting (cm.)	6,433	87.35	± 3.5	840	87.7	± 3.5
Hip Width (mm.)	6,354	284.2	± 23.5	476	285.1	± 18.3

Trait	Difference between Averages	Error of Difference
Stature (cm)	1.51	± .25
Ht. Sitting (cm.)	.32	± .13
Hip Width (mm.)	.9	± .89

These three traits do not indicate any important difference between the two series, for the difference in stature may easily be understood as due to environmental conditions, to which stature is especially responsive. The difference between the food and physical surroundings and type of exercise of the Negro, generally speaking, in the usual run of civilian life, and that which prevailed in the army, need not be dwelt on here. But one can very plausibly point to this fact and to that of the rejection of short individuals as an explanation of the average difference in stature between the two series.

The means for the series of this study may also be compared with those for the series of 100 adult male cadavera of the Western Reserve collection[1], for various measurements which both series have in common. These data,[2] represent averages and variabilities of pauper cadavera from the Cleveland, Ohio, hospitals, and may or may not represent an economic selection. Whether or not they do, a statistical comparison of the two series should be of value, even though there can be little doubt that this series is not as representative of the American Negro as the army series. For the traits of hand breadth and interpupillary distance, the Howard University series alone is used, but for all the other traits the entire series of male adults measured in the course of this study is employed.

[1] Referred to in the following tables as W. R. U.
[2] Todd and Lindala, (I).

Trait	100 W. R. U. Average	Sigma	Present Series Average	Sigma	Difference between Averages	Error of Diff.
Stature (cm.)	174.4	± 6.1	170.49	± 6.4	− 3.91	± .64
Ht. Sitting (cm.)	88.6	± 3.2	87.67	± 3.5	− .93	± .34
Head Length (mm.)	192.5	± 6.1	196.52	± 6.51	+ 4.02	± .64
Facial Width (mm.)	139.0	± 6.1	139.17	± 5.92	+ .17	± .64
Hand Width (mm.)	80.7	± 4.6	85.75	± 4.25	+ 5.05	± .49
Nose Width (mm.)	42.4	± 3.7	40.92	± 3.99	− 1.48	± .39
Lip Thickness (mm.)	21.0	± 4.9	21.24	± 4.5	+ .24	± .51
Interpupillary Dist. (mm.)	68.4	± 4.4	66.4	± 3.8	− 2.00	± .45

In this comparison, the differences between the means are less than three times their error (that is, of doubtful significance) in three out of the eight traits compared, height sitting, facial width and lip thickness, while in a fourth the difference is less than four times its error. Such a result of comparing the two series is not surprising. Even if the large numbers of Negroes who live in the northern states had weighted the series used in this study so as to make it one not representative of the Negro population of the country as a whole, it would not necessarily be the same in bodily form as a series of Negro paupers from a northern city on whom the same selective influence had presumably also been operative. Still, the fact that the army series and the one to be used in this study are so closely alike is the best proof, aside from the geographical data given above, and the inter-comparison of the component series for the traits measured, which will be given later in this work,[1] that we are actually dealing with a series that is representative of the American Negro.

3.

Before proceeding to the actual presentation of the anthropometric data and the results obtained from their consideration, it may be well, at this point, to consider the genealogical results of a classification of this type of material gathered from the Negroes who were measured. The presentation of the anthropometric differences between classes of differing genealogical composition will be undertaken in Chapter VI, and, I believe, will establish the general validity of the genealogies and methodologically justify their utilisation. A knowledge, however, of the ancestral racial components of the series as a whole, will enable us to understand the distributions which will be presented later better than if a group as mixed racially as this one were thought of merely as "Negro". The procedure in classifying the genealogies has been as follows: it was felt that a flexible classification would be most in accord with the genealogical information, and that one of this sort would yield

---

[1] In Chapter V.

the most fertile results. This is in view of the fact that persons measured who did not know some of their ancestry, were encouraged to state "I do not know", rather than to guess or to give some vague tradition which they might have overheard. It is needless to say that there was no suggestion of any kind employed in collecting the genealogies.

In the case of the New York City and West Virginia adults who were measured, each was asked whether the parents and grandparents were all Negro, all White, or mixed; in that of the students at Howard University, the information was collected on questionnaire blanks, the student writing out his answers by himself immediately after he had been measured. Before he left me, he handed the blank to me for inspection and further questioning, if there were doubtful points or inconsistencies in his replies. The genealogical and anthropometric forms on which data were collected at Howard University are given below and on p. 12; the form employed in New York City and West Virginia on p. 13. Those used by Professor von Luschan and Miss Blackwood included more traits than were measured in my research, and did not have equally extended genealogical features. I have utilized such measurements from their data as coincide with my own.

Figure 1
Form Used for Collecting Anthropometric Data, Howard University and New York City (1923—24).

Form H 1   No. ....
NAME
Address   Class
Length of Head   Width of Head   Index
Height of Nose   Width of Nose:
                                             al-al
                                             sp-tip
                                             cr-tip
Thickness of Lips: Width of Mouth
                  center
                  right
Height of Face   Bizygomatic Width
                  n-a
                  n-gn
Height of Ear   Width of Ear
Metacarpale laterale to M. mediale Phal. III to Dak. III
Skin-color:
          Inner Upper Arm   N   R   Y   W

          Outer Upper Arm   N   R   Y   W
Minimum Width of Forehead   Angle of Eyes
Distance between Inner Corners of Eyes   Outer
                                   Interpupillary Distance
Height of Head
Acromial Width   Width of Hip
Weight   Height   Height sitting
Date ....

Figure 2
Form Used for Collecting Genealogical Information (Howard University).

Form H 2   No. ....
GENEALOGICAL INFORMATION

Note: This information is strictly confidential. No reference will be made to it in any way other than by number.

By *Negro* is meant *all* Negro, that is, African or descent from African, with *no* mixture of White or Indian blood.

By *Mixed* is meant mixed Negro and White, — that is, neither all White nor all Negro.

By *White* is meant *all* White, without any mixture of Negro blood.

If you have Indian blood, indicate this in the proper place by the initial (I).

Name	Address		Class
Date of birth	Place of birth		
Are you Mixed?	Negro?		White?

What is your father's name?
When was he born?   Where?
Is he Mixed?   Negro?   White?

What is your mother's name?
When was she born?   Where?
Is she Mixed?   Negro?   White?

What was your father's father's name?
Where was he born?
Was he Mixed?   Negro?   White?

What was your father's mother's name?
Where was she born?
Was she Mixed?   Negro?   White?

What was your mother's father's name?
Where was he born?
Was he Mixed?   Negro?   White?

What was your mother's mother's name?
Where was she born?
Was she Mixed?   Negro?   White?

If you know the names and racial make-up of ancestors farther back than your grandparents, will you give this information about them on the back of this sheet?

(Anthro. data ....)

The element of lack of knowledge of certain ancestors, while it contributed to the difficulty of the problem, was, at the same time, an earnest of the willingness of the subjects to co-operate in the investigation. It is also felt that it did not detract materially from the validity of the groupings (as will be seen when the anthropometric comparisons between the traits of these groups are given later). The genealogical classifications represent, therefore, the

The Sample and Its Composition

Figure 2 a
Form Used for Collecting Anthropometric and Genealogical Data,
New York City (1926), and West Virginia

```
Form F 1              M      F              No. ..........
Name                                         Family No ..........
Address                             Place of Birth
Head Length     Width               Head Height                CI
Nose Height     Face ht., n-a            Ear Height
    Width              n-gn                  Width
                Bizygomatic Width        Lip Thickness
Pigmentation —        N    R    Y    W
Height                              Height sitting

Date ...........      Date of Birth ..........    Age ..........
Father
Mother of ..........................      Child of .............
FF  n  m  w           MF  n  m  w           F  n  m  w
FM  n  m  w           MM  n  m  w           M  n  m  w
(Bracket estimations, — place reports in parentheses.)
```

proportions of *known* Negro, White, and Indian ancestry. The amount of Indian blood present is surprising, as the table of percentages belonging to the various genealogical classes to be given shortly shows. The social prestige among the Negroes of those who can claim an Indian ancestor may have unduly increased the percentage of individuals claiming partial Indian ancestry; but this was guarded against as far as possible, for no mention of "Indian" was made where actual checking or writing had to be done. In New York, the subject had to bring up the matter himself, while at Howard the symbol for Indian had to be written in. This constitutes a proceeding which inertia makes somewhat more difficult than merely checking the symbols for Negro, White, and Mixed, which were provided on the blank. The classes, as has been said, are cast in flexible lines. Fundamentally, they are four: unmixed Negro (N), more Negro than White (NNW), about the same amount of Negro and White ancestry (NW), and more White than Negro (NWW). To these four classes were added four more, the same as the above, only with the inclusion of Indian ancestry. The symbols for these classes are N(I), NNW (I), NW (I), and NWW (I), and these, with the four given above, will be used to denote the genealogical classes from this point onward in this work.

The following cases will give an idea of how individuals were placed in the several classes:

    (H 1)   Mother's mother: mixed Negro-White
              Mother's father: mixed Negro-Indian
              Father's mother: Negro
              Father's father: not known

              Mother: Mixed Negro-Indian-White
              Father: Negro

This individual was classed as more Negro than White, with Indian: NNW(I).

(H259) Mother's mother: mixed Negro-White
Mother's father: mixed Negro-White
Father's mother: mixed Negro-White
Father's father: not known

Mother: mixed Negro-White
Father: mixed Negro-White

This man was placed in the classification of about the same amount of Negro and White: NW.

(H279) Mother's mother: mixed Negro-White
Mother's father: White
Father's mother: mixed Negro-White
Father's father: mixed Negro-White

Mother: mixed Negro-White
Father: mixed Negro-White

The classification made here was more White than Negro: NWW.

(H378) Mother's mother: not known
Mother's father: mixed Negro-White
Father's mother: not known
Father's father: Negro

Mother: mixed Negro-White
Father: Negro

Although the lacunae in this case are more extensive than was usually the case, on the basis of the information that was available this man was classified as more Negro than White, NNW.

(NY45) Mother's mother: mixed Negro-White
(father White, mother Negro)
Mother's father: mixed Negro-White
(father White, mother Negro)
Father's mother: mixed Negro-Indian-White
Father's father: mixed Negro-Indian-White

Mother: mixed Negro-White
Father: mixed Negro-Indian-White

Therefore the class to which the possessor of this genealogy belongs is that of about the same amount of Negro and White ancestry, with Indian, NW(I).

While the objection may undoubtedly be raised with some justice that the unknown portion of the ancestry of any person might have made an appreciable difference in his classification, the lines on which these classes have been drawn were purposely set with sufficient lack of rigidity so that this error would be minimized. And at best, there are bound to be considerable gaps in working with genealogical data, due to the lack of information most persons have regarding their ancestry. Therefore it has been felt that all possible precautions were taken in making the classifications on the basis of the known amounts of racial types in the ancestry of the persons measured. Finally, admitting that there are lacunae in many of the genealogies, in the light of current concepts of the extent to which the American Negro knows his ancestry, the remarkable thing is that the information is as complete as it is. There are some cases in which information, apparently quite definite (including, in the cases of some of the men measured at Howard University, names and places of birth), was given concerning ancestors of the fourth and even of the fifth generation, although this takes one so far back into the slavery period that it is not surprising that such statements number as few as they do.

The classifications having been made, the following ratios for the adults of the total series who belong to the various classes are found:

(1)	(2) Number	(3) %	(4)	(5) Number	(6) %	(7) (2) + (5) Number	(8) (3) + (6) %	% of (7) with Indian ancestry
N	342	22.0	N(I)	97	6.3	439	28.3	22.1
NNW	384	24.8	NNW(I)	106	6.9	490	31.7	21.5
NW	260	16.7	NW(I)	133	8.5	393	25.2	33.8
NWW	154	9.3	NWW(I)	75	5.5	229	14.8	32.7
Total	1140			411		1551	100.0	26.5

In the Howard series alone the percentage of those with Indian ancestry was found to be 33%.

These results are in startling disagreement with accepted opinion as to the amount of racial mixture represented in the American Negro population. In the first place, the proportion of individuals whose genealogies are represented in the table who ascribe Indian ancestry to themselves is far higher than has generally been thought to be the case, for in no consideration of the history of the Negro in America has the fact of his mixing with the American Indian been touched upon, to my knowledge. As stated before, among the American Negroes, Indian ancestry has distinct prestige value, and it may therefore be conceded that the proportion of those claiming it is somewhat higher than is actually the case, although even this may not be so in view of the precautions taken with regard to this.

In any event, the extent to which we find individuals of different amounts of Negro-White ancestry claiming mixture with Indians is of interest, and may throw some light on the matter. The last column of the table given on p. 15 shows that there seem to be more

Table III
Birthplaces of those having Indian Ancestry in the Sample of American Negroes measured at Howard University, and Percentages of Total by States

State	No.	% of those having Indian ancestry Total number
Alabama	7	4.0
Arkansas	7	4.0
Connecticut	6	3.4
Delaware	1	0.6
Florida	2	1.1
Georgia	11	6.25
Illinois	1	0.6
Indiana	3	1.7
Kansas	2	1.1
Kentucky	2	1.1
Louisiana	5	2.8
Maryland	7	4.0
Massachusetts	2	1.1
Michigan	1	0.6
Mississippi	4	2.3
Nebraska	1	0.6
New Jersey	7	4.0
New York	5	2.8
North Carolina	18	10.2
North Dakota	1	0.6
Ohio	3	1.7
Oklahoma	1	0.6
Pennsylvania	8	4.55
Rhode Island	3	1.7
South Carolina	10	5.7
Tennessee	4	2.3
Texas	8	4.55
Virginia	23	13.1
Washington	1	0.6
District of Columbia	13	7.4
British West Indies	5	2.8
British Guiana, Nicaragua, Panama, and Virgin Islands	1 each	2.4
	176	

The Sample and Its Composition

Combined by geographical groups the percentages of the total number claiming Indian blood are:

	Total No.	No. having Indian Ancestry	of those having Indian Ancestry %
New England Division (Conn., Mass., R. I.)	21	11	53
Middle Atlantic Division (N. Y., N. J., Penna.)	67	20	30
North Central Division (Ill., Ind., Kan., Mich., Neb., N. Dak., Ohio)	29	12	42
South Atlantic Division (Del., Fla., Ga., Md., N. Car., S. Car., Va., D. C.)..	258	75	26
South Central Division (Ala., Ark., Ky., La., Miss., Okla., Tenn., Texas).....	97	44	45
Miscellaneous	58	10	18
Total	530	172	33

individuals who claim Indian ancestry in the classes where there are larger amounts of White mixture in the ancestry. This would not be unexpected, were the statements actually those of fact, since mixture with the Indians, for those of lighter color and therefore presumably of mixed Negro-White racial composition, would probably have been easier than for those without mixture. As a further check, the places of birth of those of the Howard University sample who claimed Indian ancestry have been tabulated. They are given in Table III. It may be seen there that the states where such mixture with Indians might be expected to have occurred are, in general, best represented. Although I attempted to obtain the names of the actual tribes from which the Indian ancestors were supposed to have come, this was difficult, and I did not often succeed, as primary crossing with the Indians is a matter of several generations ago.

The percentage of those who have White ancestry is perhaps the most interesting point in the table of the genealogical classes given above. This is particularly true in view of the results of the enumerations of the United States Census Bureau, which, although not ordinarily accepted at their face value, are generally taken as the best available indication of the amount of crossing represented in the American Negro population. The Census returns are given in terms of "Black" and "mulatto", a distinction, which although based on a color difference of some validity, cannot be used acceptably for the classification of individual Negroes. The connotation of these terms, if not, indeed, their accepted meaning, is one denoting a more or less definite amount of racial mixture. Quite aside from the complete disregard of the factor of partial Indian descent, the genealogical percentages given above show how useless any classification of this type is for practical purposes. But that it is used again and again may be seen from any brief survey of the literature of the Negro[1], particularly in sociological and psychological studies. The Census figures, for the years for which such classification has been made, are as follows:

Year	Total Negro	Black	Mulatto	% Black	% Mulatto
1920	10,463,131	8,802,577	1,660,554	84.1	15.9
1910	9,827,763	7,777,077	2,050,686	79.1	20.9
1890	7,488,676	6,337,980	1,132,060	84.8	15.2
1870	4,880,009	4,295,960	584,049	88.0	12.0
1860	4,441,830	3,853,467	588,363	86.8	13.2
1850	3,683,808	3,233,057	405,751	88.8	11.2

This percentage for unmixed Negro ("black" expressly means "all full-blooded Negroes"[2]) is far too high. The combined percentages for the classes where the greatest amount of black pigmentation would be expected, N, N(I), NNW, and NNW(I), give us 60.4% of the individuals measured in this study from whom genealogies were obtained, a figure much lower than that of the latest census. It may even be admitted that the 20% pure Negro obtained from the genealogical statements may be too low for the whole country because of a possible social or local selection, although all the evidence is against such selection having been operative in the selection of the data of this study. Still it need only be pointed out that the four dark groups represent considerable mixture to demonstrate how fallacious any classification of Negro into "pure" and "mixed" must be, when it is made on the basis of a cursory glance at the skin by untrained observers.

---

[1] This is strikingly demonstrated in a work such as that of Dowd (I), where the distinction between "mulatto" and "full-blood" and the social significance of this difference is stressed to a fantastic degree; the earlier work of Reuter (I), and the psychological study of Ferguson (I), where color is stressed as having the greatest importance as an index of the amount of crossing represented in an individual, an assumption which the material in Chapter VI shows to be untenable. Reuter, in his more recent work (II) does not draw the broad distinction between groups of Negroes of differing skin-color which he drew in his earlier study, but he is still very vague as to the amount of mixture represented in the American Negro population, stating that "between 25% and 75%" are variously reported as having mixed ancestry.

[2] U. S. Bureau of Census, (I), states "For census purposes the term 'black' (B) includes all Negroes of full-blood, while the term 'mulatto' (Mu) includes all Negroes having some proportion of white blood."

CHAPTER II.
MEASUREMENTS AND OBSERVATIONAL ERRORS.

Before the results of the statistical investigation of the anthropometric data gathered in the course of this study may be presented, a description of the methods of taking the measurements, the instruments which were used, the measurements considered, and a discussion of the comparability of the measurements of the several observers must be undertaken.

The technique of five persons is involved. For that of two, Professor von Luschan and Miss Beatrice Blackwood, the only control available is through comparison of the averages and variabilities for the several traits measured, series for series. Measurements taken by myself constitute the bulk of the total series, for they comprise the Howard University, Harlem 1923—4, and one of the Harlem 1925—6 series. I have also made remeasurements on a sufficiently large number of individuals for all the traits considered, so that my own observational error for each of them is a known quantity. King's measurements may be referred to my own, since we both measured the same 100 individuals, and it is possible, therefore, to give the average difference between us for each measurement, and the variability of this difference, as well. In the case of Miss Hurston, who measured the selected Harlem series, there was, unfortunately, no opportunity for both of us to measure as long a series. However, there are measurements taken by both of us on the same nine individuals, and the averages of the differences between us for the various traits will give an idea of the extent to which we differ.

Another point may be mentioned before the consideration of this material is undertaken. For the Harlem 1923—4 series and the Howard University series, there were thirty traits measured; while for the later Harlem series and the one from West Virginia, only eighteen were considered. Further, von Luschan and Miss Blackwood measured many more than the eighteen traits which were studied during the later portion of this research. In the case of these last two, as has been said, only such of the eighteen measurements which are identical with those of my own series were tabulated; the others were not considered and will not be presented here. In the case of the 1923—4 series also, since this consists of children, only such measurements as could be combined with those of the children comprising the family data were tabulated, as in this way adequate numbers for the computation of growth curves from the early years of life to maturity were available. All the traits measured on the Howard University series, however, are considered and will be presented, as that series has been worked up as a unit. In the distribution tables, the Howard University group has been divided into age groups in the case of those traits which were measured on the series as a whole, — the remaining ones, twelve in number, are presented for the Howard series as a unit. For in the case of these the consideration of changes with age is not of the largest importance; besides, there was no other material for these traits to include with that from Howard. Therefore, the slight changes due to age which might have been observable in the Howard series were not felt to be of sufficient moment to call for the separation of this series into age groups, and all its members; where it was not combined with the total series of this study, were classed as adults. In all these cases, the results for the Howard series are included in the presentation of the next chapter, as they are of comparative value in describing the American Negro type.

Generally speaking, the measurements and the instruments used in taking them, for all the series measured by me or by my assistants, conform to the standards most generally used by anthropologists, and which are given by Martin in his standard "Lehrbuch".[1] Professor von Luschan's technique is not known to me, but presumably it does not differ to any appreciable extent from that which was employed by myself. Miss Blackwood's methods and instruments, again, were standard, except that her device for measuring stature differed somewhat from that used by myself, although not in such a way as to affect the results in comparison. Her own account of her technique has been given to me, and I append it to this chapter. Those measurements, or the instruments used for measuring, in the case of which there are differences between the methods employed in this study and those mentioned by Martin, will be commented on in their proper places as each trait is discussed below. The instruments we employed were:

        Sliding calipers (Martin)
        Spreading calipers (Martin)
        Head-spanner (Todd)
        Color top (Milton-Bradley)
        Anthropometer (Martin)

As for the traits which were measured, the principle of selection which was followed was to measure those which might be expected to show most promise in revealing the results of crossing of Negroes, Whites, and American Indians, the study of which is the primary aim of this research.

---

[1] Rudolf Martin, (I), *passim*.

These measurements and the technique of measuring them, as well as the comparability of the observations of the different persons who have cooperated in this study, may now be discussed.

1. STATURE.

This represents the total standing height of the individuals measured. It was not taken according to the directions given in Martin (p. 132) but differed in several respects. For purposes of making the measuring of the subjects easier, the measurements were not taken in the stocking feet, as is, of course, most desirable. Instead, the subjects were measured with the shoes on, using the anthropometer, and then the height of the heel was measured with the sliding calipers. Later the necessary deduction was made. The tabulations of stature were then made to the nearest half-centimeter. A test group measured by this method[1] and then remeasured without shoes, showed that my average error due to the use of this method of deducting heel height after measuring stature with the shoes not removed is only 4 mm.

Another respect in which the technique of this measurement differed from Martin's was that the anthropometer was placed behind the subject instead of in front of him, — a deviation of minor importance. He was always asked to stand erect with heels together, and to throw back his head and shoulders.

Comparing the measurements of the various observers we have, first, for the differences between the measurements on the same 100 cases of varying ages made by King and myself:

	Average (cm.)	σ
King	122.0	± 7.55
Herskovits	122.3	± 7.57

When the actual differences between measurements on each one of these subjects are tabulated, the mean square variability of these is ±.86 cm. The average difference between Miss Hurston's measurements and my own for this trait is .25 cm., the difference being in her favor. Comparing with the other two observers, we have, if we employ series of adult females:

	No.	Average (cm.)	σ
Blackwood	64	160.6	± 7.31
Von Luschan	26	161.7	± 6.49
Herskovits	55	158.25	± 5.87

There are, therefore, no reasons why, for this trait, the various component series should not be combined.

---

[1] Herskovits, (I).

2. HEIGHT SITTING.

This measurement[1] was also taken with the anthropometer, and includes the length of the trunk, neck, and head, — the vertical distance from the seat on which the subject is sitting to the top of his head. There are two points concerning which care has been taken regarding this measurement in the course of this research; first, that the subject sit as straight as he was able, and second, that his knees should be higher than the seat on which he was sitting. The second was secured by having a low stool on which he could put his feet, or having him place them on the rung of the chair on which he sat while being measured, or having him sit on a table and place his feet on a chair. My own average observational error, computed from repeated measurements on 48 persons, is .9 cm. Comparing measurements of the different observers, we have, first:

	No.	Average (cm.)	σ
King	100	64.4	± 3.29
Herskovits	100	64.1	± 3.36

The actual differences between these measurements on the individuals concerned, when tabulated, gave a mean square variability of ± 1.19 cm. The average difference between Miss Hurston's measurements and my own on the same nine persons for this trait is 1.64 cm., my average being the larger. For the other observers, we have the following comparison:

	No.	Average (cm.)	σ
Blackwood	63	82.0	± 3.41
Herskovits	108	82.85	± 3.33

Professor von Luschan did not measure this trait, but the other series, as shown, may be and have been combined without affecting the result.

3. WIDTH OF SHOULDER.

This measurement represents the distance between the acromial processes[2]. It is measured with the large sliding calipers, that, is, with the upper segments of the anthropometer, and it represents the width of the shoulders when they are thrown back. The source of error guarded against was the movement of the skin when the calipers were applied to the landmarks. In this series the measurement was taken with the coat removed, but over the shirt. Repeated measurements made by me on 49 persons showed my own observational error to be 6.58 mm. Since this measurement was taken only for the Howard University series, no figures comparing results of different observers are given.

---

[1] Martin, (I), p. 138.
[2] Martin, (I), p. 141.

4. WIDTH OF HIPS.

This measurement represents the distance between the labia externa of the crista iliaca, and is taken with the large sliding calipers employed in the trait last discussed. In this research it was only measured on the Howard University series, so no differences between the average measurements of observers other than myself need be given. My observational error for this dimension, computed from remeasurements of 40 persons, is 5.98 mm. The measurement was taken over the trousers, which might tend to make it slightly larger, although this difference is probably not very large.

5. LENGTH OF HEAD.

This is the maximum antero-posterior diameter of the head, from the glabella to the opisthocranion, and is measured with the spreading calipers. My own observational error, calculated from two measurements on each member of a control group of 42 individuals, is .76 mm. Comparing the averages for the same series of 100 boys measured by King and myself, we have:

	Average (mm.)	σ
King	179.5	± 7.50
Herskovits	178.7	± 7.38

while the tabulated differences between our measurements of each individual of the series show a variability (sigma) of ± 1.67 mm. These differences need not be taken into account in combining series, nor need those between Miss Hurston's measurement of this trait and my own, the average difference here being zero[1]. Comparing series of adult American Negro females measured by the other two observers and myself, we have:

	No.	Average (mm.)	σ
Blackwood	63	186.9	± 5.28
Von Luschan	102	187.6	± 6.20
Herskovits	111	187.2	± 5.92

Here again there are no differences sufficiently significant to prevent these series being combined.

6. WIDTH OF HEAD.

This represents the maximum width of the head, from euryon to euryon. It is measured with the spreading calipers, and my own average observational error, computed from repeated measurements

---

The fact that there is no difference at all is undoubtedly due to chance, the number of cases involved being so small. The difference from a larger series would, however, probably be very slight.

on 42 individuals, is .4 mm. Comparing results for the series of 100 boys measured jointly, we have:

	Average (mm.)	σ
King.........	140.5	± 5.38
Herskovits....	140.4	± 5.33

The mean square deviation of the actual differences between our individual measurements was ± 1.28 mm. When Miss Hurston's measurements of the small series we both measured are compared to mine, the difference is .33 mm., her average being the larger. As for the other observers, if we again compare means and variabilities for adult female series, we have:

	No.	Average (mm.)	σ
Blackwood....	63	145.3	± 4.70
Von Luschan..	102	145.6	± 4.82
Herskovits....	111	146.2	± 5.38

The differences have been disregarded in combining these series.

7. CEPHALIC INDEX.

This is the ratio between the length and breadth of the head. Being a ratio, any differences which would stand in the way of combining series would have to be observable in the measurements which go to make up the ratio. There is therefore no reason why series for cephalic index should not be as comparable as are those for length and breadth of head.

8. HEIGHT OF HEAD.

This measurement was taken, in the case of the series measured by me or under my direction, and in that of Miss Blackwood's series, with a special instrument called a head-spanner. It was worked out and manufactured under the direction of Professor Todd in the anatomical laboratory of the Medical College of Western Reserve University[1]. Other studies which have been made on the living have utilized other instruments in measuring this trait, such as the radiometer, or a combination of instruments which involve the attempt to obtain bregma height. The bregma, however, can only rarely be felt in the living, and therefore the resulting measurements, having few or no control points, are only slightly reliable and almost impossible to compare as between different observers. A large amount of this unreliability has been eliminated in this study through the use of the head-spanner. There is no attempt, when this instrument is employed, to measure bregma height, but

---
[1] Todd and Kuenzel, (I). An illustration of the head-spanner may be seen in the plate opposite p. 232.

rather the height of the head from a point in a line perpendicular to another line lying on the eye-ear plane, is measured. This latter is obtained by means of the projecting gadget, which is fitted at the lower border of the orbit of the eye. My mean observational error for this measurement, computed from repeated measurements on 85 individuals, is 1.25 mm. 37 cases were measured with the head-spanner and then remeasured with a radiometer which involved the location of bregma, and this process was repeated on the same persons, giving:

	Average (mm.)	σ	Observational error
W. R. U. Head-spanner	134.6	± 4.18	1.30
Radiometer	138.3	± 4.49	2.20

Thus it may be seen that the use of the head-spanner insures a far greater accuracy of results. It is, at the same time, obvious from the two averages that measurements taken with the two instruments cannot be mixed in one series, and therefore the results for head height given in the chapters which follow do not include the earlier measurements in which I used the radiometer. Comparing King's measurements of 100 boys with those made on the same individuals by myself, we have:

	Average (mm.)	σ
King	128.3	± 4.78
Herskovits	129.1	± 5.44

The mean square deviation of the tabulated differences between our individual measurements was ± 2.39 mm. Thus there is apparently no objection to combining series measured by King and myself, nor is there reason why measurements taken by Miss Hurston should not also be combined with ours, the average difference between our measurements of nine individuals for this trait being 1.22 mm, my average, in this case, being the larger. When we compare the statistical constants for series of adult females measured by Miss Blackwood and by myself, the result is:

	No.	Average (mm.)	σ
Blackwood	64	130.55	± 4.18
Herskovits	109	130.03	± 5.24

Here also there are no appreciable differences, to stand in the way of combination. Professor von Luschan did not measure this trait.

9. MINIMUM FOREHEAD WIDTH.

This trait is measured with the spreading calipers, and is the shortest horizontal distance between the lineae temporales. My own average observational error is 1.21 mm., and represents the repeated measurement of 48 individuals. Since this trait was not measured by the other observers no comparison of differences between us is undertaken.

10. DISTANCE BETWEEN INNER CORNERS OF EYES.

The data for this trait used in this study were likewise all gathered by myself, so again no comparison of the results of different observers need be considered. The trait is measured with the spreading calipers, and represents the distance between the inner corners of the eyes, where the lids end[1]. It is taken with the eyes opened wide, and my average observational error for repeated measurements on 42 individuals is .69 mm.

11. DISTANCE BETWEEN OUTER CORNERS OF EYES.

This measurement is taken in the same fashion as the one preceeding it, and represents the distance between the outer ends of the eyelids.[1] My observational error, computed from repeated measurements of 48 persons, is 1.27 mm. As in the case of the last trait, only measurements made by me are utilized in the following chapters, and therefore no comparisons of differences are given.

12. INTERPUPILLARY DISTANCE.

This trait is measured with the sliding calipers, and consists, of the distance between the mid-points of the pupils of the eyes.[2] Only measurements made by myself are to be found in the succeeding chapters, and therefore no comparisons need be made. In measuring the trait, the subject was in every case directed to look steadily at a spot straight before his eyes, over my head, and some distance away, so that there would be no convergence of the pupils of the eyes while the measurements were being made. My observational error, the average of remeasurements of 78 persons, is .68 mm.

13. HEIGHT OF NOSE.

This measurement represents the distance from the nasion (the midpoint of the nasofrontal suture) to the subnasale, or the median point in the base of the nose.[3] It is not an accurate measurement on the living, for the reason that, particularly in Negroes, it is difficult to feel the nasofrontal suture. It so happened, however,

---

[1] Martin, (I), p. 161.
[2] Growth data for this trait for American Negro boys may be found in Herskovits, (IX).
[3] Martin, (I), p. 167, gives in some detail the technique involved.

that the differences between the observers are, in the main, statistically unimportant, and those series between which there do not seem to be differences of moment have therefore been combined. My own observational error for this trait, the mean of the differences between repeated measurements of 48 individuals, is 1.77 mm. If the average measurement of nose height for the same 100 boys measured by King and myself be compared, the result is:

	Average (mm.)	σ
King	46.2	± 3.56
Herskovits	46.7	± 3.11

The variability of the actual differences between our observations on the same individuals is ± 3.59. This is somewhat larger than was the case for the other traits for which comparisons between us have been presented, and is, of course, a function of the uncertainty of finding the nasofrontal suture, but I do not feel that, in the light of the statistical coincidence of our averages, and the similarity of the variabilities, a constant error of measurement is involved, and therefore our series have been combined. At the same time, I do not wish to minimize the inaccuracies which are involved in the measurements of this trait, and certainly there must be careful analyses before combinations of different series are effected. In the case of the short series measured by Miss Hurston and myself, the average difference between us is .88 mm., that of my series being the larger. Here again the difference is not sufficiently large to rule out combining the two series. When we compare averages and variabilities of the different series of adult American Negro females measured by the other observers whose data are involved in this study, we have:

	No.	Average (mm.)	σ
Blackwood	64	44.4	± 4.16
Von Luschan	102	50.8	± 3.83
Herskovits	111	52.6	± 3.79

Here we see that there is no apparent reason why the combination of von Luschan's measurements with the other series discussed above should not be effected. In the case of those made by Miss Blackwood, however, it is obvious that her technique was such that her measurements differ consistently from those of the rest, her average value for this trait being much lower than the averages of series measured by the other two. Apparently, she locates the nasofrontal suture at a point farther down, and the low variability of her observations shows that she is consistent in utilizing her landmark. In the light of the great differences between the series, however, I considered it inadvisable to combine her measurements for this trait with those of the other observers.

14. WIDTH OF NOSE.

Nostril width is measured with the sliding calipers, and represents the points on the alae of the nose which are farthest apart.[1] It is not as difficult a measurement to take on adults as on children, since among children there is the tendency to dilate the nostrils. This, however, can be overcome. My own observational error, computed as the average of the differences between repeated measurements on 79 individuals, is .72 mm. The averages for King's measurements and my own on 100 boys for this trait are:

	Average (mm.)	σ
King	31.8	± 2.37
Herskovits	33.4	± 2.10

The difference between these averages may be disregarded for the purpose of combining our series, particularly since the variability of the actual differences between our measurements on these boys is only ± 1.48. The average difference between Miss Hurston's measurements and my own, of the same short series, is .66 mm., her measurements averaging the larger. For the other observers, the following comparisons may be made:

	No.	Average (mm.)	σ
Blackwood	64	37.2	± 2.90
Von Luschan	111	37.9	± 3.33
Herskovits	102	37.6	± 4.16

Although there is an appreciable difference in variability between our several series, the averages are very close to one another, and therefore the series obtained by these two last observers have been combined with the others especially collected for this research.

15. DEPTH OF NOSE.

This trait, measured with the sliding calipers, represents the distance from the subnasale to the pronasale, or from the base to the tip of the nose.[2] It is subject to large observational error, since the point at which to locate the tip of the nose is not readily describable in any standard fashion. The average observational error from 48 remeasurements of this trait made by me is 1.08 mm. Only the Howard University series, measured by myself, will be used in discussing it in the chapters to follow.

16. DISTANCE FROM CREASE TO TIP OF NOSE, RIGHT SIDE.

Again, this measurement is difficult to standardize, and, as far as I know, has not been employed by others. In this study, it was

[1] Martin, (I), p. 162.
[2] Martin, (I), p. 167, measurement no. 22.

taken only on the Howard University series. It represents a cross-section of the side of the nose, and, taken together with nasal depth and breadth, should help give an adequate idea of the contour of the nose. It is taken with the sliding calipers. My average observational error for this trait, computed from repeated measurements of 48 cases, is 1.12 mm.

17. UPPER FACIAL HEIGHT.

Facial height is measured with the sliding calipers, and represents the distance between the nasion (as described before) and the prosthion, or the middle point on the lower edge of the upper gum, at the upper edge of the teeth.[1] It is an inaccurate measurement at best, as are all of those involving the nasion. Unlike the height of the nose, where observations of most of the several observers were found to be comparable, the incomparability of the series of this study is marked for this trait. The reason for this is unknown to me, unless it be that the added element of lifting the upper lip in order to find the lower landmark for this measurement may have distracted the attention of the measurers from the upper point. My own mean observational error, computed from repeated measurements on 48 individuals, is 1.96 mm. Aside from the extent to which this is strikingly large, when compared to my errors for other traits and to the average absolute magnitude of the measurement itself, I have noticed that there was a tendency even in measuring this trait from year to year, where my judgement of the location of the upper landmark of this trait was involved. Thus, for two samples of 13-year old boys from the same Harlem population, which I measured two years apart, I obtained the following averages and variabilities:

	No.	Average (mm.)	σ
1923—1924 series	140	63.9	± 4.21
1925—1926 series	45	67.3	± 4.34

With such variation in the average measurements of the same observer with time, it is not strange that there should be striking differences in the results obtained by different measurers for this trait. Attention may be called to the consistency of the variabilities of my two series noted above, — I selected my upper land-mark at about the same point during each period, but quite unconsciously my idea of the location of the nasofrontal suture had changed in the interval. If we compare the measurements of King and myself on the same 100 boys for this trait, we find:

	Average (mm.)	σ
King	62.6	± 4.28
Herskovits	63.4	± 3.66

---

[1] Martin, (I), p. 165.

Here the difference between the variabilities rather than between the averages is most noticeable. And it is when the variability computed from tabulating the differences in our measurements of the individuals who made up this control series is regarded, that we see the most telling reason against combining our series. For, according to it, the chances that our average difference in the measurement of this trait will be larger than that given above are great, the mean square deviation of these actual differences being ± 4.20 mm. The average difference between the short series measured by Miss Hurston and myself is .77 mm., my average being the larger. This is not a material difference, but I feel that findings of the sort discussed above, and which will be shown immediately following, dictate that the safest method is one in which the series of different observers for this trait are not combined. Thus, when the series of adult females measured by the other two observers are compared with an adult female series measured by me, we find:

	No.	Average (mm.)	σ
Blackwood	64	60.05	± 4.29
Von Luschan ..	102	74.8	± 4.21
Herskovits	110	67.95	± 5.46

Obviously, measurements obtained by observers whose results differ thus greatly cannot be combined into one series. And therefore, in the case of this trait, such combination has not been effected. The Howard series is utilized in the following discussions instead, and that only in the light of the discussion above.

18. TOTAL FACIAL HEIGHT

Everything which was remarked concerning the unreliability of the last measurement may be more than repeated in the case of the present one. Apparently, the greater distance involved in making this measurement causes an increase of inaccuracy. Certainly this follows from a consideration of the results obtained by the various persons who contributed to the data of this study, for the unreliability of their measurements of the last trait is emphasized in those they obtained for this one. Total facial height is the distance from the nasion to the gnathion, or that point on the lower side of the mandible in the median sagittal line, a point which can be felt by working the flesh from side to side. My own observational error, from repeated measurements on 48 individuals, is 2.21 mm. King's measurements and my own on the same 100 boys gave the following:

	Average (mm.)	σ
King	103.7	± 5.91
Herskovits	101.5	± 5.07

The variability of the differences between the individual measurements taken by the two of us is ± 4.72 mm., greater than that for upper facial height. The average difference between Miss Hurston's measurement of this trait on a short series and my own is 1.11 mm., my measurements averaging the larger. When we compare series of adult females measured by the two independent observers with one measured by myself, we find:

	No.	Average (mm.)	σ
Blackwood	64	110.4	± 5.04
Von Luschan	102	116.2	± 5.94
Herskovits	111	115.7	± 6.35

Obviously, again, such test results do not allow of combination, and therefore, as far as this trait is concerned, this has not been attempted, but, as in the case of the last trait, only the data gathered by myself at Howard University will be presented in the following chapters.

19. BIZYGOMATIC WIDTH.

This measurement is given by Martin[1] as the distance between the widest places on the cheek bones. The measurement is taken with the spreading calipers, and is determined empirically, although there is always the danger that in running the tips of the calipers along the bone the flesh may "bunch" at the back and thus make the measurement larger than it should actually be. Practice, however, usually overcomes this difficulty without much trouble. My own mean observational error, from repeated measurements of 48 individuals, is .67 mm. Comparing King's measurements of 100 boys with my own, we obtain the following:

	Average (mm.)	σ
King	116.5	± 4.24
Herskovits	117.2	± 4.35

The mean square variability obtained from tabulating the differences between our measurements of the individuals of the series is ± 1.00 mm. The average difference between the measurements of Miss Hurston and myself for the short series measured by both of us is .66 mm., my measurements averaging the larger. When comparison is made for the adult female series of the independent observers and one of my own, we have:

	No.	Average (mm.)	σ
Blackwood	64	132.0	± 5.09
Von Luschan	98	132.4	± 4.89
Herskovits	111	133.1	± 5.52

---

[1] Martin, (I), p. 160.

32 *The Anthropometry of the American Negro*

20. WIDTH OF MOUTH.

This represents the distance between the corners of the mouth, when the lips are closed but not pressed together, and is described by Martin as the "gradlinige Entfernung der beiden Cheilia voneinander."[1] It is measured with the sliding calipers. My own observational error, the average of remeasurements of 48 individuals, is 1.56 mm. Since the trait was not measured on series to be combined with those measured by me, no comparisons need be presented.

21. THICKNESS OF LIPS (CENTER).

This measurement is described by Martin[2] as the distance between the labrale inferior and the labrale superior, in the median sagittal line, or between those points on the upper and lower lips where the mucous membrane meets the skin. In this measurement, which is taken with the sliding calipers, care must be exercised that the lips are in repose. This is not a difficult achievement for adults, though it is somewhat harder for children. My mean observational error, computed from remeasurements of 48 individuals, is 1.00 mm. Comparing King's measurements of 100 boys with my own for the same group, we find:

	Average (mm.)	σ
King	19.0	± 3.56
Herskovits	19.2	± 3.43

The mean square variability of the tabulated differences between our respective measurements of individuals is ± 1.96 mm. The difference between the average of Miss Hurston's measurements of eight individuals and my own for the same eight is 1.38 mm., her average being the larger one. When the series measured by the independent observers and myself for this trait are compared, we find, for adult females:

	No.	Average (mm.)	σ
Blackwood	64	21.8	± 3.27
Von Luschan	98	18.3	± 4.09
Herskovits	110	19.3	± 4.31

22. THICKNESS OF LIPS (RIGHT SIDE).

This measurement, which is not given in Martin, is essentially the same as the one just discussed, and was taken primarily as a check measurement on the one immediately preceding it. It is obtained with the lips in resting position, and represents the greatest distance on the right side of the mouth at the point where the upper and

---

[1] Martin (I), p. 163.
[2] Martin, (I), p. 168.

lower rims of the mucous portion of the lips are most widely separated. My mean observational error, calculated from a series of 48 remeasurements of this trait, is 1.08 mm. No comparative data are available or necessary, as the measurement was taken only by me.

23. PHYSIOGNOMIC HEIGHT OF EAR (EAR LENGTH).

This represents the height (or length) of the ear between those points farthest apart when the arms of the sliding calipers, with which this trait is measured, are at right angles to the base of the ear.[1] It is a measurement which can be taken with a high degree of accuracy, and my own mean observational error, computed from remeasurements made on a series of 79 individuals, is .77 mm. King's measurements and my own on the same series of 100 boys may next be considered:

	Average (mm.)	σ
King	53.0	± 4.17
Herskovits	53.4	± 4.19

The mean square variability of the differences between our measurements of this trait on these boys is ± 1.27 mm. The average difference between Miss Hurston's measurements and those of myself for the same series of nine individuals, is. 33 mm., my average being the larger. This trait was not measured by Miss Blackwood, but if von Luschan's measurements of adult females be compared with those obtained by me, we have:

	No.	Average (mm.)	σ
Von Luschan	101	58.1	± 4.43
Herskovits	110	58.9	± 4.32

24. WIDTH OF EAR.

This measurement is also taken with the sliding calipers, and in the same fashion as in the case of the trait immediately preceeding, except that the arms of the calipers in this case must be at right angles to where they were in measuring the length of the ear, — that is, parallel to the base of the ear, and with one of the arms lying along it[2]. My average observational error for this trait, the mean of the differences between repeated measurements of 48 persons, is 1.00 mm. Measurements made by King and myself on 100 boys for this trait may be compared as follows:

	Average (mm.)	σ
King	53.0	± 4.17
Herskovits	53.4	± 4.19

---

[1] Martin, (I), p. 169.
[2] Martin, (I), p. 169.

The mean square variability of our differences when tabulated, is ± 1.51 mm. The average difference between Miss Hurston's measurements of this trait on nine persons, and my own, is 1.44 mm. Further comparison, using series of adult females, is as follows:

	No.	Average (mm.)	σ
Von Luschan	101	32.0	± 2.75
Herskovits	110	32.65	± 2.88

Miss Blackwood did not measure this trait.

25. WIDTH OF RIGHT HAND.

This trait was measured on the Howard University students only, and therefore no comparisons are presented. It represents the distance between the metacarpale laterale and the metacarpale mediale[1], that is, the breadth of the hand at its widest point. It is measured with the sliding calipers, and my mean observational error, computed from remeasurements of this trait on 48 persons, 87 mm., is due mainly to the difficulty of locating exactly the joints involved, and in the fact that the skin, being loose at these points, tends to move about when the calipers are applied. Each subject was told, of course, to stretch out his hand rigidly while the measurement of this trait and the one following were taken.

26. LENGTH OF THE MIDDLE FINGER, RIGHT HAND.

This represents the distance between the phalangion of the middle finger (III) and the tip of this finger (daktylion III). Again, it is the joint which contributes in large part to the size of the observational error, since it is not easy to feel without practice, and the skin is even looser than in the case of the last trait, thus exhibiting an even greater tendency to slip under the arms of the calipers. My average observational error is 1.76 mm., computed from repeated measurements of 79 boys, and is due in large part to these factors. Since this trait was measured only by myself (on the Howard University series), comparisons between the measuring of this trait on the part of the different observers are not given.

27. PIGMENTATION, BLACK (N) ELEMENT, UPPER OUTER ARM.

The aspect of skin color is perhaps one of the most important to be treated in any study of the American Negro, representing, as he does, crosses between peoples of such differing pigmentation. My method of measuring pigmentation is the one first used by Davenport and later developed by Todd and Van Gorder in their

---

[1] Martin, (I), p. 147.

study of skin-color of Negro-White crosses. As far as is known, it is the only means devised to date for studying pigmentation in quantitative fashion. For this reason, in spite of the essential artificiality of the findings derived from its use, (since these represent no actual anatomical or physiological facts), it has been employed in this study. Since it has only been used by a very few students, the large number of researches into the subject of the pigmentation of the various races which have been made with the use of the Von Luschan color scale or with colored papers or other devices will not be referred to. That these are not comparable with the present method will soon be evident; there is the added difficulty of comparing the findings of various observers due to the differing methods employed (except where the standardized Von Luschan scale has been used) and the largely varying errors of observation for different observers which must result. This last constitutes an objection, it must be remarked, which is far from being overcome through the use of the method employed in this research.

In the collection of data for this study the Milton-Bradley color top has been exclusively used, insofar as I have been able to control the method. This color top is really a toy which was devised to teach kindergarten children the principle of color mixture, and has the advantages that it is made in quantity, is not too expensive to be used in studies such as this, and comes with color disks which, standardised after a fashion, may be frequently changed to obviate error due to their becoming soiled thru excessive handling. It was our regular practice to change the disks, after from ten to fifteen persons had been observed, this number varying according to the facilities which were available for keeping the disks clean. They were never touched by the hand, but only with a small dissecting forceps. The four disks which were used were black, white, red, and yellow, since by employing these four, the color of any skin can be very closely approximated, if not exactly matched. A sheet of paper in which a small hole (about an inch in diameter) had been cut was placed over the upper arm, thus exposing a small skin-surface, and after this the lower arm was covered by another sheet of paper. The subject was asked to rest his elbow on a table, and under the arm, near where the skin showed through the hole, a third sheet of white paper was spread. Thus only the skin at the place where the color was to be matched was visible to the observer, and the color of the spinning top was not influenced by the color of the table on which it was spun.

The top was adjusted, and then spun, and adjustments in the amount of each color showing were made until the observer was satisfied that the color of the skin being studied had been matched. The spinning was done by hand. Here, undoubtedly the objection may be raised that the color will vary with a varying spead of spinning. The answer to this, I believe, is two-fold: in the first place, all the spinning for any one component series was done by the person who measured that series, and therefore a constant initial speed may be assumed for each; in the second place, one does not look at the spinning top for more than an instant, and that when it is revolving most rapidly. As Todd and Van Gorder discovered, to continue looking at the top is to induce added uncertainty as to the extent to which the color blended by it agrees with the color of the skin being studied, and I myself found that it needed only the glance of an instant to know when the colors matched.

As has been remarked by Todd and Van Gorder, the red disks which are supplied with the tops do not represent a spectrum color. Checking these with Ridgeway's color standards, I found, as they did, that the best value for the red of the disk is that which is a spectrum red with 59% black, although the so-called "standardization" of the color by the Milton-Bradley Company is anything but reliable, and other values might easily be found for other specimens of the red disk. Yet this seemed to fit the situation best, and therefore, before the distributions for black were tabulated, the values for this color were corrected by subtracting 59% of the value of the red from the original reading of that color, and adding this amount to the original value of the black segment. The calculations, in consequence, are based on tabulation of the corrected observed values of black and red.

My own average observational error, computed from repeated estimations of skin color with the color top, on 48 individuals, is 3.2%, which compares favorably with Todd and Van Gorder's estimate of a 5% observational error as the maximum allowable. Comparing my readings of black (N) with those of King for our series, measured jointly, of 100 boys, we have:

	Average (%)	σ
King	72.9	$\pm$ 12.84
Herskovits	73.65	$\pm$ 9.28

There is a striking difference in the variabilities, and it is not surprising, therefore, in spite of the fact that the averages are relatively close, that in the series measured on this Harlem population by both of us, King's results should be consistently darker than my own. In spite of control, the personal element in the observation of color is very flexible, and it may be that although he saw consistently darker than myself, a knowledge of this (which was unavoidable to some extent through comparison of our findings on the same persons at an earlier time when instruction in taking the measurements was going on) might have unconsciously influenced our findings in the case of the test series. That King does see pigmentation differently from the way I see it I have no doubt, for his series is so much more variable than my own; the variability of the differences between us for the individual members of the series of 100 boys is as high as

± 5.98%; and the averages for the following groups of adult males, both from American-born Harlem series are:

	No.	Average (%)	σ
King	40	73.10	± 14.70
Herskovits	65	66.20	± 13.44

In all other traits of these series no differences are to be noted. All these facts show that the personal element has been important, and that in comparing results allowance must be made for this. The difference between my observation of N of the color top and Miss Hurston's are not so great, being 1.33% on the average (mine being the darker) although the shortness of the series measured by us both makes it less certain that this gives us an actual picture of the comparability of our measurements. Von Luschan did not use the color top, and, although Miss Blackwood did use it, there have been no opportunities to test the extent to which we see color in the same or in a different manner. In any event, I have restricted the combination of series to those which I myself have measured, both for the N as well as the other colors involved, as I felt that the dictates of the procedure which is methodologically most acceptable would not allow of the combination of data gathered by different observers, particularly where the differences in seeing color seem to be as great as they are in the present case.

28. PIGMENTATION, RED (R) ELEMENT, UPPER OUTER ARM.

This represents the percentage of red on the disks after the color of the skin of the individual being measured had been matched. The figures which are presented in this study, for this color, it must be remembered, are not actually those found on the top, but are corrected, since the figure which seemed best to fit the rather varying "standardized" red of the Milton-Bradley Company was that of red, 41%, black, 59%. We have, therefore, worked up our material from tabulations of the approximately true red, and not from the actual readings of the red disk. My average observational error, from 48 repeated observations, is 2.15% for this color. Comparing King's and my own observations for the control group of 100 boys, we have:

	Average (%)	σ
King	12.2	± 3.34
Herskovits	11.9	± 2.82

The mean square variability of the actual differences between our observations on the several boys was ± 2.46%. The average difference between Miss Hurston's observations and mine is 13%, the redder average being my own. However, caution again does not permit the combination of these series, since any of the colors of the top must be closely influenced by all the others, and only series measured by myself have been combined.

38   *The Anthropometry of the American Negro*

29. PIGMENTATION, YELLOW (Y) ELEMENT, UPPER OUTER ARM.

This represents the third disk on the surface of the color top, the yellow one. Here no correction is necessary, as the yellow of the disk is an unmixed color. My average observational error, computed from repeated observations of color on 48 persons, is 1.19%. When we compare measurements made by King with those made by myself on the same 100 boys, we have, for the yellow:

	Average (%)	σ
King	8.35	± 4.41
Herskovits	8.9	± 3.62

The mean square deviation of the individual differences in our observations was ± 2.15 %. Miss Hurston's average observation differs from mine not at all, according to the repeated observations of skin color on eight persons, but this is undoubtedly due to chance. As said for the other two colors discussed above, combination of the yellow has not been attempted, in spite of the apparent smallness of the differences in observation.

30. PIGMENTATION, WHITE (W) ELEMENT, UPPER OUTER ARM.

This represents the remaining portion of the color top. Again, as in the case of the yellow, there is no correction necessary. My own mean observational error, computed from repeated observations on 48 individuals, is 1.44 %. If the readings of King and myself the W on our control series of 100 boys be considered, we have:

	Average (%)	σ
King	6.5	± 5.77
Herskovits	5.4	± 4.16

The mean square variability of the differences is 3.35 %. As between Miss Hurston and myself, the difference is .38 % when the averages of readings on eight persons by each of us be compared, my reading being the lighter (greater percentage of W). Miss Blackwood's findings, as has been said, could not be compared with my own, and Von Luschan did not use the color top. So here, as before, no combination of series has been attempted.

NOTES ON TECHNIQUE USED BY B. BLACKWOOD IN MEASURING NEGRO FEMALES.[1]

Stature. From top of head to ground, without shoes, care being taken that the subject was standing in an upright position, eyes directed forwards.
Sitting height. The subject was asked to sit upright on a flat-topped desk or table (not a chair), with knees bent over the edge of it. Special attention

---

[1] Kindly furnished by Miss Blackwood to assist in judging the comparability of our measurements.

was given to posture, the subject's natural sitting position being, as a rule, bad. Directions given: "Sit up straight, make yourself as tall as you can and look straight ahead." The measurement was from top of head to ground, the height of the desk or table being subtracted afterwards. Only the corrected figure is given on the blanks.

Head length. Taken from glabella to maximum occipital extension.

Head width. Maximum, wherever found.

Minimum frontal width. Narrowest diameter between temporal crests of frontal bone, with considerable pressure.

Bizygomatic width. Greatest diameter between zygomatic arches, with considerable pressure.

Nasal width. Across widest portion of nose, with the least possible amount of constriction.

Nasal height. From nasion to akanthion (sub-nasal point). In some cases the exact position of the nasion was very difficult to determine.

Facial height. The upper, smaller figure represents the "upper facial height" from nasion to alveolar margin of upper jaw. This was difficult in cases of extreme prognathism, and probably involves a certain degree of inaccuracy in all cases. The lower, larger figure represents "total facial height", from nasion to lower margin of chin (pogonion).

Head height. Taken with the "Reserve Head Spanner" according to directions given by Dr. Wingate Todd with the instrument. Lacking in some records, as I did not possess the instrument at the beginning of the work.

Ear height and ear width. Not taken. These spaces on the blank were used in later records for recording Lip Thickness and Mouth Width.

Skin color. Estimated on the inner side of the upper arm according to Von Luschan's scale, used from memory owing to the sensitiveness of many subjects in this particular, but with frequent consultation of scale. Of questionable value, further than as an indication of lightness or darkness. Von Luschan's scale is entirely inadequate for Negroes and useless for Whites. In the later records (Tuskegee and afterwards) the Milton-Bradley color top was used, with much more satisfactory results.

CHAPTER III.

A DESCRIPTION OF THE AMERICAN NEGRO TYPE.

The first step in the consideration of anthropometric data as extensive, and as geographically representative of a population as those of the present study, is to attempt a description in terms of comparison with other populations. This is particularly important in the case of a group which has a racial background such as that of the American Negro. As has been remarked, the physical traits which have been considered are such as would give an indication of racial crossing. We measured not only the more obvious traits which would indicate the results of crossing between Whites and Negroes (not to mention between Negroes and Indians, or between all three) as, for example, nasal width, lip thickness, and skin color, but others such as interpupillary distance, head form, height sitting, and the like. As will be noticed in Chapter VI, certain of the traits measured at the inception of my research were found to be of minor importance for the problem and therefore when additional data were gathered in Harlem and West Virginia, those found to be unimportant were dropped. As has been stated, only the traits measured in the latter portion of this study have been abstracted from the data of Professor von Luschan and Miss Blackwood, and this material was consolidated with that gathered by myself or under my direction.

All traits considered at any time in this study, however, were measured on the Howard University sample. This sample may itself be considered as representative of the American Negro type, for there does not seem to have been any noticeable selection of physical traits as far as it is concerned, in spite of the fact that its members were university students. Therefore, all the thirty traits for which data were collected will be presented in this chapter, although the series is materially larger for eighteen characteristics than it is for the other twelve which were not measured in the latter portion of this research.

To "place" the American Negro type among the populations for which comparative measurements are available, particularly with respect to the populations of northern Europe, West Africa and aboriginal America from which it is derived, the adult males of the component series have been combined into one group. Where this combination has not been effected, the Howard University series is used. This procedure was felt to be wise, since, coming before further analysis of the data is undertaken, it will give an idea of the physical form of the American Negro, and the extent to which the three-way mixture he represents can be compared to other populations of the world, particularly those from which he is descended. Only the adult male portion of the entire series was selected for this purpose, since comparative material from adult male series representative of other populations is more available than measurements of adult females, or children's groupings of either sex.

It has not been a simple matter to obtain the comparative material necessary for the presentation attempted in this chapter, and particularly to obtain figures indicative of variability as well as of average values. Martin[1] has, of course, been a mine of information, but in the main Martin gives only averages, and these, it need not be remarked, are not particularly valuable without their accompanying errors. Then, too, in the case of many of the traits for which he gives tables, the sources from which he obtained his figures are not given and could not be checked, while, too often, when they are furnished to his reader, the students who originally worked out the averages have not published the raw data, or even the distributions from which these were derived. Consequently, this made it impossible for me to compute the variabilities for such series, although I have done so wherever I could.

These variabilities, quite aside from the dictates of accepted statistical procedure, are especially important in the case of the comparative analysis of a population which represents as much racial mixture as the American Negro does. I have found in all previous analyses of the data of this study[2] that the homogeneity of the American Negro population is much greater than has been thought. Representing such a vast amount of racial mixture, there has apparently been a great deal of breeding within the mixed group, and the fact that out of the genealogies assembled only a very small percentage of the present generation claim to be primary crosses between Negroes, or even Negro hybrids, and Whites, demonstrates the diminishing amount of direct crossings between these two groups of our population. The social pressure against crossing is growing to be as strong among Negroes as it is among the White population. Crossing with the Indians is a matter of some generations ago, and today is an exceptional occurrence. In other words, the tendency to breed within the Negro group is becoming progressively stronger.

A comparison of the mean square variabilities for Whites and Negroes measured by Davenport and Love shows that the Negroes,

---

[1] Martin, (I), *passim*.
[2] e. g., Herskovits, (II, IV, V), etc.

in the majority of traits considered by them, are less variable than the Whites. According to this the Whites are more variable in seven traits, the Negroes more so in three, while the two have about the same variability in three more. Todd's comparative results for 75 traits measured on 100 male Negro and 100 male White cadavera, show the Negroes more variable in 36 traits, the Whites more so in 36, and the two series the same in 3, when we use the coefficient of variability as the measure of variation.[1] And although the variability of my sample will be found to be higher in many traits than that of some of the primitive and relatively isolated groups of Africa for which variabilities are available, and sometimes, although less frequently, higher than for the comparatively homogeneous English and Scottish, it will be found to be lower in most cases than the Marquesans, for example, whom Sullivan demonstrated to be a greatly mixed type, or other populations where mixture without consolidation has occurred.

The data of this chapter, therefore, may serve to give something of an idea of the physical type of the American Negro which is being developed here. That racial crossing between Negroes and Whites in this country is diminishing is evident, I believe, to anyone who has had intimate contact with the American Negro, and I know of no other hypothesis which will fit my observations and those of Todd and of Davenport and Love.

A word must be said as to the terminology here used before presenting the results for the male adult series. As has been remarked, the use of the term "Negro" to denote the American Negro-hybrid is awkward, to say the least. I use it here only as a convenience, for to use the expression "Negro-Indian-White-hybrid" would be much too cumbersome. "American Negro" is far better, and so I shall employ either this term, or simply the word "Negro" to mean the mixed group which is the so-called "Negro" population of the United States. Obviously, from a biological point of view, to select one element of a cross and use it as a designation of the resulting mixed group is meaningless. The matter becomes somewhat clearer, if we consider the sociological reasons for the application of the word "Negro" to the American mixed Negro-White-Indian population.[2] With the foregoing in mind, and since common usage dictates its employment, therefore, "Negro" or "American Negro" will be used to indicate the mixed population studied.

In the discussions of the traits measured, I shall give, for each trait, the average, mean square variability, and the error of the mean, as well as the number of cases on which these statistical constants depend. I shall also present such averages, and, where

---

[1] Todd and Lindala (I)
[2] Herskovits, III.

A Description of the American Negro Type

possible, their variabilities, for the same traits, as I have been able to find for adult male samples from other racial groups from the American Negroes may be descended. A few data from other groups are also appended.

N	Group	Mean ± SD	Source
34	Lotuko	178.3 ± 8.18	(Seligman)
1000	Cambridge men	174.9 ± 6.46	(Macdonnell)
1078	English sons	174.4 ± 6.49	(Pearson)
100	W. R. U. cadavera	174.4 ± 6.10	(Todd and Lindala, I)
727	Old Americans	174.3 ± 5.80	(Hrdlička, II)
30	Acholi	174.0 ± 6.21	(Seligman)
56	Creek	173.9 ± 5.9	(Boas, II)
77	Half-blood Sioux	173.5 ± 6.81	(Sullivan, II)
1787	NAm. Indians tribes of 170 cm average stature or more	172.8 ± 6.1	(Boas)
479	Half-blood of the same group	173.8 ± 7.3	(Boas)
94	Iroquois	172.7 ± 5.7	(Boas, II)
612	Pure Sioux	172.6 ± 5.6	(Boas, IX)
46981	Swedes	172.2 ± 5.93	(Lundborg and Linders)
83	Somali	172.1 ± 5.73	(Puccioni)
262	Scottish	172.1 ± 6.4	(Boas, IV)

1. STATURE.

This trait was measured by all the observers except by Miss Blackwood on adult males. Her series, being composed entirely of females, is therefore not represented at all in any of the tabulations of data on which the results given in this chapter are based. The average stature is 170.49 cm with a mean error ± .21 cm. Comparison may be made with the following populations:

N	Group	Mean ± SD	Source
6454	Negro troops	171.99 ± 6.91	(Davenport and Love)
96696	White troops	171.97 ± 6.66	(Davenport and Love)
1078	English fathers	171.95 ± 6.87	(Pearson, I)
404	Foreign Swedes	171.81 ± 6.43	(Lundborg)
493	Scottish students (Aberdeen)	171.7 ± 5.94	(Schuster)
107	Indian troops	171.51 —	(Davenport and Love)
43	Delaware	171.5 ± 5.2	(Boas, II)
—	Kanuri-Bornu	171.0 —	(Martin)
100	W. R. U. White cadavera	170.6 —	(Todd and Lindala, I)
—	Mandingo	170.59 —	(Martin)
887	**American Negro**	170.49 ± 6.40	**(Present series)**
1124	NAm tribes of average stature 166—170 cm	169.4 ± 6.0	(Boas, IX)
—	Civil War Negro troops	168.99 —	(Baxter)
—	Fan	169.8 —	(Martin)
30	Kajiji	*168.3 ± 8.57	(Tremearne)
169	Alur	168.0 —	(Czekanowski)
448	Foreign-born Bohemians	167.5 ±6.4	(Boas, IV)

* In this, and the other comparative tables which follow, all series are represented by adult males, unless otherwise specified. The means and sigmas which I myself computed from raw data published by others are indicated by asterisks. The references after the statistical constants are to the papers of the authors mentioned, the titles of which are given in full in the bibliography.

—	M'Baka	167.1		—	(Martin)
20	Ekoi	*166.86	±	5.83	(Mansfeld)
284	French	166.8	±	6.47	(Pearson)
41	Montagnais-Naskapi	166.2	±	5.87	(Hallowell)
—	Togo	166.1		—	(Martin)
390	Germans	165.95	±	6.68	(Pearson)
—	Fiot	165.7		—	(Martin)
47	Ashanti	164.21	±	5.53	(Rattray)
—	Ewe	163.7		—	(Martin)
—	Yoruba	163.0		—	(Martin)
37	Kagoro	*160.11	±	5.55	(Tremearne)
78	Hawaiians	171.59	±	6.25	(Von Luschan)

Compared with American Negroes measured by others, and with African peoples, the present sample is seen to be taller than the Negroes of Civil War times, but to check in satisfactory fashion with the findings of Todd, and of Davenport and Love. They are taller than the African West Coast peoples represented in Martin's tables, with the exception of the Kanuri-Bornu, while they are of about the same stature as the Mandingo series. But they are smaller than the East Africans, in the main. They are no nearer the statures of the European Whites to whom they are generically related than they are to the Africans from whom they have presumably descended. However, it is interesting to note that the means for the White and Negro troops are so close to each other, that the Negroes of this sample are distinctly shorter than Hrdlička's Old Americans, and that while they are taller than the French, Bohemians, and Germans, they are not as tall as the English and Scottish from whom they are more probably descended. They seem to fall between the means for the Africans and Europeans, being, however, nearer the latter than the former. When we attempt to compare them with the Indians, we find that insufficient numbers of Indian populations are shown, although those available seem to demonstrate that the American Negro is shorter than the Indian. Detailed studies, particularly from Indian tribes with whom the Negroes might have mixed (not including the Sioux) show that the American Negro is shorter than his Indian ancestors. Finally, the comparative variability of this series in this trait, low when we consider the amount of crossing represented by it, is also to be noted.

2. Height Sitting.

As was seen in the last chapter, there is no objection to combining measurements of this trait taken by the different observers. The average of the total male adult series is 87.67 cm. with a mean error of ± .12 cm.:

* See note page 43.

A Description of the American Negro Type

Comparisons may be made with the following data:

96239	White troops	90.39	± 3.51	(Davenport and Love)
105	Indian troops	90.10	—	(Davenport and Love)
77	Half-blood Sioux	89.6	± 4.39	(Sullivan, II)
100	W. R. U. White cadavera	88.6	± 3.41	(Todd and Lindala)
100	W. R. U. Negro cadavera	88.6	± 3.19	(Todd and Lindala)
538	Pure Sioux	88.5	± 3.50	(Sullivan, II)
840	**American Negroes**	87.7	± **3.41**	**(Present series)**
41	Montagnais-Naskapi	87.4	± 3.01	(Hallowell)
6433	Negro troops	87.35	± 3.48	(Davenport and Love)
37	Kagoro	*86.51	± 3.00	(Tremearne)
19	Ekoi	*85.97	± 3.07	(Mansfeld)
30	Kajiji	*84.44	± 3.94	(Tremearne)
50	Bahiru	80.10	—	(Czekanowski)

These values show that the sitting height of the American Negro is smaller than that of the Indians or Whites, and that the variability, in a number of instances, is also smaller. The close correspondence between the army data, Todd's series, and this sample of Negroes is again to be noted. The significance of the position of this series in the comparative table is that the Negroid trait of long legs (small sitting height) seems to be present, though not to so great an extent as it is in the true Negro. In other words, here, as will be seen elsewhere, there seems to have been a blending of the average values of the ancestral types by the American Negro. The sitting height in percents of the total height (relative sitting height), is 51.42 %. This is close to Davenport and Love's result for Negroes: 50.79 %. Comparisons may be made with the relative sitting height of other populations, from Martin's table (p. 260), particularly those of Africa, while we may also compare this proportion in the present sample with that of various European elements represented in Davenport and Love's White population:

Ba-Binga	54.0	(Martin)
Kagoro	53.8	(Martin)
Apache	53.2	(Martin)
Swedes	53.0	(Martin)
Russian Jews	53.0	(Martin)
Pima	52.9	(Martin)
Amer. Irish troops	52.79	(Davenport and Love)
Amer. English troops	52.67	(Davenport and Love)
Amer. Scottish troops	52.60	(Davenport and Love)
Old Americans	52.6	(Hrdlička, IV)
English	52.4	(Martin)
Shoshoni	52.2	(Martin)
French	52.0	(Martin)
Togo	51.9	(Martin)
Half-blood Sioux	51.6	(Sullivan, II)
Fiot	51.5	(Martin)
American Negroes	**51.42**	**(Present series)**

---

* See note page 43.

Pure Sioux .... 51.4 (Sullivan, II)
Fan .... 51.3 (Martin)
D'chagga .... 50.5 (Martin)
M'Baka .... 50.4 (Martin)
Masai .... 48.9 (Martin)

Though many more populations might be cited, enough are given here to show that the sitting height of the American Negro is smaller in proportion to his stature than that of the Old White Americans, the Americans of European origin measured by Davenport and Love, or the European populations represented in Martin's table. The relative sitting height of my sample, on the other hand, is somewhat greater than that of the two West African tribes which are given, somewhat smaller than that of the rest of the African populations represented above, while it is less than that of most of the American Indian tribes.

3. WIDTH OF SHOULDER (Table IV).

The data for this trait are those of the Howard University series only. The mean and variability are:

Number of cases: 476
Average: 40.24 cm.
Standard deviation: ± 2.04 cm.
Error of the average: ± .09 cm.

Comparison may be made with the data gathered by Davenport and Love in their study of the troops during the late war, although this is none too satisfactory. Their measurement which most closely corresponds to acromial width as taken by myself is that given by Martin (p. 141) as the maximum shoulder breadth. It is "the horizontal distance between the two largest projections of the deltoid muscle. (This is) .. a very inexact measurement". Davenport and Love remark on its variability with the general condition of the individual and the extent to which these muscles have been developed by him, and state that the measurement was taken "at about four or five centimeters below the acromial processes, or at about the greatest thickening of the deltoid".[1] At the same time, since these measurements are the best available for American populations, and may serve in a rough way as a check on my own, they are quoted:

96167 Whites   41.41 cm.   ± 2.408
 6289 Colored 42.89 cm.   ± 2.154
  104 Indian   42.58 cm.   —

---

[1] Davenport and Love, (I), p. 203.

We see here that the Indian and Negro troops are nearer each other than are the Negro and White, and that the homogeneity of the Negro group is greater than that of the Whites. Sullivan has given us data on full and half-blood Sioux for acromial width, which, in view of the amount of Indian ancestry in the present series, should also be of interest. Other available figures for shoulder-width may be given here:

58	Hawaiians	*39.2	± 3.96	(Von Luschan)
538	Pure Sioux	38.8	± 1.92	(Sullivan, II)
76	Half-blood-Sioux	38.9	± 1.89	(Sullivan, II)
19	Ekoi	*38.3	± 2.00	(Mansfeld)
43	Micmac	37.9	± 2.00	(Boas, IX)
50	Bahiru	34.9	—	(Czekanowski)

4. WIDTH OF HIPS (Table V).

As in the case of the last measurement, the sample utilized for this trait represents only the men measured at Howard University. The mean and deviations are:

Number of cases:	476
Average:	28.51 cm.
Standard deviation:	± 1.83 cm.
Error of the average:	± .08 cm.

We may again compare measurements taken by Davenport and Love on soldiers. In this case our measurements are identical, as they quote the directions from Martin (p. 143) which were those followed by us in the present research. Their results are as follows:

95685 Whites	29.43 cm.	±2.55
6354 Colored	28.42 cm.	±2.35
107 Indians	29.71 cm.	—

We see, therefore, that the sample used in the present study checks very closely with Davenport and Love's much larger one as to the averages, although the variability of my sample is materially smaller than that of the Negro troops.

Comparison may be further made by throwing the width of the hips into terms of percentage of stature. For the series of American Negroes used in this study, this is 16.7 %. This relative transverse diameter of the pelvis is, for the groups in Davenport and Love's work:

Indian	17.3
Whites	17.1
Italian	17.33
Scottish	17.03
English	17.02
Irish	16.88
Negro	16.5

---

* See note page 43.

Table IV Width of shoulders		Table V Width of Hips	
Mm.	No.	Mm.	No.
335—340[1]	2	195—200	1
340—	1	200—	—
345—	—	205—	1
350—	1	210—	—
355—	2	215—	—
360—	9	220—	1
365—	9	225—	2
370—	24	230—	—
375—	20	235—	1
380—	35	240—	2
385—	22	245—	4
390—	50	250—	4
395—	36	255—	8
400—	48	260—	24
405—	43	265—	36
410—	40	270—	50
415—	28	275—	48
420—	43	280—	50
425—	25	285—	65
430—	13	290—	53
435	14	295—	42
440—	4	300—	23
445—	4	305	25
450—	2	310—	21
455—460	1	315—	4
		320—	3
		325—	3
		330—	1
		335—	2
		340—	—
		345—	1
		350—	—
		355—	—
		360—	—
		365—	—
		370—	—
		375—	1

This shows that relatively, as well as absolutely, the pelvic diameter is greater in the non-Negro populations represented than in those having Negro blood. Martin gives a long list (p. 269) of these relative pelvic diameters, some of which will be of interest for comparative purposes:

Bavarians	17.4
Rumanians	17.2
Germans	17.0
Colorado Indians	17.0
French	16.8
American Negroes	16.7
Norman French	16.4

---

[1] Exclusive.

Poles	16.4
Bushmen	16.4
Russians	16.3
Ba-Binga	15.6
Fan	14.6
M'Baka	14.5
Fiot (Africa)	14.2

The relative pelvic diameter is again seen to be greater in the European peoples than in the African. The American Negro falls about between these two general groupings (if we include the American Indian with the European), — that is, he is about the same in this trait as the French, greater than the Africans, (except the Bushmen) and for the most part, less than the American and European Whites and American Indians represented.

5. LENGTH OF HEAD.

This trait was measured by all the observers who have contributed data to this study, and their series have been combined. The average for men is 196.52 mm. with a mean error of $\pm$ .21. The frequency distribution may be seen in the last column of Table XXVI, p. 115.

Means and standard deviations of other populations are given for comparison as follows:

N	Group	Mean ± SD	Source
727	Old Americans	*197.28 ± 6.04	(Hrdlička, IV)
263	Scotch foreign-born	196.7 ± 5.9	(Boas, IV)
961	**American Negroes**	**196.52 ± 6.51**	**(Present series)**
959	Oxford students	196.05 ± 6.23	(Schuster)
540	Pure Sioux	194.9 ± 6.16	(Sullivan, II)
493	Aberdeen students	194.8 ± 5.73	(Schuster)
91	Masai	194.67 ± 5.28	(Leys and Joyce)
77	Half-blood Sioux	194.4 ± 7.12	(Sullivan, II)
50	Montagnais-Naskapi	194.0 ± 6.92	(Hallowell)
46975	Swedes	193.84 ± 6.19	(Lundborg and Linders)
1000	Cambridge students	193.51 ± 6.16	(Macdonnell)
34	Lotuko	192.9 ± 6.05	(Seligman)
100	W. R. U. Negro cadavera	192.6 ± 6.08	(Todd and Lindala)
55	Kajiji	*192.31 ± 6.72	(Tremearne)
27	Somali	191.81 ± 4.75	(Leys and Joyce)
19	Ekoi	*191.05 ± 4.11	(Mansfeld)
802	Cairo natives	190.52 ± 5.90	(Orensteen)
450	Foreign-born Bohemians	189.8 ± 6.4	(Boas, IV)
110	Embu	189.08 ± 6.52	(Leys and Joyce)
40	Vai	*188.85 ± 6.25	(Virchow)
384	Akikuyu	188.72 ± 6.13	(Leys and Joyce)
100	W. R. U. White cadavera	188.3 ± 7.52	(Todd and Lindala)
72	Kagoro	*188.19 ± 6.12	(Tremearne)
60	American-born Bohemians	188.0 ± 6.2	(Boas, IV)
128	Akamba	187.80 ± 5.24	(Leys and Joyce)
48	Ashanti	187.33 ± 4.66	(Rattray)
30	Acholi	187.3 ± 6.05	(Seligman)
83	Marquesans	193.2 ± 7.00	(Sullivan, I)
86	Hawaiians	*191.25 ± 7.22	(von Luschan)

* See note page 43.

50   The Anthropometry of the American Negro

These averages show that these American Negroes are, on the average, of longer absolute head-length than any of the populations except the Old Americans and the Scottish foreign-born. The difference between the mean of my series and that of the Western Reserve sample may be due to shrinkage of the tissues after death, while comparison with the African populations shows these peoples to be much shorter in absolute head-length than the American Negro sample used in this study. Comparison of the standard deviations shows that the variabilities of both the Negro groups are less than those for the American Whites of Todd's series, for the half-blood Sioux, the Montagnais-Naskapi Indians, the pure Hawaiians, or the Marquesans, which Sullivan indicated were a mixture of at least two distinct types. On the other hand, the Old White Americans are less variable; the African Negro series have about the same or smaller variabilities, as have the rest of the populations represented in the table, the Scottish excepted. However, while all of these last are less variable than the series of this study, they are not less so than Todd's series. It is interesting to note that a series of 87 Western Reserve Negro crania[1] gave a standard deviation of ± 6.51 mm., a figure somewhat nearer that for the population measured by us than that for the cadavera cited above.

6. Width of Head.

The series for this trait is that comprising all the adult males measured by all the observers. The frequencies of this combined series may be seen in the column for adults of Table XXIX, p. 121. The average value is 151.38 mm. with a mean error of ± .18 mm. Comparison with other male populations may be made as follows:

```
  450  Foreign-born Bohemians ...    159.1  ± 5.9    (Boas, IV)
   52  Montagnais-Naskapi .......    157.1  ± 4.55   (Hallowell)
   60  American-born Bohemians..     156.5  ± 5.2    (Boas, IV)
  540  Pure Sioux ...............    155.1  ± 5.39   (Sullivan, II)
   77  Half-blood Sioux .........    154.3  ± 5.04   (Sullivan, II)
 1000  Cambridge men ............    153.96 ± 5.05   (Macdonnell)
  263  Foreign-born Scottish.....    153.8  ± 4.7    (Boas, IV)
  727  Old Americans ............   *153.76 ± 5.20   (Hrdlička, IV)
  493  Aberdeen students ........    153.4  ± 4.69   (Schuster)
  959  Oxford students ..........    152.84 ± 4.92   (Schuster)
  961  American Negroes .........    151.38 ± 5.74   (Present series)
46973  Swedes ...................    150.4  ± 5.10   (Lundborg and Linders)
   48  Ashanti ..................    145.01 ± 4.41   (Rattray)
   55  Kajiji ...................   *144.56 ± 4.66   (Tremearne)
  802  Cairo-born males .........    144.45 ± 4.67   (Orensteen)
  128  Akamba ...................    143.63 ± 5.09   (Leys and Joyce)
   40  Vai ......................   *142.45 ± 5.07   (Virchow)
  384  Akikuyu ..................    143.25 ± 4.93   (Leys and Joyce)
   27  Somali ...................    143.19 ± 4.34   (Leys and Joyce)
```

* See note page 43.
[1] Todd, (I).

A Description of the American Negro Type

```
 20 Ekoi ....................... *143.16 ± 5.42 (Mansfeld)
 91 Masai ......................  142.49 ± 5.37 (Leys and Joyce)
 72 Kagoro ..................... *142.43 ± 4.07 (Tremearne)
 30 Acholi .....................  141.8  ± 4.6  (Seligman)
 34 Lotuko .....................  141.3  ± 4.7  (Seligman)
 86 Hawaiians ................. *158.93 ± 4.8  (Von Luschan)
 83 Marquesans ................  153.2  ± 4.87 (Sullivan, I)
```

Measurements on the living and on skulls are obviously different; therefore the mean for head width of Todd's Western Reserve cranial material may not be compared with that for my series. However, we may make comparison of the variabilities of the two series of crania of Whites and Negroes. Todd's sigmas of ± 6.46 mm. for 100 White male crania, and ± 6.10 mm. for 100 Negro male crania show the greater variability of his White population as against his Negroes. The variability of this series checks with that of his for Negroes. The Old Americans, as almost all other populations of the comparative table, are less variable than the sample of the present study. The mean for my series, when placed in position in the table of averages, lies lower than any of the White or Indian populations except that of the Swedes, but is higher than that of any of the Africans, whether from East or West Africa.

7. CEPHALIC INDEX.

The frequency distribution of the series utilized here may be seen in the "adult" column of Table XXXII, p. 127. The average is 77.09 with a mean error of ± .11. Comparison of these results with the averages and variabilities of other male populations may be made as follows:

```
   60 Bohemian American-born ..  84.4   ± 4.0  (Boas, IV)
  450 Bohemian foreign-born ....  83.8   ± 3.4  (Boas, IV)
   52 Montagnais-Naskapi .......  81.0   ± 2.67 (Hallowell)
  126 Delaware Indians .........  79.8   ± 3.5  (Boas, II)
   82 Laka (Cameroon) ..........  79.7   —      (Struck)
  167 W. R. U. White (skulls) ..  79.67  ± 4.74 (Todd, I)
  540 Pure Sioux ...............  79.6   ± 3.20 (Sullivan, II)
   77 Half-blood Sioux ..........  79.4   ± 2.64 (Sullivan, II)
  351 Iroquois .................  79.3   ± 2.49 (Boas, II)
  169 Alur .....................  78.55  ± 3.2  (Seligman)
 1000 Cambridge men ............  78.33  ± 2.90 (Macdonnell)
  263 Foreign-born Scottish .....  78.3   ± 2.6  (Boas, IV)
  404 Foreign-born Swedes ......  78.27  ± 3.35 (Lundborg and Linders)
  959 Oxford students ..........  78.02  ± 2.52 (Schuster)
  727 Old Americans ............ *77.95  ± 3.01 (Hrdlička, IV)
76980 Swedes .................. 77.69   ± 3.14 (Lundborg and Linders)
   48 Ashanti ..................  77.52  ± 2.47 (Rattray)
  961 American Negroes .........  77.09  ± 3.45 (Present series)
  128 Akamba ...................  76.54  ± 2.80 (Leys and Joyce)
   47 Vai ...................... *76.05  ± 2.96 (Virchow)
```

* See note page 43.

4*

384	Akikuyu	75.99	±	3.30	(Leys and Joyce)
72	Kagoro	*75.78	±	2.79	(Tremearne)
30	Acholi	75.7	±	2.3	(Seligman)
45	Banyange (Cameroon)	75.4	—		(Struck)
19	Ekoi	*75.26	±	3.27	(Mansfeld)
26	Mandingo	75.0	—		(Struck)
55	Kajiji	*75.17	±	3.07	(Tremearne)
87	W. R. U. Negro (skulls)	74.89	±	3.19	(Todd, I)
80	Somali	73.55	±	3.09	(Puccioni)
48	Asini (Gold Coast)	73.4	—		(Struck)
34	Lotuko	73.3	±	2.8	(Seligman)
86	Hawaiians	83.18	±	3.7	(Von Luschan)
83	Marquesans	79.4	±	4.52	(Sullivan)

This sample of American Negroes is mesocephalic. The mean is higher than Todd's crania, although if we make the accepted correction for difference in index between those derived from cranial measurements and those made on the heads of the living[1] by an addition of 1% to the mean cranial index, the discrepancy between the present population and Todd's sample becomes less striking. Other than Todd's series, all the averages in the table are for the living. It will be noted that, in the main, the American Negro is less dolichocephalic than most of the West African groups to whom he might be expected to be related, while his cephalic index is somewhat lower than those of the European populations, and also lower than the averages for the American Indian series. This seems to indicate once more that there has been a blending of the characteristic head forms of the various racial groups from which the American Negro is descended, particularly when the homogeneity of the distribution curve is remarked. Consideration of the mean square variabilities shows again that both those computed for American Negro series are relatively close. On the other hand, the variability of the American Negro is greater than that of the Old Americans, Africans, Scottish, and certain of the American Indian populations, while it is smaller than that of the Western Reserve sample of White cadavera, the American born Bohemians, the pure Hawaiians, Delaware Indians, and the mixed Marquesans.

8. Height of Head.

The series for this trait represented here by the constants given below comprise data from all the observers with the exception of Professor Von Luschan, and this measurement, it will be recalled, is not bregma height, but that obtained by the use of the Western Reserve head-spanner, as explained in the preceding chapter. The frequency distribution for these adult males will be found in the "adult" column of Table XXXIV, p. 131. The average is 134.02 mm. with a

---

* See note page 43.
[1] Martin, (I), p. 421; Boas, (II), p. 395.

mean error of ± .16 mm. We may compare the averages and variabilities for other male populations with these results. Comparisons must be made, however, with the reservation in mind of the unreliability of the landmark used in making these measurements (the bregma), and the difference between measurements made with the radiometer and with the headspanner.

20	Ekoi	*146.40	± 8.02	(Mansfeld)
727	Old Americans	*140.5	± 5.82	(Hrdlička, IV)
839	**American Negroes**	134.02	± **4.64**	**(Present series)**
41	Montagnais-Naskapi[1]	134.00	± 4.67	(Hallowell)
2348	English Criminals	132.29	± 8.01	(Goring)
—	Egyptians (Kharga)	132	—	(Martin
—	Lithuanians	131	—	,,
—	Chinese	124	—	,,
50	Bahiru	123.24	—	(Czekanowski)
—	Bugu	120	—	(Martin)
—	Batua	118	—	,,

The high head of the Ekoi contrasts startlingly with the other African populations that are given. If we disregard this instance, however, the African head seems to be somewhat lower than the European and Old White American, although the mean for the present sample is greater than that for any of the other populations cited, except the West African Ekoi and the Old Americans.

9. MINIMUM FOREHEAD WIDTH. (Table VI)

This trait was not measured on any but the Howard University series. The table for forehead width given in Martin for skeletal material (p. 709) shows that the African population represented, the Ashanti, is somewhat smaller in this dimension than are the Europeans. The few Indian populations do not differ from the Negro as much as do the Europeans. The average is 106.65 mm. with a mean error of ± .14 mm. We may compare the mean for this population with those for the Old Americans, Swedes, W. R. U. Negro cadavera, the Marquesans and Hawaiians and the Bahiru, as well as with those for other male populations given by Martin in a short table for this dimension in the living (p. 710):

—	Rumanians	114	—	(Martin)
—	Lithuanians	110	—	(Martin)
—	Tungus	109	—	(Martin)
48	Ashanti	107.60	± 4.07	(Rattray)
100	W. R. U. Negro cadavera	106.9	± 6.54	(Todd and Lindala)
539	**American Negroes**	**106.65**	± **5.65**	**(Present series)**
—	Polish Jews	106	—	(Martin)
247	Old Americans	*105.9	± 4.24	(Hrdlička, IV)
46794	Swedes	104.57	± 4.33	(Lundborg and Linders)

---

* See note page 43.
[1] Hallowell's measurements were made with the same instrument I used.

The Anthropometry of the American Negro

—	Bugu	104	—	(Martin)
—	Batua	103	—	(Martin)
50	Bahiru	101.12	—	(Czekanowski)
86	Hawaiians	111.31	± 5.08	(Von Luschan)
79	Marquesans	103.1	± 5.19	(Sullivan, I)

Table VI[1]		Table VII		Table VIII		Table IX	
Minimum Forehead Width		Distance between Inner Corners of Eyes		Distance between Outer Corners of Eyes		Interpupillary Distance	
Mm.	No.	Mm.	No.	Mm.	No.	Mm.	No.
91	1	21	1	91	4	56	1
92	—	22	—	92	6	57	3
93	1	23	—	93	6	58	8
94	—	24	1	94	12	59	6
95	4	25	—	95	15	60	16
96	6	26	3	96	16	61	16
97	3	27	8	97	17	62	26
98	8	28	6	98	33	63	39
99	9	29	23	99	40	64	46
100	13	30	33	100	28	65	54
01	24	31	67	01	59	66	45
02	36	32	62	02	47	67	60
03	35	33	78	03	40	68	56
04	42	34	77	04	40	69	53
105	58	35	60	105	42	70	24
06	54	36	45	06	35	71	35
07	44	37	33	07	16	72	13
08	31	38	16	08	25	73	11
09	32	39	10	09	13	74	5
110	35	40	4	110	9	75	8
11	26	41	6	11	8	76	2
12	16	42	—	12	3	77	1
13	17	43	4	13	8	78	—
14	8	44	1	14	4	79	1
115	11			115	4		
16	11			16	2		
17	2			17	—		
18	3			18	1		
19	1			19	—		
120	3			120	—		
21	—			21	—		
22	1			22	—		
				23	1		
				24	—		
				125	—		
				26	—		
				27	1		

[1] Add: 126—1; 141—1; 147—1; 150—1.

10. DISTANCE BETWEEN INNER CORNERS OF EYES
(Table VII).

This trait, like the preceding one, was only measured on the Howard University group. The average is 33.14 mm. with a mean error of ± .13 mm. Comparison of these results may be made with such reports for males as are available:

100 W. R. U. Negroes	34.8	± 2.71	(Todd and Lindala)
40 Vai	*34.58	± 2.59	(Virchow)
20 Ekoi	*33.20	± 4.71	(Mansfeld)
538 **American Negroes**	**33.14**	**± 2.99**	**(Present series)**
50 Bahiru	33.12	—	(Czekanowski)

The low bridge of the nose, which accompanies the greater distance between the eyes, and which is characteristic of the true Negro, is present in all the samples presented above; the variability of the Ekoi in this trait is much larger than might be expected. Further comparison (with European peoples particularly) may be made from the table of averages which Martin gives (p. 430):

Hottentots	37.2
Bushmen	36.0
Fan	36.0
Belgians	35.0
Rumanians	32.9
Bavarians	32.3
Greeks	32.1
Parisians	31.5

The mean for the American Negro sample seems to lie between the average values of the European populations and those of the Africans. Although it is near those for the East Africans and the Ekoi and Vai, it is much lower than that of the Fan, who are also a West African people, and somewhat higher than most of the European peoples represented. The low variability exhibited by the American Negroes, in view of its greatly mixed racial origin, is also to be noted.

11. DISTANCE BETWEEN OUTER CORNERS OF EYES
(Table VIII).

In this trait again, only the Howard University series is employed.

Number of cases:	535
Average:	102.45 mm.
Standard deviation:	± 5.02 mm.
Error of the Average:	± .22 mm.

We may compare these with similar statistical constants for the following male populations, although these do not in every case represent

---

* See note page 43.

the same measurement that I took. Thus, Tremearne's was biorbital breadth rather than the dimension measured by me. However, there is not enough difference between the two to make the direct comparison of results inadvisable.

499	English criminals	114.83	±4.92	(Goring)
55	Kajiji	*106.43	±3.83	(Tremearne)
72	Kagoro	*104.03	±4.57	(Tremearne)
20	Ekoi	*102.45	±5.08	(Mansfeld)
535	**American Negroes**	102.45	±5.02	**(Present series)**
40	Vai	* 97.15	±4.08	(Virchow)
50	Bahiru	91.66	—	(Czekanowski)

Martin gives the following averages for Europeans, (p. 430):

	European
Lithuanians	100.0
Greeks	98.0
Rumanians	96.9
Bavarians (female)	85.0

When we compare the present series with these others, we see that generally speaking, it falls between the European groups and the pure Africans, the English criminal class, however, standing out in striking exception. This is not true of the East African Bahiru, who are presumably mixed with Hamitic strains, nor is it true of the West African Vai. The mean for the Ekoi, as well as the standard deviation, is almost identical with that for the American Negroes, while the mean for this group is lower than those for the biorbital breadth measured by Tremearne on the peoples he studied. My sample however, is materially more variable than either of these.

12. INTERPUPILLARY DISTANCE. (Table IX)

Only the Howard University series is represented for this trait, as was the case of the traits preceding it. The statistical constants are:

Number of cases:	529
Average:	66.42 mm.
Standard deviation:	± 3.77 mm.
Error of the Average:	± .16 mm.

Martin gives an average for an unstated number of 20 year-old Munich boys as 52.54 mm., and one for 5000 soldiers, presumably Germans, as 62.2 mm. Both of these are appreciably smaller than that for this American Negro sample. We also may compare the above figures with those for Todd's samples of Negro and White male cadavera:

100 W. R. U. Negro cadavera 68.4 ± 4.41 mm.
100 W. R. U. White cadavera 63.4 ± 4.19 mm.

---

* See note page 43.

13. HEIGHT OF NOSE.

With this trait we return again to the full series, to obtain which it was seen that a combination of the component series could be effected, in spite of the uncertainty of the upper land-mark. The distribution may be seen in Table XXXVIII, p. 137. The mean value is 53.41 mm. with a mean error of ± .12 mm.

For comparative purposes, the following table, giving means and variabilities (where these latter are available) for other male series, may be consulted:

260	Swedes	61.37	± 2.18	(Lundborg and Linders)
539	Pure Sioux	58.3	± 3.94	(Sullivan, II)
75	Armenians (Asiatic)	56.4	± 4.9	(Boas, VI)
77	Mixed Sioux	54.9	± 3.55	(Sullivan, II)
247	Old Americans	*53.5	± 3.36	(Hrdlička, IV)
960	**American Negroes**	**53.41**	**± 3.75**	**(Present series)**
50	Bahiru	52.22	—	(Czekanowski)
41	Montagnais-Naskapi	51.8	± 3.86	(Hallowell)
34	Lotuko	50.4	± 4.5	(Seligman)
91	Masai	50.13	± 3.44	(Leys and Joyce)
27	Somali	49.90	± 2.84	(Leys and Joyce)
30	Acholi	49.8	± 3.4	(Seligman)
55	Kajiji	*49.22	± 3.84	(Tremearne)
—	Fan	48.0	—	(Martin)
72	Kagoro	*47.93	± 4.01	(Tremearne)
20	Ekoi	*47.05	± 2.76	(Mansfeld)
110	Embu	46.40	± 3.34	(Leys and Joyce)
324	Akikuyu	46.04	± 3.24	(Leys and Joyce)
128	Akamba	45.94	± 3.62	(Leys and Joyce)
48	Ashanti	45.17	± 2.48	(Rattray)
40	Vai	*42.45	± 3.59	(Virchow)
86	Hawaiians	*56.71	± 3.96	(Von Luschan)
84	Marquesans	53.5	± 3.97	(Sullivan, I)

Comparing the American Negro with these other populations, we find that he lies between the African populations, on the one hand, and the Old Americans and the Armenians, Sioux and Swedes on the other, being practically identical, on the average, with the Old Americans and the Marquesans. It is quite possible that the mean nasal height given above for the American Negroes represented in this sample is a result of a blending of the West African, White, and Indian nasal heights, and it is striking that there should be this identity with the only White population represented in the above table, while the mean is higher than the African, and lower than the Indian populations. The variability of the present sample when comparison is made, is relatively low, and again argues the homogeneity which is in accordance with the other findings which have already been mentioned as pointing to this condition.

---

* See note page 43.

14. WIDTH OF NOSE.

The frequency distribution for this trait, which is represented here by the adult males of all the component series combined into one, may be consulted in Table XL, p. 141.

Number of cases: 961
Average: 40.92 mm.
Standard deviation: ± 3.99 mm.
Error of the average: ± .13 mm.

Comparing these data with those for other male populations, we have:

55	Kajiji	*45.51	±	2.83	(Tremearne)
72	Kagoro	*44.41	±	2.78	(Tremearne)
—	Fan	44.0	—		(Martin)
20	Ekoi	*43.95	±	2.18	(Mansfeld)
30	Acholi	43.5	±	3.18	(Seligman)
48	Ashanti	42.48	±	3.20	(Rattray)
34	Lotuko	42.4	±	2.3	(Seligman)
100	W. R. U. Negro cadavera	42.4	±	3.68	(Todd and Lindala)
50	Bahiru	41.84	—		(Czekanowski)
961	**American Negroes**	**40.92**	±	**3.99**	**(Present series)**
110	Embu	40.84	±	2.87	(Leys and Joyce)
384	Akikuyu	39.93	±	2.85	(Leys and Joyce)
540	Pure Sioux	39.9	±	3.22	(Sullivan, II)
128	Akamba	39.56	±	2.77	(Leys and Joyce)
40	Vai	*38.25	±	3.19	(Virchow)
91	Masai	38.10	±	2.95	(Leys and Joyce)
77	Half-blood Sioux	37.6	±	3.04	(Sullivan, II)
41	Montagnais-Naskapi	37.6	±	3.38	(Hallowell)
75	Armenians (Asiatic)	37.2	±	2.9	(Boas, VI)
100	W. R. U. White cadavera	34.9	±	3.68	(Todd and Lindala)
227	Somali	34.70	±	3.07	(Leys and Joyce)
267	Swedes	30.18	±	3.65	(Lundborg and Linders)
84	Marquesans	43.2	±	2.70	(Sullivan, I)
86	Hawaiians	*43.13	±	2.94	(Von Luschan)

Here again we see that the American Negro population lies between the White and Indian averages, on the one hand, and those for the West African populations, with the exception of the Vai, on the other. The Western Reserve collection is somewhat broader as to nasal width than the present sample, but it is smaller than the West African peoples, and larger than the Indian or White means presented. The variability of the present sample is the highest of all those series represented, and is followed in this respect by the Western Reserve Negro series, these cadavera, however, being no more variable than the White ones.

15. DEPTH OF NOSE (Table X).

For this trait we have once more only the Howard University series represented, as this measurement was not taken on the other series. Its average and mean error are 21.33 ± .09 mm. This measurement

---

* See note page 43.

is rarely taken, and other than the short table given in Martin (p. 457), which is mainly for male populations which are not in any way related to the one under consideration, I was able to locate only two means. Martin, for those averages he gives, says nothing about the variability of the series from which they have been computed, nor the numbers of cases involved. Since he offers no references, it was not possible to work out these in the manner I did for Mansfeld's data. The averages, however, are given here for whatever comparative value they may hold:

	Polish Jews	26.0	—	(Martin)
20	Ekoi	21.45	± 2.71	(Mansfeld)
535	**American Negroes**	**21.33**	**± 2.04**	**(Present series)**
	White Russians	21.0	—	(Martin)
	Toricelli	20.0	—	,,
	Buriates	18.2	—	,,
	Nahuqua	15.5	—	,,
	Auetö	13.9	—	,,
50	Bahiru	13.38	—	(Czekanowski)
	Mawembi pygmies	13.2	—	(Martin)

Here we find what might be expected, — namely, that in the Negroid populations the depth of the nose is not as great as in European peoples, who have the narrow high nostrils. At the same time, the mean of the present sample is greater than is that of the Bahiru of East Africa, and about the same as that of the Ekoi. The variability of my series is smaller than is that of the Ekoi.

16. DISTANCE FROM CREASE TO TIP OF NOSE (RIGHT SIDE) (Table XI).

Like the trait preceding it, this measurement is represented here only by the series measured at Howard University. The average and variability for the series are:

Number of cases:	535	
Average:	35.40 mm.	
Standard deviation:	±	2.23 mm.
Error of the average:	±	.19 mm.

To my knowledge, there are no data available for comparative purposes.

17. UPPER FACIAL HEIGHT (Table XII).

It will be remembered that in the discussion of the comparability of results obtained by different observers who have contributed to the data of this study, this trait stood out as one of the few for which series could not be combined. Therefore, my own measurements of the Howard University group are the only ones which have been tabulated for comparative purposes, not because it is felt that these represent actuality to any greater extent than any of the other series, but because it constitutes the largest series of adult males measured by one observer. The average and its error are: 71.34 ± .18 mm.

Table X Nasal Depth (sn.-tip)		Table XI Nasal Depth (cr.-tip)		Tabel XII Upper Facial Height		Table XIII Total Facial Height	
Mm.	No.	Mm.	No.	Mm.	No.	Mm.	No.
16	1					102	1
17	10					03	1
18	34	28	1	54	1	04	—
19	55	29	1	55	—	105	—
20	81	30	1	56	1	06	1
21	110	31	16	57	—	07	2
22	97	32	24	58	—	08	1
23	72	33	45	59	—	09	1
24	39	34	99	60	—	110	4
25	22	35	99	61	1	11	12
26	9	36	74	62	3	12	8
27	5	37	80	63	2	13	14
		38	45	64	14	14	12
		39	28	65	24	115	19
		40	15	66	16	16	16
		41	5	67	35	17	14
		42	1	68	39	18	25
		43	—	69	39	19	25
	4	44	1	70	45	120	40
				71	62	21	41
				72	49	22	32
				73	43	23	26
				74	36	24	34
				75	44	125	30
				76	30	26	32
				77	19	27	21
				78	12	28	19
				79	11	29	26
				80	6	130	19
				81	4	31	15
				82	1	32	17
				83	1	33	6
						34	7
						135	7
						36	1
						37	—
						38	2
						39	1
						140	—
						41	2

A Description of the American Negro Type 61

Comparisons may be made with the means and sigmas for the following African male populations:

50 Bahiru	72.56	—	(Czekanowski)
538 American Negroes	**71.34**	**± 4.06**	**(Present series)**
34 Lotuko	66.1	± 4.9	(Seligman)
30 Acholi	68.5	± 4.6	(Seligman)
48 Ashanti	59.89	± 4.48	(Rattray)
20 Ekoi	*54.75	± 4.10	(Mansfeld)

It will be seen that the average value of the American Negro in this trait is greater than that for any of these African populations except the Bahiru. This is not strange, as the large upper facial height is expected in non-Negroid populations, and the Bahiru are an East African people (as are the Acholi and Lotuko, whose averages are larger than those of the West African Ekoi and Ashanti) who have Hamitic admixture, although in the light of the unreliability of this measurement, these figures cannot be taken as being of large importance, and are given only for what they may be worth. The homogeneity of the American Negro as manifested in the variability of this sample as compared to that of the other populations is apparent.

18. TOTAL FACIAL HEIGHT (Table XIII).

As in the case of the trait preceding, the measurement of this character is very unreliable, and therefore the component series have not been combined for it, but only the Howard University group is utilized.

Number of cases: 534
Average: 122.60 mm.
Standard deviation: ± 6.31 mm.
Error of the average: ± .27 mm.

Comparison with other male populations may be made from the following table:

46982	Swedes	126.57	± 6.92	(Lundborg and Linders)
537	Pure Sioux	124.6	± 6.37	(Sullivan, II)
2348	English criminals	123.73	± 7.70	(Goring)
534	**American Negroes**	**122.60**	**± 6.31**	**(Present series)**
77	Half-blood Sioux	121.5	± 6.36	(Sullivan, II)
100	Bavarians	121.3	—	(Fischer)
41	Montagnais-Naskapis	120.7	± 4.65	(Hallowell)
247	Old Americans	*119.3	± 6.72	(Hrdlička, IV)
30	Acholi	118.3	± 5.8	(Seligman)
34	Lotuko	118.2	± 5.4	(Seligman)
21	Bagirimi	118.0	—	(Talbot)
20	Ekoi	*114.45	± 6.82	(Mansfeld)
50	Bahiru	113.91	—	(Czekanowski)
72	Kagoro	*112.04	± 7.52	(Tremearne)
48	Ashanti	108.29	± 5.87	(Rattray)
40	Vai	*106.78	± 5.84	(Virchow)
86	Hawaiians	*127.78	± 5.82	(von Luschan)
81	Marquesans	124.1	± 7.80	(Sullivan, I)

* See note page 43.

This comparison places the mean for the American Negro sample above that of the Old Americans, and well above the African groups represented, whether they be true Negroes from West Africa, or East African Hamites and Nilotes. It is, however, below the Swedes, the pure Sioux, the Marquesans, the English criminals, and the Hawaiians. The same criticism of the worth of these comparisons holds, however, as in the case of the preceding trait. The population used here as representative of the American Negro does not have a high variability when comparison is made with the other groups in the table.

19. BIZYGOMATIC WIDTH.

Here again we have the adult males from all the component series of this study combined into one. The resulting frequency distribution is given in the adult column of Table XLIV, p. 147. The average and its error are 139.17 ± .19 mm. Comparison with other male populations may be made from the following table:

538	Sioux	149.1	± 5.45	(Sullivan, II)
157	Full-blood Ojibwa	147.7	—	(Boas, I)
85	$3/4$-blood Ojibwa	147.3	—	(Boas, I)
52	Montagnais-Naskapi	146.8	± 4.89	(Hallowell)
73	$3/8$-blood Ojibwa	144.7	—	(Boas, I)
75	Armenians (Asiatic)	143.6	± 5.1	(Boas, VI)
77	Half-blood Sioux	143.4	± 5.49	(Sullivan, II)
55	Kajiji	*139.49	± 5.03	(Tremearne)
263	Foreign-born Scottish	139.3	± 5.6	(Boas, IV)
956	**American Negroes**	**139.17**	**± 5.92**	**(Present series)**
120	Ekoi	*139.05	± 3.94	(Mansfeld)
100	W. R. U. Whites (cadavera)	139.0	± 6.09	(Todd and Lindala)
100	W. R. U. Negroes (cadavera)	139.0	± 6.73	(Todd and Lindala)
247	Old Americans	*138.6	± 4.82	(Hrdlička, IV)
100	Bavarians	138.0	—	(Fischer)
2348	English criminals	137.51	± 6.54	(Goring)
40	Vai	*137.17	± 4.94	(Virchow)
72	Kagoro	*136.96	± 4.05	(Tremearne)
46981	Swedes	136.02	± 4.84	(Lundborg and Linders)
50	Bahiru	135.56	—	(Czekanowski)
598	Foreign-born Bohemians	135.2	± 5.5	(Boas, IV)
48	Ashanti	134.67	± 4.28	(Rattray)
34	Lotuko	134.4	± 5.35	(Seligman)
30	Acholi	134.3	± 4.6	(Seligman)
86	Hawaiians	*145.31	± 5.30	(Von Luschan)
84	Marquesans	143.2	± 4.88	(Sullivan, II)

The mean of the present series, when compared with those for other peoples represented in the above table, places the facial width of the American Negro with that of the Kajiji and Ekoi of West Africa, the Western Reserve samples of cadavera, and also that

---

* See note page 43.

of the Old Americans and the foreign-born Scottish. It is larger than the means for the English criminals, the Swedes, the Vai and Kagoro of West Africa, and those of the other African populations. The facial widths of the American Indian populations for which we have these data (although there is little likelihood that the Indian mixture in the series studied in this research comprises any appreciable amount of Sioux) are much greater than those of other populations. Whether this signifies that the Indian influence in the racial crossing can be detected or not, cannot be stated until a more definite investigation into the influence of the Indian element in crossing with Negroes is made. The standard deviations, where we have them, show that except for the Western Reserve White cadavera and the English criminals, the sample used in this study has the highest variability of any of the populations listed above. This might result from the large number of different types which have gone to make up the American Negro and emphasizes again that low variability in one, or even a large number of traits, is not an earnest that it will be found in others which may be studied.

20. WIDTH OF MOUTH (Table XIV, p. 66).

This trait was measured for adult males only on the Howard University series. The average and its error are 53.15 ± .17 mm. The comparative table of averages (without, however, their variabilities) cited by Martin (p. 444), may be given here, together with other comparative material which I have been able to find:

—	Ba-Binga	58.0	—	(Martin)
—	Fan	57.0	—	(Martin)
100	W. R. U. Negro cadavera	56.5	± 4.05	(Todd and Lindala)
—	Polish Jews	56.0	—	(Martin)
—	Egyptians (from Charga)	54.0	—	(Martin)
—	Belgians	54.0	—	(Martin)
247	Old Americans	*53.7	± 3.78	(Hrdlička, IV)
584	**American Negroes**	**53.15**	± **4.01**	**(Present series)**
—	French	53.0	—	(Martin)
40	Vai	*52.52	± 5.04	(Virchow)
50	Bahiru	51.46	—	(Czekanowski)
—	Colorado Indians	51.0	—	(Martin)
—	Ba-Tua	51.0	—	(Martin)
20	Ekoi	*49.2	± 3.63	(Mansfeld)
—	Bavarians (female)	(47.2)	—	(Martin)

The American Negroes, in this trait, seem to place themselves at about the same average value as the Vai, the one American Indian group which is represented in Martin's table, the French and Belgians, and the Old Americans. The Fan and Ba-Binga, as well as the Polish Jews, seem to have wider mouths than these other peoples.

---

* See note page 43.

21. THICKNESS OF LIPS (CENTER).

The total combined series of adult males is available for comparison with other populations, for this trait. The mean and its error are 21.24 ± .45 mm. The frequency distribution will be found in the adult column of Table XLVI, p. 151. Comparison of these results may be made with the following averages and sigmas, for other male populations:

20 Ekoi	*25.60 ± 3.73	(Mansfeld)
40 Vai................	*24.91 ± 4.32	(Virchow)
50 Bahiru............	23.18 —-	(Czekanowski)
959 American Negroes ..	21.24 ± 4.50	**(Present series)**
100 W. R. U. Negro....	21.1 ± 4.92	(Todd and Lindala)
100 W. R. U. White ...	11.5 ± 3.70	(Todd and Lindala)

We see that means for both the American Negro groups are in close correspondence, while those for the Vai and Ekoi of West Africa and that of the East African Bahiru are materially higher. The one average available for a White series is, as would be expected, much smaller. It must be remembered that the Western Reserve measurements, however, being made on cadavera, might perhaps be smaller than those taken on the living, due to shrinkage after death, although Professor Todd has informed me that this, in his opinion, is not likely to affect the results and thus makes comparison possible in the case of this trait. The standard deviations of the Western Reserve Negroes and of the present series correspond closely.

Martin gives a table of lip measurements with averages only, and this, for males, may also be cited for comparative purposes:

Bondijo	26.2
Ba-Tua	23.8
M'Baka	23.6
Hottentots	23.1
Chinese from Setchuan .	22.0
American Negroes	**21.24**
Ba-Binga	18.8
Shoshoni	14.7
Bavarians	14.2

The means of all the African peoples (including the Hottentots, though there is, of course, no relationship between them and the American Negroes) are larger than for the mixed American Negro series represented in this study, except the average for the Ba-Binga. The European and American Indian representatives in the table, on the other hand, show average values which are much lower.

22. THICKNESS OF LIPS, (RIGHT) (Table XV, p. 66).

This, as has been said, is more of a check measurement than anything else, and when it had served its purpose on the Howard University series, was discarded in the later portion of this research.

---

* See note page 43.

It may be given here for that series, however, as a matter of record, and as a check on the statistical constants given for the trait just preceding it. The mean and variability are:

>   Number of cases: 535
>   Average: 23.26 mm.
>   Standard deviation: ± 4.22 mm.
>   Error of the average: ± .18 mm.

There are no comparative data to be had for this measurement.

23. PHYSIOGNOMIC HEIGHT OF EAR (EAR LENGTH).

Combining the adult males of all the series in which males were measured, we have the average and its error 60.70 ± .14 mm. The "adult" column of Table L, p. 157, gives the frequency distribution. Comparisons with other male populations may be made from the following table of averages and variabilities.

247	Old Americans	*66.9	±	5.72	(Hrdlička, IV)
260	Swedes	65.06	±	3.86	(Lundborg and Linders)
2383	English criminals	64.31	±	4.88	(Goring)
—	Europeans (Aryans)	64.0	—		(Karutz)
959	**American Negroes**	60.70	±	**4.82**	**(Present series)**
20	Ekoi	*59.55	±	3.96	(Mansfeld)
—	Negroes in general	58.5	±	—	(Karutz)
50	Bahiru	57.36	—		(Czekanowski)
56	Hawaiians	*69.4	±	4.65	(Von Luschan)
84	Marquesans	67.1	±	5.72	(Sullivan, I)

The size of the ear of American Negroes is relatively close to the average of the measurement for Negroes in general, computed by Karutz, and to those for the Bahiru and the Ekoi. The data from Karutz' work, though presumably comprehensive, are difficult to use and to evaluate, since he does not give the number of cases involved in his calculations, nor the persons who originally measured the subjects who are represented in his results. Martin (p. 468) gives a long table of average length of ear for many populations, and this includes the average derived from Karutz' paper. It shows that the Negroid peoples tend to have the smallest ears in relation to their stature, the largest of any of the Negro peoples represented in Martin's table being that for Negroes in general, given above. The same observation may be made in the present table, in which the averages for the Old Americans, and for Europeans in general, are materially larger than those for the Negroes. The smallness of the variability of the American Negro sample used here, when it is compared in this respect to the homogeneous Old Americans, to say nothing of the mixed Marquesans, is to be noted.

---

* See note page 43.

Table XIV		Table XV		Table XVI		Table XVII	
Width of Mouth		Thickness of Lips (right side)		Width of Hand (Met. lat. — Met. med.)		Length of Middle Finger (Phal. III — Dak. III)	
Mm.	No.	Mm.	No.	Mm.	No.	Mm.	No.
						91	2
		12	3			92	2
43	5	13	2			93	2
44	3	14	3	74	1	94	1
45	5	15	8	75	3	95	3
46	9	16	15	76	1	96	5
47	18	17	18	77	6	97	8
48	23	18	23	78	9	98	9
49	33	19	21	79	8	99	8
50	38	20	42	80	13	100	3
51	49	21	51	81	36	01	20
52	57	22	40	82	49	02	20
53	45	23	58	83	59	03	20
54	57	24	51	84	40	04	22
55	60	25	50	85	47	105	35
56	30	26	30	86	41	06	35
57	25	27	30	87	40	07	31
58	26	28	26	88	40	08	38
59	18	29	25	89	42	09	32
60	12	30	19	90	35	110	43
61	8	31	7	91	22	11	39
62	6	32	5	92	16	12	29
63	3	33	4	93	9	13	30
64	3	34	1	94	8	14	17
65	—	35	1	95	4	115	9
66	—	36	2	96	3	16	23
67	—			97	1	17	8
68	1			98	2	18	11
				99	2	19	11
				100	1	120	4
						21	5
						22	6
						23	1
						24	2
						125	1
						26	2
						27	—
						28	—
						29	—
						130	2

24. PHYSIOGNOMIC WIDTH OF EAR (WIDTH OF EAR).

Here again the series used represents the total of adult males in all series. The frequency distribution is given in the column marked "adults" of Table LII, p. 161. The average and its error are 33.79 ± .09. The following comparative averages and, in a few cases, variabilities, for male populations are available:

— Alsatians	39.1		—	(Martin, p. 469)
247 Old Americans	*37.9	±	2.52	(Hrdlička, IV)
— Egyptians from Kharga Oasis	37.0		—	(Martin)
20 Ekoi	*35.6	±	3.24	(Mansfeld)
— Germans (Hamburg)	35.5		—	(Martin)
50 Bahiru	35.2		—	(Czekanowski)
260 Swedes	34.7	±	2.17	(Lundborg and Linders)
960 **American Negroes**	**33.79**	±	**2.68**	**(Present series)**
— Great Russians	32.8		—	(Martin)
— Eskimo	31.2		—	(Martin)
56 Hawaiians	*37.2	±	3.02	(Von Luschan)
— Aino	36.4		—	(Martin)
84 Marquesans	32.7	±	2.52	(Sullivan, I)

From this table it may be seen that the ear width of the American Negro is somewhat less than that of the Europeans, and much smaller than that of the Old White Americans. It seems that the width of the ear in the American Negro tends distinctly toward the Negroid type of ear, since it is somewhat smaller than even that of the West African Ekoi and the East African Bahiru. The comparatively low variability of the sample of the present study, in spite of the amount of racial crossing it represents, should be noticed in the table above.

25. WIDTH OF RIGHT HAND (Table XVI).

This trait was only measured, as far as adult males are concerned, on the Howard University series. The average and variability are:

Number of cases: 538
Average: 85.75 mm.
Standard deviation: ± 4.25 mm.
Error of the average: ± .18 mm.

Comparison of the average and variability of this series with those of others may be made as follows:

20 Ekoi	*81.90	±	3.63	(Mansfeld)
100 W. R. U. Negro cadavera[1]	80.7	±	4.64	(Todd and Lindala)
100 W. R. U. White cadavera[1]	77.9	±	4.66	(Todd and Lindala)
50 Bahiru	77.8		—	(Czekanowski)

The average of the series used here to represent the American Negroes is greater than those for the two African populations represented, and somewhat larger than that of either figure given for the Negro

---
* See note page 43.
[1] Left hand.

or White cadavera. The standard deviation of all three samples are relatively the same. Further comparison may be made with the table given by Martin (p. 301) which, however, represents the width of the hand expressed in terms of percentage of stature. For the Howard series, this is 5.01%. For other male populations, the average relative hand-widths are:

Bugu	5.8
Yakoma	5.6
Lithuanians	5.6
Egyptians (Kharga)	5.4
Duala	5.2
French	5.1
American Negroes	**5.01**
Bavarians (female)	5.0
European Jews	4.9
Mawembi pygmies	4.8
Suaheli	4.8
Bushmen	4.4
Togo (West Africa)	4.2

Thus in relative hand-width, the American Negro may be seen to be about the same as the Europeans, but midway between the West Africans and the Hamitic peoples represented in the table.

26. LENGTH OF MIDDLE FINGER (RIGHT HAND) (Table XVII).

For this trait, as for the one preceding it, the Howard University sample alone is used to represent the American Negro. The average and its error are 108.63 ± .27 mm. Comparison may be made with the following male series:

3000	English criminals (left hand)	115.47	± 5.48	(Macdonnell)
801	Cairo native (left hand)	114.09	± 6.14	(Orensteen)
20	Ekoi	*112.50	± 5.91	(Mansfeld)
538	**American Negroes**	**108.63**	**± 6.21**	**(Present series)**
50	Bahiru	103.34	—	(Czekanowski)

The longest fingers, those of the English criminals, are appreciably longer than those of the American Negroes, and so are those of the Cairo natives and of the Ekoi, while those of the Bahiru are shorter. The variability of the Howard University sample is the highest of all those available. Further comparison of averages may be made with those below, abstracted from Martin's table for this trait (p. 303):

Letts	106
Lithuanians	105
Jews	97
Little Russians	97
Chinese	93

---

* See note page 43.

These averages are all smaller than that of the American Negro sample, and also of the West African Ekoi. The fact that the average of the present series is larger than any of them should not be strange in view of the size of the Negro hand, the middle finger of which, even here, is larger on the average than any of those for White peoples except the English criminals.

27. Pigmentation, Black (n) Element, Upper Outer Arm.

In the case of this trait, one of the most important as far as Negro-White crossing and the difference between Negroes and Whites are concerned, the combination of the various series into one large one has not been possible. As was demonstrated in the last chapter, the personal subjective element bulks too large, and the individual differences between observers, where the method was the same, makes combination hazardous. Therefore the series to be used in this and the three following aspects of this trait are those of male adults measured by myself alone, — the members of the Howard University series 20 years of age and over, and adult male Negroes measured in New York City.

The statistical constants for this series are:

Number of cases:	593
Average:	66.65%
Standard deviation: ±	13.98%
Error of the average: ±	.57%

Consideration of the frequency distribution of this trait, given in the "adult" column of Table LVI, p. 165, shows a large amount of skewness toward the lower ranges, and a massing at the upper, with the modal value well above the average. There is little evidence to be seen in the curve of the bimodality of which Davenport[1] speaks as the evidence for genetic dimorphism of the black. Davenport's conclusions are based on a series of pigmentation observations, made with the color-top, of 18 persons who declared themselves to be of unmixed Negro ancestry, and the data are not corrected for the error of 59% black which is found in the red disk, as was mentioned in the last chapter.[2] However, we shall be able to discuss the validity of Davenport's results on the basis of the data from the unmixed-Negro genealogical class of the Howard series when the results for these genealogical groups are presented in chapter VI.

As noted in the preceding chapter, comparisons with the results of others are difficult, due to the newness of the method employed in the consideration of skin color in this study. Comparison with Davenport's material has not been attempted, since it consists of a small number of cases and does not represent unselected

---

[1] Davenport, (I).
[2] For a detailed examination of Davenport's hypothesis, and its invalidation on the basis of his own data, see Barnes, (I).

material. However, Todd and Van Gorder, in their paper on pigmentation already mentioned[1] give the readings for samples of skin from the upper part of the upper left arm (superficial to the lower portion of the deltoid muscle) and therefore directly comparable to those taken in the present study. Since the average and variability for their 97 cases (excluding three given as jaundiced) were not published, I have computed these, and as a result find, for the N (black) element, the following:

Average: 82.79%
Standard deviation: ± 6.11%[2]

These results differ so radically from my own that the discrepancy demands further attention. That these differences are not the result of chance sampling is to be seen from the computation of the difference between the two averages and its error (16.14 ± .83) and of the error of the difference between the two mean square variabilities (7.87 ± .57).

Todd and Van Gorder state categorically that they do not believe that the corrected value for N is materially different in the living and in cadavera. While they assert that their conclusions are made in comparison with Davenport's materials, which, they say, are too few "to make the statement that the difference between the corrected figures is practically negligible anything more than an impression"[3] they later state that they "believe that the *corrected* N value in the skin of the cadaver gives a very close approximation to the true value of N in the living".[4] If we accept their statement, then we must turn elsewhere for an explanation of the large differences between their results and mine. They state that their population was "apparently full Negro in most instances and it is simply our desire to make no unwarrantable assumption which makes us insist upon styling them Negro-hybrids".[5] If we compare their results with those of the Howard series who, according to their genealogies, are full-blooded Negroes (the N-class), we find that the mean and sigma are 75.49 ± 10.34,[6] again a value which is materially different from theirs, although not nearly as great as that between their results and mine when my entire series is considered. One explanation of the discrepancy in the figures, therefore, might be that the greater hybridity of the sample employed in this study, (due, perhaps, to social selection acting in the case of Todd and Van Gorder's sample, since most of the individuals comprising this

---

[1] Todd and Van Gorder, (I).
[2] ibid., p. 248.
[3] More recently Todd and Lindala (I) have published statistical constants for 100 cases, the average and standard deviation being 82.0 ± 8.8%.
[4] Todd and Van Gorder, (I), p. 249.
[5] ibid., p. 248.
[6] see p. 219.

latter were paupers who might, owing to social causes, be selected from the more Negroid portion of the Negro population of Cleveland) has affected the results. As has been stated, they reject the explanation that the observations on the living and on cadavera may give different results. The third, and one which is of the greatest importance and must be thoroughly investigated before further work with the Milton-Bradley color-top is undertaken, is the question of the reliability of the results obtained through it. In the final analysis, the colors are selected arbitrarily, and have little relation to the physiological and anatomical causes of skin-color; hence they may or may not be an adequate means of describing skin color. Certainly until a further standardization of such possible sources of error as difference of speed in spinning, the personal equation (which undoubtedly bulked large in consideration of the data gathered by the various observers who contributed to this research), and the like, are worked out, the results which have been found here seem to point to too great a discrepancy to make the top available for comparative purposes.[1] Which of the explanations offered accounts for the large differences shown between the averages and deviations of our series, or whether or not all of them have contributed, I do not undertake to state.

28. PIGMENTATION, RED (R) ELEMENT, UPPER OUTER ARM.

The frequency distribution for this element of the color-top for the series used here, — i. e., those adult males measured by myself, — is given in Table LX, p. 169, in the column marked "adult". These figures, it must again be stated, are those for the red after correction, that is, after 59% of the original reading of this sector of the color-top has been deducted from it to allow for the difference between the red of the disk and true red. The curve for red, it will be noted, is not nearly as skewed as is the one for black, there being, however, a slight suggestion of bimodality which, at the same time, may be due to chance. There is a slight massing toward the upper end of the curve, the modal value being at 14%, 1.62% above the mean. The statistical constants for this color are:

Number of cases: 593
Average: 12.38%
Standard deviation: ± 2.84%
Error of the average: ± .12%

We may compare this average and sigma with those computed from the data given by Todd and Van Gorder:

Average: 7.61%
Standard deviation: ± 2.51%

---

[1] Since the above was written, the use of the color-top has been discussed in greater detail by Todd, Blackwood, and Beecher (I).

If we test the difference between these two sets of figures, we find that the error of the difference between the averages, when compared to the difference between the averages themselves (4.77 ± .28) gives us a difference which is statistically significant, and not due to chance sampling. The error of the difference between the sigmas, when compared with their difference (.33 ± .19) is, however, so large that it may be due to chance, as would be expected where the difference between these two values is as small as it is here. The difference between the averages may be easily understood, since Todd and Van Gorder's are from specimens of skin taken from cadavera. They themselves say that "examination of the R value shows that in bloody skins there may be a fairly high percentage of red and that this drops as the methaemoglobin forms.. It seems possible that we have here an indication of the difference between the skin in the living and in the cadaver... From our general experience we should imagine that a change of 5% or even more would not be unlikely." The difference between their average and mine (4.77%) attests to the accuracy of their judgement, and the smallness of the difference between our standard deviations contributes to our assurance that we may be safe in accepting the explanation given above for this difference. It is only the sentence immediately following the last one quoted that we may hesitate to accept, as has been pointed out: "The important thing is that the N value remains the same."[1]

29. Pigmentation, Yellow (y) Element, Upper Outer Arm.

The distribution of this color element for the present series may be seen in the "adult" column of Table LXII, p. 171. It represents the percentages of the entire surface of the color-top which is yellow when the skins measured have been matched, and, as has been said, this color entails no corrective factor. The curve skews off toward the upper ranges, and masses at the lower, the modal values being at 5% and 7%, materially lower than the average. This skewness would be expected, of course, from consideration of the size of the mean square variation compared to that of the average. Yet this is not strange, for from the genealogical information the distribution of ancestral type leans somewhat more heavily toward the Negro than toward the White, and since the yellow must be smaller in quantity for those skins the color of which is relatively light, we have a result that is not surprising. The average and variability for the series employed here are:

Number of cases: 593
Average: 10.81%
Standard deviation: ± 4.66%
Error of the average: ± .19%

---

[1] Todd and Van Gorder, (I), p. 254.

A Description of the American Negro Type 73

Comparing these results with those of Todd and Van Gorder for the same color, we find when we compute their values for the 94 cadavera used before:

$$\text{Average:} \quad 4.98\%$$
$$\text{Standard deviation:} \quad \pm\ 2.25\%$$

Here again we find an appreciable difference. And that it is not due to chance sampling is to be seen from the fact that the difference between the averages is 5.83 %, with an error of ± .30. Again we must turn to one of our three hypotheses, to account for the discrepancy; the greater hybridity of my sample as compared with theirs, the difference in personal equation in observation of color, plus the fact that their data are from cadavera, or the inadequacy of the method used. Granting, as we did before, that the entire present sample is of greater hybridity than theirs, we still find appreciable differences between their average and mean square variability and those of the N group of my sample, which is 7.76 % ± 3.57 %. There is, however, a closer correspondence than with the similar figures for the entire sample, and it may well be that different amounts of hybridity, always a factor in analysis of any American Negro series of unknown genealogical background, may account for some of this difference. But it cannot account for all of it. That there may be difference in the yellow element after death which makes for differences when comparisons are drawn between such data and observations on the living may be plausible, since this appeared to be the case with the red, and very possibly, despite the conclusions of Todd and Van Gorder, in the case of the black (N). They themselves say nothing as to the effect of death upon this element of pigmentation, except to remark that "there may be a slight increase in the W—Y value as the red diminishes". But this is also contradicted by comparing my results with theirs, for their average for red is well under mine, and the same is true for the values of yellow, the opposite of what should occur if this statement held true. In any event, the discrepancy in the Y values arrived at by them and by me remains; the reason for it should become apparent after further research into the problem, with an investigation as to the fundamental value of this method of quantitative determination of pigmentation.

30. Pigmentation, White (w) Element, Upper Outer Arm.

The tabulation of the data for the adult males measured by myself for this, the remaining element of the color top in our consideration of pigmentation, may be seen in Table LXIV, p. 173, in the "adult" column. The skewness is due, first, to the high variability of a low average. The modal value is at 3 %, the mean being 7 % removed from it, and the distribution skewing off toward the upper range, where it reaches 44 % as a maximum value. This may be due in part to the physical difficulty fundamental to the use of a color-top, involved in observing small differences between two fairly high amounts of White. That is, while the difference between 2 % and 4 % of white on the surfaces of two spinning tops make the resulting mixed colors readily distinguishable, two colors where the only difference is between 32 % white in the one and 34 % in the other cannot be distinguished at all. However, the skewness may also be due in part to the ancestral composition of the American Negro, as was remarked before. The statistical constants for this series are:

Number of cases: 593
Average: 10.00%
Standard deviation: ± 8.44%
Error of the average: ± .34%

The same skewness is to be seen in my computation of the mean and standard deviation of Todd and Van Gorder's material. These, for the 94 cadavera, are:

Average: 4.57%
Standard deviation: ±2.41%

Other than this skewness there is no resemblance between the two series. The difference between the means is 5.43 %; its error ± .42. The difference between the variabilities is over fifteen times its error. Thus there is again something fundamental involved, which cannot be explained by chance sampling. That this is not the case in traits other than pigmentation has been seen, for these averages have in many instances been shown to be within plus or minus one times their sigma, and it follows that the series dealt with in this study and Negro material from Western Reserve are samples of the same larger population. The difference must lie, it must again be emphasized, either in the technique, or in the fact that there are pigmentation differences between the living and cadavera material, or in the personal equation of the observers concerned, as is very likely the case when the results of the preceding chapter are considered. The mean of 6.00 % for the unmixed Negro group (N) of the Howard University sample for this color, and the standard deviation of ± 5.24 are again, as in the case of the Y values, much closer to Todd and Van Gorder's results than are the mean and sigma of my entire series of adult males, and this, too, may result from the greater hybridity of the general Negro population as represented in my series as against a pauper selection of Negroes in theirs, which, it will be remembered, they stated was called "Negro-hybrid" only as a matter of caution. But, as has been said before, this will not explain more than a portion of the difference. And while it cannot be doubted that the quantitative determination of pigmentation is the most desirable method of studying skin color, it is clear from the study of the pigmentation of these two samples of the American Negro population, both as carefully controlled as is possible in the laboratory, on the one hand,

and in the field, on the other, that we have a method that is far from satisfactory. The use of the color-top is, I believe, preferable to that of the color-scale, and it is also clear that the use of data gathered by one observer for different groups can be used very satisfactorily, as has been seen from considerations brought forward in the last chapter, or as will be shown in a later one, where comparisons will be made for skin color between groups of different genealogical classes, representing different amounts of racial crossing. But we are far from standardization, and it is reasonably clear from the material adduced above that it is inadmissible to compare quantitative results obtained by different observers, or even by the same observer at different times, for a trait where the subjective element and personal difference of observation is as great as it is in the consideration of color values.

We have concluded a description of the American Negro as represented by series of adult males for numerous physical traits, — a description made in terms of the extent to which he is like or unlike the parent populations who have contributed to his being, and the extent to which he resembles one or the other or combines the characteristics obtained from all of them. That the latter is the case is, I believe, a fair statement of what has happened as a result of the crossing that has gone into his make-up, while the homogeneity of the type which has resulted has been indicated by the low variabilities of this greatly mixed group when these are compared, trait for trait, with the available data concerning variability for the racially unmixed populations to which he is related. It is sufficient here to indicate these two points, which are of major theoretical interest in consideration of the mechanisms and the results of racial mixture among human types.

A more detailed discussion of these points, their significance for biological theory, and perhaps for the somewhat more practical problems connected with the American Negro, as well as the social mechanisms which most probably account for them, will be taken up in the last chapter of this work.

CHAPTER IV.
DIFFERENCES WITHIN THE SERIES[1].

The question as to the extent to which there are local and occupational differences represented in the series with which we have been working is one which must be considered before our analysis is carried any further. For it has long been assumed that there is a selective process at work among the Negroes; that certain physical types (dependent upon the amount of White admixture) go to college, or leave the south and migrate to the northern states, while others remain at home.

Is it true, however, that there is such a selection of the types more largely mixed with White blood; that these are the more aggressive, the more adventurous, and are therefore the ones who would comprise the bulk of the Negro population in the northern cities? Does the Negro with a large amount of White ancestry tend to go to college, while his more Negroid fellow stays at home and enters the trades or works on the farm? To what extent may it be said to be true that West Indian Negroes are of a different physical type, easily distinguished from the Negroes born in the United States?

All these questions are pertinent to our investigation. I have assumed, for instance, that the series as a whole, particularly that portion of it comprised in the combined series of adult males, may be taken as representative, by and large, of the generality of the American Negro population. But obviously, if there is a selection which sends a definite physical type to the northern cities in the migrations which have been occurring during the past ten years or so, then such an assumption is not tenable. Similarly, a large section of the series was measured at Howard University. What of the validity of our contention if the University man differs from his non-University brother? Or the West Indian Negro from the American born? It is therefore essential to investigate the extent to which the various series which comprise the entire study may or may not be alike, — and particularly to see the extent to which they are alike or different in such traits as may be indicative of the amounts of Negro blood represented in them.

It will be remembered that there are several series from New York City, composed of persons living there but, in the main, born

---

[1] The material presented in this chapter has been discussed in somewhat less detail in Herskovits (XI).

either in the West Indies or in other parts of the United States.[1] There is the Howard University series, and that from a rural community of West Virginia. There is the well-to-do and professional group living in New York City, who were measured separately from the series representing the general Negro population of that city. There are three groups from the south, composed of females, one from a university where a selection from the upper economic levels of Negro communities is generally conceded, the other two more representative of the general Negro population, measured in a normal and an industrial school. Finally, there is the series from a number of cities of the south and from southern schools, of wide geographical distribution, although in this case the extent to which the method of reaching the persons measured might have brought about an unconscious selection is not known. For the series of Miss Blackwood, my assistants, and myself, this much can be said on the last point, — any selection which occurred in obtaining the individuals represented in the groups would be a selection operative on the entire population from which a given group was measured. For we made it a rule to take without any distinction all individuals of a group we might be able to reach. Thus, in New York City, in measuring in the public schools, all the children in a given grade would be measured, and their homes later visited in order to obtain measurements from the adults and other members of their families. And since school attendance is compulsory, selection, in the sense mentioned before, is not operative.

As a first step, it may be well to consider how the genealogical analyses of the component series compare with one another. This comparison is possible only for the series measured by me or my assistants. Professor von Luschan did not take genealogies except in relatively rare cases, — not sufficient for the type of analysis to which I have subjected my own material. Miss Blackwood, who began to take genealogical information rather late in her study of Negro women, informed me that the Tuskegee girls measured did not give genealogies in which she herself would place reliability, the main difficulty being one of separating in their minds the biological and sociological implications of the word "Negro", while lack of time made for haste not conducive to carefulness in gathering genealogies.

For the adults of the other series, male and female, we have:

---

[1] We may refer again to Table II, p. 7, for the necessary details of the places of birth of the individuals composing the several series mentioned here.

78   The Anthropometry of the American Negro

Series	N		N(I)		NNW	
	No.	%	No.	%	No.	%
New York (M. J. H.)	69	23.8	11	3.9	71	24.4
New York (L. K.)	96	32.9	20	6.9	84	28.8
West Va. (L. K.)	54	24.0	25	11.0	64	28.5
Howard Univ. (M. J. H.)	109	20.3	36	6.7	129	23.8
Harlem Sel. (Z. H.)	14	7.0	5	2.5	36	17.5
Total	342	22.0	97	6.3	384	24.8

Assuming, roughly, that N and N(I) means full-blooded Negroes; NNW and NNW(I) $3/4$ Negro; NW and NW(I) $1/2$ Negro; and NWW and NWW(I) $1/4$ Negro, the groups contain the following amounts of Negro blood:

New York (M. J. H.) 63.3%
New York (L. K.) 72.8%
West Va. (L. K.) 72.8%
Howard Univ. (M. J. H.) . 69.1%
Harlem Sel. (Z. H.) 53.0%

It may well be that L. K., himself a colored man, found easier access to the darker New York families, or that the difference reflects our methods of securing genealogical information. The similarity of the West Virginia group and the L. K. New York group is of particular interest, since the former is an inbred, stable rural community, the latter a representation of the emigrants to northern cities.

The series, which is striking from the point of view both of the differences from the percentages for the genealogical classes of the component series it exhibits, and its differences from these percentages for the series as a whole, is the one measured on a selected group in Harlem. It will be remembered that the data for this series were obtained from among the well-to-do and professional classes in the New York City Negro population. In view of social conditions and the *mores* of the Negroes of America, which will be discussed in some detail later,[1] it is not strange that we find that the non-Negroid ancestry bulks so large in comparison with the other groups measured. We find large differences between this series and the others in the smallness of the percentage of unmixed Negroes and Negroes mixed with Indian but no White blood, and the relatively large proportion of persons of more White than Negro and more White than Negro with Indian ancestry. The New York series measured by myself is also somewhat larger as to percentages of these two latter groups than are the other series, but in view of the small absolute numbers

---

[1] In Chapter VIII.

Differences Within the Series

NNW(I)		NW		NW(I)		NWW		NWW(I)	
No.	%	No.	%	No.	%	No.	%	No.	%
22	7.6	45	15.5	19	6.5	49	16.3	5	1.8
15	5.2	33	11.3	15	5.1	23	7.8	6	2.0
11	5.0	33	15.0	10	4.5	11	5.0	15	7.0
51	9.6	95	17.7	57	10.6	30	5.6	31	5.7
7	3.5	54	26.0	32	15.5	42	20.0	18	8.0
106	6.7	260	16.8	133	8.5	154	10.0	75	4.8

involved, this may be due to chance or to the causes already discussed. For the other classes, all series with the exception of the selected one are remarkably consistent. In other words, this is internal evidence either that errors in giving genealogies are exceedingly consistent in all the groups represented in the different series, or that there is strikingly less selection of those who have migrated, and persons who attend colleges, in respect to ancestral background, than has been otherwise supposed. And the former explanation would be extraordinary indeed, were it actually the one that explained the consistency in the genealogical percentages which is recorded.

This is not the place for the validation of the genealogies. In Chapter VI, the Howard University series will be analyzed intensively with this problem in mind, and it will be shown that these genealogies, when tested by anthropometric criteria, at least, give us strong reason to suppose them valid. One may assume that if the genealogical percentages of the Howard University group when compared to the other series of this research are essentially the same, and the same similarity in anthropometric traits appears to hold between these series, that the genealogies of the other groups are valid to the same degree as are those of the Howard University group. The reasoning may then be carried one step farther, and we may argue that if the entire series is representative, on the whole, for such of the American Negro population as is not concentrated in small, unusually isolated, inbred communities, we may then assume that the genealogical percentages presented in the totals of the table given just above hold, by and large, for the American Negro in general. And the importance of such a realization of the amount of racial mixture represented in the American Negro population of this country, in relation to its significance for the consideration of other problems concerning the Negro, need not be enlarged on here.

We may, therefore, proceed without further discussion to an analysis of the larger series into its component parts. We shall consider in order the traits which have been measured by the various observers who have contributed data to this study. For this consideration, I shall utilize the adult male and female portions of each series, — this will give us a double check as to the extent to which the series are alike or different. The series will be presented in the following order, and I shall use the abbreviations indicated in parentheses in the tables for the individual traits which are discussed below:

1. New York City (Harlem), measured by M. J. Herskovits; born in the United States, (NY US I)
2. New York City (Harlem), measured by Louis King; born in the United States, (NY US II)
3. New York City (Harlem), measured by M. J. Herskovits; born in the West Indian islands, (NY WI I)
4. New York City (Harlem), measured by Louis King; born in the West Indian islands, (NY WI II)
5. New York City, (Harlem), measured by Zora Hurston; selected from well-to-do and professional groups, (NY Selected)
6. West Virginia series, measured by Louis King, (West Va.)
7. Howard University series, measured by M. J. Herskovits, (Howard Univ.)
8. Von Luschan series, measured by Felix von Luschan, (Von Luschan)
9. Fisk University series, measured by Beatrice Blackwood, (Fisk)
10. Agricultural and Industrial State Normal College series, measured by Beatrice Blackwood at Nashville, Tenn., (A & I SN)
11. Tuskegee Institute series, measured at Tuskegee, Ala., by Beatrice Blackwood, (Tuskegee)

This means that every locality represented in the total series has been treated separately, and that the work of every measurer has been considered by itself, even where two persons have measured in the same local population. This was done in working up the data as a procedure methodologically advisable, but its value will become apparent as consideration of the results for these separate populations, or portions of them measured by more than one person, proceeds.

1. STATURE.

Considering the results for male and female adults, the series comprising the material gathered in this study give the following statistical constants:

Series	Males			Females		
	No.	Average, (cm.)	σ	No.	Average, (cm.)	σ
NY US I	64	168.39	± 6.19	109	157.66	± 5.85
NY US II	47	167.43	± 5.37	104	157.56	± 6.22
NY WI I	56	170.34	± 5.69	81	159.22	± 5.74
NY WI II	58	169.71	± 6.07	92	157.66	± 5.33
NY Selected ...	106	173.74	± 5.76	130	160.43	± 5.71
West Va.	97	167.87	± 6.84	129	155.63	± 5.27
Howard Univ. .	412	171.01	± 6.18	—	—	—
Von Luschan ..	54	171.37	± 6.40	100	160.87	± 5.92
Fisk	—	—	—	24	157.83	± 6.98
A & I S N	—	—	—	82	160.29	± 7.54
Tuskegee	—	—	—	64	160.58	± 7.31

There are slight differences among the several New York series, the West Indians seeming to be somewhat taller than the American-born Negroes represented. The well-to-do series shows the effect of better economic circumstances, however, as this series gives us the tallest males, on the average, and some of the tallest females. The university series comes next in stature (except in the case of the Fisk series, and the von Luschan, the economic situation of the members of which are unknown to me). Generally speaking, it may be said that those differences between the series occur that would be expected with better or worse economic circumstances, — thus, the West Virginia series represents a poor farming community, where the food is none too good, while the New York selected series lives under the most favorable conditions of any of those reported. Other than this, there are no distinct differences represented between northern and southern Negroes, — nothing, certainly, that may not be put down to the effect of environmental conditions. It will be remembered that the difference between the Civil War Negroes and those measured in the army during the late war, as shown in the table of averages for this trait contained in the last chapter, argued that the present-day Negroes are, generally speaking, appreciably taller than those of somewhat earlier times. This, again, is most probably due to better environment as the Negro has come out of his background of slavery, — in any event, it demonstrates that we are dealing here with a trait that has a relatively high susceptibility to change.

2. HEIGHT SITTING.

For this trait, the various series show the following averages and variabilities:

Series	Males			Females		
	No.	Average, (cm.)	σ	No.	Average, (cm.)	σ
NY US I	65	87.46	± 3.53	108	82.85	± 3.33
NY US II	47	86.11	± 2.60	103	82.00	± 3.15
NY WI I	56	87.27	± 3.29	81	82.78	± 3.18
NY WI II	58	86.60	± 3.70	89	81.80	± 3.20
NY Selected	105	88.30	± 3.45	129	62.60	± 3.00
West Va.	91	86.30	± 3.85	122	81.00	± 3.30
Howard Univ.	412	88.15	± 3.13	—	—	—
Fisk	—	—	—	24	79.79	± 3.39
A & I S N	—	—	—	80	83.83	± 3.46
Tuskegee	—	—	—	63	82.02	± 3.41

Here again it will be noticed that there is a large degree of correspondence between the component series. The outstanding difference is that of the Fisk University series of females, which I am at a loss to explain. It may be only remarked that stature and height sitting of the Fisk students are low. The two tables are consistent thoughout, — the New York selected series is among the tallest in this trait as it was in the last, the University groups are also large, while the poorer ones are smaller. This trait was not measured by Professor von Luschan. The variabilities are even more alike than the averages, all differences being statistically insignificant.

3. Length of Head.

For the component series, we have the following statistical constants as regards this trait:

Series	Males			Females		
	No.	Average, (mm.)	σ	No.	Average, (mm.)	σ
NY US I	67	197.35	± 6.9	111	187.2	± 5.9
NY US II	46	196.8	± 6.4	104	187.5	± 5.6
NY WI I	58	194.9	± 6.4	80	184.65	± 5.1
NY WI II	58	192.8	± 6.2	93	184.8	± 6.2
NY Selected	106	196.0	± 5.7	131	189.8	± 5.4
West Va.	91	196.6	± 6.0	124	189.5	± 7.0
Howard Univ.	475	197.1	± 6.7	—	—	—
Von Luschan	53	196.2	± 6.96	102	187.6	± 6.2
Fisk	—	—	—	24	184.6	± 6.4
A & I S N	—	—	—	82	186.2	± 5.95
Tuskegee	—	—	—	63	186.9	± 5.3

This measurement is one for which the error of observation is lower than in most of those taken on the living, and therefore differences between groups are important, since the measurements of the different observers are comparable to an unusual extent. There seems, from the table given above, to be a considerably shorter absolute head-length for the West Indian than for the American-born Negroes of New York, while, in the case of the females, the shorter length of the Fisk series is noticeable. I have no explanation to offer for these two differences; others are due to chance.

4. Width of Head.

The averages and variabilities for the series of male and female adults for head-width are:

Series	Males			Females		
	No.	Average, (mm).	σ	No.	Average, (mm).	σ
NY US I	67	151.9	± 6.0	111	146.2	± 5.4
NY US II	46	150.7	± 5.45	104	145.5	± 5.1
NY WI I	58	152.0	± 4.4	80	145.5	± 4.0
NY WI II	58	151.6	± 6.2	93	145.8	± 5.0
NY Selected ...	106	149.3	± 5.5	130	144.4	± 5.1
West Va.	91	150.0	± 5.6	124	146.15	± 4.7
Howard Univ. .	475	151.9	± 5.8	—	—	—
Von Luschan ..	53	152.1	± 6.2	102	145.6	± 4.8
Fisk	—	—	—	24	145.5	± 4.5
A & I S N	—	—	—	82	143.6	± 5.0
Tuskegee	—	—	—	63	145.3	± 4.7

Here again there are no significant differences between these series.

5. Cephalic Index.

For the various series, the following results were obtained:

Series	Males			Females		
	No.	Average, (%)	σ	No.	Average, (%)	σ
NY US I	67	77.1	± 3.6	111	78.1	± 3.0
NY US II	46	76.7	± 3.7	104	77.7	± 3.15
NY WI I	58	78.9	± 3.4	80	79.0	± 3.1
NY WI II	58	78.1	± 3.4	93	78.9	± 2.8
NY Selected ...	106	76.2	± 2.7	130	77.0	± 2.85
West Va.	91	76.4	± 3.3	127	77.2	± 3.2
Howard Univ. .	475	77.2	± 3.5	—	—	—
Von Luschan ..	53	77.6	± 3.7	102	77.8	± 3.1
Fisk	—	—	—	24	78.6	± 3.7
A & I S N......	—	—	—	82	77.2	± 2.7
Tuskegee	—	—	—	63	77.8	± 3.0

The shape of the head, as can be seen from this table, shows little regional or occupational variation. The well-to-do New York series is longer-headed than any of the other populations measured, for both sexes. The variabilities of the series scatter as we should expect those of unselected samples of a population to scatter, — there is no significant difference visible. As far as head-form is concerned, therefore, no striking differences between these various American Negro populations is discernible. Of course, it is quite true that this trait alone is not of sufficient weight to be decisive, — far too much importance has been ascribed to it in anthropological studies of population differences. But it is a ratio of the two diameters of the head which comprise the most exact measurements that can be taken on the living, and since it has been given such importance in other anthropometric studies, it is especially interesting to see that in this trait no differences of significance are to be noted which would point to selection of Negroes through migration, or attendance at college, or remaining at the place of birth.

6. Height of Head.

Only the populations which were measured with the Western Reserve head-spanner are represented in this table. Von Luschan did not measure this trait, nor was Miss Blackwood able, because of the exigencies of the situation in which she found herself at Fisk University, to measure it on enough of the Fisk women to make an appreciable series. We have the data for the trait for the other series, however, as follows:

Series		Males			Females	
	No.	Average, (mm.)	σ	No.	Average, (mm.)	σ
N Y US I	66	133.3	± 4.8	109	130.0	± 5.2
NY US II	46	132.2	± 4.2	100	128.9	± 4.9
NY WI I	57	134.0	± 4.8	76	131.3	± 5.6
NY WI II	58	133.4	± 4.6	91	129.7	± 4.1
NY Selected ...	105	135.4	± 4.9	131	130.0	± 5.1
West Va.	91	133.7	± 5.4	123	129.0	± 5.7
Howard Univ. .	410	134.2	± 4.2	—	—	—
A & I S N......	—	—	—	51	131.2	± 6.0
Tuskegee	—	—	—	64	130.55	± 4.2

Again, as in the other traits presented thus far, there are no great differences between the groups represented. The height of the head of the New York selected series is somewhat larger on the average, for males, than for the other male series, the difference between it and the lowest value being one not due to chance sampling, but this does not hold for females. The variabilities are as consistent as the averages.

7. Height of Nose.

In this trait we are dealing once more with the first of those where there is the difficulty of locating the upper landmark, a deficiency which makes for inaccuracy of result. It will be remembered that in discussing the personal equations of the various persons who measured this trait, it was stated that while there were no reasons why the series of all the others besides Miss Blackwood should not be combined, her measurements seemed to be so consistently smaller than those of the rest of us that it was felt best not to effect combination with her series. This may now be seen in the following presentation of the statistical constants:

Differences Within the Series

Series	Males			Females		
	No.	Average, (mm.)	σ	No.	Average, (mm.)	σ
NY US I	67	55.4	± 3.8	111	52.6	± 3.8
NY US II	46	53.9	± 4.1	102	51.2	± 4.5
NY WI I	58	54.3	± 3.15	81	52.75	± 4.4
NY WI II	58	52.6	± 4.7	93	50.5	± 4.6
NY Selected ...	106	54.0	± 3.2	131	52.1	± 3.3
West Va.	91	50.3	± 3.8	124	45.5	± 3.0
Howard Univ. .	475	53.6	± 3.4	—	—	—
Von Luschan ..	52	53.3	± 3.7	102	50.8	± 3.8
Fisk	—	—	—	24	42.8	± 4.4
A & I S N......	—	—	—	82	43.7	± 3.75
Tuskegee	—	—	—	64	44.3	± 4.2

As has been remarked, the male series seem to be comparable — that is, there are no striking differences between the various series except that between the NY US I and the West Virginia, between which the difference is a significant one. Of course, it may be maintained that this is arguing two ways at once, and that the very likeness of these male series may be due to personal errors which vary in such a way as to effect this similarity. I rather doubt this, but I should not insist on the point, and I merely indicate that the lack of decisive differences in the other traits discussed thus far in this chapter at least makes it reasonable to suppose that since there is no significant difference here (with one exception noted), we are again simply witnessing the same similarity of general type manifesting itself for nasal height. With the female series, there are large differences of statistical importance between those measured by my assistants and myself in New York, and the Von Luschan series, on the one hand, and the Blackwood series and that of King for West Virginia, on the other. While these may or may not be due to the personal differences in technique involved, not only between us and Miss Blackwood, but between King measuring this trait in New York and later differently in West Virginia, it may perhaps be assumed with reasonable safety that these differences are caused rather by the latter than the former cause. The variabilities are quite alike. And the averages of Miss Blackwood's several series may also be observed to be quite similar, when the three of them are compared one with another, even though all contrast so strikingly with those of the series measured by others.

8. Width of Nose.

Comparison of the averages and mean square variabilities for the groups which have gone to make up the total series of this study may be made in the table appended as follows:

Series	Males			Females		
	No.	Average, (mm.)	σ	No.	Average, (mm.)	σ
NY US I	67	41.3	± 3.1	111	37.9	± 3.4
NY US II	46	41.5	± 4.2	103	36.6	± 3.65
NY WI I	58	42.6	± 3.7	79	38.3	± 3.0
NY WI II	58	41.9	± 3.75	93	36.8	± 3.9
NY Selected ...	106	37.5	± 3.9	131	34.3	± 3.5
West Va.	91	41.6	± 2.8	124	38.0	± 3.3
Howard Univ. .	475	41.0	± 3.9	—	—	—
Von Luschan ..	53	40.9	± 4.45	102	37.6	± 4.2
Fisk	—	—	—	24	36.1	± 2.6
A & I S N......	—	—	—	82	36.5	± 3.8
Tuskegee	—	—	—	64	37.2	± 2.9

This trait shows interesting differences between the series. It is to be regarded as one of the "key" traits in a study of Negro-White crossing, and if important differences with respect to racial background were present in any of these groups, testimony derived from the behavior of a trait such as this would certainly weigh more heavily than, let us say, genealogical information. We find first, that none other than those due to chance sampling are apparent, except between the selected well-to-do and professional group from the Harlem district and the others. Thus the testimony of the genealogies, that there is more White blood present in this group than in the general population, is borne out, for the narrower nose-widths are Caucasoid, when compared to the other groups represented. The theory that there is a selection according to which the less Negroid go to the colleges, is not upheld when the mean for the Howard University sample for this trait is compared with the non-University groups, for it is statistically identical with them, and the same holds true for women as for men. As a matter of fact, when the table is consulted, none of the groups appears to be distinctly Negroid, but all of them partake of the characteristic which was noticed in the last chapter, when the mean for the total male series was compared to African and Caucasian and Indian populations. They seem to fall between these two, and, so far as this trait offers a criterion, to exhibit about the same amount of mixture; only the Harlem series, which is more Caucasoid than the others, is to be excepted. There are, further, no significant differences between the mean square variability of any one of the series and those of the others, which argues a comparable amount of homogeneity for them all.

9. Upper Facial Height.

As has been remarked, the difficulty of locating the nasion for this trait plays havoc with any accuracy that may be striven for by those taking this measurement. The differences between the series indicated below, therefore, are not surprising:

Differences Within the Series

Series	Males			Females		
	No.	Average, (mm.)	σ	No.	Average, (mm.)	σ
NY US I	67	72.2	± 5.6	110	67.95	± 5.5
NY US II	46	69.9	± 5.4	103	66.7	± 6.0
NY WI I	58	71.7	± 4.1	81	68.8	± 3.6
NY WI II	58	69.3	± 5.3	93	66.6	± 5.7
NY Selected	106	70.9	± 3.7	130	67.6	± 3.1
West Va.	91	66.5	± 4.85	124	61.55	± 4.3
Howard Univ.	474	71.4	± 4.11	—	—	—
Von Luschan	53	77.9	± 4.7	102	74.8	± 4.2
Fisk	—	—	—	24	58.3	± 3.1
A & I S N	—	—	—	82	57.9	± 4.3
Tuskegee	—	—	—	64	60.05	± 4.3

Generally speaking, as far as the variabilities are concerned, there is a reasonable degree of consistency in both the male and female series. But when we consider averages, the observational differences bulk large. Von Luschan, obviously, measured from a point which was quite different from that employed by the rest of us. So did Miss Blackwood, and the same seems to have been true of King when he was working in West Virginia. Other than this the series may be compared, although it is noticeable that the tendency of King to measure this trait smaller than I did, as is to be remarked in the West Virginia series, was operative to a lesser degree when he measured his Harlem series. Comparing West Indians measured by him with American-born Negroes of his series, and the two sets of persons of those respective origins measured by myself, there seems to be discernible no appreciable difference, either for males or for females. Similarly, as between the southern series measured by Miss Blackwood, there seem to be no differences that are of importance.

10. TOTAL FACIAL HEIGHT.

The observational error for this trait is even larger than for the other two involving the nasion, the distance measured being greater, and the element of the manner in which the teeth are put together also making for uncertainty. With this in mind, the results for the component series of this study may be considered:

Series	Males			Females		
	No.	Average, (mm.)	σ	No.	Average, (mm.)	σ
NY US I	67	123.8	± 6.9	111	115.7	± 6.35
NY US II	46	123.65	± 7.1	103	117.0	± 6.4
NY WI I	58	122.0	± 7.0	81	116.2	± 5.2
NY WI II	58	123.4	± 7.3	93	116.8	± 6.5
NY Selected	106	123.9	± 5.9	129	116.7	± 4.9
West Va.	91	120.2	± 7.35	124	110.1	± 6.2
Howard Univ.	472	122.6	± 6.3	—	—	—
Von Luschan	53	123.74	± 6.7	102	116.2	± 5.9
Fisk	—	—	—	24	109.1	± 4.9
A & I S N	—	—	—	82	109.2	± 5.5
Tuskegee	—	—	—	64	110.3	± 5.0

When we consider the nature of this measurement, there is a surprising degree of similarity between the means of these series. It is obvious that there are no differences between the American-born and the West Indian Negroes in this trait, and apparently, unless there are observational errors operative, none between these and the well-to-do inhabitants of Harlem, and the Howard University students. Whether the difference between these various series and the one measured in West Virginia is the actual statement of a real difference, or due to an observational difference, I cannot say. On the one hand, the correspondences between King's New York series and my own in the measurement of this trait would argue that here we have the statement of an actual difference, but the extent to which the other traits are similar in these groups would argue against this conclusion. The Von Luschan measurements in this case show agreement with the other series, but again I cannot determine whether this is chance or the expression of a real likeness. Miss Blackwood, in this trait as in the one preceding it, measured differently from the rest of us, but her series show no differences between themselves. The variabilities, as may be seen, are statistically similar for all the series.

11. BIZYGOMATIC WIDTH.

For this trait, the statistical constants for the component series are:

Series	Males			Females		
	No.	Average, (mm.)	σ	No.	Average, (mm.)	σ
NY US I	67	140.9	± 5.5	111	133.1	± 5.5
NY US II	46	138.7	± 5.9	103	131.1	± 5.2
NY WI I	58	142.0	± 4.5	80	134.8	± 4.7
NY WI II	57	139.3	± 4.7	91	131.65	± 4.95
NY Selected	104	137.7	± 6.1	126	131.0	± 5.5
West Va.	91	138.8	± 5.7	123	132.2	± 5.7
Howard Univ.	473	139.2	± 6.1	—	—	—
Von Luschan	53	138.6	± 6.8	98	132.4	± 4.9
Fisk	—	—	—	24	132.0	± 4.5
A & I S N	—	—	—	82	131.1	± 5.0
Tuskegee	—	—	—	64	132.0	± 5.1

While there seem to be observational differences, these are not, statistically considered, outside the realm of probability, although there is a slight chance that the selected New York series, as far as males are concerned, may show significance in the difference between its average and the averages of the other male series. This is not, however, corroborated when comparison is made between the female groups. There are no differences between the variabilities that are statistically important, and all of them are consistently low for this trait.

12. THICKNESS OF LIPS.

The averages and variabilities of the several series for this trait are:

Series	Males			Females		
	No.	Average, (mm.)	σ	No.	Average, (mm.)	σ
NY US I	67	20.8	± 5.5	111	19.3	± 4.3
NY US II	46	20.35	± 4.2	103	18.7	± 3.9
NY WI I	58	22.7	± 4.8	81	20.1	± 4.7
NY WI II	57	21.1	± 3.8	93	19.3	± 3.6
NY Selected ...	106	19.8	± 3.8	131	17.6	± 3.6
West Va.	91	20.0	± 4.2	124	18.5	± 4.1
Howard Univ. .	475	22.1	± 4.4	—	—	—
Von Luschan ..	52	19.7	± 3.85	98	16.8	± 4.1
Tuskegee	—	—	—	64	21.8	± 3.3

Lip thickness was not measured by Miss Blackwood either at Fisk University or the Normal School at Nashville. However, we have interesting differences apparent between the other series. Between the general population and the well-to-do section of it, there is one which holds statistical significance, and again shows the result which the genealogical analysis and a knowledge of social conditions within the Negro community would lead one to expect, — a more Caucasoid type than the general population exhibits. The results for the Von Luschan series are also of interest, and are of a nature such as to lead me to suspect that Professor Von Luschan's series may consist, to a large extent, of a selected group from the professional and like groups of the southern cities which he visited. The means, for both males and females, are distinctly non-Negroid when compared with the other series. Of course, I must again confess ignorance of the exact technique he employed in obtaining these measurements, but the results for this series as they stand are very interesting. The Howard University group exhibits a more Negroid aspect as regards this trait, but this may be due to the factor of difference in average age, that for Howard being lower with resulting fuller lips. The variabilities of all the series listed in the table above are very consistent. In a word, if we except the selected series from Harlem, and the one measured by Von Luschan — more or less of an unknown quantity — it may be said that as far as this trait is concerned, there seem to be no differences of importance between the series constituting this study. And the importance of lip thickness in any study of Negro-White mixture need not again be stressed.

13. HEIGHT OF EAR.

The statistical constants for the several series of this study for this trait are:

Series	Males			Females		
	No.	Average, (mm.)	σ	No.	Average, (mm.)	σ
NY US I	67	62.0	± 4.7	110	58.9	± 4.3
NY US II	46	60.4	± 4.1	103	57.2	± 4.2
NY WI I	58	60.2	± 3.4	80	58.9	± 4.7
NY WI II	58	60.0	± 4.1	93	57.9	± 3.9
NY Selected ...	106	61.0	± 3.6	131	59.0	± 3.7
West Va.	91	62.1	± 5.0	124	57.9	± 4.9
Howard Univ. .	474	60.2	± 4.15	—	—	—
Von Luschan ..	52	61.2	± 5.2	101	58.1	± 4.4

No measurements of this trait were taken by Miss Blackwood. Extended comments are not necessary regarding the table given above. There is a close likeness between the averages for the series which are represented, and the variabilities are also quite similar, the differences not being such as may be ascribed to any reason other than chance. In a word, we have again in this trait an indication of the similarity which holds between these samples of the American Negro population.

14. Width of Ear.

The means and variabilities for the various series of this study, for this trait, are as follows:

Series	Males			Females		
	No.	Average, (mm.)	σ	No.	Average, (mm.)	σ
NY US I	67	35.2	± 2.7	110	32.65	± 2.9
NY US II	46	34.0	± 2.7	103	32.7	± 2.5
NY WI I	58	33.35	± 2.6	80	31.9	± 2.4
NY WI II	58	33.5	± 2.1	93	32.1	± 2.2
NY Selected ...	106	32.6	± 2.6	131	31.95	± 1.9
West Va.	91	34.2	± 2.55	123	32.8	± 2.3
Howard Univ. .	475	33.4	± 2.8	—	—	—
Von Luschan ..	52	33.2	± 2.9	101	32.0	± 2.75

This measurement on the ear, like the last, was not measured at all by Miss Blackwood. There are no more distinctive differences between the groups in this case than there were in that of ear-height. The averages and variabilities are both, statistically, quite as would be expected from samples of the same general population (except for the New York selected males), and we have, therefore, once again testimony on the question as to the extent to which an American Negro type, described in the last chapter, is an actuality.

15. Pigmentation, Black (N) Element, Upper Outer Arm.

It must be remembered that in the discussions of the means and variabilities of the colors comprising the disk of the color top used in evaluating skin color, the element of personal judgement bulks very large. Therefore, the differences in the following table must be considered with this in mind:

Series	Males			Females		
	No.	Average, (%)	σ	No.	Average, (%)	σ
NY US I	65	66.2	± 13.4	111	67.55	± 12.5
NY US II	40	73.1	± 14.7	97	73.0	± 12.8
NY WI I	58	71.6	± 11.85	81	69.9	± 10.4
NY WI II	52	79.5	± 12.0	88	70.2	± 16.7
NY Selected	106	56.7	± 11.8	130	54.6	± 11.2
West Va.	88	73.7	± 13.0	122	71.3	± 12.45
Howard Univ.	470	65.4	± 14.4	—	—	—
Tuskegee	—	—	—	53	67.3	± 8.25

Considering the table given above, the most striking difference which may be seen in it is the lowness of the average value of black (that is, lightness of skin-color) in the Harlem well-to-do and professional series. This is not an unexpected result, and it is quite permissible, I believe, to rely on the testimony of the table as far as this is concerned, since it has been corroborated by the behavior of all the other traits which might be indicative of the amount of Negro-White crossing involved, and by the genealogical information given by this group. We may next compare the three series measured by myself, — that of the New York Negroes born in the United States and the West Indies, and that from Howard University. In doing this, we see that there is little difference in skin-color between the first and the last of these, but that the West Indian Negroes who have come to New York seem to be slightly darker — more Negroid, on the average — than their American-born neighbors, and that this seems to hold for comparisons between Americans and West Indians of both sexes. If we further compare the two groups of the same origins measured by King, we find that, in part, the same relationship holds as to color, — that here, in the case of the males, the latter are the darker, though this is not true for the females. Statistically these differences between the American-born and West Indian series are chance ones, yet there seems to be a consistency about the results, with some slight corroboration from the other traits already discussed, that would seem to argue a very slightly greater Negroidness on the part of the West Indians.

When we compare King's New York American-born series with the group he measured in West Virginia, we find that there are no significant differences. Since, in regard to all other traits, the differences between the groups both of us measured prove them to be practically from the same Harlem population, we may conclude that the differences in pigmentation between his series and mine are only the expression of personal differences in the perception of color. Finally, considering Miss Blackwood's results with the color-top (for the only series for which she used it) the result is sufficiently like my own for the Howard series and for the New York females that we may, perhaps, in very tentative fashion, compare the series.[1] This last, however, must only be done while bearing in mind the fact that there has been no opportunity for her to repeat measurements on an identical series with any one whose data are represented in this study, and that therefore the difference in personal error between her and any of the rest of us is an unknown quantity.

Summing up the findings for this trait, therefore, it may be said that, by and large, we have further testimony for the unity of the American Negro sample gathered from all parts of this country; that there does not seem to be any difference between city Negroes, rural Negroes, and University men as far as skin-color is concerned; that the professional and well-to-do Negroes are lighter than the general Negro population; and that, while the West Indians may be slightly more Negroid than the American-born, one cannot be sure that this finding is one which would be confirmed by the measurement of a larger series of West Indians.

16. PIGMENTATION, RED (R) ELEMENT, UPPER OUTER ARM.

This series of averages and variabilities represents those for the corrected readings of red on the color-top for the series of this study:

Series	Males			Females		
	No.	Average, (%)	σ	No.	Average, (%)	σ
NY US I	65	12.8	± 2.6	111	13.3	± 3.0
NY US II	40	11.6	± 3.7	97	11.9	± 4.6
NY WI I	58	12.5	± 2.9	81	13.2	± 3.2
NY WI II	52	9.6	± 3.7	88	12.2	± 5.0
NY Selected ...	106	13.85	± 2.2	130	14.3	± 2.1
West Va.	87	12.1	± 3.2	122	13.8	± 3.7
Howard Univ. .	470	12.3	± 2.9	—	—	—
Tuskegee	—	—	—	53	13.9	± 2.05

Few remarks are necessary after the discussion of the results for black given in the table for that color. All the disks of the top are, of course, interrelated, and it is not surprising that we find here much the same results that were found for the black: that the series measured by myself show about the same average values, that those measured by King are reasonably alike, that the selected Harlem series measured by Hurston differ relatively much from all the others, and that the Blackwood series agrees in the main with those measured by me.

---

[1] As demonstrated by Todd, Blackwood, and Beecher (I).

17. PIGMENTATION, YELLOW (Y) ELEMENT, UPPER OUTER ARM.

The results for this color of the top are:

Series	Males			Females		
	No.	Average, (%)	σ	No.	Average, (%)	σ
NY US I	65	12.1	± 4.8	111	11.2	± 4.6
NY US II	40	8.35	± 4.4	97	9.05	± 4.3
NY WI I	58	9.8	± 4.65	81	10.8	± 4.6
NY WI II	52	6.6	± 4.4	88	9.65	± 5.1
NY Selected ...	106	15.4	± 5.1	128	16.2	± 4.6
West Va.	87	8.1	± 4.6	122	8.8	± 4.4
Howard Univ. .	470	10.8	± 4.6	—	—	—
Tuskegee	—	—	—	53	9.6	± 3.8

The yellow contributes to lightness much more noticeably than the red does, and almost as much as the white. Therefore, the inverse manner in which the average values act, when they are compared to those of the black, are not surprising. The outstanding distinction in the series, here as before, is in the mean of the selected series, while King's Harlem series have less of this color, on the average, than the comparable Harlem series measured by myself. This would, of course, be expected from the fact that he sees colors darker than I do. All of the series measured by him are quite like one another, as are those measured by me, and these last, here as was the case with the other two colors considered, are matched by Miss Blackwood's findings. The West Indians show smaller percentages of this color than the American-born Negroes do, but other than this and the mean of the series which was actually selected by Miss Hurston, there is little selection evidenced by these results, which rather argue again a unity of type as a characteristic of the American Negro population.

18. PIGMENTATION, WHITE (W) ELEMENT, UPPER OUTER ARM.

It will be remembered that this color presents statistical difficulties, inherent in the fact that all curves resulting from tabulations for it, as is the case with yellow to a lesser degree, are markedly skew. At the same time, presentation may be made of the results obtained by computing the data on hand for it, as it is of interest to note the extent to which these findings check with the results for the other three colors used on the color-top:

Series	Males			Females		
	No.	Average, (%)	σ	No.	Average, (%)	σ
NY US I	65	9.2	± 8.3	111	8.5	± 6.9
NY US II	40	6.5	± 7.25	97	6.1	± 5.8
NY WI I	58	6.2	± 5.5	81	6.5	± 5.1
NY WI II	52	4.2	± 5.0	88	7.6	± 7.7
NY Selected ...	106	13.8	± 7.5	127	15.1	± 7.3
West Va.	87	5.5	± 5.2	122	6.0	± 5.6
Howard Univ. .	470	10.6	± 8.6	—	—	—
Tuskegee	—	—	—	53	9.2	± 4.3

The West Indian series of a given observer show less white on the average than the American-born Negro series measured by the same man, with the exception of the female series measured by King, where the opposite holds, though not so emphatically as to remove this from the realm of chance difference. King's West Virginia series again checks with the findings for the other colors, being about the same degree of lightness as his American-born Harlem series, while the Howard University and Miss Blackwood's series are about the same in this respect as the American-born New York Negroes measured by myself. If we make the same assumption made in the case of the other colors, that the difference between King's findings and my own for samples of the same New York population is due to a difference in personal observation of color, then all the unselected series may be said to be about the same, for this color as for the others. The variabilities of the several series are much alike, there being no difference between any two that cannot be laid to chance, while all the series exhibit the same phenomenon of skewness, and to about the same degree.

If the findings of this chapter be summarized, therefore, it is apparent that as far as the testimony of the traits measured and which are comparable is concerned, as well as of the genealogical information given, there are few significant differences between such of these samples of the American Negro as were not selected by the observer. This is more impressive when it is recalled that these unselected groups were measured in different parts of the country, among University and non-University people; in a sedentary rural population and a city group which has resulted from extensive migration; among Negroes of the north and of the south.

That an economic and social mechanism seems to be at work, one which allows the Negro of non-Negroid appearance to occupy the more favorable positions among his own people, is the interpretation which comparison of the results for the selected Harlem group with those for the other Harlem (unselected) series brings to mind. Of course, there is an other explanation of the matter,—a biological rather than a sociological one. This, however, will be discussed in the last chapter, where all the evidence which I have been able to assemble seems strikingly to point to the correctness of the sociological interpretation. Whichever is true, there is little doubt that there are differences in the racial make-up of such a group as compared to the general Negro population of which it forms a part.

The most interesting point involved, however, is perhaps that which throws light on the claim so often made that there is a selection on the basis of the amount of racial crossing represented in an individual, which causes the less Negroid person to be the more aggressive and to move from his place of residence in the south to the northern cities. There does not seem to be any basis for this assumption as far as the comparative results which have been adduced here are concerned, and while it cannot be denied that local districts in the far south might yield types which are more Negroid than the southern groups represented in this study (which are drawn from all over the south), the comparison of the West Virginia series with those from the north makes one wonder concerning the extent to which even this may be true. At the same time, I do not assume that this West Virginia population represents a group as might be found in a similar rural district in the far south. It is to be hoped that fuller investigation of local groups, and particularly of such groups among which migration has not been a decisive factor in changing the composition of the population, will be undertaken. Until some of these peoples are investigated, however, and until it is shown that there is a selection in migration so that there are significant differences in physical type between the Negroes who go north and those who remain at home in the south, I feel that there is little basis for such an hypothesis, when the data presented in this chapter are given due consideration. And from this, it further seems to follow that we may regard the sample comprising the entire series as a valid representation of the American Negro population as a whole.

CHAPTER V.
GROWTH CURVES AND SEX DIFFERENCES[1].

The next aspect of the American Negro population studied in this research, which must be considered, is that of the manner in which the traits that have been discussed in the last two chapters develop with growth, and the ways in which they differ in the two sexes, both as to growth and as to differences in the measurements of these traits in the adult. For this purpose, the component series were combined for each sex-age group into one large series, and the total numbers thus achieved were sufficiently large that such differences as manifest themselves are removed from the realm of chance.

Naturally, the entire number of traits studied at any time during this research are not represented in the tables given below. In the first place, those which were measured only on the New York children's and Howard University series do not give a long enough age range, while there are, for all practical purposes, no measurements of females for them, since few of this sex were measured before the family data were collected. Further, the traits of upper and total facial height have had to be excluded from the data of this chapter, even though they were measured on the entire series, because, as discussed at some length in Chapter II, they differ so largely for different observers. The component series could not be combined, and no one series is large enough, nor can we be sure enough of its accuracy as against the findings of the others, to make it worthy of presentation.

In the case of skin-color, although the same objections against the presentation of the results for the facial heights hold, I felt that this trait is of such major importance in our consideration of Negro-White crossing, that the material gathered for pigmentation by myself alone has been utilized. By this means an age-sex series has been obtained, which, if regrettably small for certain of the age-sex classes, is at the same time sufficiently large to indicate whatever change takes place in development, and what differences, if any, exist between the sexes.

The computation of age for the purpose of classifying the age groups was made in the following manner: every individual was placed in his age group according to his last birthday at the time he was measured. Therefore, the five-year-old age class includes

---

[1] The averages and variabilities in this chapter have been presented in Herskovits, (XII).

all individuals who, at the time of their measurement, were between the ages of five years, no months, and no days, and that of five years, eleven months, and thirty days. This causes the average age for each class to fall on the half-year point — that is, for this five-year series, it would be five and one half years. As to the accuracy of the dates of birth given there is little doubt in my own mind. In the case of the children measured in the New York Public Schools, a sufficiently large sample checked with the school records to an extent which convinced me that the children in the schools where we measured knew their correct ages. And the school records themselves, I may say, are based on official certificates of birth. For the younger children, the ages were obtained by questioning the parents, who frequently corrected an age given voluntarily by the child himself; for the adults, since all above the age of twenty have been combined into one group (except in the case of stature) the exact age makes no great difference for the purpose in hand, although I have no good reason to be unduly doubtful as to the accuracy of the ages given me by the adults.

With these essential explanations, we may turn to the consideration of the data themselves.

Tables XVIII—LXVI and figs. 3—20 contain the averages and distributions for age and sex. The inequality of numbers of observations in the various tables has been discussed before (Chap. II). These are due in part to the personal equations in some of the measurements that forbade the combination of the various series, in part to the lack of certain measurements in some of the schedules. The irregularities in the curves are in all probability due to the inadequacy of numbers, not to differences in the composition of the series for each age.

The well known sex differences appear in all the series: the intercrossing of male and female statures during the adolescence of girls, and the increased variability for both sexes during adolescence in all measurements that increase rapidly, (here particularly in stature and height sitting); the somewhat closer approach in others that have only a slight amount of annual growth. The slowly increasing measurements show the characteristic sex differences of the adult also to be present in childhood, as has been pointed out by Boas and Sawtell.[1]

The average stature (Table XVIII, fig. 3) of both males and females reaches its maximum at the end of the second decade of life. Loss of stature sets in at a remarkably early age. Among American Indians the maximum stature has been shown to occur in the fourth decade of life.[2] The same phenomenon occurs in height sitting (Table XXI, fig. 4). The ratio between height sitting and

---

[1] See Boas, (X), and Sawtell, (I, II).
[2] See Boas, (II).

stature (Table XXIV, fig. 5) shows first a decrease, later an increase, due to the early rapid growth of the limbs and the later rapid growth of the trunk. This phenomenon has been pointed out by G. West.[1]

The length, width and height of head show no decrease after the adult stage has been reached (Tables XXV, XXVIII, XXXVI, figs. 6, 7, 10). This might be expected, since the soft tissues contribute very little to these measurements.

The cephalic index (Table XXXI, fig. 9) shows a distinct decrease with increasing age, due presumably to the development of the frontal sinuses. This agrees with numerous previous observations and contradicts the opinion expressed by Pearson[2] which is based on a single short series of observations.

In the main, we see that for the adult groups the males are longer-headed than the females, and that this is consistent from the 16th year onward. Before then, from about the 8th year, the reverse is true, the girls being the longer-headed. Earlier in life than this, there is not sufficient consistency in the sex differences, and it is difficult to see where these lie. It was felt that this point might be made somewhat less obscure were a running average, computed on the basis of a three-year period, to be applied to the age means. The results, with the graph drawn on the basis of them, are shown for the smoothed curve and new averages in Table XXXI—A, fig. 9. According to this we can see that, by and large, it may be said that there are three principal periods of sex differences and growth. In early childhood, on the whole, the males are longer-headed than the females.[3] There is then an intermediate period, from about eight to sixteen years, when the reverse is true, and from then on the original relationship of the sexes is restored. This may well be a function of the earlier coming to maturity on the part of the girls, due to an earlier growth of the frontal sinuses. The resultant overtaking of the female indices by the male series would restore the original longer-headedness of this sex which seems to be the normal sex difference; and this is actually what occurs.

The measurement of the height of nose (Table XXXVII, fig. 11) suffers by the inaccuracy of the determination of the naso-frontal suture as well as by the lack of a definite lower point.

The width of nose (Table XLII, fig. 12) and bizygomatic width (Table XLIII, fig. 13) do not call for any comment.

The thickness of the lips (Table XLVIII, fig. 14) begins to decrease when the adult stage is reached. The lips of the adult male are thicker than those of the female.

---

[1] See West (I).
[2] Pearson (IV). For an example which contradicts his findings and is in accord with mine, see Boas, (IV).
[3] A paper by Wissler (III) discussing this point with particular application to the Hawaiian material collected by the late Louis Sullivan, may be consulted for comparative purposes.

In the height and width of the ear (Tables XLIX and LIV, figs. 15 and 16) there is a continued increase during adult life, due probably to the flabbiness of the lobe of the ear.

In the tables which give the averages and mean square variabilities for the four colors of the color-top with which pigmentation was studied in this research (as explained in Chapter II), it will be noticed that the numbers of cases for the various age groups are materially smaller than is the case for the other traits which have been considered in this chapter (LV, LX, LXI, and LXVI and figs. 17—20). This is because of the fact discussed above, that the determination of skin-color, although a quantitative method is employed, rests so largely on personal differences involved in the estimation of color values that to combine series measured by different persons is methodologically inadvisable. As has been explained, the data which make up the tables for skin-color were all gathered by myself alone, and I have not included in them data from any other source. It will be noticed, in the case of the black (N), that there seems to be a decrease in this element until the fifth year, perhaps a steady increase to the age of sixteen or seventeen, and finally a decrease again into the adult group. In terms of actual appearance of the skin-color of these American Negroes, this means that there is first an early lightness, then a darkening, and finally a slight lightening with increasing age after puberty. If the column which gives the numbers of cases is consulted, however, it will be found that no age group is large enough to give reliable results before the fifth year, and therefore we need accept the findings for the earlier changes in skin-color in only a very tentative fashion, if at all.

Confirmation of the results for later years, however, is seen in the curve for females, which, for the years six through twelve, follows that for the male groups quite faithfully, and, after the intervening years to the adult group, for which the numbers of cases of females are too small to give the results any great value, the correspondence with the result for males again occurs. All this is also true, but inversely, for the other colors of the color-top, the red, yellow, and white, as would be expected. The increasing darkness with age agrees with the material of Todd and Van Gorder, and that of Davenport, who have all noticed this phenomenon. But their data disagree with mine in that the time of greatest darkness seems to be, according to their results, at about forty years of age, while that of my series is much earlier. However, the numbers of cases which they have at their disposal are not as large as are those of the present series, although it may also be true that a further analysis of these data into age groups above the age of twenty, — the group which I have put under the heading "adult" — might show a result for this series which would correspond to theirs. But this I feel, is somewhat doubtful, since most of my adult data come from persons who are between twenty and forty, in the case of females, and twenty and forty-five for males.[1] At any event, we may conclude without much hesitation from the skin-color data presented here, that, whatever its exact time of occurrence, there is change in pigmentation with age among the American Negroes.

The problem of sex differences is an especially interesting one in the case of skin color, for, as will be discussed in some detail later, there is a color selection among the American Negroes which is of the greatest importance as furnishing a mechanism for the establishment of the American Negro type. The argument for such a selection hinges to an important degree on the existence or non-existence of an inherent linkage of pigmentation and sex. I feel that the series presented here and the curves of age-changes developed from it show quite definitely that there is no such sex-linkage, but that whatever differences between the sexes at any given age (particularly between the two sexes for such ages at which there are sufficiently large numbers of cases available to rule out the operation of chance) are not due to significant cause.

The detailed frequency distributions for the age-sex classes for the black are to be seen in Tables LVI and LVII, for the red, in LVIII and LIX, for the yellow in LXII and LXIII, and for the white in Tables LXIV and LXV. The skewness for the curves for black, yellow and white, which has already been remarked on above, is apparent in all the tabulations. In the case of the red, here, as before, we more nearly approximate the normal type of distribution.

---

[1] Barnes, (I) made such an analysis of these same data, plus those of the other series of this study. Her results as regards age changes in pigmentation confirm what is maintained here.

Table XVIII
Stature (cm.)

Age	Males No.	Males Average	σ	Females No.	Females Average	σ
1	10	74.9	± 6.52	3	83.7	—
2	21	89.1	± 5.88	21	85.9	± 4.12
3	31	95.2	± 6.01	35	95.8	± 4.68
4	54	102.0	± 5.67	23	100.6	± 6.29
5	52	110.0	± 5.67	60	109.85	± 5.69
6	139	116.2	± 6.21	77	116.3	± 6.46
7	179	120.3	± 5.82	94	120.8	± 7.72
8	178	125.8	± 6.38	79	124.6	± 6.95
9	167	130.8	± 6.29	54	131.3	± 6.43
10	171	135.3	± 6.99	54	135.15	± 7.55
11	206	140.85	± 6.06	52	141.15	± 8.73
12	234	144.18	± 7.96	62	149.0	± 6.47
13	300	150.1	± 8.25	44	153.7	± 8.25
14	258	156.5	± 8.37	49	154.65	± 7.26
15	192	161.0	± 7.73	69	158.1	± 5.87
16	66	163.6	± 7.47	104	157.75	± 5.82
17	45	167.1	± 5.87	125	158.5	± 6.46
18	38	170.1	± 6.64	176	159.2	± 5.68
19	61	172.0	± 7.60	155	159.9	± 6.46
20—24	286	171.1	± 6.37	248	159.4	± 7.36
25—29	157	171.0	± 6.18	89	159.3	± 6.16
30—39	187	170.0	± 6.17	316	158.8	± 6.43
40—49	179	170.6	± 6.50	164	158.7	± 5.81
50—59	54	167.8	± 6.36	61	158.3	± 5.76
60—69	15	169.5	± 6.58	21	150.8	± 11.40
70—79	9	166.8	± 7.40	10	155.1	—
80—89	—	—	—	6	153.3	—

Table XIX
Stature (Males)

Age Cm.	1[1]	2		1	2		1	2
70—71	1	—	80—81	—	1	90—91	—	5
72—73	3	—	82—83	1	1	92—93	—	3
74—75	1	—	84—85	1	2	94—95	—	3
76—77	—	1	86—87	1	2	96—97	—	—
78—79	—	2	88—89	—	—	98—99	—	2

[1] Add: 65—1, 69—1.

Table XIX (continued).

Stature (Males)

Age Cm.	3[1]	4	5	6	7	8	9	10	11	12	13
90—91	3	—	—	—	—	—	—	—	—	—	—
92—93	3	1	—	—	—	—	—	—	—	—	—
94—95	4	8	—	—	—	—	—	—	—	—	—
96—97	5	4	1	—	—	—	—	—	—	—	—
98—99	5	7	2	—	—	—	—	—	—	—	—
100—101	2	9	—	—	3	1	—	—	—	—	—
102—103	2	5	4	—	1	—	—	—	—	—	—
104—105	—	5	4	6	1	—	—	—	—	—	—
106—107	1	5	5	5	3	—	—	—	—	—	—
108—109	—	1	9	10	1	—	—	—	—	—	—
110—111	1	4	6	9	1	1	—	—	—	—	—
112—113	—	5	6	14	5	4	—	—	—	—	—
114—115	—	—	7	20	19	5	2	1	—	—	—
116—117	—	—	4	19	15	4	1	2	—	—	—
118—119	—	—	1	16	25	10	3	—	—	—	—
120—121	—	—	2	17	21	18	3	—	—	—	—
122—123	—	—	—	11	35	16	9	2	1	—	—
124—125	—	—	1	4	19	26	16	9	1	—	—
126—127	—	—	—	2	12	25	19	10	3	2	—
128—129	—	—	—	1	9	19	14	9	1	2	1
130—131	—	—	—	3	1	17	23	15	4	4	4
132—133	—	—	—	—	5	9	23	15	16	4	2
134—135	—	—	—	1	3	11	23	23	17	12	6
136—137	—	—	—	—	—	5	8	27	14	6	4
138—139	—	—	—	—	—	5	10	16	27	22	10
140—141	—	—	—	1	—	2	6	14	28	27	14
142—143	—	—	—	—	—	—	1	8	28	28	21
144—145	—	—	—	—	—	—	3	8	21	28	29
146—147	—	—	—	—	—	—	3	2	18	19	22
148—149	—	—	—	—	—	—	—	3	13	19	30
150—151	—	—	—	—	—	—	—	3	4	10	28
152—153	—	—	—	—	—	—	—	3	5	17	35
154—155	—	—	—	—	—	—	—	1	3	15	19
156—157	—	—	—	—	—	—	—	—	2	6	21
158—159	—	—	—	—	—	—	—	—	—	4	16
160—161	—	—	—	—	—	—	—	—	—	2	11
162—163	—	—	—	—	—	—	—	—	—	3	10
164—165	—	—	—	—	—	—	—	—	—	1	5
166—167	—	—	—	—	—	—	—	—	—	1	5
168—169	—	—	—	—	—	—	—	—	—	—	2
170—171	—	—	—	—	—	—	—	—	—	—	3
172—173	—	—	—	—	—	—	—	—	—	1	1
174—175	—	—	—	—	—	—	—	—	—	—	1

[1] Add: 82—83, 1; 84—85, 1; 86—87, 2; 88—89, 1.

Table XIX (continued)
Stature (Males)

Age Cm.	14	15	16	17	18	19	20—24	25—29	30—39	40—49	50—59	60—69	70+
136—137	3	—	—	—	—	—	—	—	—	—	—	—	—
138—139	2	—	—	—	—	—	—	—	—	—	—	—	—
140—141	7	2	1	—	—	—	—	—	—	—	—	—	—
142—143	7	2	1	—	—	—	—	—	—	—	—	—	—
144—145	7	4	—	—	—	—	—	—	—	—	—	—	—
146—147	5	1	1	—	—	—	—	—	—	—	—	—	—
148—149	15	6	—	—	—	—	—	—	—	—	—	—	—
150—151	18	7	—	—	—	—	1	—	1	—	—	—	—
152—153	28	12	1	—	—	—	—	—	—	1	—	—	—
154—155	29	17	3	1	—	3	—	1	2	—	1	—	1
156—157	23	7	1	2	—	1	4	2	2	1	1	1	—
158—159	32	14	3	4	—	—	4	2	2	5	2	—	1
160—161	19	17	7	1	2	1	9	8	11	7	8	—	—
162—163	13	24	9	4	5	3	13	5	12	14	6	2	—
164—165	13	23	9	4	6	1	19	11	15	10	2	1	2
166—167	7	19	9	8	4	8	28	16	21	22	5	2	1
168—169	15	12	9	4	4	3	37	18	19	16	6	1	—
170—171	5	7	5	3	1	5	30	21	24	23	7	2	1
172—173	4	10	1	7	3	5	37	11	14	20	7	1	2
174—175	2	5	2	5	3	14	38	19	24	19	—	2	—
176—177	2	1	1	1	2	6	22	23	23	19	5	1	—
178—179	—	2	1	1	5	5	17	9	9	7	3	1	1
180—181	1	—	—	—	2	1	13	5	5	5	—	1	—
182—183	1	—	2	—	—	1	7	4	1	4	1	—	—
184—185	—	—	—	—	—	1	4	1	2	4	—	—	—
186—187	—	—	—	—	1	1	1	—	—	2	—	—	—
188—189	—	—	—	—	—	2	1	1	—	—	—	—	—
190—191	—	—	—	—	—	—	—	—	—	—	—	—	—
192—193	—	—	—	—	—	—	—	—	—	—	—	—	—
194—195	—	—	—	—	—	—	1	—	—	—	—	—	—

Table XX
Stature (Females)

Age Cm.	1	2		1	2		1	2
76—77	1	—	86—87	—	2	96—97	1	—
78—79	1	1	88—89	—	4			
80—81	—	2	90—91	—	3			
82—83	—	3	92—93	—	1			
84—85	—	4	94—95	—	1			

Table XX (continued)
Stature (Females)

Age Cm.	3[1]	4[2]	5	6	7	8	9	10	11	12	13
90— 91	3	—	—	—	—	—	—	—	—	—	—
92— 93	5	—	—	—	—	—	—	—	—	—	—
94— 95	5	2	1	—	—	—	—	—	—	—	—
96— 97	4	4	—	—	—	—	—	—	—	—	—
98— 99	7	4	2	—	—	—	—	—	—	—	—
100—101	3	2	2	—	—	—	—	—	—	—	—
102—103	4	1	4	1	1	—	—	—	—	—	—
104—105	1	3	6	—	—	—	—	—	—	—	—
106—107	—	3	6	5	—	—	—	—	—	—	—
108—109	—	2	6	3	1	1	—	—	—	—	—
110—111	—	1	12	8	4	3	—	—	—	—	—
112—113	—	—	9	11	6	—	—	—	—	—	—
114—115	—	—	1	11	13	2	1	—	—	—	—
116—117	—	—	6	14	8	5	1	—	—	—	—
118—119	—	—	4	3	9	6	1	—	—	—	—
120—121	—	—	1	6	12	11	1	2	—	—	—
122—123	—	—	1	4	11	10	1	3	—	—	—
124—125	—	—	—	4	6	7	5	4	1	—	—
126—127	—	—	—	2	9	3	5	1	1	—	—
128—129	—	—	—	2	6	12	7	3	6	—	—
130—131	—	—	—	2	2	8	4	4	1	—	1
132—133	—	—	—	—	2	4	7	5	3	—	—
134—135	—	—	—	—	2	2	6	4	4	1	—
136—137	—	—	—	—	—	3	7	7	1	1	2
138—139	—	—	—	1	—	—	2	3	4	2	—
140—141	—	—	—	—	—	—	3	5	4	4	1
142—143	—	—	—	—	—	2	2	3	5	3	2
144—145	—	—	—	—	—	—	1	6	6	6	—
146—147	—	—	—	—	—	—	—	3	2	8	2
148—149	—	—	—	—	—	—	—	1	3	11	4
150—151	—	—	—	—	—	—	—	—	4	7	4
152—153	—	—	—	—	2	—	—	—	3	7	6
154—155	—	—	—	—	—	—	—	—	2	2	1
156—157	—	—	—	—	—	—	—	—	1	2	2
158—159	—	—	—	—	—	—	—	—	1	5	9
160—161	—	—	—	—	—	—	—	—	—	—	4
162—163	—	—	—	—	—	—	—	—	—	1	2
164—165	—	—	—	—	—	—	—	—	—	1	2
166—167	—	—	—	—	—	—	—	—	—	1	—
168—169	—	—	—	—	—	—	—	—	—	—	2

[1] Add: 86—87, 3. [2] Add: 80—81, 1.

Growth Curves and Sex Differences

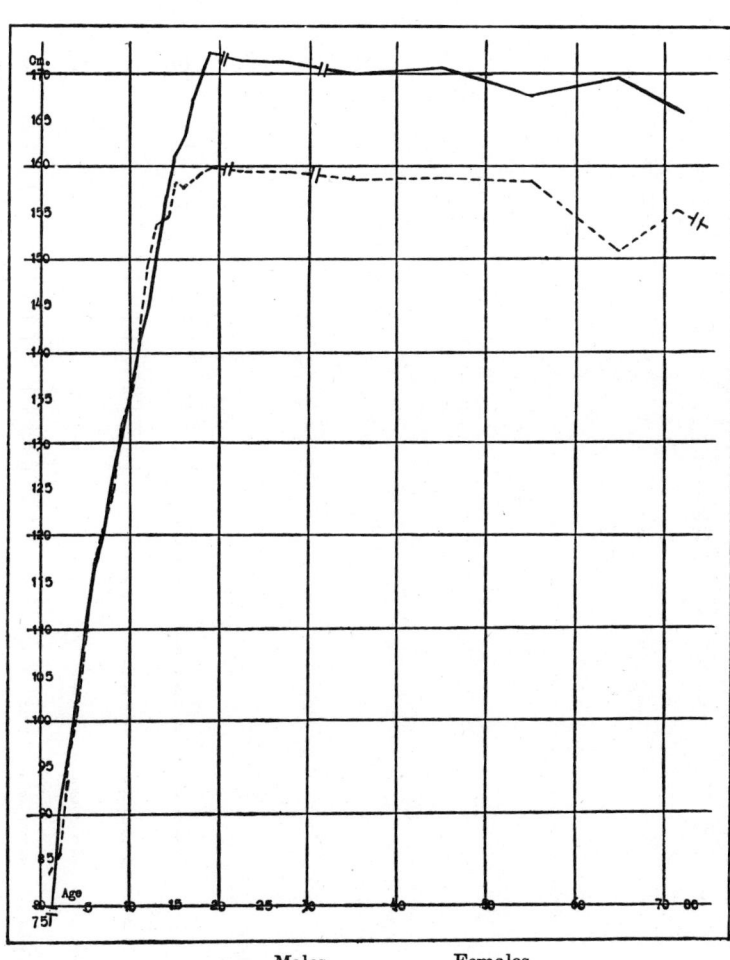

——— Males ----- Females.
Fig. 3.
Growth in Stature.

Table XX (continued)
Stature (Females)

Age Cm.	14	15	16	17	18	19	20—24	25—29	30—39	40—49	50—59	60—69[1]	70—79	80+
130—131	1	—	—	—	—	—	—	—	—	—	—	—	—	—
132—133	—	—	—	—	—	—	—	—	—	—	—	—	—	—
134—135	—	—	—	—	—	1	—	—	—	—	—	—	—	—
136—137	—	—	—	1	—	—	—	—	1	—	—	—	—	—
138—139	2	—	—	—	—	1	2	—	—	—	—	1	—	—
140—141	—	—	—	1	—	—	1	—	1	—	—	—	—	—
142—143	—	1	1	—	—	—	3	—	—	—	—	—	—	—
144—145	2	2	—	1	2	—	2	—	1	2	1	1	—	—
146—147	2	1	2	3	1	—	4	3	6	2	1	1	—	1
148—149	2	1	5	2	5	3	10	3	11	3	3	—	—	1
150—151	4	4	8	4	6	6	10	3	22	7	2	1	—	1
152—153	5	7	9	7	12	18	18	9	16	13	5	5	5	—
154—155	5	6	10	12	18	9	27	6	36	27	7	3	1	1
156—157	7	3	14	13	23	20	25	9	49	19	6	2	2	—
158—159	9	15	14	24	29	14	20	10	35	22	13	1	1	1
160—161	3	8	15	20	23	18	23	14	41	18	5	2	1	—
162—163	3	7	11	18	19	14	29	10	31	19	6	2	—	—
164—165	2	8	6	9	13	18	24	10	31	12	3	—	—	1
166—167	—	4	3	6	10	18	16	5	13	7	4	—	—	—
168—169	2	2	4	2	9	4	18	1	9	8	5	—	—	—
170—171	—	—	1	—	3	7	4	4	8	1	—	—	—	—
172—173	—	—	—	2	1	3	5	—	1	1	—	—	—	—
174—175	—	—	—	—	1	1	4	1	1	1	—	—	—	—
176—177	—	—	—	—	—	—	1	1	2	2	—	—	—	—
178—179	—	—	—	—	1	—	1	—	—	—	—	—	—	—
180—181	—	—	—	—	—	—	1	—	1	—	—	—	—	—

[1] Add: 114—1, 128—1.

Table XXI
Height Sitting (cm.)

Age	Males			Females		
	No.	Average	σ	No.	Average	σ
1	8	45.4	—	2	46.5	—
2	20	49.9	± 4.01	17	48.5	± 2.06
3	29	53.55	± 2.72	30	53.5	± 3.00
4	49	56.7	± 3.75	23	55.0	± 2.81
5	53	59.45	± 2.56	59	58.8	± 2.78
6	130	61.7	± 4.35	75	61.7	± 3.21
7	178	63.6	± 3.11	92	62.8	± 3.26
8	173	66.0	± 2.88	76	65.45	± 3.24
9	163	67.25	± 3.02	50	68.1	± 3.36
10	166	69.15	± 3.36	46	70.0	± 4.10

Growth Curves and Sex Differences

Table XXI (continued)
Height Sitting (cm.)

Age	Males			Females		
	No.	Average	σ	No.	Average	σ
11	203	71.5	± 2.97	49	72.0	± 4.68
12	232	72.6	± 3.47	55	75.9	± 3.80
13	294	74.8	± 4.07	32	78.8	± 4.07
14	248	77.6	± 4.24	44	79.7	± 2.78
15	190	80.5	± 4.41	57	80.9	± 2.40
16	62	81.55	± 4.89	93	81.2	± 3.48
17	37	83.6	± 4.07	114	81.15	± 2.94
18	32	87.0	± 3.42	164	81.9	± 3.58
19	56	88.3	± 4.04	141	82.7	± 3.22
Adult	840	87.67	± 3.50	808	82.2	± 3.39

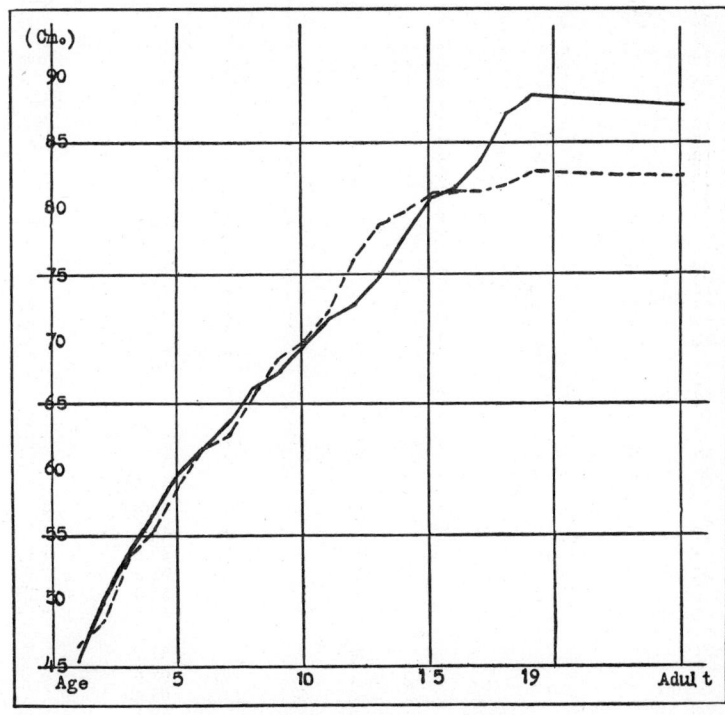

——— Males   ------ Females

Fig. 4.
Growth in Height Sitting.

Table XXII
Height Sitting (Males)

Age Cm.	1	2	3	4	5	6[1]	7	8	9	10
40	—	1	—	—	—	—	—	—	—	—
41	—	—	—	—	—	1	—	—	—	—
42	2	—	—	—	—	—	—	—	—	—
43	1	1	—	—	—	—	—	—	—	—
44	1	1	—	1	—	—	—	—	—	—
45	—	—	—	—	—	—	—	—	—	—
46	1	—	1	—	—	—	—	—	—	—
47	1	—	—	—	—	—	—	—	—	—
48	1	4	1	—	—	—	—	—	—	—
49	—	2	1	—	—	—	—	—	—	—
50	—	1	1	—	—	1	—	—	—	—
51	1	2	1	—	—	—	—	—	—	—
52	—	2	2	1	—	—	—	—	—	—
53	—	2	6	4	—	—	1	—	—	—
54	—	1	5	6	1	—	—	—	—	—
55	—	3	3	7	3	1	—	1	—	—
56	—	—	5	2	5	3	3	—	1	—
57	—	—	2	10	2	7	2	—	—	—
58	—	—	1	7	4	10	3	—	—	—
59	—	—	—	2	12	12	1	2	1	—
60	—	—	—	3	5	12	14	3	1	1
61	—	—	—	3	6	18	14	4	3	1
62	—	—	—	—	5	12	27	5	2	2
63	—	—	—	—	2	13	24	14	7	5
64	—	—	—	1	2	16	30	24	11	6
65	—	—	—	2	—	11	16	17	15	4
66	—	—	—	—	—	4	18	27	24	13
67	—	—	—	—	—	2	13	26	22	21
68	—	—	—	—	1	2	3	20	23	19
69	—	—	—	—	—	—	5	12	17	25
70	—	—	—	—	—	1	3	6	13	12
71	—	—	—	—	—	—	1	7	12	12
72	—	—	—	—	—	1	—	3	4	19
73	—	—	—	—	—	1	—	2	4	8
74	—	—	—	—	—	—	—	—	2	8
75	—	—	—	—	—	—	—	—	1	6
76	—	—	—	—	—	—	—	—	—	3
77	—	—	—	—	—	—	—	—	—	—
78	—	—	—	—	—	—	—	—	—	—
79	—	—	—	—	—	—	—	—	—	1

[1] Add: 86—2.

Table XXII (continued)
Height Sitting (Males)

Age Cm.	11	12	13[1]	14	15	16	17	18	19	Adult
60	—	1	—	—	—	—	—	—	—	—
61	—	1	—	—	—	—	—	—	—	—
62	—	1	—	—	—	—	—	—	—	—
63	1	1	—	—	—	1	—	—	—	—
64	1	—	1	—	—	—	—	—	—	—
65	2	—	—	—	—	—	—	—	—	—
66	5	3	1	1	—	1	—	—	—	—
67	5	5	3	1	—	—	—	—	—	—
68	19	11	4	1	—	—	—	—	—	—
69	18	16	8	3	—	—	—	—	—	—
70	28	17	13	1	3	1	—	—	—	—
71	28	27	18	10	1	—	—	—	—	—
72	24	35	35	9	4	—	—	—	—	—
73	20	30	22	14	7	—	—	—	—	—
74	18	20	38	15	6	2	—	—	—	—
75	14	19	30	24	8	—	1	—	—	—
76	12	20	25	28	4	1	1	—	—	—
77	5	7	20	26	15	—	1	—	—	2
78	1	6	21	20	15	4	3	—	1	1
79	1	5	20	12	17	6	1	—	—	12
80	1	3	10	14	10	4	—	—	—	12
81	—	3	9	26	18	7	3	—	3	11
82	—	1	7	12	15	6	5	4	2	27
83	—	—	3	10	14	9	4	2	2	39
84	—	—	1	8	14	6	2	—	3	43
85	—	—	1	6	17	5	2	5	1	71
86	—	—	1	3	10	1	4	6	3	93
87	—	—	—	2	2	2	2	2	2	81
88	—	—	1	—	6	3	2	2	5	96
89	—	—	—	—	1	2	4	4	9	110
90	—	—	—	1	3	1	2	1	7	85
91	—	—	—	—	—	—	—	3	8	64
92	—	—	—	—	—	—	—	1	2	36
93	—	—	—	—	—	—	—	1	3	21
94	—	—	—	1	—	—	—	—	4	19
95	—	—	—	—	—	—	—	—	—	10
96	—	—	—	—	—	—	—	1	—	6
97	—	—	—	—	—	—	—	—	—	1
98	—	—	—	—	—	—	—	—	1	—

[1] Add: 52—1; 59—1.

Table XXIII
Height Sitting (Females)

Age Cm.	1	2	3	4	5	6	7	8	9	10
45	—	1	—	—	—	—	—	—	—	—
46	1	2	—	—	—	—	—	—	—	—
47	1	3	—	—	—	—	—	—	—	—
48	—	3	1	1	—	—	—	—	—	—
49	—	3	4	—	—	—	—	—	—	—
50	—	1	—	1	—	1	—	—	—	—
51	—	2	4	1	—	—	—	—	—	—
52	—	2	1	1	—	—	1	—	—	—
53	—	—	5	1	3	—	—	—	—	—
54	—	—	3	3	3	—	1	—	—	—
55	—	—	4	3	4	1	—	—	—	—
56	—	—	2	5	2	2	1	—	—	—
57	—	—	3	4	5	1	1	—	—	—
58	—	—	2	2	7	7	1	—	—	—
59	—	—	1	—	8	5	6	1	—	—
60	—	—	—	—	9	8	7	4	1	—
61	—	—	—	1	10	8	16	5	1	2
62	—	—	—	—	4	9	11	5	1	—
63	—	—	—	—	2	14	7	7	2	1
64	—	—	—	—	2	7	14	9	2	2
65	—	—	—	—	—	4	6	4	4	2
66	—	—	—	—	—	3	10	13	4	2
67	—	—	—	—	—	2	2	9	7	3
68	—	—	—	—	—	2	4	8	7	5
69	—	—	—	—	—	1	3	4	5	3
70	—	—	—	—	—	—	—	2	4	5
71	—	—	—	—	—	—	1	1	4	4
72	—	—	—	—	—	—	—	3	3	3
73	—	—	—	—	—	—	—	—	1	3
74	—	—	—	—	—	—	—	—	2	5
75	—	—	—	—	—	—	—	1	—	2
76	—	—	—	—	—	—	—	—	1	2
77	—	—	—	—	—	—	—	—	1	1
78	—	—	—	—	—	—	—	—	—	1
79	—	—	—	—	—	—	—	—	—	—

Growth Curves and Sex Differences

Table XXIII (continued)
Height Sitting (Females)

Age Cm.	11	12	13	14	15	16	17	18[1]	19	Adult
60	—	—	—	—	—	—	—	—	—	—
61	—	—	—	—	—	—	—	—	—	—
62	1	—	—	—	—	—	—	—	—	—
63	1	—	—	—	—	—	—	—	—	—
64	1	—	—	—	—	—	—	—	—	—
65	4	—	—	—	—	—	—	—	—	—
66	—	—	—	—	—	—	—	—	—	—
67	3	—	—	—	—	—	—	—	—	—
68	4	2	—	—	—	—	—	—	—	—
69	2	2	—	—	—	—	—	—	—	—
70	—	1	1	—	—	—	—	—	—	2
71	4	1	1	—	—	—	1	—	—	—
72	4	4	1	—	—	—	—	—	—	2
73	5	4	1	—	—	2	—	1	—	3
74	2	4	2	—	—	—	1	—	1	6
75	3	6	1	2	—	3	2	4	1	9
76	6	6	3	4	2	3	4	8	1	15
77	4	9	1	6	3	4	5	2	4	24
78	2	4	1	4	6	6	9	12	8	49
79	2	2	2	4	5	10	9	10	10	60
80	1	4	7	10	9	8	12	14	13	79
81	—	2	4	4	9	14	11	21	13	81
82	—	1	2	1	8	11	20	26	10	100
83	—	1	1	2	6	8	18	19	20	81
84	—	1	1	5	4	9	9	15	17	104
85	—	1	2	2	5	8	8	13	18	71
86	—	—	1	—	—	2	3	8	9	45
87	—	—	—	—	—	2	1	3	7	34
88	—	—	—	—	—	2	1	4	3	21
89	—	—	—	—	—	1	—	—	5	9
90	—	—	—	—	—	—	—	1	1	5
91	—	—	—	—	—	—	—	1	—	5
92	—	—	—	—	—	—	—	—	—	3
93	—	—	—	—	—	—	—	—	—	—
94	—	—	—	—	—	—	—	1	—	—

[1] Add: 99—1.

Table XXIV
Ratio between Height Sitting and Stature (%)

Age	Males	Females
1	60.58	55.58
2	55.97	56.50
3	56.27	55.86
4	55.64	54.71
5	54.05	53.51
6	53.07	53.07
7	52.87	52.00
8	52.47	52.52
9	51.40	51.88
10	51.09	51.78
11	50.75	51.01
12	50.12	50.96
13	49.74	51.27
14	49.58	51.52
15	49.98	51.17
16	49.83	51.48
17	50.04	51.19
18	51.17	51.43
19	51.34	51.72
Adult	51.42	51.81

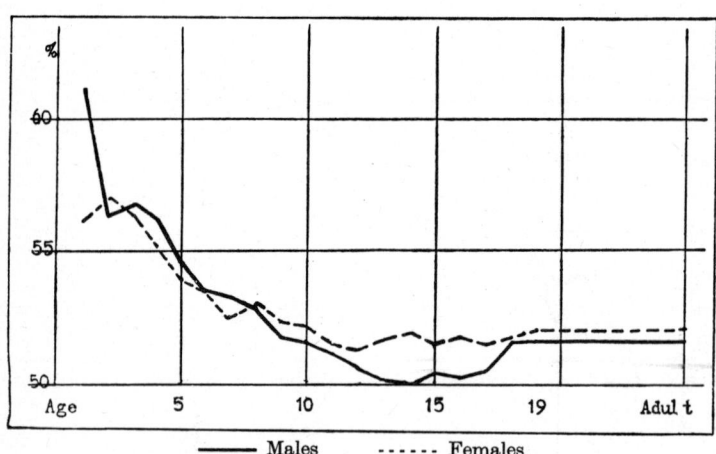

Fig. 5.
Age-changes in Ratio between Height Sitting and Stature.

Growth Curves and Sex Differences

Table XXV
Length of Head (mm.)

Age	Males			Females		
	No.	Average	σ	No.	Average	σ
1	11	160.4	± 6.64	5	160.4	± —
2	24	170.25	± 7.02	19	167.8	± 5.64
3	31	172.1	± 6.28	36	168.5	± 6.94
4	54	176.9	± 6.93	23	172.2	± 6.23
5	53	175.8	± 5.94	62	172.6	± 6.15
6	140	178.0	± 6.99	78	176.4	± 5.99
7	172	179.2	± 6.51	97	174.3	± 6.00
8	176	180.0	± 6.41	79	176.1	± 7.25
9	166	181.6	± 5.43	55	179.0	± 5.08
10	169	182.1	± 6.60	52	178.7	± 7.76
11	205	184.3	± 5.91	52	180.3	± 6.02
12	233	184.8	± 6.13	64	183.6	± 6.52
13	301	186.55	± 6.05	44	182.4	± 6.26
14	257	188.0	± 6.27	50	185.5	± 6.56
15	192	189.2	± 6.68	69	188.7	± 6.51
16	68	190.3	± 5.79	104	186.4	± 6.23
17	47	193.2	± 7.40	125	185.7	± 5.55
18	38	194.55	± 7.69	176	186.4	± 5.96
19	61	194.9	± 7.43	156	186.5	± 5.64
Adult	961	196.5	± 6.51	929	187.0	± 6.16

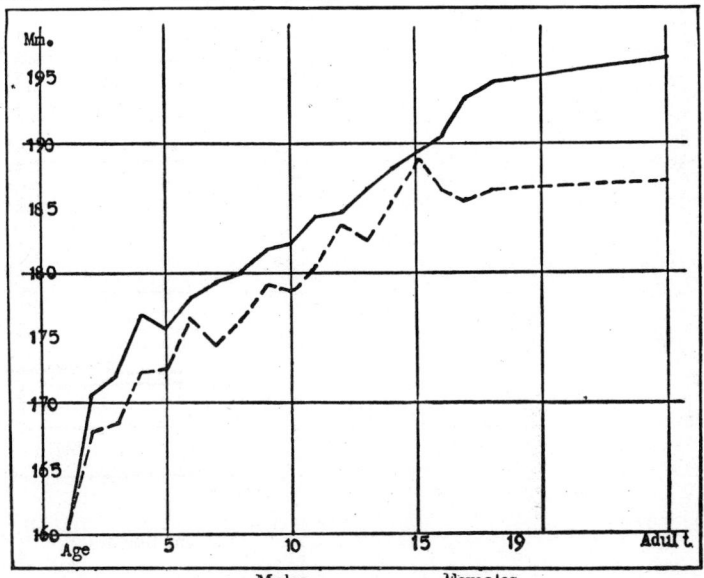

——— Males ------ Females.

Fig. 6.
Growth in Length of Head.

Table XXVI
Length of Head (Males)

Age Mm.	1[1]	2	3	4	5	6	7	8[2]	9	10[3]
153	—	1	—	—	—	—	—	—	—	—
54	1	—	—	—	—	—	—	—	—	—
55	—	—	—	—	—	—	—	—	—	—
56	—	—	—	—	—	—	—	—	—	—
57	—	—	—	—	—	—	—	—	—	—
58	—	—	—	—	—	—	—	—	—	—
59	1	1	1	—	—	1	—	—	—	—
160	1	—	1	—	1	1	—	—	—	—
61	1	—	—	1	—	—	—	—	—	—
62	1	1	—	—	—	—	—	—	—	—
63	1	2	1	—	—	—	—	2	—	—
64	—	—	—	1	—	1	—	—	1	—
65	1	—	1	4	—	2	—	—	—	—
66	—	1	3	1	—	1	2	1	1	2
67	—	1	2	—	1	1	4	1	—	—
68	—	2	—	2	3	4	4	1	—	2
69	1	—	3	3	3	7	1	3	—	3
170	—	2	1	2	2	4	3	3	1	—
71	1	3	1	2	—	7	8	4	2	2
72	—	1	2	—	7	2	6	7	2	2
73	—	2	—	5	5	4	12	4	5	5
74	—	2	2	1	2	6	4	6	7	8
75	—	—	1	2	5	9	6	5	2	2
76	—	1	2	3	1	7	9	8	7	4
77	—	1	6	1	4	9	9	12	6	7
78	—	—	—	3	2	11	15	16	9	8
79	—	1	—	3	1	6	13	15	12	13
180	—	1	2	4	2	7	7	11	12	10
81	—	—	—	6	5	5	8	7	11	8
82	—	—	—	2	—	10	8	9	13	17
83	—	—	1	—	2	2	10	9	20	10
84	—	—	1	3	2	9	5	14	10	10
85	—	—	—	1	—	4	7	8	11	6
86	—	1	—	1	4	3	2	6	5	10
87	—	—	—	2	1	7	5	6	9	5
88	—	—	—	—	—	3	7	3	5	7
89	—	—	—	—	—	—	5	4	3	3
190	—	—	—	—	—	2	6	1	3	8
91	—	—	—	—	—	—	2	3	3	4
92	—	—	—	1	—	1	3	3	2	4
93	—	—	—	—	—	1	—	1	—	2
94	—	—	—	—	—	3	—	—	—	2
95	—	—	—	—	—	—	—	—	4	1
96	—	—	—	—	—	—	—	1	—	—
97	—	—	—	—	—	—	1	1	—	—
98	—	—	—	—	—	—	—	—	—	1
99	—	—	—	—	—	—	—	—	—	2

[1] Add: 146—1; 148—1; 152—1.
[2] Add: 206—1.   [3] Add: 200—1.

Table XXVI (continued)
Length of Head (Males)

Age Mm.	11	12[1]	13[2]	14	15	16	17	18	19	Adult[3]
170	—	—	1	—	—	—	—	—	—	—
71	1	2	—	—	2	—	—	—	—	—
72	3	—	1	—	—	—	—	—	—	—
73	4	2	2	3	—	—	—	—	—	—
74	3	—	2	1	—	—	—	—	—	—
75	4	6	4	—	1	—	—	—	—	—
76	5	3	4	3	1	—	—	—	—	—
77	—	4	8	2	1	2	1	—	1	1
78	13	15	6	12	—	—	—	—	—	—
79	13	9	6	10	6	3	—	2	—	1
180	10	12	10	5	4	1	1	—	—	—
81	14	11	12	6	10	—	—	—	—	3
82	12	12	14	3	6	—	1	—	2	8
83	16	20	19	13	4	1	—	2	1	11
84	14	9	21	19	13	2	—	—	—	10
85	7	16	13	10	11	1	3	2	3	9
86	16	17	27	16	14	4	1	1	3	21
87	9	13	18	16	8	4	1	—	3	27
88	8	14	26	14	17	7	2	2	3	24
89	6	15	14	16	7	8	6	1	3	25
190	8	8	10	16	10	1	2	2	1	25
91	13	7	19	20	11	3	1	1	1	39
92	6	10	11	12	11	8	6	—	2	34
93	9	8	10	12	7	5	1	2	2	69
94	4	7	13	11	5	4	3	3	2	65
95	1	—	7	5	6	1	1	2	2	56
96	1	2	6	10	8	3	3	2	2	51
97	4	2	4	3	6	3	2	2	3	65
98	1	2	5	7	6	2	2	2	5	59
99	—	2	4	4	5	3	1	2	2	58
200	—	—	1	1	3	—	3	—	5	39
01	—	—	—	3	2	—	1	2	3	52
02	—	—	1	1	2	1	—	3	1	37
03	—	1	—	1	2	—	—	2	3	40
04	—	—	—	2	—	1	1	—	2	25
05	—	—	—	—	1	—	1	1	2	20
06	—	—	1	—	—	—	—	—	2	24
07	—	—	—	—	1	—	2	—	—	17
08	—	—	—	—	—	—	—	1	2	12
09	—	—	—	—	—	—	—	—	—	12
210	—	—	—	—	—	—	—	—	—	6
11	—	—	—	—	1	—	—	—	—	4
12	—	—	—	—	—	—	—	1	—	3
13	—	—	—	—	—	—	1	—	—	2

[1] Add: 167—2; 168—2. [2] Add: 168—1.
[3] Add: 214—2; 215—2; 216—1; 218—1; 219—1.

8*

Table XXVII
Length of Head (Females)

Age Mm.	1	2	3	4	5	6	7	8	9	10
154	—	—	1	—	—	1	—	—	1	—
55	2	—	—	—	—	—	—	—	—	—
56	—	—	—	—	—	—	—	—	—	—
57	—	—	—	—	—	—	—	1	—	—
58	—	1	2	—	—	—	—	—	—	—
59	—	1	1	—	—	—	1	—	—	—
160	—	—	—	1	1	—	—	—	—	—
61	1	—	—	1	—	2	1	—	—	—
62	—	—	4	—	4	1	3	1	—	1
63	1	1	2	—	—	4	—	—	—	1
64	—	4	—	—	2	1	—	—	—	—
65	—	—	2	1	3	—	4	2	—	—
66	—	1	2	2	3	2	3	3	—	—
67	—	3	3	1	—	2	1	1	—	—
68	1	—	3	—	4	3	6	3	—	1
69	—	1	1	2	3	3	4	3	1	1
170	—	2	1	1	1	1	3	2	—	—
71	—	1	4	1	5	6	3	4	—	—
72	—	—	3	—	4	4	4	4	3	1
73	—	1	—	4	4	5	8	6	6	5
74	—	1	—	—	4	7	4	5	3	2
75	—	—	—	2	3	4	6	1	3	4
76	—	—	1	—	5	2	9	5	3	2
77	—	1	1	3	—	6	7	5	4	3
78	—	—	1	1	5	6	7	3	2	5
79	—	—	—	1	3	8	7	8	5	1
180	—	—	2	—	—	1	3	2	6	3
81	—	1	—	1	2	3	1	4	3	3
82	—	—	1	—	3	1	3	2	3	1
83	—	—	1	—	1	2	3	5	3	3
84	—	—	—	—	—	1	3	—	2	4
85	—	—	—	—	2	—	2	3	4	2
86	—	—	—	1	—	—	—	3	—	2
87	—	—	—	—	—	1	1	—	1	2
88	—	—	—	—	—	—	—	2	—	—
89	—	—	—	—	—	—	—	—	1	1
190	—	—	—	—	—	1	—	—	—	1
91	—	—	—	—	—	—	—	—	1	—
92	—	—	—	—	—	—	—	—	—	—
93	—	—	—	—	—	—	—	—	1	1
94	—	—	—	—	—	—	—	(207—1)	(201—1)	

Growth Curves and Sex Differences 117

Table **XXVII** (continued)
Length of Head (Females)

Age Mm.	11	12	13	14	15	16	17	18	19	Adult
168	(163—1)	—	—	—	—	—	—	—	—	(164—1)
69	(165—1)	3	—	—	—	—	—	—	—	1
170	—	—	—	—	—	—	—	1	—	—
71	1	—	—	—	—	—	—	1	—	—
72	1	—	2	3	1	—	2	—	—	6
73	1	—	2	1	—	—	1	2	1	6
74	4	1	—	—	—	—	1	—	1	5
75	4	1	1	—	1	3	2	3	4	6
76	1	2	1	1	4	3	1	2	—	13
77	2	4	2	—	—	1	4	—	2	7
78	4	3	6	—	3	2	2	3	4	17
79	1	2	3	3	2	5	6	4	1	24
180	4	5	2	2	5	6	5	16	8	46
81	3	2	2	5	4	5	1	6	4	34
82	5	1	5	3	3	7	6	10	14	50
83	2	7	1	2	5	3	9	12	8	50
84	3	9	3	—	2	7	10	11	18	65
85	3	1	3	6	4	5	13	6	9	53
86	2	4	1	1	4	6	6	16	15	58
87	1	3	2	2	6	3	5	12	3	65
88	5	3	1	2	5	10	8	11	9	60
89	1	2	—	3	5	5	4	4	6	55
190	2	—	1	4	3	12	18	14	15	52
91	—	3	2	3	2	4	5	2	7	43
92	—	3	—	2	1	4	4	6	5	46
93	—	3	—	3	3	1	3	6	3	39
94	—	—	—	2	2	3	4	7	6	27
95	—	1	2	—	1	—	2	10	3	21
96	—	—	2	—	—	1	1	6	1	13
97	—	—	—	—	—	2	—	2	4	18
98	—	—	—	1	—	1	—	2	2	13
99	—	—	—	—	—	—	2	—	1	13
200	—	—	—	—	—	1	—	1	1	2
01	—	—	—	1	1	2	—	—	—	5
02	—	—	—	—	—	—	—	—	—	3
03	—	—	—	—	—	1	—	—	1	6
04	—	—	—	—	1	1	—	—	—	2
05	—	1	—	—	—	—	—	—	—	1
06	—	—	—	—	—	—	—	—	—	—
07	—	—	—	—	—	—	—	—	—	1
08	—	—	—	—	(209—1)	—	—	—	—	2

Table XXVIII

Width of Head (mm.)

Age	Males			Females		
	No.	Average	σ	No.	Average	σ
1	11	129.9	± 6.92	5	129.2	—
2	24	135.1	± 5.78	19	130.6	± 4.44
3	31	134.7	± 4.54	36	134.6	± 4.70
4	54	137.6	± 4.69	23	134.6	± 5.07
5	53	139.0	± 5.23	62	135.6	± 4.65
6	140	140.1	± 5.84	78	136.2	± 5.08
7	172	140.0	± 5.01	96	137.25	± 4.77
8	176	140.8	± 5.31	78	137.9	± 4.68
9	166	141.9	± 5.15	55	138.4	± 4.90
10	166	142.1	± 5.30	53	138.2	± 5.16
11	206	143.0	± 4.80	52	139.4	± 4.71
12	233	143.8	± 4.94	64	142.0	± 4.03
13	301	144.65	± 5.52	44	141.8	± 6.18
14	257	146.0	± 5.05	50	143.4	± 6.99
15	192	146.9	± 5.10	69	143.4	± 5.03
16	68	147.2	± 5.02	104	144.3	± 4.97
17	47	148.3	± 4.75	125	143.9	± 4.96
18	38	149.0	± 4.70	176	144.2	± 4.85
19	61	148.2	± 5.24	156	144.3	± 4.58
Adult	961	151.4	± 5.74	928	145.4	± 4.99

Growth Curves and Sex Differences 119

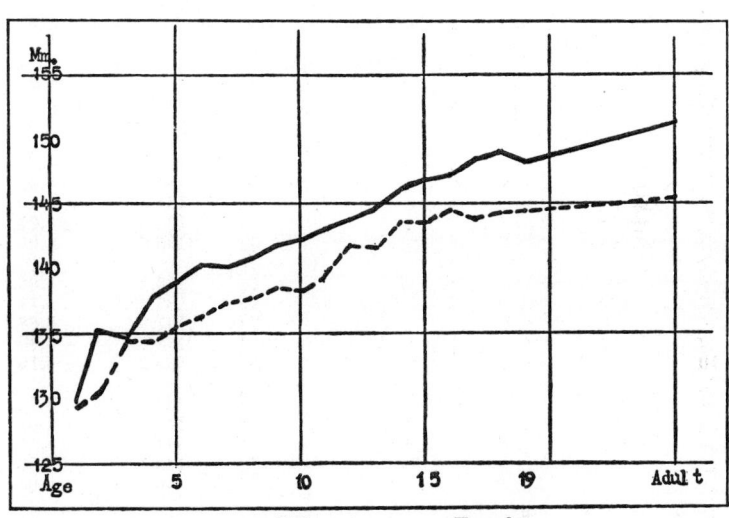

Fig. 7.
Growth in Width of Head.

Table
Width of Head

Age Mm.	1[1]	2	3	4	5	6	7	8	9	10
124	—	—	—	—	—	—	1	—	—	—
25	2	1	—	—	—	—	—	—	—	—
26	—	3	—	—	1	—	—	2	—	—
27	—	1	—	—	—	—	2	1	1	—
28	1	—	1	3	—	3	—	2	—	—
29	1	—	3	1	1	—	2	—	—	1
130	—	1	2	—	—	4	2	1	1	—
31	1	—	4	3	2	3	6	1	—	3
32	1	1	2	1	1	2	3	5	—	2
33	—	—	2	4	3	—	6	3	1	4
34	—	3	3	2	3	6	—	5	9	5
35	1	—	2	2	2	13	7	6	6	8
36	2	4	1	4	5	11	8	5	7	4
37	—	1	1	3	4	10	8	11	6	10
38	—	2	2	5	4	7	11	13	15	5
39	1	1	4	6	2	10	17	12	12	12
140	—	2	1	3	5	9	15	16	9	7
41	—	1	—	8	4	8	15	14	10	6
42	—	1	—	3	1	10	12	12	14	14
43	—	—	2	1	3	7	13	11	14	21
44	—	1	—	2	4	7	13	16	11	10
45	—	1	1	1	2	2	5	8	14	5
46	—	—	—	—	1	2	13	8	9	14
47	—	—	—	1	1	9	5	5	5	10
48	—	—	—	1	2	3	4	7	3	8
49	—	—	—	—	2	6	2	3	8	4
150	—	—	—	—	—	2	1	7	2	6
51	—	—	—	—	—	2	1	—	3	2
52	—	—	—	—	—	2	—	—	1	2
53	—	—	—	—	—	1	—	—	2	2
54	—	—	—	—	—	—	—	1	—	—
55	—	—	—	—	—	—	—	—	1	—
56	—	—	—	—	—	—	—	1	1	—
57	—	—	—	—	—	—	—	—	—	1
58	—	—	—	—	—	1	—	—	1	—
59	—	—	—	—	—	—	—	—	—	—
160	—	—	—	—	—	—	—	—	—	—
61	—	—	—	—	—	—	—	—	—	—
62	—	—	—	—	—	—	—	—	—	—
63	—	—	—	—	—	—	—	—	—	—
64	—	—	—	—	—	—	—	—	—	—
65	—	—	—	—	—	—	—	—	—	—
66	—	—	—	—	—	—	—	—	—	—
67	—	—	—	—	—	—	—	—	—	—
68	—	—	—	—	—	—	—	—	—	—
69	—	—	—	—	—	—	—	—	—	—
170	—	—	—	—	—	—	—	—	—	—

[1] Add: 113 = 1.

XXIX
(Males)

11	12	13	14	15	16	17	18	19	Adult
—	—	—	—	—	—	—	—	—	—
—	—	—	—	—	—	—	—	—	—
—	—	—	—	—	—	—	—	—	1
1	—	1	—	—	—	—	—	—	—
1	—	—	—	—	—	—	—	—	—
—	—	1	—	1	—	—	—	—	2
—	1	2	1	—	—	1	—	—	—
1	4	3	—	—	—	—	—	—	1
2	1	3	1	3	—	—	—	—	3
2	3	5	2	—	—	—	—	1	1
9	4	7	1	1	—	—	—	1	1
7	9	6	3	1	1	—	—	1	3
15	6	9	6	3	1	—	—	2	3
13	15	12	9	—	1	1	—	1	7
11	9	14	11	7	2	1	1	1	3
18	18	21	23	6	1	—	—	—	3
16	25	19	12	11	5	—	1	1	20
23	25	32	14	19	4	—	4	5	23
15	22	19	19	18	5	5	2	6	34
11	18	18	16	8	6	4	—	1	24
16	18	19	21	14	2	5	5	3	55
9	11	20	25	12	13	3	3	3	51
6	6	17	17	17	4	3	2	2	46
9	9	16	16	10	7	6	3	7	80
6	5	10	15	11	2	1	2	2	66
4	7	11	11	9	2	5	1	4	54
6	7	13	11	12	1	7	5	4	71
2	1	9	7	12	3	—	3	10	85
2	1	3	5	5	4	2	3	3	55
—	3	4	1	3	1	—	—	1	34
1	—	2	1	3	2	1	1	1	54
—	2	2	3	3	—	1	1	—	54
—	1	2	2	2	—	—	—	2	38
—	2	—	1	—	—	—	—	—	29
—	—	—	1	1	—	1	—	—	12
—	—	—	2	—	—	—	—	—	13
—	—	—	—	—	—	—	1	—	5
—	—	—	—	—	—	—	—	—	7
—	—	—	—	—	—	—	—	—	6
—	—	1	—	—	—	—	—	—	6
—	—	—	—	—	—	—	—	—	5
—	—	—	—	—	—	—	—	—	2
—	—	—	—	—	1	—	—	—	2
—	—	—	—	—	—	—	—	—	1
—	—	—	—	—	—	—	—	—	1

Table
Width of Head

Age Mm.	1	2	3	4	5	6	7	8	9	10
120	—	—	—	—	1	—	—	—	—	—
21	—	—	—	—	—	—	—	—	—	—
22	—	—	—	—	—	—	—	—	—	—
23	1	1	—	—	—	—	1	—	—	—
24	—	1	—	—	—	—	—	—	—	—
25	—	1	—	1	—	2	—	1	—	—
26	—	1	—	—	1	1	—	—	—	1
27	2	3	2	—	—	2	1	—	—	—
28	—	—	1	1	2	3	1	—	—	1
29	—	—	2	3	2	2	1	2	1	1
130	1	1	3	1	4	—	—	2	1	—
31	—	3	4	1	2	2	6	4	1	2
32	—	—	1	4	2	3	2	5	1	2
33	—	2	2	1	4	4	7	1	3	2
34	—	1	4	—	3	7	8	2	6	4
35	—	3	3	—	6	7	11	3	5	3
36	—	1	2	1	8	7	6	7	3	3
37	—	—	2	2	6	5	12	6	5	4
38	—	—	4	1	6	11	7	6	3	5
39	1	1	—	2	2	6	6	9	5	2
140	—	—	1	1	3	4	1	9	5	5
41	—	—	2	1	4	2	4	6	4	5
42	—	—	1	3	3	1	5	2	1	4
43	—	—	—	—	1	2	6	5	2	3
44	—	—	—	—	2	2	6	2	3	2
45	—	—	2	—	—	2	—	2	2	—
46	—	—	—	—	—	1	3	2	—	—
47	—	—	—	—	—	—	1	—	—	—
48	—	—	—	—	—	1	—	2	1	2
49	—	—	—	—	—	1	—	—	1	1
150	—	—	—	—	—	—	1	—	1	—
51	—	—	—	—	—	—	—	—	1	1
52	—	—	—	—	—	—	—	—	—	—
53	—	—	—	—	—	—	—	—	—	—
54	—	—	—	—	—	—	—	—	—	—
55	—	—	—	—	—	—	—	—	—	—
56	—	—	—	—	—	—	—	—	—	—
57	—	—	—	—	—	—	—	—	—	—
58	—	—	—	—	—	—	—	—	—	—
59	—	—	—	—	—	—	—	—	—	—
160	—	—	—	—	—	—	—	—	—	—
61	—	—	—	—	—	—	—	—	—	—
62	—	—	—	—	—	—	—	—	—	—
63	—	—	—	—	—	—	—	—	—	—

XXX
(Females)

11	12	13	14	15	16	17	18	19	Adult
—	—	—	—	—	—	—	—	—	—
—	—	—	—	—	—	—	—	—	—
—	—	—	—	—	—	—	—	—	—
—	—	—	—	—	—	—	—	—	—
—	—	—	—	—	—	—	—	—	—
—	—	—	—	—	—	1	—	—	—
—	—	—	—	—	—	—	—	—	—
—	—	—	1	—	—	—	—	—	—
—	—	—	1	—	—	—	—	—	—
—	—	—	1	—	—	—	—	—	—
2	—	—	1	1	—	1	1	—	1
—	—	2	1	—	1	—	1	—	3
—	1	1	—	1	1	1	1	1	—
3	—	—	4	—	—	1	1	1	2
3	—	2	—	—	1	—	1	—	7
2	—	1	—	2	—	2	2	2	5
6	1	2	2	2	2	1	4	1	13
2	4	6	1	3	3	3	3	2	12
6	7	1	1	1	3	6	8	6	24
8	7	2	4	3	4	6	2	3	39
—	3	3	1	7	6	8	12	22	48
1	11	—	3	4	7	8	11	6	53
5	4	5	4	4	14	11	16	16	59
2	5	1	2	6	9	6	16	10	76
3	7	3	5	3	4	10	14	12	72
3	3	5	3	9	9	11	11	11	59
3	2	1	1	4	7	8	12	13	65
1	1	2	1	6	7	10	11	12	84
—	4	2	1	3	5	11	15	9	70
1	3	—	4	2	4	5	9	2	46
—	—	1	1	2	5	6	13	13	59
1	—	—	1	3	5	3	2	2	25
—	—	—	2	1	2	2	4	3	34
—	—	2	3	—	1	1	2	2	26
—	—	—	—	—	1	3	2	5	11
—	—	—	1	1	2	—	—	1	10
—	1	2	1	1	—	—	—	—	11
—	—	—	1	—	—	—	2	1	4
—	—	—	—	—	1	—	—	—	4
—	—	—	—	—	—	—	—	—	1
—	—	—	—	—	—	—	—	—	1
—	—	—	—	—	—	—	—	—	—
—	—	—	—	—	—	—	—	—	4

Table XXXI
Cephalic Index

Age	Males			Females		
	No.	Average	σ	No.	Average	σ
1	11	81.2	± 4.11	5	80.5	—
2	24	79.3	± 3.22	19	77.9	± 3.38
3	31	78.5	± 4.16	36	80.0	± 4.27
4	54	78.4	± 4.22	23	78.3	± 3.27
5	52	79.0	± 3.69	62	78.7	± 3.83
6	138	79.1	± 3.98	78	78.55	± 3.33
7	168	78.2	± 3.60	96	78.9	± 3.56
8	175	78.3	± 3.86	78	78.55	± 3.95
9	166	78.2	± 3.72	55	77.4	± 3.13
10	164	78.1	± 3.58	52	77.4	± 3.49
11	206	77.7	± 3.37	52	77.35	± 2.52
12	232	77.9	± 3.60	64	77.4	± 3.01
13	301	77.6	± 3.42	44	77.7	± 3.27
14	257	78.1	± 3.55	50	77.3	± 3.79
15	192	77.8	± 3.12	69	77.5	± 3.13
16	68	77.3	± 3.27	104	77.4	± 2.94
17	47	76.9	± 3.59	125	77.6	± 3.26
18	38	76.8	± 3.96	176	77.55	± 2.84
19	61	76.3	± 2.71	156	77.5	± 2.88
Adults	961	77.1	± 3.45	928	77.8	± 3.10

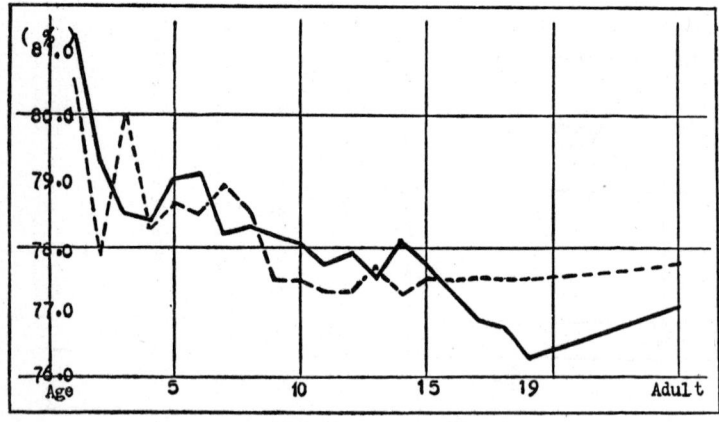

Fig. 8.
Age-changes in Cephalic Index.

Growth Curves and Sex Differences

Table XXXI—A
Cephalic Index

(Norms derived from three-year running average.)

Age	Males	Females
1	79.8	78.2
2	79.3	79.3
3	78.7	78.9
4	78.65	79.0
5	78.9	78.7
6	78.7	78.7
7	78.5	78.7
8	78.2	78.4
9	78.2	77.8
10	78.0	77.4
11	77.9	77.4
12	77.7	77.5
13	77.85	77.5
14	77.8	77.5
15	77.9	77.4
16	77.55	77.5
17	77.05	77.5
18	76.6	77.5
19	77.0	77.7
Adult	77.0	77.8

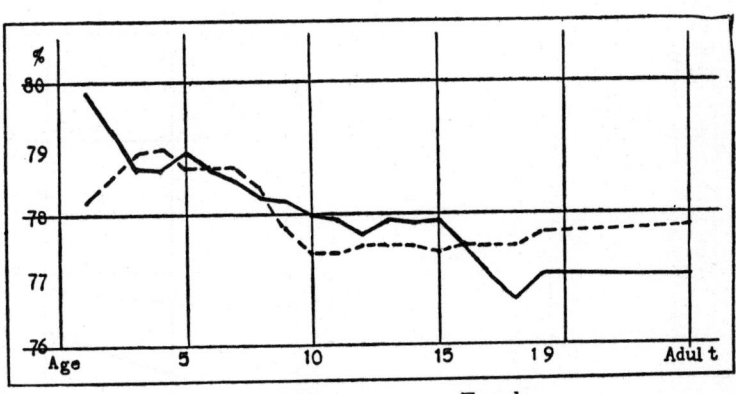

Fig. 9.
Age-changes in Cephalic Index, smoothed.

Table
Cephalic In-

Age %	1	2	3	4	5	6	7	8	9	10
62.5[1]	—	—	—	—	—	—	—	—	1	—
63.5	—	—	—	—	—	—	—	—	—	—
64.5	—	—	—	—	—	—	—	—	—	—
65.5	—	—	—	—	—	—	—	—	—	—
66.5	—	—	—	—	—	—	1	2	1	—
67.5	—	—	—	—	—	—	—	—	—	2
68.5	—	—	—	1	—	2	1	—	—	—
69.5	—	—	—	—	—	3	—	4	1	—
70.5	—	1	—	2	—	—	4	2	1	2
71.5	—	—	1	1	2	—	—	—	2	2
72.5	—	—	1	1	3	3	5	6	4	5
73.5	—	1	—	4	—	6	9	4	8	7
74.5	2	—	5	1	1	5	11	11	12	10
75.5	—	—	3	7	4	12	15	16	13	13
76.5	—	2	2	4	5	15	13	13	16	24
77.5	—	3	3	6	7	10	21	21	14	13
78.5	—	4	4	2	2	11	15	25	27	23
79.5	2	4	5	5	6	17	16	16	20	16
80.5	2	2	—	5	7	14	17	18	13	12
81.5	1	1	1	3	5	15	17	12	9	16
82.5	—	3	1	4	3	4	10	9	10	9
83.5	—	1	2	2	3	6	7	8	5	4
84.5	2	2	1	2	1	4	4	1	4	1
85.5	1	—	1	3	2	5	—	1	2	2
86.5	—	—	—	1	—	1	1	1	—	—
87.5	—	—	—	—	—	4	—	2	2	1
88.5	1	—	—	—	1	—	—	2	1	1
89.5	—	—	—	—	—	1	1	1	—	—
90.5	—	—	—	—	—	—	—	—	—	1
91.5	—	—	1	—	—	—	—	—	—	—

[1] i. e. 62.0—62.99, etc.

XXXII
dex (Males)

11	12	13	14	15	16	17	18	19	Adult
—	—	—	—	—	—	—	—	—	1
—	—	—	—	—	—	—	—	—	1
1	—	—	—	—	—	—	—	—	—
—	—	—	—	—	—	—	—	—	2
—	—	—	—	—	—	1	—	—	2
—	—	1	—	1	1	—	—	—	3
—	2	1	—	—	—	—	—	—	13
3	1	4	—	2	2	2	1	—	12
4	5	12	2	3	—	2	1	—	23
2	5	7	15	4	4	1	4	5	47
14	13	16	17	10	3	3	5	7	55
15	18	22	19	13	4	4	3	12	75
24	27	43	29	20	8	3	4	8	121
39	27	29	32	25	12	9	3	9	119
20	33	38	26	22	2	7	4	7	110
16	26	25	24	30	13	3	4	4	125
12	26	33	34	23	5	4	4	2	72
14	12	25	21	14	5	1	—	3	67
13	12	13	16	7	3	3	1	2	43
11	4	13	8	10	3	2	1	—	24
10	4	6	10	4	2	—	2	1	18
4	6	6	2	2	1	2	—	1	14
1	5	5	2	—	—	—	—	—	8
1	1	2	—	—	—	—	—	—	4
—	2	—	—	—	—	—	—	—	1
—	—	—	—	1	—	—	—	—	1
—	1	—	—	1	—	—	—	—	—
—	2	—	—	—	—	—	1	—	—
—	—	—	—	—	—	—	—	—	—

Table

Cephalic In-

Age %	1	2	3	4	5	6	7	8	9	10
62.5[1]	—	—	—	—	—	—	—	1	—	—
63.5	—	—	—	—	—	—	—	—	—	—
64.5	—	—	—	—	—	—	—	—	—	—
65.5	—	—	—	—	—	—	—	—	—	—
66.5	—	—	—	—	—	—	—	—	1	—
67.5	—	—	—	—	—	—	—	—	—	—
68.5	—	—	—	—	—	—	—	—	—	—
69.5	—	—	—	—	1	—	1	—	—	—
70.5	—	—	—	—	1	—	—	1	—	2
71.5	—	1	2	1	1	—	—	1	—	2
72.5	—	—	—	—	—	2	2	1	4	1
73.5	—	1	2	—	1	4	4	2	3	3
74.5	—	2	1	3	5	2	6	4	3	3
75.5	1	1	2	4	6	16	5	6	5	8
76.5	1	3	1	—	8	5	12	12	6	5
77.5	—	2	4	3	5	7	10	7	8	6
78.5	—	1	3	2	6	11	15	8	5	6
79.5	—	5	1	4	7	8	9	8	9	4
80.5	—	1	4	1	6	5	4	11	7	5
81.5	1	—	1	2	3	2	6	5	2	1
82.5	—	—	7	1	5	6	10	2	1	4
83.5	1	—	3	—	2	4	5	2	1	—
84.5	—	1	3	1	1	1	4	2	—	—
85.5	1	1	—	—	1	5	—	—	—	1
86.5	—	—	—	1	2	—	2	4	—	1
87.5	—	—	1	—	—	—	—	1	—	—
88.5	—	—	—	—	—	—	—	—	—	—
89.5	—	—	—	—	1	—	—	—	—	—
90.5	—	—	1	—	—	—	1	—	—	—

[1] i. e. 62.0—62.99, etc.

XXXIII
dex (Females)

11	12	13	14	15	16	17	18	19	Adult
—	—	—	—	—	—	—	—	—	—
—	—	—	—	—	—	1	—	—	—
—	—	—	—	—	—	—	—	—	—
—	—	—	—	—	—	—	1	—	1
—	—	—	1	—	—	—	—	—	—
—	1	—	1	1	1	—	—	1	3
—	—	1	—	1	—	1	1	1	5
1	—	—	1	2	2	1	—	1	11
2	3	3	3	1	2	6	4	7	33
1	4	3	3	4	9	8	10	9	50
5	5	5	3	5	7	7	13	12	65
7	9	3	7	6	8	16	28	16	84
7	8	4	6	8	19	13	22	18	116
7	10	1	5	9	11	15	21	17	133
10	7	6	4	13	16	19	27	26	117
5	5	8	3	6	13	12	14	17	106
3	5	4	3	6	6	5	14	13	77
2	2	2	5	3	2	11	10	11	47
1	1	1	3	2	4	3	5	3	33
1	3	2	1	1	2	5	3	2	20
—	—	—	—	—	—	1	2	2	13
—	—	1	—	—	2	1	1	—	4
—	1	—	—	—	—	—	—	—	5
—	—	—	—	1	—	—	—	—	3
—	—	—	1	—	—	—	—	—	1
—	—	—	—	—	—	—	—	—	1
—	—	—	—	—	—	—	—	—	—

Table
Height of

Age Mm.	1	2	3	4	5	6	7	8	9	10
110	—	—	1	—	—	—	—	—	—	—
11	—	—	1	—	—	—	—	—	—	—
12	—	—	—	1	—	—	—	—	—	—
13	—	1	—	1	1	—	—	—	—	—
14	—	—	1	2	—	—	—	1	—	—
15	—	—	1	—	1	1	—	1	—	—
16	—	—	1	—	1	1	2	—	—	—
17	—	—	1	—	1	2	1	1	—	—
18	—	1	3	1	—	4	1	—	—	—
19	—	—	1	4	—	3	1	1	1	—
120	—	—	5	1	1	1	3	2	1	1
21	—	1	2	4	1	2	4	5	—	6
22	—	—	—	5	1	4	5	2	2	—
23	—	—	—	2	—	7	3	3	3	3
24	—	1	—	2	1	4	5	5	4	8
25	—	1	4	4	3	6	9	7	10	6
26	—	2	—	6	4	10	9	4	10	5
27	—	1	1	2	2	6	5	2	10	7
28	—	1	1	2	3	7	10	5	10	9
29	—	1	1	3	5	9	14	7	3	11
130	—	—	1	1	2	8	7	6	5	7
31	—	—	—	1	1	12	7	12	11	5
32	—	1	2	1	3	5	10	13	8	6
33	—	—	1	2	—	3	7	5	5	11
34	—	—	—	2	—	4	6	3	3	7
35	—	—	—	—	1	6	2	6	1	6
36	—	—	—	—	—	4	4	2	5	4
37	—	—	—	—	—	8	2	2	3	4
38	—	—	—	—	—	4	1	1	2	3
39	—	—	—	—	1	—	—	—	3	4
140	—	—	—	—	—	—	1	2	2	1
41	—	—	—	—	—	—	—	—	1	1
42	—	—	—	—	—	2	—	—	—	—
43	—	—	—	—	—	—	—	—	—	—
44	—	—	—	—	—	—	—	—	—	1
45	—	—	—	—	—	—	—	—	—	—
46	—	—	—	—	1	—	—	—	—	—
47	—	—	—	—	—	—	—	—	—	—
48	—	—	—	—	—	—	—	—	—	—

XXXIV
Head (Males)

11	12	13	14	15	16	17	18	19	Adult
—	—	—	—	—	—	—	—	—	—
—	—	—	1	—	—	—	—	—	—
—	—	—	—	—	—	—	—	—	—
—	—	—	—	—	—	—	—	—	—
—	1	—	—	—	—	—	—	—	—
—	1	—	—	—	—	—	—	—	—
—	1	—	—	—	—	—	—	—	—
—	—	1	1	—	—	—	—	—	—
1	1	—	1	—	1	—	—	—	1
4	4	2	2	—	—	—	—	—	1
2	5	2	2	1	—	—	—	—	3
2	5	3	—	1	—	—	—	3	5
3	4	4	3	6	1	—	—	—	5
2	8	6	7	3	—	—	1	2	11
7	5	11	9	7	—	1	—	—	10
6	5	13	5	3	2	—	—	1	16
6	10	23	7	6	3	1	2	5	20
13	10	9	11	7	3	—	2	1	24
9	16	15	11	5	4	3	—	5	37
15	10	12	11	12	6	3	—	2	48
11	16	18	20	10	2	3	2	4	60
13	10	16	16	12	3	3	2	3	56
8	15	23	19	10	1	5	3	1	71
13	13	13	16	10	3	1	4	4	70
5	11	16	11	10	4	3	3	4	52
9	10	12	12	14	5	—	1	3	89
4	4	13	6	3	1	1	2	5	72
1	5	6	6	6	1	2	1	5	64
5	5	2	3	3	1	2	3	4	42
2	2	4	4	4	1	—	3	2	28
1	1	2	2	4	—	—	1	—	20
—	—	—	—	1	—	—	—	—	12
—	—	1	—	2	—	—	—	—	5
—	—	1	—	1	—	—	—	—	6
—	—	—	—	—	—	—	—	1	6
—	—	—	—	1	—	1	—	—	2
—	—	—	—	—	—	—	—	1	1
—	—	—	—	—	—	—	—	—	2

(157—1)

Table
Height of

Age Mm.	1	2	3	4	5	6	7	8	9	10
107	—	1	—	—	—	—	—	—	—	—
08	—	—	1	—	—	—	—	—	—	—
09	—	—	—	—	—	—	—	—	—	—
110	—	—	—	1	—	—	—	—	—	—
11	—	1	—	—	—	—	—	—	—	—
12	—	—	—	—	2	—	1	—	3	—
13	—	—	—	—	1	—	1	2	1	1
14	—	—	1	1	—	1	2	—	1	—
15	—	—	—	—	1	1	—	—	—	1
16	—	1	1	2	3	3	1	1	—	2
17	—	2	2	2	—	5	3	—	—	1
18	—	—	1	—	2	2	—	2	2	3
19	—	1	3	—	—	3	—	2	4	2
120	—	—	1	2	4	1	3	6	5	1
21	—	—	4	3	1	8	6	3	5	—
22	—	1	2	4	4	6	5	5	6	3
23	—	—	2	2	6	3	6	3	—	—
24	—	—	2	—	4	3	5	8	1	4
25	—	4	1	1	1	5	5	5	3	1
26	—	—	—	—	—	6	2	2	5	4
27	—	—	1	1	2	4	7	4	1	5
28	—	—	—	1	6	4	4	3	2	4
29	—	—	—	—	2	3	4	4	2	1
130	—	—	—	—	1	4	4	4	2	3
31	—	—	—	—	2	2	3	1	2	—
32	—	—	—	—	—	—	5	4	1	1
33	—	—	—	—	—	2	2	2	—	1
34	—	—	—	—	1	—	—	4	1	—
35	—	—	1	—	—	3	2	—	1	—
36	—	—	—	—	—	—	1	1	1	2
37	—	—	—	—	—	—	1	1	—	2
38	—	—	—	—	—	—	—	—	—	—
39	—	—	—	—	—	—	—	—	—	—
140	—	—	—	—	—	1	—	—	—	—
41	—	—	—	—	—	—	—	—	—	—
42	—	—	—	—	—	—	—	—	—	1
43	—	—	—	—	—	—	—	—	—	—
44	—	—	—	—	—	—	—	—	—	—
45	—	—	—	—	—	—	—	—	—	—
46	—	—	—	—	—	—	—	—	—	—

XXXV
Head (Females)

11	12	13	14	15	16	17	18	19	Adult
—	—	—	—	—	—	—	—	—	—
—	—	—	—	—	—	—	—	—	—
—	—	—	—	—	—	—	—	—	—
1	—	—	—	—	—	—	—	—	—
—	—	—	—	—	—	—	—	—	—
—	—	—	—	—	1	—	—	—	—
2	—	—	—	—	—	1	—	—	1
1	—	—	2	—	1	—	—	—	3
3	3	—	2	—	—	—	—	1	4
2	—	—	—	1	1	1	1	—	5
3	4	2	—	1	2	3	2	2	10
—	4	—	—	1	—	2	2	1	18
4	3	1	1	1	1	3	—	4	22
1	4	1	1	1	1	4	1	—	22
4	3	4	2	5	3	4	2	8	33
3	4	2	4	4	6	3	7	3	39
4	7	3	2	3	5	4	7	3	46
2	1	2	2	4	4	5	11	2	48
1	1	—	5	3	5	8	11	4	50
1	4	1	2	4	3	5	8	9	68
3	3	4	3	5	13	1	6	4	55
3	4	2	1	2	7	3	8	7	56
4	2	3	4	6	3	11	3	8	44
2	—	1	1	4	3	2	7	2	41
1	2	—	2	1	5	9	17	8	39
—	3	1	3	3	2	6	12	10	45
1	3	2	2	3	2	1	5	3	22
—	—	1	3	2	5	1	2	5	30
—	—	—	—	1	2	3	2	—	17
—	—	1	1	—	2	1	5	1	11
—	—	—	1	1	1	—	2	3	13
—	—	—	—	—	—	1	1	—	4
1	—	—	—	—	—	1	—	1	7
—	1	—	—	—	—	—	—	—	1
—	—	—	—	—	—	—	—	—	2
—	—	—	—	—	—	—	1	—	—
—	—	—	—	—	—	—	—	1	2

Table XXXVI
Height of Head (mm.)

Age	Males			Females		
	No.	Average	σ	No.	Average	σ
1	—	—	—	—	—	—
2	11	124.4	± 5.09	11	119.0	± 6.09
3	28	121.75	± 6.12	23	120.7	± 4.98
4	49	124.6	± 5.65	20	120.35	± 4.23
5	34	127.0	± 6.44	43	123.0	± 5.30
6	123	128.6	± 5.87	70	124.2	± 5.48
7	119	128.2	± 4.89	73	125.3	± 5.50
8	98	128.9	± 5.27	67	125.5	± 5.38
9	103	129.6	± 4.77	49	123.3	± 5.84
10	116	130.2	± 5.10	43	125.6	± 6.50
11	142	130.45	± 4.72	47	125.5	± 6.11
12	178	130.15	± 5.27	56	126.8	± 5.62
13	229	131.1	± 5.02	31	128.6	± 4.96
14	186	131.2	± 4.81	44	129.2	± 5.87
15	150	132.4	± 5.03	56	129.4	± 4.84
16	42	131.5	± 4.36	78	129.7	± 5.19
17	29	133.1	± 4.07	84	129.4	± 5.44
18	30	134.2	± 4.35	123	131.0	± 4.95
19	56	133.0	± 5.56	90	130.7	± 5.44
Adult	839	134.0	± 4.64	758	129.9	± 5.25

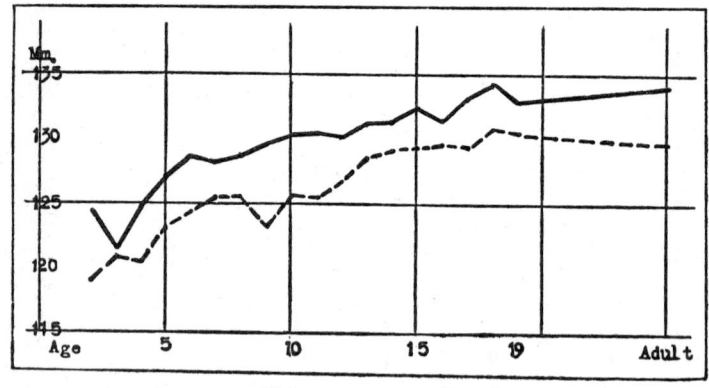

——— Males   - - - - - Females

Fig. 10.
Growth in Height of Head.

Table XXXVII
Height of Nose (mm.)

Age	Males			Females		
	No.	Average	σ	No.	Average	σ
1	11	34.3	± 4.75	4	33.25	—
2	23	36.3	± 4.32	19	33.3	± 4.50
3	31	36.3	± 4.38	36	36.25	± 5.07
4	54	37.85	± 4.39	23	37.0	± 5.35
5	53	40.3	± 4.25	62	39.3	± 3.96
6	140	42.3	± 4.53	78	41.0	± 4.81
7	179	42.5	± 4.31	97	41.8	± 4.30
8	178	42.35	± 3.56	79	42.1	± 3.73
9	167	42.3	± 3.86	54	42.0	± 5.25
10	171	43.35	± 3.42	52	43.6	± 4.22
11	207	44.6	± 3.56	52	44.0	± 4.46
12	233	46.1	± 3.76	64	45.85	± 4.70
13	301	47.3	± 4.42	38	47.1	± 3.67
14	258	47.6	± 4.36	35	46.8	± 3.98
15	192	49.9	± 4.09	40	48.9	± 3.68
16	68	50.8	± 4.82	37	49.7	± 4.41
17	47	50.7	± 3.46	37	48.7	± 4.08
18	38	52.95	± 4.29	28	50.3	± 4.81
19	61	52.7	± 3.71	24	49.3	± 4.70
Adult	960	53.4	± 3.75	759	50.6	± 4.57

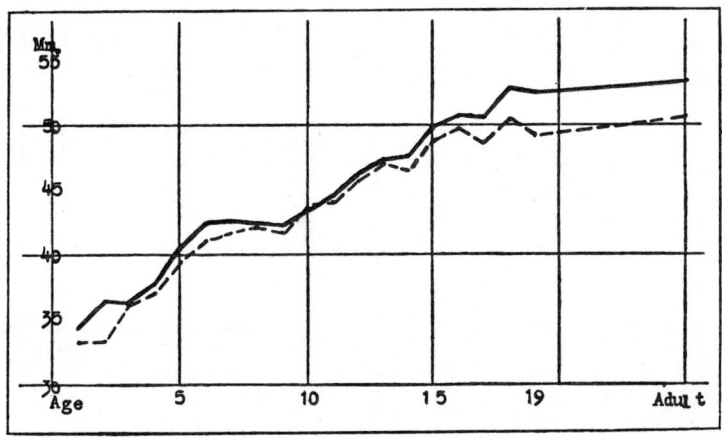

——— Males   - - - - - Females

Fig. 11.
Growth in Height of Nose.

Table
Height of

Age Mm.	1	2	3	4	5	6	7	8	9	10
26	1	—	—	—	—	—	—	—	—	—
27	—	—	—	—	—	—	—	—	—	—
28	—	—	1	—	—	—	—	—	—	—
29	1	1	1	—	—	—	—	—	1	—
30	1	1	—	1	—	—	—	—	1	—
31	1	2	—	3	—	—	—	—	—	—
32	1	2	5	4	—	—	—	—	—	—
33	1	1	1	4	1	3	1	—	—	—
34	1	1	4	2	2	3	1	2	1	—
35	—	3	4	4	4	4	2	1	2	1
36	2	2	1	3	5	5	6	3	5	2
37	—	1	1	4	1	7	9	9	8	1
38	—	1	3	3	8	6	15	9	10	8
39	1	—	3	6	5	7	11	14	9	8
40	1	3	2	5	5	12	17	19	14	17
41	—	1	2	3	2	10	14	21	21	14
42	—	2	1	4	4	16	20	17	14	22
43	—	2	1	3	2	17	17	21	19	17
44	—	—	—	1	6	9	11	19	12	18
45	—	—	—	1	2	10	9	12	15	20
46	—	—	—	2	3	5	19	10	15	15
47	—	—	—	—	2	7	5	4	7	12
48	—	—	—	1	—	6	6	6	6	8
49	—	—	1	—	—	2	7	3	4	1
50	—	—	—	—	—	7	4	2	—	2
51	—	—	—	—	—	2	2	3	—	1
52	—	—	—	—	—	1	—	3	3	—
53	—	—	—	—	—	—	1	—	—	2
54	—	—	—	—	—	—	—	—	—	2
55	—	—	—	—	1	—	—	—	—	—
56	—	—	—	—	—	—	1	—	—	—
57	—	—	—	—	—	—	1	—	—	—
58	—	—	—	—	—	1	—	—	—	—
59	—	—	—	—	—	—	—	—	—	—
60	—	—	—	—	—	—	—	—	—	—
61	—	—	—	—	—	—	—	—	—	—
62	—	—	—	—	—	—	—	—	—	—
63	—	—	—	—	—	—	—	—	—	—
64	—	—	—	—	—	—	—	—	—	—
65	—	—	—	—	—	—	—	—	—	—

XXXVIII
Nose (Males)

11	12	13	14	15	16	17	18	19	Adult
—	—	—	—	—	—	—	—	—	—
—	—	—	—	—	—	—	—	—	—
—	—	—	—	—	—	—	—	—	—
—	—	—	—	—	—	—	—	—	—
—	—	—	—	—	—	—	—	—	—
—	1	—	—	—	—	—	—	—	—
—	—	—	1	—	—	—	—	—	—
—	—	—	—	—	—	—	—	—	—
1	1	1	—	—	—	—	—	—	—
1	1	3	—	—	—	—	—	—	—
1	3	3	—	—	—	—	—	—	—
8	3	2	1	1	—	—	—	—	—
10	7	7	4	—	—	1	—	—	—
18	7	10	2	3	2	—	—	—	1
23	17	18	9	3	1	—	—	—	2
27	21	13	9	6	1	—	1	1	3
26	19	24	13	8	1	2	—	1	10
22	19	29	13	7	—	2	1	1	8
17	27	27	21	7	3	1	—	—	6
12	29	26	36	15	7	2	1	1	21
11	20	25	30	20	6	—	2	1	25
8	13	19	16	21	10	3	4	2	55
5	14	18	24	23	9	5	2	8	71
6	14	29	18	11	4	12	2	7	105
5	8	9	12	18	4	10	3	9	97
5	6	17	15	19	3	4	5	8	86
1	1	6	12	5	3	—	5	6	96
—	—	3	8	4	3	1	2	8	94
—	1	5	9	8	3	1	3	1	74
—	1	3	—	3	2	2	3	1	71
—	—	1	—	7	1	—	1	1	44
—	—	1	5	3	2	1	1	—	44
—	—	2	—	—	—	—	—	3	21
—	—	—	—	—	—	—	1	1	15
—	—	—	—	—	—	—	—	—	7
—	—	—	—	—	1	—	—	1	3
—	—	—	—	—	2	—	—	—	1
—	—	—	—	—	—	—	1	—	—

Table
Height of

Age Mm.	1	2	3	4	5	6	7	8	9	10
23	—	1	—	—	—	—	—	—	—	—
24	—	—	—	—	—	—	—	—	—	—
25	—	—	—	—	—	—	—	—	—	—
26	—	—	1	—	—	—	—	—	—	—
27	1	—	—	—	—	—	—	—	1	—
28	—	1	1	1	—	—	—	—	—	—
29	—	1	1	1	—	—	—	—	—	—
30	—	3	1	1	—	1	—	—	—	—
31	—	3	—	—	—	1	—	—	—	—
32	—	—	5	2	1	—	1	—	—	—
33	2	—	2	2	4	2	—	—	—	—
34	—	2	1	2	3	1	1	—	—	—
35	—	1	4	3	3	5	4	2	4	—
36	—	2	5	1	7	4	7	3	2	2
37	—	1	3	—	6	6	5	5	3	1
38	—	2	4	6	—	3	5	4	2	2
39	—	1	—	1	3	6	7	5	5	3
40	1	—	1	2	1	7	8	12	8	6
41	—	—	1	1	7	7	7	6	3	4
42	—	1	2	—	8	5	10	8	4	5
43	—	—	1	2	5	7	12	5	4	5
44	—	—	1	1	3	6	3	2	3	7
45	—	—	—	3	1	5	10	11	3	2
46	—	—	—	—	1	2	2	8	1	2
47	—	—	—	—	1	3	4	3	—	2
48	—	—	1	—	2	3	3	—	5	2
49	—	—	1	—	—	1	3	3	1	3
50	—	—	—	—	—	—	3	1	2	3
51	—	—	—	—	—	1	1	1	1	1
52	—	—	—	—	—	1	1	—	—	1
53	—	—	—	—	—	—	—	—	—	—
54	—	—	—	—	—	—	—	—	1	1
55	—	—	—	—	—	1	—	—	1	—
56	—	—	—	—	—	—	—	—	—	—
57	—	—	—	—	—	—	—	—	—	—
58	—	—	—	—	—	—	—	—	—	—
59	—	—	—	—	—	—	—	—	—	—
60	—	—	—	—	—	—	—	—	—	—
61	—	—	—	—	—	—	—	—	—	—
62	—	—	—	—	—	—	—	—	—	—
63	—	—	—	—	—	—	—	—	—	—
64	—	—	—	—	—	—	—	—	—	—
65	—	—	—	—	—	—	—	—	—	—
66	—	—	—	—	—	—	—	—	—	—

XXXIX
Nose (Females)

11	12	13	14	15	16	17	18	19	Adult
—	—	—	—	—	—	—	—	—	—
—	—	—	—	—	—	—	—	—	—
—	—	—	—	—	—	—	—	—	—
—	—	—	—	—	—	—	—	—	—
—	—	—	—	—	—	—	—	—	—
—	—	—	—	—	—	—	—	—	—
—	—	—	—	—	—	—	—	—	—
—	—	—	—	—	—	—	—	—	—
—	—	—	—	—	—	—	—	—	—
—	—	—	—	—	—	—	—	—	—
1	—	—	—	—	—	—	—	—	—
—	—	—	—	—	—	—	—	—	—
—	—	—	—	—	—	—	—	—	—
2	—	—	—	—	—	—	—	—	—
—	2	—	—	—	—	—	—	1	1
1	2	—	1	—	—	—	—	—	3
6	3	—	—	—	—	—	—	—	4
7	7	1	4	1	2	2	1	—	9
3	4	6	1	1	1	—	1	2	16
6	4	3	1	3	1	—	—	—	14
5	6	1	2	—	1	4	2	1	25
3	5	2	3	3	2	4	—	—	28
4	3	2	5	3	1	1	1	3	33
5	6	3	4	6	3	2	2	—	57
2	4	4	3	4	3	5	2	3	47
2	6	7	3	1	5	5	4	2	72
—	1	4	2	3	2	3	2	1	76
—	4	1	2	2	1	3	3	2	58
3	—	1	2	4	3	2	2	2	59
1	3	1	1	5	3	1	3	1	57
—	1	1	—	—	4	2	1	4	57
—	1	1	—	3	2	1	—	1	39
1	—	—	—	—	1	1	—	—	27
—	1	—	—	1	1	—	1	—	29
—	—	—	1	—	1	—	1	1	22
—	1	—	—	—	—	—	—	—	9
—	—	—	—	—	—	1	1	—	6
—	—	—	—	—	—	—	1	—	5
—	—	—	—	—	—	—	—	—	2
—	—	—	—	—	—	—	—	—	2
—	—	—	—	—	—	—	—	—	—
—	—	—	—	—	—	—	—	—	1
—	—	—	—	—	—	—	—	—	(76—1)

140 The Anthropometry of the American Negro

Table
Width of

Age Mm.	1	2	3	4	5	6	7	8	9	10
23	—	1	—	—	—	—	—	—	—	—
24	1	—	1	1	—	—	—	—	—	—
25	1	4	4	1	1	—	—	—	—	—
26	2	2	4	1	—	—	—	—	—	—
27	1	3	2	4	2	2	2	3	—	—
28	1	6	7	12	3	8	2	2	1	1
29	1	2	4	9	9	9	6	6	4	1
30	3	1	4	10	8	12	12	5	8	3
31	—	2	4	6	9	17	23	17	8	13
32	—	1	1	5	9	23	18	23	12	11
33	—	—	—	2	1	20	32	22	18	17
34	—	—	—	1	4	18	29	36	23	28
35	—	1	—	1	2	17	24	26	31	34
36	—	—	—	—	3	10	14	17	18	24
37	—	—	—	1	1	2	4	13	19	17
38	—	—	—	—	—	1	3	6	10	10
39	—	—	—	—	1	—	1	1	7	5
40	—	—	—	—	—	1	3	—	4	3
41	—	—	—	—	—	—	—	—	1	2
42	—	—	—	—	—	—	—	—	2	—
43	—	—	—	—	—	—	—	—	—	1
44	—	—	—	—	—	—	—	—	1	—
45	—	—	—	—	—	—	—	—	—	—
46	—	—	—	—	—	—	—	—	—	—
47	—	—	—	—	—	—	—	—	—	—
48	—	—	—	—	—	—	—	—	—	—
49	—	—	—	—	—	—	—	—	—	—
50	—	—	—	—	—	—	—	—	—	—
51	—	—	—	—	—	—	—	—	—	—
52	—	—	—	—	—	—	—	—	—	—
53	—	—	—	—	—	—	—	—	—	—
54	—	—	—	—	—	—	—	—	—	—
55	—	—	—	—	—	—	—	—	—	—
56	—	—	—	—	—	—	—	—	—	—

XL
Nose (Males)

	11	12	13	14	15	16	17	18	19	Adult
	—	—	—	—	—	—	—	—	—	—
	—	—	—	—	—	—	—	—	—	—
	—	—	—	—	—	—	—	—	—	—
	—	—	—	—	1	—	—	—	—	—
	1	—	—	—	—	—	—	—	—	—
	4	4	3	1	—	—	—	—	—	1
	4	10	3	1	—	—	—	—	—	4
	9	7	9	4	1	—	—	—	—	4
	12	16	10	7	8	1	—	—	3	12
	22	25	15	8	6	3	—	—	—	17
	26	24	25	15	11	1	—	3	1	27
	26	37	27	20	13	5	2	1	2	30
	31	26	40	28	14	3	1	3	3	44
	30	25	45	42	11	4	4	6	5	50
	16	21	31	28	25	8	3	5	6	74
	9	11	31	30	18	7	6	5	7	69
	5	10	29	22	24	7	9	3	5	83
	4	8	11	17	17	11	3	4	7	101
	4	4	8	10	11	7	6	1	8	109
	2	2	10	11	12	3	3	2	2	89
	—	—	3	7	7	1	4	2	7	81
	—	1	—	2	8	1	2	2	2	51
	1	1	1	4	4	6	3	—	1	37
	—	—	1	1	—	—	1	1	1	40
	—	—	—	—	1	—	—	—	—	14
	—	—	—	—	—	—	—	—	1	13
	—	—	—	—	—	—	—	—	—	2
	—	1	—	—	—	—	—	—	—	4
	—	—	—	—	—	—	—	—	—	3
	—	—	—	—	—	—	—	—	—	1
	—	—	—	—	—	—	—	—	—	—
	—	—	—	—	—	—	—	—	—	—
	—	—	—	—	—	—	—	—	—	1

142   The Anthropometry of the American Negro

Table
Width of

Age Mm.	1	2	3	4	5	6	7	8	9	10
23	—	1	1	1	—	1	—	—	—	—
24	—	—	1	1	—	—	1	—	—	—
25	—	2	2	3	—	1	—	—	—	—
26	1	4	4	—	1	—	—	—	—	—
27	1	6	5	1	3	2	2	2	1	1
28	—	1	6	5	4	9	4	1	—	1
29	1	4	2	3	6	9	10	7	3	3
30	—	1	7	2	11	12	12	6	3	1
31	—	—	2	3	16	17	9	9	10	3
32	1	—	4	3	8	9	14	10	13	6
33	—	—	1	1	7	7	19	9	3	8
34	—	—	—	—	6	7	7	14	8	8
35	—	—	—	—	—	3	9	8	3	5
36	—	—	1	—	—	1	4	3	5	8
37	—	—	—	—	—	—	4	6	1	4
38	—	—	—	—	—	—	1	1	2	3
39	—	—	—	—	—	—	—	3	1	2
40	—	—	—	—	—	—	—	—	2	—
41	—	—	—	—	—	—	1	—	—	—
42	—	—	—	—	—	—	—	—	—	—
43	—	—	—	—	—	—	—	—	—	—
44	—	—	—	—	—	—	—	—	—	—
45	—	—	—	—	—	—	—	—	—	—
46	—	—	—	—	—	—	—	—	—	—
47	—	—	—	—	—	—	—	—	—	—
48	—	—	—	—	—	—	—	—	—	—
49	—	—	—	—	—	—	—	—	—	—
50	—	—	—	—	—	—	—	—	—	—
51	—	—	—	—	—	—	—	—	—	—

XLI
Nose (Females)

11	12	13	14	15	16	17	18	19	Adult
—	—	—	—	—	—	—	—	—	—
—	—	—	—	—	—	—	—	—	—
—	—	—	—	—	—	—	—	1	2
—	—	—	—	—	—	—	—	—	1
—	—	—	—	—	—	—	—	—	2
—	—	—	—	1	—	1	—	1	6
2	—	—	—	—	—	—	1	1	4
2	1	1	1	—	1	2	2	2	15
1	6	4	—	1	3	6	3	2	24
11	3	2	2	1	5	3	9	11	50
6	3	4	1	4	9	9	7	4	58
5	9	4	10	7	13	15	15	11	74
8	6	6	6	7	16	17	15	18	81
2	14	5	5	10	9	14	26	17	104
5	5	1	8	11	8	14	20	18	107
6	7	7	4	9	11	15	22	20	95
2	6	2	3	12	6	11	12	11	84
—	3	2	3	1	13	8	24	15	62
—	1	5	1	2	4	4	7	4	54
2	—	—	2	3	3	4	6	8	34
—	—	—	1	—	1	—	1	6	35
—	—	—	1	—	2	2	2	2	19
—	—	1	1	—	—	—	2	3	8
—	—	—	1	—	—	—	1	—	2
—	—	—	—	—	—	—	—	—	3
—	—	—	—	—	—	—	—	—	3
—	—	—	—	—	—	—	1	—	2
—	—	—	—	—	—	—	—	—	—
—	—	—	—	—	—	—	—	—	1

Table XLII
Width of Nose (mm)

Age	Males			Females		
	No.	Average	σ	No.	Average	σ
1	10	27.3	± 2.15	4	28.5	—
2	23	27.9	± 2.64	19	27.0	± 1.68
3	31	28.1	± 2.14	36	28.6	± 2.72
4	54	29.0	± 2.17	23	28.6	± 2.71
5	53	31.2	± 2.72	62	30.8	± 1.94
6	140	32.4	± 2.47	78	30.8	± 2.35
7	173	33.2	± 2.41	97	32.1	± 2.75
8	177	33.6	± 2.43	79	32.9	± 2.78
9	167	34.8	± 2.82	55	33.05	± 2.79
10	170	34.8	± 2.42	53	33.9	± 2.77
11	206	35.4	± 2.94	52	34.5	± 2.98
12	233	35.6	± 3.28	64	35.6	± 2.65
13	302	37.0	± 3.15	44	36.1	± 3.40
14	258	37.9	± 3.27	50	36.9	± 3.38
15	192	38.9	± 3.63	69	36.7	± 2.62
16	68	39.6	± 3.43	104	36.5	± 3.12
17	47	40.8	± 2.97	125	36.55	± 3.06
18	38	39.2	± 3.23	176	37.1	± 3.15
19	61	40.15	± 3.63	155	37.0	± 3.55
Adult	961	40.9	± 3.99	930	37.0	± 3.73

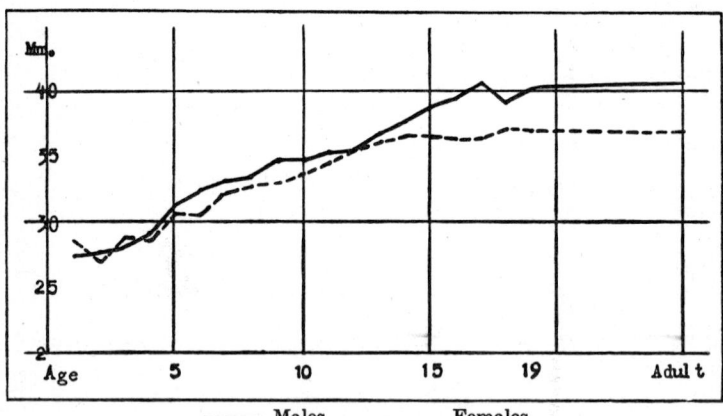

Fig. 12.
Growth in Width of Nose.

Table XLIII
Bizygomatic Width (mm)

Age	Males			Females		
	No.	Average	σ	No.	Average	σ
1	10	103.3	± 6.03	4	104.75	—
2	24	109.8	± 4.78	19	104.9	± 3.74
3	31	110.2	± 4.00	36	109.25	± 5.74
4	54	111.6	± 5.01	23	108.5	± 4.66
5	52	114.2	± 4.90	61	112.75	± 3.42
6	140	116.2	± 4.80	78	113.97	± 4.12
7	177	116.6	± 4.58	95	115.8	± 4.72
8	178	119.0	± 4.96	78	117.4	± 5.08
9	167	120.55	± 5.98	54	118.9	± 4.91
10	171	121.4	± 5.26	53	120.3	± 4.65
11	207	123.3	± 5.29	51	121.7	± 5.40
12	233	124.4	± 4.82	63	124.25	± 4.58
13	301	126.4	± 5.42	44	126.7	± 5.44
14	257	129.1	± 4.90	50	128.0	± 5.56
15	192	131.0	± 5.27	69	130.2	± 5.69
16	68	132.2	± 5.33	104	130.5	± 5.36
17	47	134.5	± 5.46	125	130.6	± 4.67
18	38	136.2	± 6.54	176	131.1	± 4.92
19	61	136.8	± 6.76	156	131.9	± 5.18
Adult	956	139.2	± 5.92	917	132.2	± 5.25

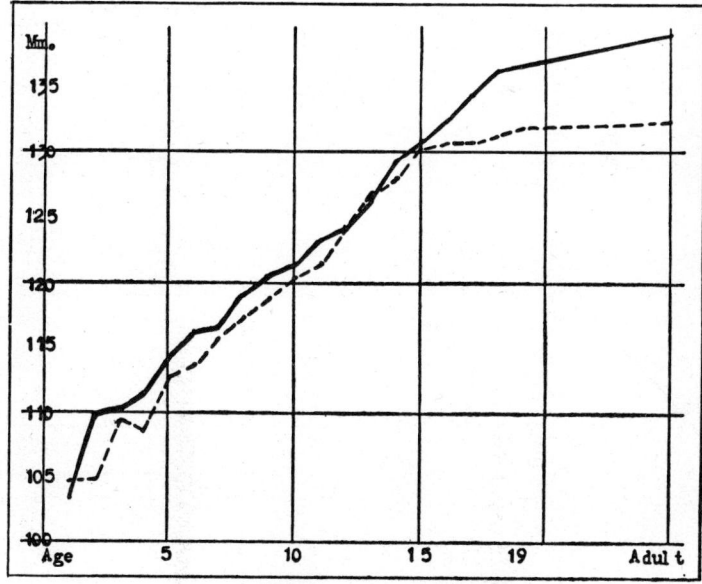

——— Males ------ Females
Fig. 13.
Growth in Bizygomatic Width.

Table XLIV
Bizygomatic Width (Males)

Age Mm.	1	2	3	4	5	6	7	8	9	10
97 (94—1)	—	—	—	—	—	—	—	—	—	—
98 (96—1)	—	—	—	—	—	—	—	—	—	—
99 (97—1)	—	—	—	—	—	—	—	—	—	—
100	1	—	—	2	—	—	—	—	—	—
01	—	1	—	—	—	—	—	—	—	—
02	—	—	—	1	—	—	—	1	—	—
03	—	2	1	—	1	—	—	—	—	2
04	1	—	—	2	2	—	2	—	—	—
05	—	3	4	2	1	—	—	—	2	—
06	2	1	2	1	1	1	1	—	—	—
07	—	2	3	3	—	3	1	—	1	—
08	2	1	2	3	—	3	2	—	1	—
09	—	—	2	2	1	4	6	3	—	—
110	—	2	2	5	3	5	3	1	2	2
11	—	3	2	7	6	6	7	3	1	1
12	—	2	5	2	8	9	9	7	4	3
13	—	1	—	4	1	14	11	6	1	2
14	1	2	2	5	4	8	11	16	7	9
15	—	1	3	3	3	13	20	9	5	4
16	—	1	2	2	5	11	16	17	10	9
17	—	—	—	4	2	13	15	10	14	11
18	—	1	—	2	2	7	14	7	4	6
19	—	1	1	1	3	9	13	15	12	10
120	—	—	—	2	4	8	13	16	19	14
21	—	—	—	—	2	6	12	9	17	7
22	—	—	—	—	1	7	6	5	9	10
23	—	—	—	—	1	4	7	19	21	21
24	—	—	—	1	1	2	4	12	13	15
25	—	—	—	—	—	2	—	10	4	10
26	—	—	—	—	—	3	3	2	9	6
27	—	—	—	—	—	1	1	4	1	6
28	—	—	—	—	—	—	—	1	—	11
29	—	—	—	—	—	—	—	3	4	5
130	—	—	—	—	—	—	—	—	—	3
31	—	—	—	—	—	—	—	1	1	3
32	—	—	—	—	—	—	—	—	—	—
33	—	—	—	—	—	1	—	—	1	1
34	—	—	—	—	—	—	—	—	1	—
35	—	—	—	—	—	—	—	—	1	—
36	—	—	—	—	—	—	—	1 (147—6)	—	—
37	—	—	—	—	—	—	—	— (156—1)	—	—

Table XLIV (continued)
Bizygomatic Width (Males)

Age Mm.	11	12	13	14	15	16	17	18	19	Adult
111	2	—	1	—	—	—	—	—	—	—
12	—	—	—	—	—	—	—	—	—	1
13	1	—	—	—	—	—	—	—	1	—
14	2	—	1	—	—	—	—	—	—	—
15	3	—	3	—	—	—	—	—	—	—
16	11	5	5	1	2	—	—	—	—	—
17	8	5	4	—	—	—	—	—	—	—
18	7	5	5	2	—	—	—	—	—	—
19	7	14	8	1	—	—	—	—	—	—
120	20	17	15	2	3	1	—	—	—	—
21	12	26	9	10	3	1	—	—	—	—
22	8	17	15	7	3	1	—	2	1	—
23	20	21	24	12	10	2	1	—	—	2
24	19	17	24	19	7	—	—	1	—	4
25	19	15	28	11	8	4	1	1	—	5
26	10	18	21	13	6	2	2	—	1	4
27	15	14	16	19	8	3	1	—	1	10
28	14	15	26	20	12	3	3	2	3	12
29	7	12	17	19	7	4	3	1	1	10
130	8	6	15	26	9	2	1	—	1	14
31	3	3	10	13	15	6	3	—	2	24
32	4	8	13	16	12	8	1	3	1	33
33	1	6	8	17	16	2	7	2	6	45
34	1	3	11	16	15	7	2	5	4	45
35	3	—	7	8	15	5	1	3	4	52
36	1	2	9	10	11	1	1	4	4	53
37	—	—	1	4	9	1	4	3	5	53
38	—	1	1	3	6	5	2	2	3	61
39	—	2	—	5	9	5	3	1	1	57
140	—	—	1	1	1	1	4	—	4	66
41	—	—	—	1	2	3	4	2	1	59
42	—	—	—	—	2	—	—	1	2	68
43	—	—	2	—	—	1	2	1	2	56
44	—	—	—	—	1	—	—	1	3	55
45	—	—	—	—	—	—	—	—	1	26
46	—	—	—	1	—	—	1	—	4	33
47	—	—	1	—	—	—	—	2	2	38
48	—	—	—	—	—	—	—	—	1	28
49	—	—	—	—	—	—	—	1	—	12
150	—	—	—	—	—	—	—	—	—	10
51	—	—	—	—	—	—	—	—	—	5
52	—	—	—	—	—	—	—	—	—	5
53	—	—	—	—	—	—	—	—	—	4
54	—	—	—	—	—	—	—	—	—	—
55	—	—	—	—	—	—	—	—	—	1
56	—	—	—	—	—	—	—	—	2	2
57	—	—	—	—	—	—	—	—	—	1
58	—	—	—	—	—	—	—	—	—	(162—1)
59	—	—	—	—	—	—	—	—	—	(168—1)

Table XLV
Bizygomatic Width (Females)

Age Mm.	1	2	3	4	5	6	7	8	9	10
99	—	(97—1)	(98—1)—	—	—	—	—	—	—	—
100	—	—	1	—	—	—	—	—	—	—
01	—	2	—	—	—	—	—	—	—	—
02	2	1	2	2	—	—	—	—	—	—
03	1	4	3	1	—	—	1	—	—	—
04	—	1	—	4	—	1	—	—	—	—
05	—	3	2	2	1	—	2	—	—	—
06	—	2	1	1	1	1	—	—	—	—
07	—	1	3	1	2	2	1	1	—	—
08	1	—	4	—	1	1	—	—	—	—
09	—	2	3	1	3	3	3	—	1	—
110	—	1	2	3	11	6	2	6	1	—
11	—	—	3	1	6	8	5	6	2	—
12	—	—	2	1	7	7	11	3	1	1
13	—	—	2	3	4	9	8	4	3	4
14	—	1	1	—	5	7	4	4	2	1
15	—	—	2	—	8	5	7	6	3	3
16	—	—	1	2	2	10	8	4	1	3
17	—	—	1	1	5	3	8	7	7	4
18	—	—	1	—	1	7	7	8	5	7
19	—	—	—	—	1	3	8	4	6	2
120	—	—	—	—	2	1	5	6	4	4
21	—	—	—	—	—	2	5	3	4	2
22	—	—	—	—	1	1	5	1	3	—
23	—	—	—	—	—	—	3	2	3	6
24	—	—	—	—	—	—	—	4	3	4
25	—	—	—	—	—	—	—	1	1	5
26	—	—	—	—	—	—	—	5	—	2
27	—	—	—	—	—	—	1	2	—	2
28	—	—	1	—	—	—	—	1	1	2
29	—	—	—	—	—	—	—	—	—	—
130	—	—	—	—	—	—	—	—	1	—
31	—	—	—	—	—	1	—	—	2	1
32	—	—	—	—	—	—	1	—	—	—
33	—	—	—	—	—	—	—	—	—	—

Table XLV (continued)
Bizygomatic Width (Females)

Age Mm.	11[1]	12	13	14	15	16	17	18	19	Adult
111	1	—	—	—	—	—	—	(97—1)	(105—1)	—
12	—	—	—	—	—	—	—	—	—	—
13	1	—	—	—	—	—	—	—	—	—
14	1	2	1	—	—	—	—	1	—	1
15	—	1	—	—	—	—	—	—	—	—
16	1	1	—	1	—	—	—	—	—	—
17	3	1	—	—	—	—	—	—	—	1
18	4	1	—	1	2	—	—	—	—	—
19	5	3	—	2	—	—	—	—	—	2
120	7	2	3	1	2	—	—	1	1	5
21	4	5	2	1	—	1	2	1	—	9
22	4	5	5	3	—	4	4	3	1	11
23	3	8	3	1	2	7	1	1	—	14
24	1	5	4	3	4	1	4	5	5	28
25	3	3	3	3	3	5	8	3	5	28
26	3	6	3	8	5	4	8	11	5	49
27	2	7	3	1	4	7	7	12	6	40
28	1	3	2	3	7	9	18	11	18	59
29	2	2	1	1	6	5	3	7	7	65
130	—	2	3	3	5	15	9	21	17	66
31	2	—	1	4	5	6	7	12	7	51
32	—	3	5	3	3	10	8	22	17	78
33	—	2	1	2	3	2	6	6	6	64
34	2	1	1	1	3	9	12	14	15	62
35	—	—	—	1	4	6	10	12	7	68
36	—	—	—	3	3	4	2	11	11	54
37	—	—	—	3	—	2	6	5	8	39
38	—	—	2	—	2	1	4	6	6	24
39	—	—	—	1	1	1	1	2	2	21
140	—	—	—	—	3	—	3	1	3	33
41	—	—	1	—	—	—	2	3	4	14
42	—	—	—	—	—	2	—	2	2	8
43	—	—	—	—	—	—	—	1	—	8
44	—	—	—	—	—	2	—	1	—	5
45	—	—	—	—	1	—	—	—	1	4
46	—	—	—	—	—	—	—	—	1	3
47	—	—	—	—	—	—	—	—	—	1
48	—	—	—	—	—	—	—	—	—	(149—1)
49	—	—	—	—	(152—1)	(154—1)	—	—	—	(152—1)

[1] Add: 106—1.

Table
Thickness of Lips

Age Mm.	1	2	3	4	5	6	7	8	9	10
9	—	—	—	—	—	1	—	1	—	—
10	1	—	1	2	2	1	—	—	—	—
11	—	—	1	2	—	1	1	—	1	—
12	—	2	4	4	1	4	1	2	1	—
13	1	3	3	6	2	2	3	4	1	—
14	1	1	4	5	5	14	8	2	4	—
15	—	2	5	6	7	8	10	7	6	9
16	1	2	5	5	6	9	17	6	6	7
17	—	—	2	4	5	16	19	18	13	12
18	—	1	2	5	3	20	28	18	18	20
19	1	1	1	3	7	13	23	15	11	15
20	—	—	2	6	3	19	17	24	16	22
21	—	1	—	2	6	11	13	26	26	21
22	—	—	1	2	1	8	14	17	18	20
23	—	2	—	1	1	6	7	19	16	12
24	—	—	—	—	3	3	9	9	9	17
25	—	—	—	—	1	1	4	3	12	12
26	—	—	—	—	—	1	2	3	5	3
27	—	—	—	—	—	—	2	2	3	1
28	—	—	—	—	—	1	1	1	—	—
29	—	—	—	—	—	—	—	—	—	—
30	—	—	—	—	—	—	—	—	—	—
31	—	—	—	—	—	—	—	—	—	—
32	—	—	—	—	—	—	—	—	—	—
33	—	—	—	—	—	—	—	—	—	—
34	—	—	—	—	—	—	—	—	—	—
35	—	—	—	—	—	—	—	—	—	—
36	—	—	—	—	—	—	—	—	—	—
37	—	—	—	—	—	—	—	—	—	—
38	—	—	—	—	—	—	—	—	—	—
39	—	—	—	—	—	—	—	—	—	—

XLVI
(Males)

11	12	13	14	15	16	17	18	19	Adult
—	—	—	—	—	—	—	—	—	—
—	—	—	—	—	—	—	—	—	7
—	—	—	—	—	—	—	—	—	5
—	—	1	—	1	—	—	—	—	17
—	1	—	—	—	—	—	—	—	17
2	3	3	1	2	—	1	—	—	13
4	8	2	1	1	2	—	—	1	43
1	5	6	7	2	2	—	—	1	43
16	11	10	12	3	—	2	1	3	55
15	18	14	7	10	3	3	3	4	59
12	16	22	14	11	4	2	5	3	81
15	24	20	23	16	5	4	1	3	92
26	31	34	32	17	8	2	4	8	80
35	30	29	24	14	3	8	8	8	83
22	21	52	31	21	6	5	4	10	71
21	23	38	24	22	10	1	3	6	82
14	21	24	24	17	6	5	2	2	43
7	9	13	15	18	5	5	1	—	48
8	6	9	17	11	4	2	1	3	43
6	5	11	13	7	3	2	2	4	33
—	1	4	7	7	3	1	1	1	17
—	1	2	2	6	2	2	1	2	6
1	—	1	2	3	—	1	—	1	10
—	—	3	—	3	2	1	1	—	4
—	—	2	2	—	—	—	—	—	1
—	—	—	—	—	—	—	—	—	2
—	—	—	—	—	—	—	—	1	3
—	—	—	—	—	—	—	—	—	—
—	—	—	—	—	—	—	—	—	—
—	—	—	—	—	—	—	—	—	—
—	—	—	—	—	—	—	—	—	1

Table
Thickness of Lips

Age Mm.	1	2	3	4	5	6	7	8	9	10
7	—	—	—	—	—	—	—	—	—	—
8	—	—	—	—	—	—	—	—	—	—
9	—	1	2	1	—	—	1	—	—	—
10	—	2	1	1	1	—	—	—	—	—
11	—	—	1	2	1	3	—	—	—	—
12	—	2	4	2	2	1	—	—	—	—
13	—	3	1	2	4	2	5	—	—	1
14	—	1	3	1	6	9	6	2	1	2
15	—	1	5	2	8	6	8	8	1	3
16	—	3	8	2	7	9	13	7	3	2
17	—	1	1	4	6	9	5	10	5	4
18	—	—	5	1	10	8	13	10	8	6
19	—	—	3	—	4	12	8	15	10	6
20	—	1	1	3	4	2	8	5	3	8
21	—	1	1	1	2	6	7	8	7	9
22	—	—	—	—	3	5	5	4	5	2
23	—	—	—	1	1	1	9	6	5	3
24	—	—	—	—	1	2	5	2	5	3
25	—	—	—	—	—	2	—	2	1	3
26	—	—	—	—	—	1	—	—	1	1
27	—	—	—	—	—	—	1	—	—	—
28	—	—	—	—	1	—	—	—	—	1
29	—	—	—	—	—	—	—	—	—	—
30	—	1	—	—	—	—	—	—	—	—
31	—	—	—	—	—	—	—	—	—	—
32	—	—	—	—	—	—	—	—	—	—
33	—	—	—	—	—	—	—	—	—	—
34	—	—	—	—	—	—	—	—	—	—
35	—	—	—	—	—	—	—	—	—	—
36	—	—	—	—	—	—	—	—	—	—
37	—	—	—	—	—	—	—	—	—	—

XLVII
(Females)

11	12	13	14	15	16	17	18	19	Adult
—	—	—	—	—	—	—	—	—	2
—	—	—	—	—	—	—	—	—	1
—	—	—	—	—	—	—	—	—	7
—	—	—	—	—	—	—	—	—	7
—	—	—	—	—	—	1	—	—	15
1	—	1	—	—	—	2	—	1	22
—	2	—	—	—	1	2	1	—	26
2	1	—	—	2	2	3	—	4	52
2	1	1	3	—	1	—	—	—	41
2	3	1	3	8	3	4	1	1	51
1	7	4	1	2	4	5	1	3	81
4	2	8	3	6	2	7	5	3	78
4	6	6	3	4	7	7	6	10	65
10	9	3	4	2	10	8	17	8	70
8	8	5	8	8	10	2	8	8	77
5	4	1	7	8	9	12	15	7	62
3	6	4	3	7	5	6	12	8	50
5	7	4	3	5	9	3	10	4	30
1	4	1	—	2	7	6	5	2	33
2	2	—	4	3	3	3	8	4	28
1	1	—	3	2	3	2	3	1	6
—	—	1	2	1	3	4	7	—	2
—	1	1	1	1	—	—	1	2	7
—	—	—	—	1	—	1	—	—	4
—	—	—	—	—	—	—	1	2	—
—	—	—	—	—	—	1	—	1	—
—	—	—	—	—	—	—	—	—	—
—	—	—	—	—	—	—	—	—	—
—	—	—	—	—	—	—	—	—	—
—	—	—	—	1	—	—	—	1	—

Table XLVIII
Thickness of Lips (mm)

Age	Males			Females		
	No.	Average	σ	No.	Average	σ
1	5	15.0	—	—	—	—
2	15	16.2	± 3.65	17	15.1	± 4.73
3	31	15.2	± 2.74	36	15.3	± 2.98
4	53	16.1	± 3.32	23	15.5	± 3.70
5	53	17.5	± 3.49	61	17.0	± 3.29
6	139	18.1	± 3.31	78	17.7	± 3.36
7	179	18.95	± 3.19	94	18.4	± 3.41
8	177	19.9	± 3.12	79	18.8	± 2,71
9	166	20.4	± 3.26	55	20.0	± 2.73
10	171	20.7	± 2.98	54	19.8	± 3.13
11	205	21.7	± 3.12	51	20.35	± 3.21
12	234	21.4	± 3.28	64	20.7	± 3.25
13	300	22.5	± 3.43	41	20.15	± 3.34
14	258	22.8	± 3.52	48	21.5	± 3.67
15	192	23.3	± 3.92	63	21.35	± 4.19
16	68	23.3	± 3.88	79	21.5	± 3.42
17	47	23.3	± 3.96	78	20.9	± 4.15
18	38	22.6	± 3.52	102	22.4	± 3.34
19	61	22.7	± 3.92	70	21.6	± 4.42
Adult	959	21.2	± 4.50	817	18.9	± 4.12

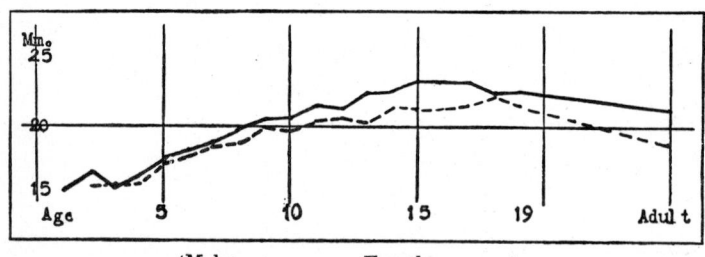

(Males ——— Females - - - - -)
Fig. 14.
Growth in Thickness of Lip

Table XLIX
Physiognomic Height of Ear, (Ear Length) (mm)

Age	Males			Females		
	No.	Average	σ	No.	Average	σ
1	9	45.0	± 3.83	4	46.0	—
2	23	49.6	± 4.41	19	47.95	± 4.09
3	31	50.8	± 4.55	36	49.7	± 3.11
4	54	51.8	± 3.44	23	50.0	± 3.46
5	53	51.3	± 4.64	61	52.1	± 4.22
6	139	53.1	± 4.31	78	51.7	± 3.47
7	173	53.7	± 3.48	78	52.9	± 3.38
8	177	54.5	± 3.55	79	53.6	± 4.18
9	166	54.8	± 4.45	55	54.95	± 3.92
10	170	55.7	± 3.87	54	53.8	± 3.46
11	206	56.7	± 3.94	52	54.35	± 3.60
12	233	56.8	± 3.97	63	55.9	± 3.69
13	302	56.9	± 3.92	39	56.3	± 3.92
14	256	57.2	± 4.02	35	55.6	± 3.66
15	192	58.0	± 3.99	40	56.05	± 4.60
16	68	57.9	± 3.59	37	56.2	± 4.21
17	47	58.1	± 3.83	37	55.7	± 3.14
18	38	58.8	± 3.22	28	56.0	± 2.94
19	60	59.9	± 4.46	23	56.4	± 5.34
Adult	959	60.7	± 4.32	757	58.3	± 4.31

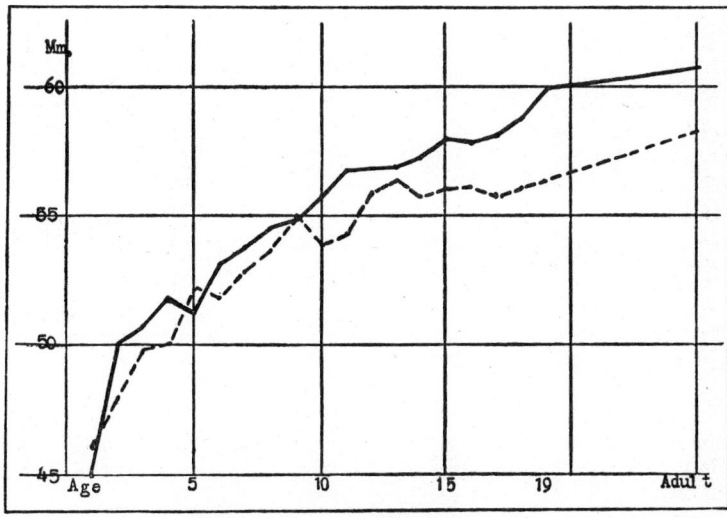

(Males ——— Females - - - - -)

Fig. 15.
Growth in Height of Ear

156   *The Anthropometry of the American Negro*

Table
Physiognomic Height of Ear

Age Mm.	1	2	3	4	5	6	7	8	9	10
40	(39—1)	1	(32—1)	—	—	—	—	—	—	—
41	—	—	—	—	—	1	—	—	—	—
42	1	—	—	—	3	1	—	—	1	—
43	2	—	—	—	—	3	—	—	—	—
44	1	1	—	2	3	1	—	—	—	1
45	1	1	1	1	1	1	2	2	2	—
46	—	3	1	1	4	1	1	3	3	1
47	1	2	2	—	1	6	4	1	4	4
48	—	2	3	1	1	5	5	2	5	2
49	—	2	2	11	5	9	2	3	10	5
50	1	1	2	6	4	7	22	6	8	5
51	—	5	1	3	3	9	17	17	6	8
52	1	—	5	6	5	17	15	21	8	3
53	—	2	4	8	2	13	14	15	8	13
54	—	—	6	3	6	7	16	18	19	11
55	—	—	1	1	6	16	16	21	19	24
56	—	—	1	6	4	11	19	21	11	17
57	—	—	1	4	3	14	20	13	14	19
58	—	3	—	—	—	4	9	14	10	17
59	—	—	—	—	—	1	6	6	12	14
60	—	—	—	1	1	6	1	8	6	9
61	—	—	—	—	—	5	1	1	12	11
62	—	—	—	—	1	1	1	1	5	3
63	—	—	—	—	—	—	2	1	2	—
64	—	—	—	—	—	—	—	3	—	—
65	—	—	—	—	—	—	—	—	1	2
66	—	—	—	—	—	—	—	—	—	1
67	—	—	—	—	—	—	—	—	—	—
68	—	—	—	—	—	—	—	—	—	—
69	—	—	—	—	—	—	—	—	—	—
70	—	—	—	—	—	—	—	—	—	—
71	—	—	—	—	—	—	—	—	—	—
72	—	—	—	—	—	—	—	—	—	—
73	—	—	—	—	—	—	—	—	—	—
74	—	—	—	—	—	—	—	—	—	—
75	—	—	—	—	—	—	—	—	—	—
76	—	—	—	—	—	—	—	—	—	—

L
(Ear Length) (Males)

11	12	13	14	15	16	17	18	19	Adult
—	—	—	—	—	—	—	—	—	—
—	—	—	—	—	—	—	—	—	—
—	—	—	—	—	—	—	—	—	—
1	2	—	—	—	—	—	—	1	1
3	—	—	2	2	—	—	—	—	—
—	2	2	—	—	—	—	—	—	—
1	1	1	2	1	1	—	—	—	—
2	—	1	3	—	—	—	—	—	1
4	1	2	2	—	—	—	—	—	—
1	5	11	5	3	1	—	1	1	2
5	9	9	3	4	1	4	—	1	7
6	9	23	11	11	1	—	—	—	15
14	16	9	15	6	1	2	1	—	19
13	18	20	17	2	5	3	1	1	32
15	27	24	22	17	7	3	3	3	28
26	18	28	26	16	6	2	3	3	59
29	18	33	26	26	9	4	4	4	44
25	38	36	26	18	6	5	3	7	71
20	13	30	23	26	7	9	6	5	74
12	14	21	23	10	8	5	3	11	120
6	13	22	13	14	4	1	6	7	86
10	12	17	15	7	6	2	3	1	93
5	8	5	7	13	1	4	2	1	73
4	2	5	7	5	3	1	—	4	66
1	5	—	3	5	—	1	2	3	57
1	1	2	3	3	—	—	—	3	32
1	1	1	1	1	—	—	—	1	23
1	—	—	1	2	1	1	—	1	16
—	—	—	—	—	—	—	—	1	15
—	—	—	—	—	—	—	—	1	7
—	—	—	—	—	—	—	—	—	4
—	—	—	—	—	—	—	—	—	6
—	—	—	—	—	—	—	—	—	4
—	—	—	—	—	—	—	—	—	2
—	—	—	—	—	—	—	—	—	1
—	—	—	—	—	—	—	—	—	1

158 The Anthropometry of the American Negro

Table
Physiognomic Height of Ear

Age Mm.	1	2	3	4	5	6	7	8	9	10
42	1	—	—	—	—	1	—	1	—	—
43	—	3	1	—	—	—	—	2	—	—
44	—	1	2	—	3	—	—	—	1	—
45	—	2	—	2	2	2	2	1	1	—
46	1	1	2	1	1	2	2	1	—	1
47	—	1	2	4	2	1	—	1	—	1
48	2	2	5	2	5	4	4	2	1	1
49	—	2	6	3	5	12	5	1	2	1
50	—	3	6	1	5	8	6	5	2	4
51	—	1	3	3	4	10	5	5	2	6
52	—	—	1	1	6	5	10	13	4	5
53	—	1	2	3	5	8	9	6	4	7
54	—	—	5	1	4	9	9	9	10	8
55	—	1	—	—	6	5	5	12	4	6
56	—	—	—	—	3	5	10	1	3	3
57	—	—	1	1	2	3	6	2	3	2
58	—	1	—	1	5	2	2	7	7	3
59	—	—	—	—	—	—	2	4	4	3
60	—	—	—	—	2	—	—	4	4	2
61	—	—	—	—	1	—	1	1	2	—
62	—	—	—	—	—	—	—	—	1	—
63	—	—	—	—	—	1	—	—	—	—
64	—	—	—	—	—	—	—	1	—	1
65	—	—	—	—	—	—	—	—	—	—
66	—	—	—	—	—	—	—	—	—	—
67	—	—	—	—	—	—	—	—	—	—
68	—	—	—	—	—	—	—	—	—	—
69	—	—	—	—	—	—	—	—	—	—
70	—	—	—	—	—	—	—	—	—	—
71	—	—	—	—	—	—	—	—	—	—
72	—	—	—	—	—	—	—	—	—	—
73	—	—	—	—	—	—	—	—	—	—

LI
(Ear Length) (Females)

11	12	13	14	15	16	17	18	19	Adult
—	—	—	—	—	—	—	—	—	—
—	—	—	—	—	1	—	—	—	—
—	—	—	—	—	—	—	—	—	1
1	—	—	—	—	—	—	—	1	—
—	1	—	—	1	—	—	—	—	1
2	1	—	1	—	—	—	—	—	2
—	—	3	—	1	1	—	—	1	6
2	2	1	—	1	1	—	—	—	5
2	3	1	—	2	—	2	—	2	8
3	1	1	6	1	2	3	2	1	17
7	1	—	—	3	1	1	1	1	29
3	8	2	1	1	2	5	2	2	32
8	5	2	7	6	3	3	5	—	30
2	4	5	3	2	3	2	5	—	59
5	8	3	3	5	3	5	1	3	65
5	5	3	3	2	4	5	2	3	58
6	7	4	2	3	6	4	3	2	64
4	4	4	4	3	3	2	2	1	65
1	9	5	2	3	3	2	4	1	91
—	2	4	1	1	1	3	—	2	55
1	2	1	—	2	1	—	1	1	53
—	—	—	2	2	1	—	—	1	38
—	—	—	—	—	1	—	—	—	24
—	—	—	—	—	—	—	—	—	16
—	—	—	—	—	—	—	—	1	9
—	—	—	—	—	—	—	—	—	13
—	—	—	—	—	—	—	—	—	5
—	—	—	—	1	—	—	—	—	3
—	—	—	—	—	—	—	—	—	4
—	—	—	—	—	—	—	—	—	—
—	—	—	—	—	—	—	—	—	1
—	—	—	—	—	—	—	—	—	3

160   *The Anthropometry of the American Negro*

Table
Physiognomic Width of Ear

Age Mm.	1	2	3[1]	4	5	6	7[2]	8	9	10
25	—	—	—	—	—	—	1	—	2	—
26	—	1	—	1	—	2	—	1	1	—
27	1	—	2	2	2	3	2	1	5	—
28	2	3	2	2	2	6	8	3	4	4
29	1	—	2	5	4	12	8	7	8	8
30	1	3	3	4	7	16	23	23	11	18
31	2	4	8	12	10	15	25	28	18	27
32	—	4	4	9	8	10	43	35	23	24
33	1	3	5	10	7	21	23	23	31	31
34	1	2	3	6	6	18	25	28	24	19
35	—	1	1	1	4	13	7	13	19	16
36	—	1	—	1	2	8	5	12	14	10
37	—	1	—	—	—	4	6	2	4	7
38	—	—	—	—	1	—	2	1	2	5
39	—	—	—	1	—	1	—	—	—	2
40	—	—	—	—	—	—	—	1	—	—
41	—	—	—	—	—	—	—	—	—	—
42	—	—	—	—	—	—	—	—	—	—

Table
Physiognomic Width of Ear

Age Mm.	1	2	3	4	5	6	7	8	9	10
22	—	—	—	—	—	1	—	—	—	—
23	—	—	—	—	—	—	—	—	—	—
24	—	—	—	—	—	—	—	—	—	—
25	—	—	1	—	1	—	—	—	—	—
26	—	3	2	—	1	2	3	1	—	1
27	1	—	3	1	1	5	2	3	1	1
28	1	2	6	3	2	5	5	6	2	3
29	1	5	5	7	9	12	11	9	5	7
30	—	6	7	4	13	19	21	11	12	9
31	—	—	6	6	15	16	23	8	9	10
32	—	2	3	2	9	11	17	15	8	7
33	—	—	2	—	6	4	6	14	5	8
34	—	—	1	—	1	—	3	6	8	3
35	—	—	—	—	2	—	1	5	1	4
36	—	1	—	—	1	1	3	—	3	1
37	—	—	—	—	—	1	—	1	—	—
38	—	—	—	—	—	1	—	—	—	—
39	—	—	—	—	—	—	—	—	—	—
40	—	—	—	—	—	—	—	—	—	—
41	—	—	—	—	—	—	—	—	1	—

[1] Add 16—1.   [2] Add 23—1.

LII
(Males)

11	12	13	14	15	16	17	18	19	Adult
—	—	—	—	1	—	—	—	—	2
2	—	—	—	—	—	1	—	1	2
1	2	3	4	—	1	—	1	1	3
1	6	3	6	3	—	—	1	—	14
8	7	11	6	3	1	1	2	3	36
16	18	17	13	15	6	6	2	3	60
18	37	34	19	16	4	6	2	5	108
41	33	52	40	28	13	6	4	7	114
40	34	52	52	30	12	3	9	11	147
35	36	45	40	32	12	4	3	10	125
24	27	31	29	13	12	7	9	5	130
12	14	33	26	22	3	5	3	7	82
4	13	11	10	11	1	3	2	3	61
1	3	6	10	9	—	2	5	2	32
3	3	1	1	4	2	1	1	1	26
—	1	3	—	4	1	—	1	1	10
—	—	—	—	—	—	2	—	—	4
—	—	—	—	—	—	—	—	—	4

LIII
(Females)

11	12	13	14	15	16	17	18	19	Adult
—	—	—	—	1	—	—	—	—	—
—	—	—	—	—	—	—	1	—	—
1	—	—	—	—	—	—	—	—	2
—	1	1	—	2	1	1	—	—	8
—	—	2	3	—	3	2	3	—	8
1	3	2	2	3	2	3	—	2	21
6	4	4	4	3	1	3	6	—	51
7	9	6	2	7	5	6	3	6	82
8	10	7	10	7	7	5	2	4	107
10	15	7	5	3	8	6	5	5	143
9	9	4	4	7	3	6	3	2	105
7	6	4	3	2	6	2	3	1	95
2	4	1	1	—	—	2	—	2	56
1	1	1	—	4	—	—	2	1	34
—	1	—	1	1	—	1	—	—	16
—	—	—	—	—	1	—	—	—	16
—	—	—	—	—	—	—	—	—	10
—	—	—	—	—	—	—	—	—	1
—	—	—	—	—	—	—	—	—	1

Table LIV
Physiognomic Width of Ear (mm)

Age	Males			Females		
	No.	Average	σ	No.	Average	σ
1	9	30.1	± 2.23	3	28.0	± —
2	23	31.6	± 2.54	19	29.4	± 2.28
3	31	30.7	± 3.36	36	29.5	± 2.09
4	54	31.6	± 2.31	23	29.7	± 1.33
5	53	31.8	± 2.34	61	30.75	± 1.98
6	139	32.15	± 2.55	78	30.2	± 2.30
7	179	32.0	± 2.34	95	30.5	± 1.67
8	178	32.4	± 2.19	79	31.3	± 2.27
9	166	32.6	± 2.56	55	31.65	± 2.44
10	171	32.8	± 2.41	54	31.2	± 2.18
11	206	32.9	± 2.18	52	31.65	± 2.06
12	234	33.0	± 2.43	63	31.75	± 2.08
13	302	33.2	± 2.34	39	31.1	± 2.24
14	257	32.9	± 2.24	35	31.1	± 2.29
15	191	33.65	± 2.66	40	31.2	± 2.93
16	68	33.15	± 2.09	37	31.2	± 2.44
17	47	33.6	± 3.16	37	31.1	± 2.42
18	38	34.0	± 3.20	28	30.8	± 2.88
19	60	33.4	± 2.74	23	31.6	± 2.04
Adult	960	33.8	± 2.68	756	32.3	± 2.54

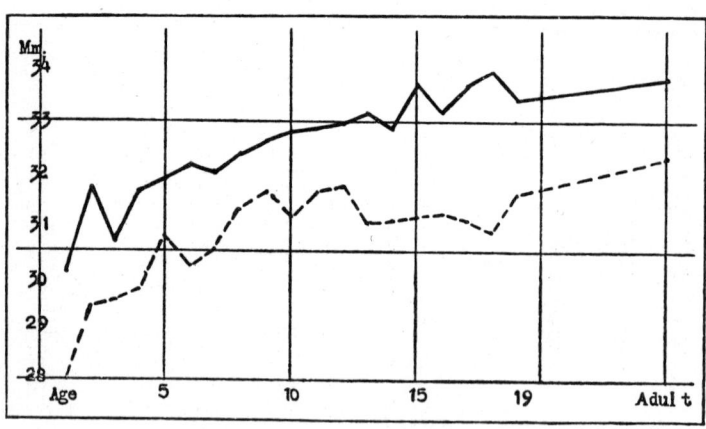

(Males ——— Females -----)

Fig. 16.
Growth in Width of Ear

Growth Curves and Sex Differences

Table LV
Pigmentation, Upper Outer Arm, % N

Age	Males			Females		
	No.	Average	σ	No.	Average	σ
1	4	80.0	—	1	83.0	—
2	9	71.9	—	7	68.9	—
3	5	65.6	—	10	70.4	—
4	15	73.8	± 10.17	7	75.2	—
5	31	64.6	± 14.76	32	70.6	± 11.49
6	105	68.9	± 13.50	43	70.2	± 7.50
7	150	70.9	± 11.4	62	70.7	± 10.11
8	146	69.9	± 13.17	50	71.1	± 9.39
9	148	71.1	± 12.66	16	69.9	± 8.70
10	141	70.8	± 11.43	17	72.2	± 7.77
11	156	72.6	± 10.38	15	74.0	± 6.30
12	156	71.3	± 11.85	16	73.25	± 9.30
13	186	74.63	± 8.94	4	65.0	—
14	144	72.6	± 10.62	5	71.0	—
15	98	74.2	± 12.15	6	69.5	—
16	36	74.3	± 10.59	7	74.4	—
17	21	72.4	± 10.50	5	75.8	—
18	25	66.8	± 10.62	4	70.2	—
19	40	69.05	± 10.40	1	71.0	—
Adult	593	66.65	± 13.89	192	68.4	± 12.03

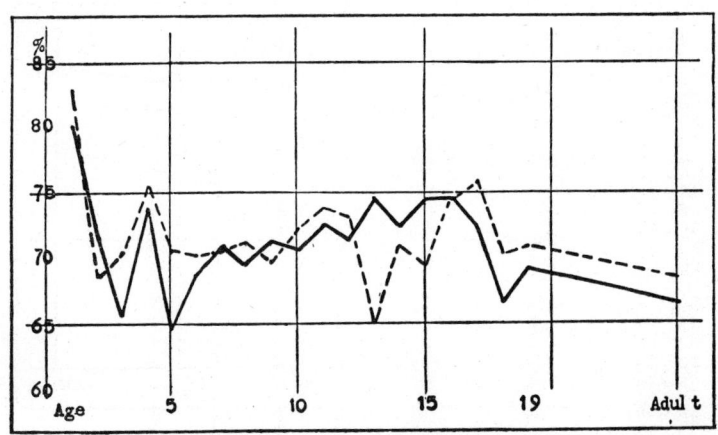

(Males ——— Females - - - - -)

Fig. 17.

Age-changes in Pigmentation, Black (N) Element, Upper Outer Arm.

Table
Pigmentation, Upper Outer Arm,

Age %	1	2	3	4	5	6	7	8	9	10
25—27	—	—	—	—	—	—	—	—	—	—
28—30	—	—	—	—	—	—	—	1	1	—
31—33	—	—	—	—	—	1	—	—	—	—
34—36	—	—	—	—	1	2	1	2	1	1
37—39	—	—	—	—	1	3	1	—	2	2
40—42	—	—	—	—	1	2	1	3	3	2
43—45	—	—	—	—	1	—	—	4	2	—
46—48	—	—	—	—	—	1	5	6	—	1
49—51	—	—	—	—	1	3	3	1	2	5
52—54	—	—	—	1	2	4	5	2	5	4
55—57	—	1	—	—	1	4	5	5	7	5
58—60	—	1	—	—	1	3	5	6	7	5
61—63	—	—	2	2	2	7	11	10	9	8
64—66	—	—	—	2	3	8	11	12	5	7
67—69	—	—	3	1	3	10	9	9	10	12
70—72	—	1	—	—	—	6	11	9	8	16
73—75	—	4	—	1	2	13	17	15	19	12
76—78	1	—	—	—	5	10	22	13	11	20
79—81	2	1	—	2	2	9	17	19	27	21
82—84	1	—	—	6	4	10	16	15	16	12
85—87	—	1	—	—	1	6	6	12	10	6
88—90	—	—	—	—	—	3	4	2	3	2
91—93	—	—	—	—	—	—	—	—	—	—

Table
Pigmentation, Upper Outer Arm,

Age %	1	2	3	4	5	6	7	8	9	10
34—36	—	—	—	—	1	—	—	—	—	—
37—39	—	—	—	—	—	—	—	—	—	—
40—42	—	—	—	—	—	—	—	—	—	—
43—45	—	—	—	—	—	—	—	—	—	—
46—48	—	—	—	—	1	—	2	—	—	—
49—51	—	—	—	—	—	—	2	1	—	—
52—54	—	—	—	—	2	2	—	2	—	—
55—57	—	1	1	—	1	1	3	3	1	2
58—60	—	—	—	1	—	3	5	1	1	—
61—63	—	—	2	1	1	2	4	6	3	—
64—66	—	2	1	1	2	6	3	2	3	1
67—69	—	1	—	1	5	7	5	6	—	3
70—72	—	—	1	—	3	3	6	2	1	1
73—75	—	1	1	1	2	5	10	7	2	4
76—78	—	2	3	1	4	8	6	6	1	2
79—81	—	—	—	—	5	3	8	9	2	2
82—84	1	—	1	1	5	2	5	3	2	2
85—87	—	—	—	—	—	1	2	2	—	—
88—90	—	—	—	—	—	—	1	—	—	—

LVI
Black (N) Element, (Males)

11	12	13	14	15	16	17	18	19	Adult
—	—	—	—	—	—	—	—	—	1
—	—	—	—	—	—	—	—	—	3
—	—	—	—	1	—	—	—	—	4
—	1	—	—	—	—	—	—	1	12
—	1	—	1	—	—	—	—	—	9
—	2	—	1	2	—	—	—	—	17
2	1	—	2	2	1	1	—	—	9
1	5	2	3	1	1	—	1	—	17
1	1	2	1	1	—	—	2	—	24
4	4	3	—	—	—	—	1	2	19
10	7	4	6	3	2	1	3	4	34
6	8	3	2	2	—	—	—	1	34
11	9	13	10	4	1	1	3	3	38
6	6	6	9	7	1	3	1	4	40
11	12	7	14	4	3	—	2	2	42
14	14	23	15	5	2	4	3	5	45
15	14	25	14	9	5	2	2	6	53
22	21	20	15	8	5	4	3	6	53
21	19	32	18	18	7	2	3	2	58
16	17	29	20	15	3	—	1	3	41
11	8	16	11	12	3	2	—	1	34
4	6	1	2	3	2	—	—	—	6
1	—	—	—	1	—	1	—	—	—

LVII
Black (N) Element, (Females)

11	12	13	14	15	16	17	18	19	Adult
—	—	—	—	—	—	—	—	—	—
—	—	—	—	—	—	—	—	—	1
—	—	—	—	—	—	—	—	—	4
—	—	—	—	—	—	—	—	—	3
—	—	—	—	—	—	—	1	—	9
—	—	—	—	—	—	—	—	—	5
—	1	—	—	1	—	—	—	—	6
—	1	1	1	—	—	—	—	—	9
—	—	—	1	1	—	—	—	—	17
1	1	—	—	—	1	—	—	—	13
1	1	1	—	—	1	—	—	—	12
2	—	1	—	—	—	1	—	—	10
3	1	1	—	1	—	—	—	1	11
1	3	—	—	1	—	1	1	—	21
1	3	—	2	1	3	1	1	—	28
5	1	—	1	—	1	2	—	—	20
1	4	—	—	1	1	—	1	—	16
—	—	—	—	—	—	—	—	—	5
—	—	—	—	—	—	—	—	—	2

Table LVIII
Pigmentation, Upper Outer Arm, % R

Age	Males			Females		
	No.	Average	σ	No.	Average	σ
1	4	10.25	—	1	9.0	—
2	9	13.3	—	7	14.3	—
3	5	14.4	—	10	13.1	—
4	15	12.2	± 3.09	7	13.0	—
5	31	12.7	± 3.22	32	12.2	± 2.89
6	105	12.4	± 3.18	43	13.8	± 2.60
7	150	11.9	± 2.71	62	12.6	± 3.19
8	146	11.8	± 3.13	50	12.8	± 2.80
9	148	11.8	± 3.19	16	13.2	± 2.74
10	141	11.9	± 2.91	17	12.9	± 2.62
11	156	11.6	± 2.90	15	12.7	± 3.00
12	156	11.9	± 2.90	16	11.6	± 2.23
13	185	11.3	± 2.78	4	14.5	—
14	144	11.8	± 2.97	5	12.0	—
15	98	11.0	± 3.23	6	12.0	—
16	36	10.6	± 2.82	7	12.6	—
17	21	10.9	± 2.93	5	12.0	—
18	25	13.0	± 2.63	4	12.7	—
19	40	12.7	± 1.94	1	12.0	—
Adult	593	12.4	± 2.84	192	13.3	± 3.07

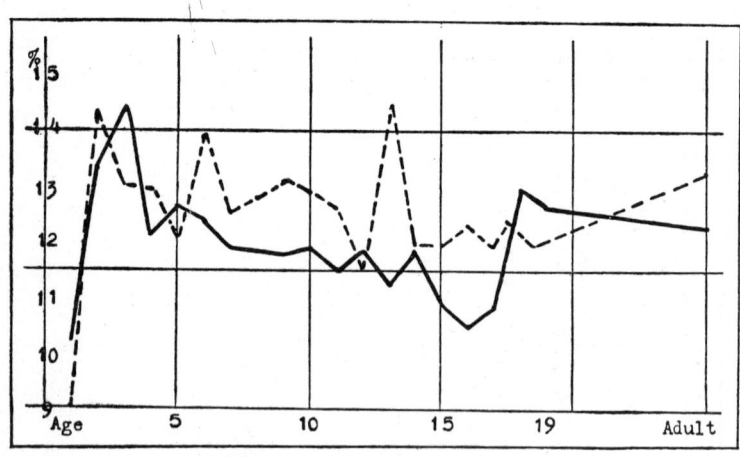

(Males ——— Females - - - - -)

Fig. 18.

Age-Changes in Pigmentation, Red (R) Element, Upper Outer Arm

Growth Curves and Sex Differences

Table LIX
Pigmentation, Upper Outer Arm, % Y

Age	Males			Females		
	No.	Average	σ	No.	Average	σ
1	4	6.75	—	1	5.0	—
2	9	9.65	—	7	10.6	—
3	5	13.0	—	10	10.4	—
4	15	8.7	± 3.36	7	10.6	—
5	31	10.45	± 4.31	32	8.9	± 3.16
6	105	10.2	± 5.15	43	10.3	± 3.37
7	150	9.2	± 4.25	62	9.7	± 4.14
8	146	9.4	± 4.76	50	10.0	± 3.74
9	148	9.0	± 4.39	16	10.3	± 3.39
10	141	9.0	± 4.59	17	8.9	± 3.56
11	156	8.3	± 3.94	15	8.3	± 2.60
12	156	8.8	± 4.30	16	9.2	± 4.37
13	186	7.6	± 3.35	4	14.0	—
14	144	8.1	± 3.71	5	10.6	—
15	98	7.5	± 3.82	6	12.7	—
16	36	7.6	± 3.83	7	9.1	—
17	21	9.1	± 4.25	5	8.2	—
18	25	11.4	± 4.40	4	11.0	—
19	40	10.6	± 3.71	1	10.0	—
Adult	593	10.8	± 4.66	192	11.2	± 4.90

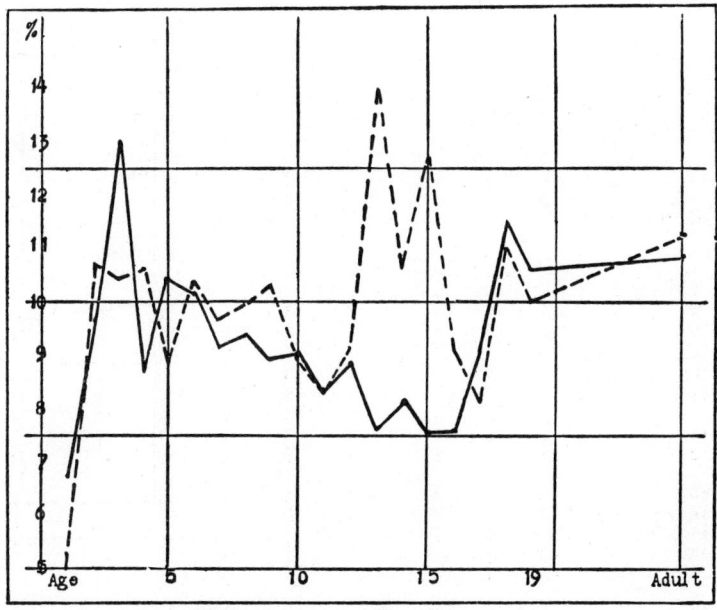

(Males ——— Females - - - - -)
Fig. 19.
Age-Changes in Pigmentation, Yellow (Y) Element, Upper Outer Arm

168   The Anthropometry of the American Negro

Table
Pigmentation, Upper Outer Arm,

Age %	1	2	3	4	5	6	7	8	9	10
3	—	—	—	—	—	—	—	—	—	—
4	—	—	—	—	—	—	—	—	—	—
5	—	—	—	—	—	2	2	3	3	1
6	—	—	—	—	—	1	4	1	2	2
7	—	—	—	—	1	6	5	14	7	8
8	—	1	—	1	2	3	5	5	12	8
9	1	1	—	3	4	8	11	19	20	8
10	1	—	—	2	3	7	12	9	10	21
11	2	1	1	1	2	12	26	8	16	21
12	—	2	—	1	2	14	20	19	15	11
13	—	—	—	1	2	13	19	20	14	9
14	—	1	2	4	6	10	20	16	16	24
15	—	—	1	—	1	14	9	16	14	12
16	—	1	—	—	5	8	15	9	11	10
17	—	—	—	1	2	1	1	4	2	2
18	—	1	1	—	—	3	1	2	4	4
19	—	—	—	1	—	—	—	1	1	—
20	—	1	—	—	1	3	—	—	1	—

Table
Pigmentation, Upper Outer Arm,

Age %	1	2	3	4	5	6	7	8	9	10
5	—	—	—	—	—	—	1	—	—	—
6	—	—	—	—	—	—	2	—	—	—
7	—	—	—	—	1	—	—	1	—	—
8	—	—	—	—	3	1	7	3	—	—
9	1	—	2	1	1	2	3	2	3	2
10	—	—	1	—	3	3	1	5	—	2
11	—	1	1	—	9	2	8	7	1	2
12	—	—	1	1	2	4	6	3	4	1
13	—	2	1	—	2	7	8	7	1	2
14	—	1	1	2	4	6	8	10	—	4
15	—	1	—	1	2	5	5	3	1	1
16	—	1	1	1	2	9	8	3	5	1
17	—	—	—	1	1	1	2	4	1	1
18	—	1	1	—	2	1	1	1	—	1
19	—	—	1	—	—	2	1	1	—	—
20	—	—	—	—	—	—	1	—	—	—

LX
Red (R) Element (Males)

11	12	13	14	15	16	17	18	19	Adult
—	—	—	—	—	—	1	—	—	—
1	—	—	—	1	—	—	—	—	1
1	2	—	1	1	1	—	—	—	3
2	4	8	3	2	2	1	—	—	1
9	6	10	7	11	3	2	—	—	27
10	9	10	8	4	2	—	1	—	18
19	12	31	15	19	3	1	2	3	58
15	19	15	16	12	6	1	—	2	42
20	25	35	24	13	8	6	5	8	80
21	10	7	9	8	3	—	3	5	66
16	15	20	12	6	3	1	4	4	65
13	21	25	22	11	3	5	4	12	100
13	14	10	10	4	—	2	1	3	52
12	13	11	8	3	1	1	4	3	41
1	3	3	6	2	—	—	—	—	21
2	1	—	2	1	1	—	—	—	11
1	2	—	1	—	—	—	—	—	4
—	—	—	—	—	—	—	1	—	3

LXI
Red (R) Element (Females)

11	12	13	14	15	16	17	18	19	Adult
—	—	—	—	—	—	—	—	—	—
—	—	—	—	—	—	—	—	—	4
1	1	—	—	1	—	—	—	—	4
2	2	—	—	—	1	—	—	—	12
—	3	—	—	1	1	—	—	—	17
3	3	1	3	1	1	2	2	—	25
1	1	—	1	1	1	2	1	1	21
3	3	—	—	—	—	—	—	—	23
2	1	1	—	1	1	1	—	—	21
1	1	—	1	—	1	—	—	—	15
—	1	1	—	—	—	—	1	—	20
—	—	1	—	1	1	—	—	—	13
1	—	—	—	—	—	—	—	—	5
1	—	—	—	—	—	—	—	—	5
—	—	—	—	—	—	—	—	—	7

Table
Pigmentation, Upper Outer Arm,

Age %	1	2	3	4	5	6	7	8	9	10
2	—	—	—	—	—	1	—	1	—	1
3	—	—	—	—	—	5	9	10	7	7
4	—	1	—	—	1	7	8	8	17	8
5	—	—	—	4	3	6	13	14	20	17
6	1	—	—	3	4	11	12	17	16	11
7	3	1	—	1	3	9	17	15	10	14
8	—	1	—	—	2	7	20	9	16	27
9	—	2	—	—	1	9	14	13	11	9
10	—	1	—	2	—	6	11	8	10	9
11	—	1	1	1	3	9	4	5	3	1
12	—	—	1	2	6	5	7	13	7	8
13	—	—	1	1	1	8	9	6	7	6
14	—	1	1	—	2	1	5	3	7	4
15	—	1	1	1	1	1	6	5	5	6
16	—	—	—	—	1	2	3	5	6	4
17	—	—	—	—	1	7	5	3	3	—
18	—	—	—	—	—	3	2	2	1	2
19	—	—	—	—	—	2	1	5	—	1
20	—	—	—	—	1	1	4	1	—	—
21	—	—	—	—	1	2	—	1	1	2
22	—	—	—	—	—	1	—	—	1	2
23	—	—	—	—	—	1	—	1	—	1
24	—	—	—	—	—	—	—	1	—	—
25	—	—	—	—	—	1	—	—	—	1
26	—	—	—	—	—	—	—	—	—	—
27	—	—	—	—	—	—	—	—	—	—
28	—	—	—	—	—	—	—	—	—	—

Table
Pigmentation, Upper Outer Arm,

Age %	1	2	3	4	5	6	7	8	9	10
2	—	—	—	—	—	—	1	—	—	—
3	—	—	—	—	1	1	—	—	—	—
4	—	—	—	—	1	—	6	2	—	—
5	1	1	—	—	4	—	2	3	1	3
6	—	—	1	1	3	5	5	8	2	3
7	—	—	1	—	1	5	7	3	2	2
8	—	1	2	2	5	6	8	5	—	2
9	—	2	1	1	4	2	4	2	2	—
10	—	1	—	—	3	4	8	6	1	1
11	—	—	—	—	3	2	1	3	—	1
12	—	—	2	1	4	4	3	4	4	3
13	—	1	1	—	—	5	1	4	2	—
14	—	—	1	—	1	3	5	1	—	—
15	—	—	1	1	1	4	5	4	1	—
16	—	—	—	1	1	1	2	3	—	2
17	—	—	—	—	—	1	2	2	1	—
18	—	—	—	—	—	—	1	—	—	—
19	—	—	—	—	—	—	1	—	—	—
20	—	1	—	—	—	—	—	—	—	—
21	—	—	—	—	—	—	—	—	—	—
22	—	—	—	—	—	—	—	—	—	—

LXII
Yellow (Y) Element (Males)

11	12	13	14	15	16	17	18	19	Adult
2	1	1	—	—	—	1	—	—	4
4	7	6	9	9	4	—	—	—	15
12	13	20	16	11	5	3	—	1	24
26	25	32	16	19	3	1	3	—	46
22	10	29	11	13	7	—	—	7	35
22	16	25	23	8	2	2	2	3	53
10	17	14	12	7	3	3	4	1	44
8	11	11	7	5	3	2	1	2	36
6	8	13	16	5	3	4	2	9	43
8	9	5	10	2	1	—	1	2	34
11	5	8	4	3	—	—	1	3	35
4	10	5	8	6	1	2	2	3	34
7	2	9	4	4	—	—	2	2	30
3	6	5	4	2	2	2	3	2	42
6	9	1	1	2	1	—	—	1	41
1	1	1	—	2	1	—	1	2	30
2	3	1	1	—	—	—	1	2	25
—	—	—	—	—	—	—	1	—	12
2	—	—	—	—	—	1	1	—	6
—	3	—	—	—	—	—	—	—	—
—	—	—	1	—	—	—	—	—	2
—	—	—	1	—	—	—	—	—	—
—	—	—	—	—	—	—	—	—	1
—	—	—	—	—	—	—	—	—	—
—	—	—	—	—	—	—	—	—	—
—	—	—	—	—	—	—	—	—	1

LXIII
Yellow (Y) Element, (Females)

11	12	13	14	15	16	17	18	19	Adult
—	—	—	—	—	—	—	—	—	—
—	—	—	—	—	—	—	—	—	3
—	2	—	—	—	—	—	1	—	5
2	3	—	—	—	1	1	—	—	15
4	—	—	1	—	—	1	—	—	13
1	4	—	1	—	2	—	—	—	15
1	—	—	1	—	—	2	1	—	22
1	—	—	—	—	2	—	—	—	10
2	2	—	—	1	—	—	—	1	13
2	1	—	—	1	—	—	—	—	11
1	—	—	—	2	1	1	1	—	9
1	1	2	—	—	1	—	—	—	16
—	—	1	—	—	—	—	—	—	7
—	1	—	1	1	—	—	—	—	12
—	—	1	—	1	—	—	—	—	16
—	2	—	1	—	—	—	—	—	11
—	—	—	—	—	—	—	—	—	5
—	—	—	—	—	—	—	—	—	2
—	—	—	—	—	—	—	1	—	1
—	—	—	—	—	—	—	—	—	3
—	—	—	—	—	—	—	—	—	3

Table

Pigmentation, Upper Outer Arm,

Age %	1	2	3	4	5	6	7	8	9	10
1	—	—	—	—	—	1	—	1	—	—
2	2	1	—	5	2	8	5	5	4	3
3	1	3	—	4	2	11	21	11	9	7
4	—	2	1	1	2	12	23	17	26	16
5	1	—	—	—	4	10	18	19	9	29
6	—	1	1	—	1	7	5	12	26	14
7	—	—	1	—	5	11	14	16	16	13
8	—	1	1	—	3	8	14	12	17	11
9	—	—	1	1	1	3	11	5	6	10
10	—	—	—	—	1	9	5	10	3	8
11	—	1	—	2	1	3	3	7	5	6
12	—	—	—	1	—	3	5	3	4	—
13	—	—	—	1	2	2	4	3	6	3
14	—	—	—	—	1	2	5	3	4	7
15	—	—	—	—	—	1	1	3	2	3
16	—	—	—	—	—	2	2	2	—	—
17	—	—	—	—	—	1	2	1	2	1
18	—	—	—	—	1	3	3	1	1	3
19	—	—	—	—	1	1	—	1	1	—
20	—	—	—	—	1	—	—	—	—	1
21	—	—	—	—	—	1	—	2	—	1
22	—	—	—	—	—	—	6	1	2	—
23	—	—	—	—	—	—	—	1	—	1
24	—	—	—	—	—	2	—	—	—	—
25	—	—	—	—	—	—	—	1	2	—
26	—	—	—	—	—	—	—	3	—	1
27	—	—	—	—	1	—	1	2	1	1
28	—	—	—	—	—	—	1	—	—	1
29	—	—	—	—	—	—	—	1	1	—
30	—	—	—	—	—	—	—	—	1	—
31	—	—	—	—	—	2	—	—	—	—
32	—	—	—	—	1	—	—	—	—	—
33	—	—	—	—	—	—	—	2	—	1
34	—	—	—	—	1	1	1	—	—	—
35	—	—	—	—	—	—	—	—	—	—
36	—	—	—	—	—	—	—	—	—	—
37	—	—	—	—	—	—	—	1	1	—
38	—	—	—	—	—	—	—	—	—	—
39	—	—	—	—	—	1	—	—	—	—
40	—	—	—	—	—	—	—	—	—	—
41	—	—	—	—	—	—	—	—	—	—
42	—	—	—	—	—	—	—	—	—	—
43	—	—	—	—	—	—	—	—	—	—
44	—	—	—	—	—	—	—	—	1	—

LXIV
White (W) Element (Males)

11	12	13	14	15	16	17	18	19	Adult
—	1	—	—	—	—	—	—	—	3
4	6	5	5	8	2	—	1	—	23
13	14	30	15	11	5	1	1	5	81
19	20	34	18	17	6	4	5	2	65
24	24	22	20	19	4	5	2	10	70
23	23	24	15	11	3	1	2	1	36
15	15	21	16	3	3	3	4	3	42
13	8	14	14	5	3	—	3	2	30
6	5	7	11	4	2	1	—	2	31
9	6	7	7	3	1	—	—	2	21
7	2	3	2	4	—	3	—	2	21
3	4	4	6	2	3	—	1	3	13
4	4	4	3	2	1	1	1	1	18
6	6	1	1	1	—	1	—	1	12
3	—	3	1	—	—	—	—	1	11
—	2	—	—	1	—	—	1	4	13
2	3	2	2	—	1	—	1	—	19
2	2	1	2	1	—	—	1	—	7
—	—	—	1	—	1	—	—	—	5
—	1	1	—	—	—	—	—	—	5
—	1	1	1	—	—	—	1	—	2
—	2	2	—	1	—	—	—	—	4
1	2	—	—	—	—	1	—	—	8
—	2	—	2	—	—	—	—	—	4
1	—	—	—	—	—	—	—	—	2
—	—	—	—	—	—	—	—	—	3
—	2	—	—	—	—	—	—	—	3
1	—	—	—	1	1	—	—	—	5
—	1	—	1	—	—	—	—	—	3
—	—	—	—	—	—	—	—	—	9
—	—	—	1	3	—	—	—	—	4
—	—	—	—	—	—	—	—	—	1
—	—	—	—	—	—	—	—	—	4
—	—	—	—	—	—	—	—	—	2
—	—	—	—	—	—	—	—	1	2
—	—	—	—	—	—	—	—	—	2
—	—	—	—	—	—	—	—	—	—
—	—	—	—	—	—	—	—	—	2
—	—	—	—	—	—	—	—	—	2
—	—	—	—	—	—	—	—	—	1
—	—	—	—	—	—	—	—	—	1
—	—	—	—	—	—	—	—	—	—
—	—	—	—	1	—	—	—	—	1
—	—	—	—	—	—	—	—	—	2

174   The Anthropometry of the American Negro

Table
Pigmentation, Upper Outer Arm,

Age %	1	2	3	4	5	6	7	8	9	10
1	—	—	—	—	1	—	—	1	—	—
2	—	—	—	1	3	6	4	4	3	1
3	1	1	3	1	1	7	9	11	2	3
4	—	2	2	—	3	5	7	2	—	2
5	—	1	—	1	7	7	8	5	2	5
6	—	—	—	—	2	4	5	8	—	1
7	—	2	—	1	2	4	7	4	1	1
8	—	—	4	1	3	2	5	4	4	2
9	—	—	—	1	4	3	5	3	2	1
10	—	1	—	—	—	1	3	1	—	—
11	—	—	—	1	—	1	2	—	—	—
12	—	—	—	—	—	—	1	2	1	1
13	—	—	—	—	2	2	—	2	—	—
14	—	—	1	—	—	—	3	1	1	—
15	—	—	—	—	1	1	—	—	—	—
16	—	—	—	—	—	—	—	2	—	—
17	—	—	—	—	—	—	1	—	—	—
18	—	—	—	—	—	—	1	—	—	—
19	—	—	—	—	1	—	1	—	—	—
20	—	—	—	—	—	—	—	—	—	—
21	—	—	—	—	—	—	—	—	—	—
22	—	—	—	—	—	—	—	—	—	—
23	—	—	—	—	—	—	—	—	—	—
24	—	—	—	—	1	—	—	—	—	—
25	—	—	—	—	—	—	—	—	—	—
26	—	—	—	—	—	—	—	—	—	—
27	—	—	—	—	—	—	—	—	—	—
28	—	—	—	—	—	—	—	—	—	—
29	—	—	—	—	(35—1)	—	—	—	—	—

LXV
White (W) Element, (Females)

11	12	13	14	15	16	17	18	19	Adult
—	—	—	—	—	—	—	—	—	4
—	5	—	—	1	3	—	1	—	24
4	4	—	1	1	2	1	1	—	39
3	2	1	1	—	—	2	1	—	29
1	1	2	1	1	—	2	—	—	11
5	1	—	—	—	1	—	—	—	9
1	—	—	—	—	—	—	—	1	12
1	—	—	—	—	—	—	—	—	5
—	—	—	—	—	1	—	—	—	6
—	—	—	—	—	—	—	—	—	8
—	1	1	1	—	—	—	—	—	7
—	—	—	—	1	—	—	—	—	9
—	—	—	—	—	—	—	—	—	5
—	—	—	—	—	—	—	—	—	1
—	—	—	1	1	—	—	—	—	—
—	—	—	—	1	—	—	1	—	1
—	2	—	—	—	—	—	—	—	3
—	—	—	—	—	—	—	—	—	6
—	—	—	—	—	—	—	—	—	1
—	—	—	—	—	—	—	—	—	2
—	—	—	—	—	—	—	—	—	1
—	—	—	—	—	—	—	—	—	3
—	—	—	—	—	—	—	—	—	—
—	—	—	—	—	—	—	—	—	2
—	—	—	—	—	—	—	—	—	1
—	—	—	—	—	—	—	—	—	(28—1)
—	—	—	—	—	—	—	—	—	(30—1)
—	—	—	—	—	—	—	—	—	(39—1)
—	—	—	—	—	—	—	—	—	—

Table LXVI
Pigmentation, % W

Age	Males			Females		
	No.	Average	σ	No.	Average	σ
1	4	2.50	—	1	3.00	—
2	9	4.89	—	7	5.70	—
3	5	6.80	—	10	6.30	—
4	15	5.47	± 4.32	7	6.40	—
5	31	10.42	± 7.99	32	8.19	± 6.87
6	105	8.69	± 7.02	43	5.70	± 3.31
7	150	8.10	± 5.75	62	6.89	± 3.95
8	146	9.13	± 6.90	50	6.32	± 3.72
9	150	8.48	± 6.39	16	6.56	± 3.51
10	141	8.27	± 5.36	17	5.65	± 2.61
11	156	7.72	± 4.27	15	4.93	± 1.48
12	156	8.01	± 5.72	16	5.38	± 4.91
13	186	6.51	± 3.85	4	6.20	—
14	144	7.64	± 4.75	5	7.60	—
15	98	7.48	± 6.98	6	8.30	—
16	36	7.33	± 5.09	7	3.90	—
17	21	7.76	± 4.65	5	4.20	—
18	25	8.44	± 5.18	4	6.20	—
19	40	8.68	± 5.96	1	7.00	—
Adult	593	10.00	± 8.44	192	7.33	± 6.32

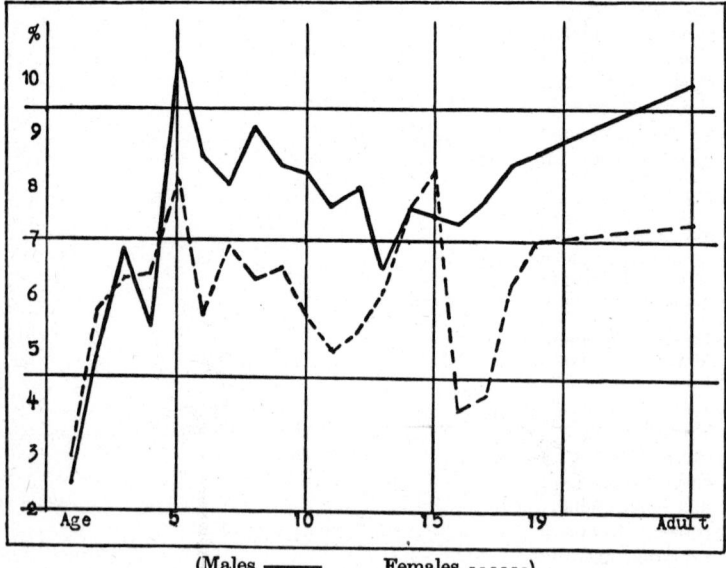

(Males ——— Females -----)

Fig. 20.
Age-Changes in Pigmentation, White (W) Element, Upper Outer Arm

CHAPTER VI
THE VALIDITY OF THE GENEALOGIES.

In the first chapter an analysis of the genealogical information furnished by the adults measured in the course of this research, was presented. Each person was classified according to his *known* (or, if the term is preferable, his *stated*) ancestry. In other words, the individual was placed in a given genealogical class according to the information he was able or willing to give. It is not claimed that the classes represent hard and fast lines; that, for example, the class "about the same amount of Negro and White ancestry" is exactly one-half Negro and one-half White. There may be fairly large variations from this rigid standard, as there must be in any series of genealogical data.

Let us first briefly repeat the results of the classification of the genealogical data for the entire adult series. There are four principal classes, based on divisions involving varying amounts of Negro-White mixture, with Indian ancestry as well. To take this properly into consideration, the Indian element has been separated into four more classes, the same as the general ones, but with Indian added to the various amounts of Negro-White. I repeat a portion of the table from Chapter I, giving the classes, the letters indicating them (which will be used henceforth instead of the somewhat involved designations they have had to be given), the numbers of persons in the classes, and the percentage of the total represented by each:

Unmixed Negro	N	342	22.0%
Negro, mixed with Indian	N(I)	97	6.3%
More Negro than White	NNW	384	24.8%
More Negro than White, with Indian	NNW(I)	106	6.9%
About the same amount of Negro and White	NW	260	16.7%
About the same amount of Negro and White, with Indian	NW(I)	133	8.5%
More White than Negro	NWW	154	9.3%
More White than Negro, with Indian	NWW(I)	75	5.5%

That such a large amount of crossing as is shown by this table should exist is hardly strange, in view of our knowledge of historical facts. Except for the figures of the Census Bureau, which are not to be taken too seriously as indicating the amount of crossing which has been occurring in this country as far as Negroes are concerned, there is no consideration of the Negro by any student which has not included comment on the fact of mixture among this population. But the amount of Indian mixture is surprising, although it is readily understood in the light of the opportunities which must have presented themselves for contact between Indians and Negroes. There are colonies in existence today in New York, New Jersey, and New England (to say nothing of the southern states) which are composed principally of persons of Negro-Indian mixture. Indeed, Professor Speck, long a student of the Negro-Indian colonies found in some of the southern states, in a letter to me, expressed surprise that the percentage of those claiming part Indian descent was not greater than it was among my sample of American Negroes, and even hazarded a tentative opinion that in fact there might be more crossing than was represented in the table given above.

The genealogical classifications, however, cannot be expected to be accepted of themselves. There is a general opinion current that Negro genealogies have all the unreliability of any genealogical statements, plus that which comes from the putatively large amount of illegitimacy represented in the Negro population, especially from pre-Civil War times. And such a widespread opinion may not be disregarded unless proof is brought which will demonstrate it to be untenable. As far as I know, no genealogies of Negroes have ever been collected, — certainly none which might be checked by anthropometric data. I therefore determined to undertake this in the present study.

Other reasons, also, made this desirable. In a study of racial crossing, it is imperative to know as exactly as possible between what racial groups the crossing has occurred, and when; and it is only through records, in the main non-existent as far as the American Negro is concerned, or through genealogies, that such information can be obtained. Therefore, the latter procedure had to be utilized. Further, I felt that there was another important point involved on which light might be sought by the genealogical method. Physical characteristics, such as skin-color, nose form, lip form, and the like, have been used to distinguish Negroes of various amounts of crossing with White, — and this holds especially true for skin-color. It seemed to me that a genealogical investigation such as the present one might throw some light on the extent to which such judgements as to identification of the racial background of an individual, on the basis of his physical appearance, might have validity.

In this chapter, therefore, an attempt will be made to investigate two points: the validity of the Negro genealogies, and the extent to which an individual may be "placed" as having a definite percentage of Negro or White mixture in his ancestral history through the use of anthropological characteristics. Detailed information regarding the exact nature of the crossing and the time of its occurrence, is essentially a matter for historical research, and lies outside the province of this study.

Of all the series in my possession, the genealogies gathered by myself at Howard University seemed peculiarly fitted for this

The Validity of the Genealogies 179

portion of the investigation. In the first place, all these genealogies were taken by myself, and I used especial care in gathering them. Secondly, the Howard University series is composed only of males, and is therefore available in its entirety, and since there are so few individuals under twenty years of age contained in it, no consideration need be given to possible age-changes. Finally, the percentages of the several classifications for the Howard genealogies check so closely with those of the total series given above, and with those of the genealogical divisions of the various component series, that they may be regarded as fully representative.

I shall restate the classification of the Howard series, and then, without further qualification, proceed to the analysis of the data themselves. Since the correspondence in anthropometric traits, as well as in genealogical percentages of the Howard group with the other series is so uniform, validation of the genealogies of the series treated in this chapter may be considered to apply to the total.

N	109	20.3%
N(I)	36	6.7%
NNW	129	23.8%
NNW(I)	51	9.6%
NW	95	17.7%
NW(I)	57	10.6%
NWW	30	5.6%
NWW(I)	31	5.7%

The method of analysis of the Howard genealogies was as follows: the individuals of the series who had been measured and classified according to the method described in Chapter I were placed in one of the eight genealogical classes, and the averages and variabilities (sigmas) for each of these classes in each of the thirty traits measured, were then computed. If the genealogies are valid, there should be continuous differences between the means for the various classes according to the amount of Negro blood present, which should range from averages about the same as those manifested by the peoples of West Africa for that group which represented itself as being unmixed Negro, to least Negroid for the classes claiming more White than Negro ancestry. We may now turn to the presentation of the results of the analysis, in consideration of the problems which have been posed.

1. Stature (Table LXVII).

Stature, as seen from the discussion of it in Chapter III, is greater in Whites than in most West African Negroes. This is particularly true in the case of those North European populations for whom measurements of stature were available when compared with the Negroes from the west of Africa. The average of the sample of males used in this study, considered as a whole, and of other American Negro groups which have been measured for this trait, is, as has been seen, somewhat less than the means for Whites, and particularly for Indian tribes of the eastern United States, from whom the Indian ancestry of the members of this sample presumably came. If we turn to the averages and mean square variabilities for the genealogical divisions of the Howard series, we find:

Class	Without Indian			With Indian		
	No.	Average (cm.)	σ	No.	Average (cm.)	σ
N	102	170.4	± 5.65			
N(I)				34	169.7	± 6.49
NNW	115	170.4	± 6.77			
NNW(I)				44	171.7	± 5.65
NW	87	171.7	± 5.93			
NW(I)				44	172.1	± 5.29
NWW	23	172.15	± 7.05			
NWW(I)				26	171.6	± 7.54
W[1]	727	174.3	± 5.80			

A regular change in the averages is to be seen in this table, as might be expected were the genealogical statements reliable. In the groups without Indian admixture the stature becomes consistently larger with increasing proportions of stated White ancestry. The same holds true for the classes having Indian ancestry, with the exception that the tallest of these four is the NW (I) group instead of the NWW (I). If we consider the pairs with similar amounts of Negro ancestry, with and without Indian, we see that in two cases the groups mixed with Indian are taller than those without Indian mixture, and the opposite is the case for the other two. Here, as elsewhere, the influence of the Indian blood is very difficult to detect, although since the numbers of cases in the classes with partial Indian ancestry are in the main materially smaller than the corresponding groups without Indian, the element of chance as the determinant of mean values is present to a greater extent. The NWW(I) class shows the highest variability, and the NW(I) the lowest. The N group has the same variability as the NNW(I), and these are second and third lowest, the fourth lowest in variability being the NW. It is impossible to decide in these cases whether the increase in stature with increase of White blood is due to heredity or to the more favorable economic conditions of the lighter group.

One may compare the results obtained from these groups of various degrees of mixture with those obtained from the only other study of this kind which has been made. This is the classical piece of research by Eugen Fischer, who worked with the Rehobother Bastards of South Africa. In his work, which will be referred

---

[1] "W" used in this and following tables will indicate the use of the mean and mean square variability for Hrdlička's (IV) sample of Old White Americans. It must be remembered that this group is by no means identical with the White ancestry of the Negroes.

The Validity of the Genealogies

Table LXVII
Stature

Cm.	N	N(I)	NNW	NNW(I)	NW	NW(I)	NWW	NWW(I)
151.5	—	—	—	1	—	—	—	—
152.5	—	—	—	—	—	—	—	—
153.5	—	—	1	—	—	—	—	—
154.5	—	—	—	—	—	—	—	—
155.5	—	1	2	—	—	—	1	—
156.5	1	1	—	—	—	—	—	1
157.5	—	—	—	—	—	—	—	—
158.5	2	—	2	—	—	—	1	—
159.5	—	—	1	—	1	—	—	—
160.5	3	2	4	1	2	2	—	—
161.5	2	—	2	—	2	1	—	1
162.5	1	1	5	2	3	—	1	—
163.5	4	—	3	—	2	—	—	—
164.5	7	3	4	—	5	1	—	—
165.5	6	3	5	1	3	3	—	2
166.5	5	1	5	5	6	1	1	2
167.5	11	2	7	—	2	—	—	1
168.5	7	1	3	1	2	4	2	2
169.5	5	1	9	5	3	4	1	3
170.5	2	2	8	2	5	2	2	4
171.5	4	2	10	1	4	1	2	2
172.5	2	2	3	4	6	1	2	—
173.5	5	4	8	6	7	3	1	2
174.5	6	2	6	2	6	7	—	—
175.5	6	1	11	3	6	1	3	1
176.5	6	1	1	1	6	3	1	1
177.5	6	2	3	4	4	—	1	—
178.5	6	—	—	1	3	2	1	1
179.5	2	—	2	4	4	2	1	—
180.5	1	—	2	—	3	3	1	—
181.5	—	—	3	—	—	1	—	—
182.5	1	1	—	—	—	2	—	—
183.5	1	1	—	—	2	—	—	1
184.5	—	—	1	—	—	—	—	—
185.5	—	—	2	—	—	—	—	—
186.5	—	—	—	—	—	—	—	—
187.5	—	—	—	—	—	—	—	1
188.5	—	—	2	—	—	—	1	—
189.5	—	—	—	—	—	—	—	—
190.5	—	—	—	—	—	—	—	—
191.5	—	—	—	—	—	—	—	—
192.5	—	—	—	—	—	—	—	—
193.5	—	—	—	—	—	—	—	1

to again for other traits measured by Fischer, the subjects were the descendants of Europeans (in the main Dutch Boers) and Hottentots. The group he measured was divided on the basis of genealogies, obtained for the most part from parish registers, into three classes: "mitt" *(mittlere)*, or those individuals who had equal amounts of Hottentot and European ancestry, "eu" *(überwiegend europäische)* or those predominantly European in blood, and "hott", *(überwiegend hottentottische)* or those predominantly Hottentot in origin. The results obtained by Fischer for stature are not unlike those given by the sample of American Negroes utilized here, and in this tend to confirm the validity of my results. In the population he studied, the Hottentot ancestry is shorter, as in the case of the one studied here, than the European. Therefore, the following results are what would be demanded from crosses between these two racial groups, since the "eu" class is distinctly the tallest:

Class	No.	Average, (mm.)	σ
"Eu"	12	1744	± 73.34
"Mitt"	32	1671	± 67.93
"Hott"	23	1679	± 60.57

2. HEIGHT SITTING (Table LXVIII).

In the discussion of this trait in Chapter III, it was shown that the mean of the sample of all the adult male American Negroes of this study falls between the sitting height of the Old White Americans (though near to it) and that of the populations of Africa for which averages and variabilities were worked out for this trait. It is higher than the latter, while it stands below the means for Indian populations for which data were available. It was further shown, through a consideration of relative sitting height (that is, the percentage of stature represented by the height of the trunk) of various populations, that the percentages for the Africans were, in this proportion, usually lower than those for Indian and White peoples. In other words, the legs of the Negroes are longer in relation to the trunk than are those of the Europeans and Indians, a characteristic that has been generally recognized. If we consider the statistical constants for the genealogical groups, we find them to be:

	Without Indian				With Indian			
Class	No.	Average, (cm.)	σ	% Stature	No.	Average, (cm.)	σ	% Stature
N	102	87.3	± 3.07	51.4				
N(I)					34	87.2	± 3.36	51.5
NNW	115	88.1	± 3.30	51.8				
NNW(I)					44	88.6	± 2.45	51.6
NW	87	88.35	± 3.27	51.4				
NW(I)					45	89.1	± 3.05	51.8
NWW	23	89.1	± 3.19	51.8				
NWW(I)					26	88.0	± 2.92	52.0
W	727	91.8	—	52.6				

The Validity of the Genealogies

The absolute heights for the classes without Indian mixture show an unbroken change from greatest sitting height on the part of the group more White than Negro, to least for that of the unmixed Negro class. That is what we might expect if the genealogies were actual statements of amounts of crossing. The classes mixed with Indian, except the NWW(I) series, behave in the same way. This class, with the greatest amount of White blood, falls somewhat lower than the NW(I) group, but otherwise there is the same change from class to class observable in the groups without Indian ancestry.

The relative sitting height of the various groups shows similar results, although the change from low to high is less regular than for the absolute height. The lowest are the N and NW, which show the same proportions, while the NWW(I) is highest. The groups with Indian mixture show greater consistency of change than those without it, for in the case of the latter the total difference between the highest and lowest is not so great, and there is no regularity of change between the groups of differing amounts of White ancestry. However, the unmixed Negro group has the lowest, and the more White than Negro classes, both with and without Indian mixture, the highest relative sitting height. The NNW(I) group has the lowest variability, the N(I) the highest, while the unmixed Negro group is fourth lowest in this respect.

Table LXVIII
Height Sitting

Cm.	N	N(I)	NNW	NNW(I)	NW	NW(I)	NWW	NWW(I)
79	—	—	—	—	1	—	—	—
80	1	—	—	—	—	—	—	—
81	1	1	2	—	—	1	—	—
82	3	4	4	—	3	—	1	—
83	8	1	3	1	5	2	—	1
84	7	2	8	—	1	2	—	2
85	12	—	3	4	5	2	—	1
86	11	5	16	2	9	2	3	2
87	7	6	7	6	9	5	1	1
88	11	3	17	11	10	5	2	3
89	14	4	16	5	14	4	4	6
90	13	3	11	6	4	5	5	3
91	6	3	12	4	14	7	1	2
92	4	—	3	1	5	3	2	2
93	1	1	5	2	2	3	2	1
94	3	—	4	2	2	2	1	2
95	—	—	1	—	2	1	—	—
96	—	1	2	—	1	1	1	—
97	—	—	—	—	—	—	—	—
98	—	—	1	—	—	—	—	—

Fischer's results for this trait show a similar change from greatest sitting height in the Bastards who are preponderantly European in ancestry to least in those who are mostly of Hottentot origin. His results are:

Class	No.	Average, (mm.)	σ
"Eu"	12	814	± 32.76
"Mitt"	32	804	± 24.28
"Hott"	23	803	± 35.07

Here, as in the case of the preceding trait, he does not give, for purposes of comparison, the mean height for a pure European population related to the European ancestors of the Bastards, or for a Hottentot one, but there appears to be a definite difference between the group with most European mixture, and the other two which do not have as large a proportion of this stock in their ancestry. The differences, of course, are not as significant as they would be if the number of cases were larger, but are directly in line with the results obtained from the genealogical classes of the sample used in this chapter.

3. WIDTH OF SHOULDERS (Table LXIX).

The comparison of shoulder width between the various peoples represented in the table given for this trait in Chapter III showed that there is little difference between the American Negroes, Whites, and Indians in it. The mean for the sample as a whole, and that for the Sioux Indians published by Sullivan, are, for example, not much different. With this in mind, we may turn to the averages and variabilities for the genealogical groups of the Howard sample:

	Without Indian			With Indian		
Class	No.	Average, (mm.)	σ	No.	Average, (mm.)	σ
N	102	403.9	± 20.80			
N(I)				34	402.0	± 20.55
NNW	115	401.4	± 21.55			
NNW(I)				44	399.5	± 16.70
NW	87	403.1	± 20.90			
NW(I)				45	405.2	± 20.05
NWW	23	395.7	± 18.10			
NWW(I)				26	405.0	± 19.15

There seems to be little relationship between the amount of racial mixture and the average measurements of this trait. The means seem to group themselves more or less by chance about the average for the entire sample represented. The variability of the NNW(I) is the smallest, while that of the NNW is highest. Next highest in this respect comes the NW, while the unmixed Negroes follow as the third most variable.

Table LXIX
Width of Shoulders

Mm.	N	N(I)	NNW	NNW(I)	NW	NW(I)	NWW	NWW(I)
335—339	—	1	1	—	—	—	—	—
340—344	—	—	1	—	—	—	—	—
345—349	—	—	—	—	—	—	—	—
350—354	1	—	—	—	—	—	—	—
355—359	1	—	—	1	—	—	—	—
360—364	1	—	3	1	3	1	—	—
365—369	4	1	1	—	1	2	—	—
370—374	2	—	10	2	6	1	2	1
375—379	2	1	5	2	2	3	3	2
380—384	12	2	8	2	4	2	2	3
385—389	2	3	5	2	5	2	3	—
390—394	8	5	11	4	13	2	5	2
395—399	7	2	8	8	6	3	—	2
400—404	15	5	6	8	5	3	2	4
405—409	8	—	12	4	12	3	2	2
410—414	7	5	9	2	8	7	—	2
415—419	7	3	7	2	4	4	—	1
420—424	7	3	13	3	6	6	1	3
425—429	8	—	8	2	1	3	2	2
430—434	3	1	3	1	4	1	—	—
435—439	4	2	2	—	4	1	1	2
440—444	1	—	1	—	—	—	—	—
445—449	1	—	1	—	1	1	—	—
450—454	1	—	—	—	1	—	—	—
455—459	—	—	—	—	1	—	—	—

4. WIDTH OF HIPS (Table LXX).

The hip width of Europeans and Indians is greater than that of the Africans, as was seen in Chapter III. The same was observed for the existing populations in this country, as measurements of the troops during the last war demonstrated. With such differences in mind, the statistical constants for the series of individuals of differing amounts of racial mixture may be considered for this trait:

Class	Without Indian			With Indian		
	No.	Average, (mm.)	σ	No.	Average, (mm.)	σ
N	102	286.1	± 18.25			
N(I)				34	283.8	± 16.15
NNW	115	283.2	± 17.85			
NNW(I)				44	284.1	± 16.35
NW	87	286.5	± 17.15			
NW(I)				45	283.9	± 18.90
NWW	23	289.0	± 22.15			
NWW(I)				26	290.4	± 23.00

The differences between the means shown here are not regular, but in general, the change from a low average for the class with more Negro blood, to a high one in the group which is more White than Negro in ancestry, is to be remarked. It is only in the high norms for the last two classes, — those with the most White ancestry, — that we find a decisive indication of what might be expected after consulting the comparative tables. The variability of the N group is the fifth lowest, the highest in this respect being the NWW(I), the lowest the N(I).

Table LXX
Width of Hips

Mm.	N[1]	N(I)	NNW	NNW(I)	NW[2]	NW(I)	NWW	NWW(I)
210—214	—	—	—	—	—	—	—	1
215—219	—	—	—	—	—	—	—	—
220—224	—	—	1	—	—	—	—	—
225—229	—	—	1	—	—	1	—	—
230—234	—	—	—	—	—	—	—	—
235—239	—	—	—	—	—	1	—	—
240—244	—	—	2	—	—	—	—	—
245—249	1	—	2	1	—	—	—	—
250—254	—	1	—	—	—	—	2	1
255—259	2	—	1	1	—	3	1	—
260—264	8	1	7	2	5	2	—	—
265—269	8	2	7	3	9	3	2	1
270—274	9	6	16	5	7	3	2	2
275—279	12	8	8	6	10	2	1	1
280—284	10	5	14	5	8	6	1	—
285—289	11	2	20	8	13	6	3	3
290—294	14	2	9	6	7	7	1	7
295—299	12	2	9	1	9	3	4	2
300—304	3	—	5	2	9	2	1	1
305—309	4	1	6	3	6	1	2	2
310—314	4	2	4	—	2	5	1	3
315—319	1	1	1	—	—	—	—	1
320—324	1	—	1	—	—	—	—	1
325—329	—	1	1	—	1	—	—	—
330—334	—	—	—	—	—	—	1	—
335—339	1	—	—	—	—	—	1	—
340—344	—	—	—	—	—	—	—	—
345—349	—	—	—	1	—	—	—	—

[1] Add 375—379, 1. [2] Add 195—199, 1.

The Validity of the Genealogies

5. LENGTH OF HEAD (Table LXXI, page 188).

The results of the computations based on the frequencies of this trait for the several genealogical classifications are as follows:

Class	Without Indian			With Indian		
	No.	Average, (mm.)	σ	No.	Average, (mm.)	σ
N	109	198.0	± 6.54			
N(I)				36	198.4	± 6.40
NNW	129	196.9	± 7.06			
NNW(I)				51	198.0	± 7.59
NW	95	196.1	± 6.40			
NW(I)				57	197.0	± 5.86
NWW	30	195.9	± 6.98			
NWW(I)				31	195.6	± 7.00
W	727	197.4	± 6.04			

As may be seen from the above table, the length of head decreases with increasing amounts of White blood. Addition of the White series to the table, however, does not continue the difference, but rather takes us back to a figure very near the average for the N class. The "Old Americans", however, must not be identified with the White ancestors of the mixed Negro population. The Indian element has no noticeable effect upon the averages. A comparison of mean square deviations, in view of the reiterated statement that increasing variability is an indication of greater racial mixture, is of interest: the N group, which represents no crossing, is fourth from the lowest in variability, while the lowest sigma is that of the NW(I) class, one in which there has been a great deal of mixture.

6. WIDTH OF HEAD (Table LXXII).

There is very little difference to be seen between the various groups, while the White series, the mean and mean square variability for which is included for comparative purposes, is larger in this diameter than any of the classes of American Negroes:

Class	Without Indian			With Indian		
	No.	Average, (mm.)	σ	No.	Average, (mm.)	σ
N	109	151.9	± 5.23			
N(I)				36	151.4	± 5.43
NNW	129	151.7	± 6.44			
NNW(I)				51	151.6	± 5.93
NW	95	151.4	± 4.78			
NW(I)				57	151.4	± 5.37
NWW	30	153.2	± 6.76			
NWW(I)				31	149.9	± 6.40
W	727	153.8	± 5.20			

The standard deviation for the N class in this case is the second lowest of the series.

Table LXXI
Length of Head

Mm.	N	N(I)	NNW	NNW(I)	NW	NW(I)	NWW	NWW(I)
179	1	—	—	1	—	—	—	—
180	—	—	—	—	—	—	—	—
181	—	—	—	—	—	—	—	—
182	—	—	2	2	—	—	1	1
183	—	—	2	1	1	1	2	—
184	2	—	3	1	—	—	—	1
185	1	—	1	—	2	1	—	1
186	1	—	2	2	2	1	1	1
187	2	1	6	—	3	—	—	1
188	3	1	3	—	7	—	—	1
189	3	2	2	1	4	1	1	1
190	—	2	4	1	2	—	1	—
191	4	2	5	—	2	5	4	3
192	1	1	—	—	5	2	—	—
193	12	—	7	4	5	7	—	—
194	5	2	7	3	7	3	—	2
195	4	2	7	1	8	4	2	3
196	3	—	10	6	3	4	3	2
197	7	3	7	2	5	2	—	4
198	12	2	7	1	5	5	3	1
199	5	1	10	5	5	4	2	1
200	6	1	4	1	2	2	1	1
201	7	2	8	2	3	3	3	1
202	5	1	4	2	6	1	1	—
203	5	6	8	4	6	4	2	1
204	4	1	5	—	3	1	2	—
205	3	1	1	4	1	2	—	2
206	2	1	2	3	4	1	—	1
207	3	1	3	—	1	1	—	1
208	5	1	3	—	1	—	—	—
209	—	1	3	3	1	—	—	—
210	1	1	—	1	—	1	—	1
211	1	—	—	—	—	—	—	—
212	—	—	—	—	—	—	1	—
213	—	—	—	—	—	1	—	—
214	—	—	1	—	1	—	—	—
215	—	—	1	—	—	—	—	—
216	—	—	1	—	—	—	—	—
217	—	—	—	—	—	—	—	—
218	1	—	—	—	—	—	—	—

Table LXXII
Width of Head

(Mm.)	N	N(I)	NNW	NNW(I)	NW	NW(I)	NWW	NWW(I)
131	—	—	1	—	—	—	—	—
132	—	—	—	—	—	—	—	—
133	—	—	—	—	—	—	—	1
134	—	—	1	1	—	—	—	—
135	—	—	—	—	—	—	—	—
136	—	—	—	—	—	—	—	1
137	—	—	1	—	—	—	—	—
138	1	—	1	—	—	—	—	—
139	1	—	—	2	—	—	1	1
140	—	1	1	—	—	—	—	—
141	—	1	—	—	—	1	—	—
142	—	1	3	1	2	1	1	1
143	4	1	—	—	4	2	—	—
144	2	3	6	1	6	3	—	—
145	1	—	4	2	—	1	—	—
146	5	—	6	2	5	2	2	3
147	4	—	12	4	4	5	3	1
148	7	1	6	1	2	3	—	4
149	16	3	8	3	7	5	2	3
150	7	3	4	3	5	3	2	1
151	4	2	6	3	7	2	2	2
152	8	5	12	3	13	3	3	2
153	13	3	10	6	13	9	2	2
154	6	2	7	5	7	3	—	3
155	2	—	3	2	5	1	1	1
156	9	2	7	2	6	3	2	1
157	4	2	6	3	2	2	2	—
158	6	3	6	3	3	—	1	3
159	2	2	7	1	—	3	—	—
160	—	—	2	—	—	3	1	—
161	3	1	1	1	2	—	—	—
162	1	—	2	1	—	1	—	—
163	—	—	1	1	—	—	1	—
164	—	—	2	—	—	—	2	1
165	1	—	—	—	1	1	1	—
166	1	—	1	—	—	—	1	—
167	1	—	—	—	1	—	—	—
168	—	—	1	—	—	—	—	—
169	—	—	1	—	—	—	—	—

7. CEPHALIC INDEX (Table LXXIII).

As shown in Chapter III, the indices of the Africans are distinctly lower, on the whole, than even those for the long-headed European populations, such as the Scottish and English, and for the American Indian populations represented, some of which, such as the Delaware, might well have mingled their strains with those of the American Negroes. The genealogical groups have the following values:

Class	Without Indian			With Indian		
	No.	Average,(%)	σ	No.	Average,(%)	σ
N	109	76.9	± 3.22			
N(I)				36	76.4	± 2.98
NNW	129	77.1	± 3.77			
NNW(I)				51	76.9	± 4.27
NW	95	77.2	± 2.88			
NW(I)				57	77.0	± 3.29
NWW	30	78.3	± 3.58			
NWW(I)				31	76.8	± 3.86
W	727	77.95	± 3.01			

There is a somewhat irregular progression from the longest head (lowest average index) in the N and N(I) classes (those without any White mixture) to those groups with greater amount of White blood present, differences which are confirmed when we add the White American series to the table. In every instance, also, the Indian element seems to contribute to longer-headedness and lower average indices.

Whether this signifies that the influence was mainly from those Indian peoples who were themselves long-headed I cannot say. It is, however, of interest to quote Hrdlička's summary of the distribution of head-form as far as it concerns the eastern and southern tribes[1]: "Among the extremely dolichocephalic were the Delawares.. moderate dolichocephaly, with occasional extreme forms, was and is very prevalent, being found in the Algonquin and Plains tribes ... Pure brachycephaly existed in Florida, and prevailed in the mound region ... It is .. represented ... in a lesser degree among ... the Seminole. Mesocephaly existed principally among the ... Cherokee, and some of the Sioux and Iroquois." Wissler[2], in his table for cephalic index arranged according to culture areas, gives for the southeastern area, one tribe with an index of 75, 2 with 77, 1 with 79, 1 with 80, and 3 with 84, while for the eastern woodlands, there is 1 with an average index of 71, 1 with 72, 3 with 73, 1 with 75, 4 with 78, 1 with 79, 1 with 82, 1 with 83, and 1 with 86. Thus it might be possible that the Indian influence could account for this increased tendency toward dolichocephaly manifested on the

---

[1] Hrdlička, (III), pp. 55—56.
[2] Wissler, (I), p. 322.

part of the groups who have partial Indian ancestry; certainly the influence of the White and Negro ancestors toward changing the index with differing amounts of racial mixture seems to be clearly apparent.

Table LXXIII
Cephalic Index

%	N	N(I)	NNW[1]	NNW(I)[2]	NW	NW(I)	NWW	NWW(I)
65.5	—	—	—	—	—	—	—	—
66.5	1	—	—	—	—	—	—	—
67.5	—	—	—	—	—	—	—	—
68.5	—	—	—	—	—	—	1	—
69.5	—	1	2	1	—	2	—	1
70.5	3	—	2	—	1	—	—	—
71.5	2	1	2	4	2	1	1	1
72.5	7	3	7	1	5	2	—	4
73.5	3	1	12	2	5	4	1	2
74.5	8	5	10	4	9	6	2	3
75.5	16	8	15	7	12	7	4	5
76.5	20	4	13	9	12	5	2	2
77.5	12	2	12	5	10	12	1	1
78.5	16	3	15	6	14	6	5	1
79.5	7	3	11	4	5	3	2	4
80.5	3	3	10	2	12	3	3	2
81.5	2	1	4	2	5	2	2	3
82.5	3	—	4	—	1	1	3	—
83.5	3	1	4	—	1	1	2	—
84.5	2	—	2	—	1	1	1	1
85.5	1	—	2	—	—	—	—	1
86.5	—	—	—	1	—	1	—	—
87.5	—	—	1	—	—	—	—	—
88.5	—	—	—	1	—	—	—	—

The variability of the N class, for this index, is only third lowest. the NW being the least variable, and the N(I) next lowest. Fischer (p. 63) gives the following results for cephalic index in his comparable study of the Bastards:

Class	No.	Average, (%)	σ
"Eu"	12	76.2	± 2.09
"Mitt"	32	75.5	± 2.51
"Hott"	23	76.1	± 2.31

Here the longest-headed class is that which represents equal amounts of mixture between the component ancestral elements, a result which approximates that of my series. The class nearest the Hottentots in racial make-up has an insignificantly longer head, on the average, than that nearest the Europeans in ancestry. The variability of all these classes is smaller than that of any of the genealogical groups of American Negroes being considered in this chapter.

---

[1] Add 62.5—1.   [2] Add 64.5—1; 90.5—1.

8. Height of Head (Table LXXIV).

Little difference between the averages of the various classes is to be noticed in the following table of the statistical constants for the genealogical groups. They are all concentrated very closely about the average for the entire Howard University series, which is 134.06 mm.

Class	Without Indian			With Indian		
	No.	Average, (mm.)	σ	No.	Average, (mm.)	σ
N	102	134.2	± 4.19			
N(I)				33	132.3	± 4.67
NNW	113	134.0	± 4.63			
NNW(I)				44	134.3	± 3.92
NW	87	134.4	± 4.01			
NW(I)				45	134.3	± 4.46
NWW	23	134.8	± 3.56			
NWW(I)				26	133.7	± 4.21

Table LXXIV
Height of Head

Mm.	N	N(I)	NNW[1]	NNW(I)	NW	NW(I)	NWW	NWW(I)
121	—	—	3	—	—	—	—	—
22	2	1	1	—	—	—	—	—
23	1	—	1	—	—	—	—	1
24	2	2	1	—	1	1	—	—
125	1	—	—	1	1	—	—	1
26	—	2	2	—	1	—	—	—
27	1	1	1	3	2	3	—	—
28	2	1	3	1	1	3	—	—
29	4	2	2	—	4	2	2	4
130	5	2	7	2	6	1	—	—
31	7	2	9	3	5	4	3	—
32	3	3	7	2	8	2	5	2
33	10	3	11	6	5	1	—	4
34	8	4	9	3	8	3	1	1
135	9	1	6	3	6	3	1	1
36	12	3	16	10	9	2	1	4
37	16	1	11	2	7	5	3	4
38	7	2	4	2	8	9	1	2
39	5	2	8	2	7	1	5	1
140	5	—	4	1	3	3	1	1
41	2	1	5	2	5	2	—	—
42	—	—	1	1	—	—	—	—

Comparison for the mean of the entire series of this study was made in the third chapter with those for the populations given by Martin, and with those for other peoples available. Such comparison, with

---

[1] Add 145—1.

the consideration of the average values of the table above, shows us that the small differences between the groups of different genealogical background are what might be expected. The difference in head height of the Old Americans (138.64 mm.), as has been explained, is probably due to the difference between Hrdlička's technique of measurement and mine. In Martin's table, the Bugu have an average ear height of the head of 120, the Swiss of 121 mm., while in bregma-basion height on skulls, the Swiss have an average height of 131 mm., the Sioux the same, the Spaniards one of 133 mm., and the Fan also 133 mm., with the Bavarians at 134 mm. Thus, the small and irregular differences between groups of differing amounts of Negro, White, and Indian ancestry would not be expected to show decisive differences in their average values for height of the head. There is no change, however small, even if we separate those groups with Indian ancestry from those which are without it; nor does the consideration of all the eight means change matters in this respect. The NWW class is least variable, the N(I) the most so, while the N group is fourth lowest in this respect.

9. MINIMUM FRONTAL WIDTH (Table LXXV).

In the discussion of this trait for the sample as a whole in Chapter III, the mean for the entire Howard series was found to be somewhat smaller than that for the Old Americans, though greater than the average of the Ashanti, a West African people. The differences, however, are slight, as they are in Martin's table which gives values for various peoples. There also the American Indian populations (represented by skeletal material) are close to the Africans, although both are smaller in this dimension than the Europeans. For the genealogical groups of the Howard series, the statistical constants are:

Series	Without Indian			With Indian		
	No.	Average, (mm.)	σ	No.	Average, (mm.)	σ
N	109	106.2	± 6.44			
N(I)				36	106.0	± 5.88
NNW	129	106.55	± 5.15			
NNW(I)				51	108.2	± 7.18
NW	95	106.4	± 5.55			
NW(I)				57	106.5	± 5.36
NWW	30	105.7	± 4.40			
NWW(I)				31	104.2	± 5.18
W	247	105.9	± 4.24			

There is almost no consistency in the differences between the averages of this series, although all the means for those classes with smaller amounts of White ancestry than is comprised in the NWW and NWW(I) exhibit larger average forehead widths than do the

Old Americans. Nor is there any light thrown on the meaning of the differences between the class averages when they are separated into those groups with and without Indian ancestry. The probability seems to be that this trait holds little significance in the consideration of the validity of genealogies in Negro-White crosses, due to the lack of racial differences between unmixed populations representing the two races. A survey of the mean square deviations in the table above shows that the N group have the second largest variation, the NNW(I) being most variable, and the lowest being found in the NWW, the NNW following it in this respect.

Table LXXV
Minimum Frontal Width

Mm.	N[1]	N(I)[2]	NNW[3]	NNW(I)[4]	NW[5]	NW(I)	NWW	NWW(I)[6]
95	1	—	—	—	1	—	—	2
96	—	—	3	—	1	2	—	—
97	—	1	1	—	—	—	—	1
98	—	1	2	1	1	2	—	1
99	1	1	1	1	3	1	1	—
100	1	—	6	—	1	3	2	—
01	4	2	4	2	3	1	5	3
02	3	4	10	3	10	3	2	1
03	7	3	9	1	6	5	—	4
04	8	3	9	6	7	2	4	2
105	15	4	17	2	12	6	—	2
06	17	1	12	3	10	6	2	4
07	10	3	8	7	9	3	2	1
08	7	2	4	5	5	2	3	3
09	2	2	6	4	5	7	5	1
110	9	1	9	5	6	1	1	3
11	5	1	7	3	6	4	—	—
12	6	1	5	1	—	3	—	—
13	5	—	3	1	3	2	1	2
14	—	—	3	2	2	—	1	—
115	3	1	4	2	1	—	1	—
16	1	3	3	1	1	1	1	—
17	1	—	—	—	—	1	—	—
18	1	—	1	—	1	—	—	—
19	—	—	—	—	—	1	—	—
120	1	—	1	—	—	1	—	—
21	—	—	—	—	—	—	—	—
22	—	1	—	—	—	—	—	—

[1] Add 147—1.   [2] Add 93—1.
[3] Add 126—1.   [4] Add 150—1.
[5] Add 141—1.   [6] Add 91—1.

10. Distance between Inner Corners of Eyes
(Table LXXVI).

This trait is one in which distinct differences are manifested between White and Negro populations. It has not been recorded, to my knowledge, for Indians. For the genealogical groups, we have the following averages and mean square deviations:

Class	Without Indian			With Indian		
	No.	Average, (mm.)	σ	No.	Average, (mm.)	σ
N	109	34.4	± 2.20			
N(I)				36	34.2	± 3.78
NNW	129	33.4	± 2.04			
NNW(I)				51	33.6	± 2.57
NW	95	32.6	± 3.62			
NW(I)				57	32.9	± 3.21
NWW	30	32.3	± 1.90			
NWW(I)				31	32.0	± 2.53

Here we have a result that is directly in keeping with those for the other traits discussed; there is a consistency between the means of the genealogical classes, and what would be expected were they representative of actual amounts of crossing. There are slight divergences from an even trend from the unmixed Negro to the groups of least Negro ancestry, but this disappears if the two groupings with and without Indian be made. We see that there is a steady difference from larger to smaller distance between the inner corners of the eyes from the N through the NNW, NW and NWW classes, and the same is true if we take only those groups where there has been Indian admixture. Except in the case of the two classes where there is more White than Negro ancestry, the Indian-mixed are, for the other three pairs, greater in this dimension that the corresponding ones without Indian blood. Whether this represents a definite influence exerted by the Indian cannot be said. The variability of the N group is the third lowest, that of the NWW is lowest, and between them lies the NNW. The greatest variability is that of the N(I) group. The measurement taken by Fischer on the Bastards, which is called "Interorbitalbreite", is not, as was the case in the series quoted from Tremearne in Chapter III, an interorbital width measured to the outer edges of the orbital rims, but rather a distance which corresponds even more closely to the one measured by myself between the inner corners of the eyes. Fischer finds, for the Bastards, as I have found in the case of the American Negroes, that this distance is greater in the Negroid type than in the White, and that the mixed types stand between the two unmixed groups:

Bavarians:			32.3
Bastards	{ "Eu"	34.5 }	34.9
	{ "Mitt"	34.4 }	
	{ "Hott"	35.9 }	
Hottentots:			37.3

Table LXXVI
Distance between Inner Corners of Eyes

Mm.	N	N(I)	NNW	NNW(I)	NW	NW(I)	NWW	NWW(I)
21	—	—	—	—	1	—	—	—
22	—	—	—	—	—	—	—	—
23	—	—	—	—	—	—	—	—
24	—	—	—	—	1	—	—	—
25	—	—	—	—	—	—	—	—
26	—	—	1	—	1	1	—	—
27	1	—	2	—	2	1	—	2
28	—	—	1	—	3	2	—	—
29	1	—	8	4	3	2	2	3
30	3	1	9	2	7	5	2	5
31	9	5	14	6	13	7	8	4
32	9	5	16	8	10	7	5	1
33	16	6	16	4	14	10	5	7
34	18	6	17	6	13	6	5	6
35	18	4	18	6	6	6	2	—
36	17	2	8	8	6	3	—	1
37	8	2	9	5	5	2	—	2
38	4	2	2	1	4	2	1	—
39	3	2	3	1	1	—	—	—
40	—	—	2	—	2	—	—	—
41	2	—	2	—	2	—	—	—
42	—	—	—	—	—	—	—	—
43	—	1	1	—	—	2	—	—
44	—	—	—	—	1	—	—	—

11. Distance between Outer Corners of Eyes
(Table LXXVII).

There is not as decisive a difference between populations of pure White and unmixed Negro stocks for which we have records of measurements of this trait as was the case with the one just discussed. The data which have been gathered for African populations seem to be about the same, on the average, as for Europeans, as far as this trait is concerned, while figures for Indian groups seem to be lacking. The average for this sample of Howard University students given in Chapter III, it will be remembered, was the greatest of any of the populations recorded in the comparative table given there. The averages and mean square variabilities for the several genealogical groups may now be considered for this trait:

The Validity of the Genealogies

Class	Without Indian			With Indian		
	No.	Average, (mm.)	σ	No.	Average, (mm.)	σ
N	109	104.1	± 4.42			
N(I)				36	103.1	± 5.97
NNW	126	101.9	± 5.64			
NNW(I)				51	103.4	± 4.79
NW	95	102.2	± 4.30			
NW(I)				56	101.5	± 4.82
NWW	30	100.8	± 4.10			
NWW(I)				31	100.4	± 4.63

Table LXXVII
Distance between Outer Corners of Eyes

Mm.	N	N(I)[1]	NNW[2]	NNW(I)	NW	NW(I)	NWW	NWW(I)
91	—	1	3	—	—	—	—	—
92	—	—	2	—	1	2	—	1
93	—	1	1	—	—	2	—	2
94	1	1	4	1	2	1	1	1
95	2	—	6	2	1	1	3	—
96	—	2	8	2	2	—	1	1
97	2	1	3	1	2	2	4	2
98	8	1	6	1	7	5	1	4
99	7	1	9	3	7	8	2	3
100	2	2	5	4	9	2	1	3
01	7	6	12	6	15	6	4	3
02	6	2	11	3	15	6	2	2
03	12	3	11	2	3	5	2	2
04	13	2	8	3	6	3	4	1
105	12	2	13	5	6	2	1	2
06	8	3	5	6	4	4	3	2
07	5	—	3	4	3	1	—	—
08	9	1	5	2	6	2	—	—
09	3	2	4	—	2	1	—	1
110	4	—	1	2	1	1	—	—
11	1	2	1	1	1	—	1	—
12	1	—	—	1	1	—	—	—
13	3	1	2	—	—	1	—	1
14	—	1	1	1	1	—	—	—
115	3	—	—	1	—	—	—	—
16	—	—	—	—	—	1	—	—

In this table a somewhat irregular change from greatest width between the outer corners of the eyes in the unmixed Negro group, to a lesser average value for this distance in the more White than Negro classes, may be noted. The trait maintains its irregular amount of difference from one class to another even when we separate the averages above into those for groups with and without

[1] Add 119—1.   [2] Add 122—1; 127—1.

Indian, and consider each alone. The average for the unmixed Negro group is larger than that for the Vai of West Africa, or for any of the populations contained in the comparative table given by Martin, either for African or European populations. Indeed, the lowest mean given is as large as the largest in Martin's table. The significance of this, in the absence of any kind of control as to the exact measurement meant by Virchow and by the students who measured the other populations, cannot be evaluated, but the most likely hypothesis is that there has been some difference in the technique of measuring it between myself and other students. Here again the N group is the third least variable, the NWW being the least, and the NW next. The greatest variability is exhibited by the N(I) class, as was the case in the trait of distance between the inner corners of the eyes, also.

12. INTERPUPILLARY DISTANCE (Table LXXVIII, p. 199).

The measurements of interpupillary distance might be expected to follow the general tendency which was seen in the preceding two traits, to change from largest in the unmixed Negro class to smallest in the more White than Negro. Following are the statistical constants for the genealogical classifications:

Class	Without Indian			With Indian		
	No.	Average, (mm.)	σ	No.	Average, (mm.)	σ
N	108	68.1	± 3.03			
N(I)				36	67.0	± 4.05
NNW	125	66.4	± 3.68			
NNW(I)				51	67.2	± 3.66
NW	93	66.4	± 3.40			
NW(I)				56	65.3	± 3.91
NWW	29	64.6	± 3.10			
NWW(I)				31	63.5	± 3.71
W[1]	100	63.4	± 4.19			

In general, the tendency which is exhibited is that which might be expected both in the groups with and without Indian admixture. The N class exhibits the lowest of the eight variabilities, while the N(I) group show the greatest variation.

13. HEIGHT OF NOSE (Table LXXIX, p. 200).

The height of the nose is a characteristic which is quite different in Negroes, on the one hand, and Whites and Indians on the other. This difference is obvious and holds despite the difficulty of obtaining an accurate measurement of the distance. The differences in it as a racial trait came out strongly when comparison was made in

---

[1] The series used here for W is that of the Western Reserve White male cadavera.

The Validity of the Genealogies

Chapter III between various populations for the trait. Passing to our genealogical classes, we find the means and variabilities for them to be:

	Without Indian			With Indian		
Class	No.	Average, (mm.)	σ	No.	Average, (mm.)	σ
N	109	53.1	± 3.16			
N(I)				36	53.75	± 3.62
NNW	129	53.3	± 3.71			
NNW(I)				51	54.1	± 2.93
NW	95	54.7	± 3.24			
NW(I)				57	54.15	± 3.15
NWW	30	53.7	± 3.45			
NWW(I)				31	52.4	± 2.97
W	247	53.5	± 3.36			

The results are ambiguous. I do not know whether this is due to an actual equality of the height of the nose in all the groups, or whether the differences in nose form give the result of an apparent equality of all the groups. It is very likely that the low value for W

Table LXXVIII
Interpupillary Distance

Mm.	N	N(I)	NNW	NNW(I)	NW	NW(I)	NWW	NWW(I)
56	—	—	—	—	—	1	—	—
57	—	1	1	—	—	—	—	—
58	—	—	1	—	—	1	1	5
59	—	—	2	—	1	1	1	2
60	1	1	4	3	3	1	1	2
61	1	1	4	2	3	3	—	1
62	2	2	7	—	5	6	4	1
63	3	1	10	4	9	4	4	4
64	7	3	11	3	7	7	5	3
65	13	6	9	5	9	8	3	3
66	9	2	10	6	10	5	1	1
67	12	3	17	4	10	7	1	6
68	12	5	12	4	14	1	5	2
69	18	2	14	5	9	4	1	—
70	6	1	7	4	3	1	2	—
71	10	5	7	7	3	3	—	—
72	6	—	3	1	1	1	—	1
73	2	—	4	1	3	1	—	—
74	1	1	—	1	2	—	—	—
75	3	2	1	1	1	—	—	—
76	1	—	1	—	—	—	—	—
77	1	—	—	—	—	—	—	—
78	—	—	—	—	—	—	—	—
79	—	—	—	—	—	1	—	—

may be due to a difference between Hrdlička's method of measuring and my own. The mean square deviation of the N class is the fourth lowest of the series (although that for the NW(I) is only .01 mm. lower than it), while the lowest variability is that for the NWW(I), and the next lowest that of the NNW(I).

Table LXXIX
Height of Nose

Mm.	N	N(I)	NNW	NNW(I)	NW	NW(I)	NWW	NWW(I)
42	—	—	1	—	—	—	—	—
43	—	1	—	—	1	—	—	—
44	1	—	1	—	1	—	—	—
45	1	—	1	—	—	—	—	—
46	—	—	—	—	—	—	—	—
47	2	—	6	—	—	—	1	1
48	2	1	3	2	1	1	—	1
49	5	—	7	2	2	1	2	1
50	4	2	7	1	3	6	4	4
51	19	5	18	4	7	3	1	3
52	18	7	9	6	20	5	3	4
53	12	3	9	4	11	6	4	3
54	11	2	14	10	10	15	3	4
55	10	3	13	9	10	4	4	3
56	8	5	13	2	10	5	1	1
57	3	2	10	4	6	5	4	—
58	5	1	6	3	5	1	1	2
59	7	1	7	2	4	1	—	1
60	1	1	1	1	2	1	—	—
61	—	2	3	1	2	1	1	—
62	—	—	—	—	—	—	1	—
63	—	—	—	—	—	2	—	—

14. WIDTH OF NOSE (Table LXXX).

In this trait, if in any, we should expect to find clear distinctions between the means of the genealogical groups were the genealogies on which they are based themselves reliable. The difference between the White and the Negro nose, as regards width, is so characteristic that reference to the average values for the various populations given in Chapter III is almost unnecessary. The Indian alae are characteristically somewhat broader than those of the Whites, but not so broad as are those of the Negroes. The genealogical groups give the following statistical constants for this trait:

The Validity of the Genealogies

Class	Without Indian			With Indian		
	No.	Average,(mm.)	σ	No.	Average,(mm.)	σ
N	109	43.4	± 2.81			
N(I)				36	41.2	± 4.26
NNW	129	41.35	± 3.44			
NNW(I)				51	40.85	± 4.08
NW	95	40.0	± 3.01			
NW(I)				57	39.7	± 4.76
NWW	30	37.5	± 3.86			
NWW(I)				31	39.2	± 4.53
W	247	36.1	± 2.51			

Table LXXX
Nasal Width (al.-al.)

Mm.	N	N(I)	NNW	NNW(I)	NW	NW(I)	NWW	NWW(I)
29	—	—	—	—	—	1	—	—
30	—	—	—	1	—	—	—	—
31	—	—	—	—	—	1	—	1
32	—	1	—	1	—	—	2	—
33	—	2	1	—	1	—	2	1
34	—	—	1	—	4	4	4	3
35	—	—	1	3	2	2	2	1
36	—	1	2	2	4	1	5	5
37	2	2	8	5	8	4	3	2
38	3	2	13	5	12	6	2	3
39	4	5	9	1	13	9	1	1
40	7	2	18	5	8	5	1	1
41	8	4	14	3	13	6	1	5
42	16	3	16	5	11	4	3	3
43	20	3	9	3	9	4	2	—
44	10	3	5	8	3	6	1	—
45	15	3	12	4	3	1	—	2
46	11	3	5	3	3	—	—	—
47	5	—	8	—	1	3	1	1
48	2	—	2	—	—	--	—	2
49	5	1	1	2	—	—	—	—
50	—	—	1	—	—	—	—	—
51	—	—	—	—	—	—	—	—
52	1	1	—	—	—	—	—	—

When the range of the width of the nose for the entire Howard series is considered (29—52 mm.) the fact that we have in the table above a difference of almost 6 mm. between the N and the NWW classes seems highly significant, as is the further fact that the White series employed to continue the comparison is entirely consistent with the changes between the different genealogical classes. Except for the NWW(I) group, which tends to exhibit a somewhat wider average nose than the corresponding class without

Indian admixture (a difference without statistical significance), the groups with partial Indian ancestry have narrower noses than their corresponding classes without this mixture. Such a result would also be expected, since the Indian nose as has been remarked, is narrower than that of the Negro but not as narrow as that of the White. The mean square variability of the N class in this trait is smaller than that of any of the other groups.

Fischer (p. 92) obtained the following values:

Bavarians:		33.3
Bastards	"Eu"	40.0
	"Mitt"	40.9
	"Hott"	42.0
Hottentotts:		41.0

The numbers of cases from which these averages were computed, and the standard deviations are, unfortunately, not given. But if we compare the means with the results presented above for the American Negro genealogical groups, we see at once that there is the same impressive change from greatest breadth on the part of the least Caucasoid class, to smallest nasal width on that of the most White, that manifests itself when differences between groups having the greatest amount of Hottentot ancestry, and lesser amounts of it are compared.

15 and 16. DEPTH OF NOSE.

(sn. — tip), (Table LXXXI), and *(cr.— tip)*, (Table LXXXII).

In these traits, as well as in the preceding, differences between the Negro groups and those liberally mixed with White and Indian would be expected to be found. Although as has been said in Chapter III, there are but few comparative data, the averages for such populations as Martin gives show that the Caucasian nose is more elevated than the Negroid, which is typically flat in the true Negro of West Africa. The statistical constants for the genealogical groups follow:

Sn.-tip.

	Without Indian			*With Indian*		
Class	No.	Average, (mm.)	σ	No.	Average, (mm.)	σ
N	109	21.7	± 2.14			
N(I)				36	21.7	± 1.91
NNW	126	21.0	± 1.86			
NNW(I)				51	21.2	± 2.08
NW	94	20.5	± 1.78			
NW(I)				57	21.5	± 2.23
NWW	30	21.4	± 2.79			
NWW(I)				31	21.3	± 1.73

The Validity of the Genealogies

	Without Indian			Cr.-tip With Indian		
Class	No.	Average,(mm.)	σ	No.	Average,(mm.)	σ
N	109	35.9	± 2.29			
N(I)				36	35.9	± 2.48
NNW	126	35.1	± 2.17			
NNW(I)				51	35.1	± 1.93
NW	94	35.5	± 1.90			
NW(I)				57	35.65	± 2.67
NWW	30	35.1	± 2.10			
NWW(I)				31	35.3	± 2.20

The results do not show any significant differences. In the former measurement the N group is the third most variable; the NWW(I) the least variable. In the latter the most variable class is the NW(I), the least the NW, the N class being the third highest in this respect.

Table LXXXI
Nasal Depth (sn.-tip)

Mm.	N	N(I)	NNW	NNW(I)	NW	NW(I)	NWW	NWW(I)
16	—	—	—	1	—	—	—	—
17	1	1	3	—	2	—	3	—
18	9	1	7	6	2	6	2	1
19	12	4	16	4	4	6	3	6
20	6	9	27	7	18	5	5	4
21	24	6	24	8	28	13	2	5
22	20	5	23	12	14	12	4	6
23	19	6	15	6	12	3	4	7
24	8	2	5	5	10	8	1	—
25	5	1	5	1	3	2	3	2
26	2	1	1	1	—	1	3	—
27	3	—	—	—	1	1	—	—
28	—	—	—	—	—	—	—	—

Table LXXXII
Nasal Depth (cr.-tip)

Mm.	N	N(I)	NNW	NNW(I)	NW	NW(I)	NWW	NWW(I)
28	1	—	—	—	—	—	—	—
29	—	—	1	—	—	—	—	—
30	—	—	—	—	—	—	—	1
31	2	2	3	1	1	2	3	2
32	2	1	10	3	4	4	—	—
33	8	2	12	7	7	5	3	1
34	16	5	28	9	17	11	6	7
35	20	7	22	11	19	9	4	6
36	18	4	14	7	14	7	5	5
37	15	5	16	7	20	7	6	4
38	11	4	13	3	9	2	1	2
39	8	4	4	3	—	4	2	3
40	7	1	2	—	1	4	—	—
41	1	—	1	—	2	1	—	—
42	—	1	—	—	—	—	—	—
43	—	—	—	—	—	—	—	—
44	—	—	—	—	—	1	—	—

17. Upper Facial Height (Table LXXXIII).

As has been remarked in the third chapter, there are few comparative data available for this trait, and these are only precariously comparable because of the use of the naso-frontal sutures as one of the landmarks for the heights of the face. The available averages for West African peoples fall well below the average for the entire adult male sample of this study. The Negroid face seems to be somewhat larger in most dimensions than that of the White or Indian. The results of the following table are inconclusive:

	Without Indian			With Indian		
Class	No.	Average,(mm)	σ	No.	Average,(mm.)	σ
N	108	71.7	± 4.01			
N(I)				36	71.0	± 5.69
NNW	129	71.0	± 4.23			
NNW(I)				51	72.2	± 3.87
NW	95	71.45	± 3.93			
NW(I)				57	71.75	± 3.35
NWW	30	70.3	± 4.17			
NWW(I)				31	70.3	± 3.25

Table LXXXIII
Upper Facial Height

Mm.	N	N(I)[1]	NNW	NNW(I)	NW	NW(I)	NWW	NWW(I)
61	1	—	—	—	—	—	—	—
62	—	—	1	—	1	—	1	—
63	—	—	1	—	1	—	—	—
64	2	—	1	1	5	1	2	2
65	3	4	13	1	2	—	—	1
66	4	—	4	1	1	3	3	—
67	5	2	12	4	3	3	3	3
68	8	2	8	4	9	4	3	1
69	8	1	10	2	5	4	—	9
70	13	—	14	2	8	3	4	1
71	13	6	10	8	12	7	2	4
72	8	3	8	3	13	9	3	2
73	9	5	9	6	5	5	3	1
74	8	3	7	3	6	6	—	3
75	6	2	11	6	10	4	2	2
76	4	—	5	3	7	6	3	2
77	8	1	5	4	1	—	—	—
78	1	3	3	—	4	1	—	—
79	3	—	4	3	1	—	—	—
80	3	—	2	—	—	—	1	—
81	1	2	—	—	—	1	—	—
82	—	—	—	—	1	—	—	—
83	—	—	1	—	—	—	—	—

[1] Add 54—1; 56—1.

The N group is the fourth most variable, the lowest variability being shown by the NWW(I) class, it being followed in this respect by the NW(I), NNW(I), and NW groups, respectively.

18. TOTAL FACIAL HEIGHT (Table LXXXIV).

The total facial height of the Whites and Indians is greater on the average than that of the Africans. With this in mind, and not forgetting the unreliability of this measurement, which has been stressed so often in the preceding pages, the comparison of the genealogical classes in this trait may be undertaken:

Class	Without Indian			With Indian		
	No.	Average, (mm.)	σ	No.	Average, (mm.)	σ
N	108	123.9	± 5.59			
N(I)				36	123.25	± 7.34
NNW	127	122.7	± 6.20			
NNW(I)				51	123.45	± 5.86
NW	95	122.6	± 6.03			
NW(I)				56	121.9	± 7.13
NWW	30	120.1	± 5.93			
NWW(I)				31	119.45	± 5.94
W	247	119.3	± 6.72			

In this table a general change in the means of the classes from that of unmixed Negro to the one more White than Negro, in a direction opposite to that which would be expected, is to be noted; from the highest face for the N group to the lowest in the NWW(I). What might make for such results, assuming, on the basis of the averages derived from the other traits measured and presented thus far that the genealogies are reliable is, in the main, difficult to state. There is always the possibility to be taken into consideration that adequate African material might change the expectation of our results, or there might be other causes of equal importance, one of which would seem, indeed, to be the unreliability of this measurement. The first hypothesis becomes somewhat more significant when we add to the series of means for the genealogical classes of this sample that of the Old White Americans. Here, we see, we have a result which carries out the tendency toward a lower face as one approaches a condition of greater White ancestry. However, since the comparability of Hrdlička's technique and mine is unknown, conclusions drawn from comparison of his White data with mine are precarious. All that can be said on the basis of the data of this study and what comparative material has been found, is that in this trait the averages for the genealogical classes do not follow our expectations.

Table LXXXIV
Total Facial Height

Mm.	N	N(I)	NNW	NNW(I)	NW	NW(I)	NWW	NWW(I)
102	—	—	—	—	—	1	—	—
03	—	—	—	—	—	1	—	—
04	—	—	—	—	—	—	—	—
105	—	—	—	—	—	—	—	—
06	—	—	—	—	—	1	—	—
07	—	—	—	1	1	—	—	—
08	—	1	—	—	—	—	—	—
09	—	—	—	—	1	—	—	—
110	1	—	1	—	—	—	1	1
11	1	—	2	—	3	2	1	3
12	—	2	1	1	2	1	—	—
13	1	2	3	—	1	2	2	4
14	1	—	3	1	2	3	2	—
115	2	1	7	2	4	—	2	1
16	2	—	6	1	2	1	1	3
17	4	2	3	—	2	1	1	1
18	7	1	9	3	1	1	2	1
19	6	2	6	4	1	2	3	1
120	8	2	6	5	11	3	2	3
21	4	3	14	—	10	5	4	1
22	10	1	11	1	7	1	1	2
23	4	1	4	7	5	3	—	—
24	12	1	5	2	7	3	2	2
125	5	2	4	2	7	8	—	2
26	3	3	10	7	5	4	—	—
27	7	2	2	2	1	3	2	2
28	5	2	2	3	2	2	1	2
29	7	2	7	2	4	2	—	2
130	4	1	5	2	5	1	1	—
31	4	1	3	—	5	1	1	—
32	5	1	2	3	4	2	—	—
33	2	—	3	1	—	—	—	—
34	—	1	5	—	—	—	1	—
135	2	—	1	—	2	2	—	—
36	—	—	1	—	—	—	—	—
37	—	—	—	—	—	—	—	—
38	—	1	1	—	—	—	—	—
39	—	—	—	1	—	—	—	—
140	—	—	—	—	—	—	—	—
41	1	1	—	—	—	—	—	—

The Validity of the Genealogies

The smallest variability is that of the N class. Fischer's material follows the line of change from most to least European ancestry in the manner which might be expected from the comparative table of averages in the last chapter. This can be seen also from his averages for Bavarians, mixed groups, and unmixed Hottentots (p. 77):

100 Bavarians:			121.3
Bastards	"Eu"	119.1	
	"Mitt"	112.9	114.2
	"Hott"	114.7	
8 and 7 Hottentots:			106.1

Here there is change from the greatest facial height on the part of the group with most European ancestry to a smaller value for the trait on the part of those with more Hottentot blood. However, this is not as regular as complete accordance with what would be expected would require, since the class preponderantly Hottentot has a higher facial height than the class with about the same amount of Hottentot and European ancestry. This result, therefore, while not as contrary to the expected results as is that for the genealogical groups of my sample, is at the same time of such a nature as to allow the statement that the result obtained by me is not dissimilar to that given by a similar analysis of the Bastard mixed Negroid-White population, and that the trait under consideration is one in which irregular action may perhaps be expected in a study of racial crossing.

19. BIZYGOMATIC WIDTH (Table LXXXV).

In this trait there seems to be little racial difference between Negroes and Whites, while the Indian populations are distinguished by the large measurement. As might be expected from the table of averages in the third chapter, the statistical constants follow generally the same change from wider to narrower facial widths:

Class	Without Indian			With Indian		
	No.	Average, (mm.)	σ	No.	Average, (mm.)	σ
N	108	140.7	± 5.40			
N(I)				36	139.6	± 7.07
NNW	129	138.4	± 6.87			
NNW(I)				51	139.75	± 5.32
NW	95	139.0	± 6.00			
NW(I)				57	139.5	± 5.60
NWW	30	137.3	± 7.18			
NWW(I)				31	137.1	± 5.82
W	247	138.6	± 4.80			

If the American Indian elements in this Negro-White series had influenced the facial width, it would be expected to be visible in the differences in the average values between the class having Indian ancestry and not having it. But this apparently is not the case. This may be accounted for either by the fact that the Indian crossing has occurred so long ago that the Indian trait has diffused with considerable thoroughness throughout the descendants and is not

Table LXXXV
Bizygomatic Width

Mm.	N	N(I)[1]	NNW[2]	NNW(I)	NW	NW(I)	NWW	NWW(I)
123	—	—	—	—	1	—	—	—
24	—	—	2	—	—	—	—	—
25	—	—	2	—	—	—	—	—
26	—	—	—	—	—	—	1	—
27	2	1	—	—	—	—	1	1
28	—	2	2	1	4	2	2	—
29	—	—	4	—	—	—	—	1
130	—	—	1	2	2	—	1	—
31	3	2	4	—	2	4	2	3
32	2	—	3	2	7	3	—	2
33	2	1	10	1	5	3	2	3
34	4	4	6	3	3	2	2	3
35	2	1	5	2	2	8	3	2
36	9	2	12	2	6	3	—	2
37	7	—	9	4	5	1	—	1
38	9	3	6	2	7	6	4	1
39	5	2	5	6	4	2	1	2
140	8	2	8	6	5	—	1	2
41	6	1	6	3	4	3	1	1
42	9	2	7	1	7	4	1	3
43	8	2	10	1	10	2	—	—
44	8	5	8	4	6	7	2	—
45	2	2	3	1	4	1	1	1
46	7	—	2	2	4	1	2	—
47	5	1	2	4	1	2	3	1
48	5	1	5	—	1	—	—	—
49	2	—	3	1	—	1	—	—
150	—	—	—	—	3	1	—	1
51	—	—	—	1	1	1	—	1
52	—	—	1	1	—	—	—	—
53	1	1	—	—	—	—	—	—
54	—	—	—	—	—	—	—	—
55	—	—	1	—	—	—	—	—
56	2	—	—	—	1	—	—	—

[1] Add 162—1.   [2] Add 113—1; 168—1.

The Validity of the Genealogies 209

discernible, or that the amount of Indian ancestry in each family represented in the series has been too small in comparison with the amounts of Negro and White strains to influence the physical make-up of the resulting children to any appreciable degree. There is a definite difference between the groups, however, from greater width on the part of the unmixed Negro class to a smaller average value on the part of those with more White blood; the average width of the Old Americans being, as shown, 138.6, while for other related peoples we have the mean values of 136.35 for English criminals, 132.1 for American-born Scottish, and 139.5 for foreign-born Scottish, all of which may be of some value in offering a clue. The fact, however, that the African peoples also have facial widths as narrow or narrower than these, somewhat vitiates its value as an explanatory factor. The mean square variability of the N class is the second lowest of the eight given. The Hottentot face, as may be seen from Fischer's data given below, follows much more closely than do my data the results which would be expected to follow crossing with different proportions of White. As may be noticed, the Hottentot face is much narrower than that of the White man, and therefore the difficulty inherent in my data and arising from the fact that Negro and White faces have so nearly the same average width is not present:

100 Bavarians:			141.4
Bastards	"Eu"	138.0	
	"Mitt"	135.6	136.6
	"Hott"	136.6	
8 and 7 Hottentots:			130.8

The Bastards, when the average for the entire series is given, are between the Europeans and Hottentots, and the "Eu" group has a wider face than the "Hott". The "Mitt" group have narrower faces than the "Eu" and "Hott" groups, but the difference is not decisive enough to place it outside the range of being a chance variation.

20. Width of Mouth (Table LXXXVI).

In the table given in the discussion of this trait for the entire series in Chapter III, little difference was apparent between the African and European peoples represented, as well as the Indian ones, although certain of the West African peoples seemed to show somewhat the wider mouths. Comparing the means and variabilities for the genealogical groups in our sample, we have:

210 The Anthropometry of the American Negro

Class	Without Indian			With Indian		
	No.	Average,(mm.)	σ	No.	Average,(mm.)	σ
N	107	54.95	± 3.77			
N(I)				36	53.35	± 4.40
NNW	126	52.9	± 4.23			
NNW(I)				51	52.9	± 4.01
NW	95	52.4	± 3.21			
NW(I)				57	52.5	± 3.99
NWW	30	52.1	± 3.46			
NWW(I)				31	52.1	± 3.72
W	247	53.7	± 3.78			

The N and N(I) groups have wider mouths, on the average, than the others which show a slight decrease with increasing amount of White blood. Hrdlička's W do not carry on the downward trend. The variability of the N group is fourth lowest, the NW being least variable, the NWW next, and the NWW(I) third.

Table LXXXVI
Width of Mouth

Mm.	N	N(I)	NNW	NNW(I)	NW	NW(I)	NWW	NWW(I)
43	—	—	3	1	—	—	—	1
44	1	—	1	—	1	—	—	—
45	—	1	1	—	1	—	2	1
46	1	—	3	1	—	2	1	1
47	1	1	3	4	4	3	—	2
48	4	1	7	4	3	2	1	1
49	3	3	11	2	6	6	1	1
50	1	3	7	1	15	7	3	1
51	4	3	11	4	10	7	7	3
52	14	6	10	3	13	6	2	3
53	7	2	16	7	4	3	2	4
54	12	2	9	8	10	5	4	6
55	14	8	10	4	12	6	4	2
56	6	1	9	3	5	2	1	3
57	7	1	5	2	8	1	—	1
58	13	—	6	4	2	1	—	—
59	7	1	6	1	—	2	1	—
60	4	—	4	1	—	1	1	1
61	6	1	—	—	—	1	—	—
62	1	—	3	—	1	1	—	—
63	1	1	—	1	—	—	—	—
64	—	—	1	—	—	1	—	—
65	—	—	—	—	—	—	—	—
66	—	—	—	—	—	—	—	—
67	—	—	—	—	—	—	—	—
68	—	1	—	—	—	—	—	—

21. THICKNESS OF LIPS, CENTER (Table LXXXVII).

Again, in this trait, one would expect to find appreciable differences between the averages for groups of varying amounts of racial mixture. In the discussion of this trait and its distribution for the sample as a whole in Chapter III, it was seen that the difference between (living) West Africans and (cadavera) American Whites was over 13 mm., while that between the former and (living) Bavarians was 10 mm. The thickness of the lips is a marked characteristic of the Negro. The means and variabilities of the genealogical groups are:

Class	Without Indian			With Indian		
	No.	Average, (mm.)	σ	No.	Average, (mm.)	σ
N	109	23.9	± 4.16			
N(I)				36	22.9	± 4.85
NNW	129	22.5	± 4.31			
NNW(I)				51	23.0	± 3.20
NW	95	22.0	± 3.94			
NW(I)				57	21.0	± 4.57
NWW	30	18.8	± 3.77			
NWW(I)				31	19.7	± 3.48

With the exception of the statistically insignificant gain in the average of the NNW(I) after the NNW, and of the NWW(I) after that of the NWW, there is a steady decrease in the average lip thickness of the genealogical classes according to the increase in the amount of White blood they represent. The group in which there is the most White blood, the NWW, still has an average thickness of lips that is greater than the European lip, but the N group stands very close to the mean for the 40 Vai of West Africa, and for the other West African peoples quoted on p. 64. Consideration of the averages given above affords another striking demonstration of the differences between these groups, the individuals composing which, it must be again emphasized, were classified on the basis of their own genealogical statements. The N class ranks high with respect to variability, it being fourth highest, the NNW(I) being least variable, and being followed in lowness of variation by the NWW(I), NWW, and NW classes, respectively. We may again compare results from this series of genealogical groups with those of Fischer. For thickness of the lips (p. 93) those are:

	Class	No.	Average, (mm.)	σ
Bavarians:		—	14.2	—
Bastards	"Eu"	12	15.1	± 2.25
	"Mitt"	32	16.0	± 3.98
	"Hott"	23	18.1	± 4.59
Hottentots:		—	23.1	—

Here are the same results which were found to hold for the groups of American Negroes of various degrees of White ancestry of the Howard series. Obviously, the phenomenon of Negro-White mixture and Hottentot-White mixture has had the same result in both these groups which have been studied, however different the stocks which have gone toward making up the cross.

Table LXXXVII
Thickness of Lips (center)

Mm.	N	N(I)	NNW	NNW(I)	NW	NW(I)	NWW	NWW(I)
10	—	—	—	—	—	1	1	—
11	—	—	1	—	1	—	—	—
12	—	1	1	—	—	—	1	—
13	—	—	2	—	2	2	1	2
14	—	—	—	—	—	1	—	1
15	2	2	2	—	1	2	4	2
16	1	1	5	—	2	2	2	—
17	3	1	6	2	6	4	3	2
18	6	2	4	3	7	4	4	4
19	3	2	9	3	7	2	4	4
20	7	1	14	3	9	10	—	3
21	9	2	13	6	5	4	1	6
22	8	2	7	6	15	7	3	1
23	9	5	9	6	8	2	2	2
24	13	4	12	6	7	7	4	2
25	7	2	10	3	7	2	—	—
26	9	5	10	3	3	1	—	—
27	12	2	5	3	5	2	—	2
28	9	1	8	2	5	1	—	—
29	2	—	6	2	3	—	—	—
30	2	—	2	1	1	1	—	—
31	2	2	2	—	1	—	—	—
32	3	—	1	—	—	1	—	—
33	—	—	—	—	—	—	—	—
34	—	1	—	—	—	—	—	—
35	2	—	—	—	—	1	—	—

22. THICKNESS OF LIPS, RIGHT SIDE (Table LXXXVIII).

As was remarked in Chapter III, this measurement was taken as a check on the preceding one. The correspondence between the two is as close when the sample is split into genealogical classes as when it is considered as a whole, as may be seen from the following table of the statistical constants for the genealogical groups:

		Without Indian			With Indian	
Class	No.	Average, (mm.)	σ	No.	Average, (mm.)	σ
N	108	25.1	± 3.91			
N(I)				36	23.8	± 4.79
NNW	127	23.6	± 4.15			
NNW(I)				51	24.0	± 3.65
NW	94	22.8	± 3.73			
NW(I)				57	22.1	± 4.09
NWW	30	21.0	± 3.56			
NWW(I)				31	20.4	± 3.58

There is the same general change from more to less Negroid lip thickness with the infusion of greater amounts of White ancestry into the groups, the difference from the preceding lip measurement being that there is one instead of two exceptions to the smoothness of the change, — only the NNW(I) group has a greater average value than its corresponding genealogical class without Indian. The variability of the N class in this trait as was the case in the corresponding trait before it, is fifth lowest, the smallest sigma being that of the NWW group, this being followed in this respect by the NWW(I), NNW(I), and NW groups, and exhibiting again a close resemblance between the two traits.

Table LXXXVIII
Thickness of Lips (right)

Mm.	N	N(I)	NNW	NNW(I)	NW	NW(I)	NWW	NWW(I)
12	—	—	—	—	—	1	1	1
13	—	—	1	—	1	—	—	—
14	—	1	2	—	—	—	—	—
15	—	—	1	—	1	2	2	2
16	2	1	2	2	2	2	2	2
17	1	4	3	1	2	3	2	2
18	2	—	4	—	8	2	4	3
19	5	—	8	1	4	1	2	—
20	4	3	7	4	7	8	5	4
21	6	5	12	6	7	4	5	6
22	3	—	9	5	12	7	1	3
23	16	2	18	2	7	10	1	2
24	9	2	9	7	16	5	—	3
25	12	3	12	5	9	6	2	1
26	6	4	6	7	3	1	2	1
27	12	4	6	4	3	—	1	—
28	10	3	8	1	3	1	—	—
29	5	—	9	3	5	2	—	1
30	7	1	7	—	3	—	—	—
31	4	1	—	2	—	—	—	—
32	—	1	2	—	1	1	—	—
33	3	—	—	1	—	—	—	—
34	—	—	1	—	—	—	—	—
35	—	1	—	—	—	—	—	—
36	1	—	—	—	—	1	—	—

23. Physiognomic Height of Ear (Ear Length)
(Table LXXXIX).

The European ear, according to Karutz, who has made a general study of the shape of the ear in racial groups[1], is higher than the African, which is the smaller of the two types. When we regard the means for the genealogical classes of the present sample we find:

Class	Without Indian			With Indian		
	No.	Average,(mm.)	σ	No.	Average,(mm.)	σ
N	108	59.8	± 4.57			
N(I)				36	58.9	± 5.44
NNW	129	59.7	± 4.00			
NNW(I)				51	60.6	± 3.53
NW	94	60.9	± 3.79			
NW(I)				57	60.6	± 3.80
NWW	30	60.4	± 3.45			
NWW(I)				31	61.3	± 3.74
W	247	66.9	± 5.72			

Table LXXXIX
Physiognomic Height of Ear

Mm.	N[2]	N(I)[3]	NNW	NNW(I)	NW	NW(I)	NWW	NWW(I)
51	1	1	—	1	—	—	—	—
52	2	2	4	—	1	—	—	—
53	1	1	2	—	1	3	—	1
54	5	2	8	1	2	1	—	—
55	3	1	8	1	4	3	2	1
56	11	2	10	2	5	2	2	2
57	4	3	7	4	4	2	3	—
58	8	2	10	3	6	7	1	3
59	3	7	10	7	7	3	—	4
60	13	3	17	6	14	4	8	4
61	17	1	13	8	9	8	1	2
62	10	2	8	4	15	7	7	—
63	9	1	10	4	6	5	—	1
64	6	2	6	3	6	4	—	5
65	2	2	7	4	5	3	2	5
66	4	2	2	1	3	2	2	1
67	1	—	2	—	1	2	2	1
68	2	—	2	1	1	—	—	1
69	1	—	2	—	2	—	—	—
70	2	—	1	—	1	—	—	—
71	—	—	—	1	—	—	—	—
72	—	—	—	—	1	1	—	—

[1] See the discussion of this trait in Chapter III.
[2] Add 44—2; 48—1.   [3] Add 44—1; 75—1.

The Validity of the Genealogies

This again, is what would be expected if the genealogies had been correctly given. There is a gradual change in the means from the group having no White ancestry to those in which the White blood predominates, from smaller to larger ears, and this tendency is carried on if we add the average of the unmixed White series to our list, although the difference between the mean for this latter series and that of any of the genealogical groups is noticeably large. There is an exception to the general manner of change represented in the NWW group, the average value of which is smaller than both the NW(I), NW, and NNW(I). Other than this, however, the change is quite regular, and again tends to confirm the accuracy of the genealogical statements. The mean square variability of the N class is next to the highest of the eight, the N(I) group having the greatest variability, and the NWW having the lowest.

24. Physiognomic Width of Ear
(Table XC).

While the ears of the Europeans listed in the comparative table for this trait in Chapter III are on the average wider than those of this sample considered as a whole, there are few available data which may be used for comparative purposes, there being only one norm for a West African, and none for an Indian people. Therefore, the most one can say is that the ear of the African seems to be about the same in breadth as that of the European. The following means and variabilities for the genealogical classes seem to scatter in chance fashion about the average for the entire sample which they compose:

Class	Without Indian			With Indian		
	No.	Average,(mm).	σ	No.	Average,(mm.)	σ
N	108	33.8	± 3.21			
N(I)				36	33.05	± 3.01
NNW	129	33.2	± 2.58			
NNW(I)				51	34.1	± 2.88
NW	95	33.1	± 2.67			
NW(I)				57	34.0	± 2.67
NWW	30	32.7	± 2.06			
NWW(I)				31	33.4	± 2.79
W	247	37.9	± 2.52			

For this trait, as for the one preceding, the variability of the unmixed Negro group is seen to be large when it is compared to the variation of the other seven groups, — it is highest in this respect, in fact, the NWW class again showing itself least variable.

216 The Anthropometry of the American Negro

Table XC
Physiognomic Width of Ear

Mm.	N	N(I)	NNW	NNW(I)	NW	NW(I)	NWW	NWW(I)
25	1	—	—	—	—	—	—	—
26	2	—	—	—	1	—	—	—
27	—	1	—	—	—	1	—	—
28	2	—	4	1	4	—	—	—
29	5	4	7	—	4	—	1	2
30	6	—	6	4	7	4	2	4
31	6	6	16	5	8	6	8	2
32	15	3	15	5	13	7	3	4
33	16	12	23	10	14	6	6	5
34	11	1	19	6	14	10	5	4
35	10	2	11	4	17	10	1	7
36	14	1	16	4	5	3	3	—
37	9	4	5	3	4	3	—	—
38	4	—	3	5	2	4	1	—
39	1	1	3	2	1	1	—	1
40	4	—	1	2	—	1	—	1
41	1	—	—	—	—	1	—	—
42	1	1	—	—	1	—	—	1

25. WIDTH OF RIGHT HAND (Table XCI).

Though there are few comparative data available on hand width, it will be remembered that the discussion of this trait in Chapter III showed that the mean for the White Americans in this trait is higher than that for the present sample considered as a whole, and also higher than that for the African population represented in the comparative table there. The European peoples for which averages could be obtained were very much nearer the mean of this series of American Negroes, and smaller than that for the White Americans. The statistical constants for our genealogical classes are as follows:

Class	Without Indian			With Indian		
	No.	Average, (mm.)	σ	No.	Average, (mm.)	σ
N	109	86.2	± 3.71			
N(I)				36	85.9	± 4.87
NNW	129	86.0	± 4.54			
NNW(I)				51	85.8	± 3.97
NW	94	85.0	± 3.97			
NW(I)				57	86.7	± 4.33
NWW	30	84.6	± 4.54			
NWW(I)				31	85.1	± 3.73

There is a slight trend from a wider hand in the unmixed Negro group to a somewhat narrower one in the classes having the largest amount of White ancestry. In variability, the N class is the lowest of the eight, being followed by the NWW(I), while the highest variability is that of the N(I) group.

The Validity of the Genealogies

Fischer's results are somewhat confusing, and do not seem to follow the results which would be expected at all. The hand width of the European group he uses for comparison with the Hottentot is greater than the latter, but the resulting crosses have, without exception, greater hand widths than either of the stocks from which they are derived. There is this much consistency, — the "Hott" class has a hand that is noticeably smaller than that of the "Eu" group, although, at the same time, the "Mitt" class is smaller than either of these, on the average. Fischer's results are as follows:

```
100 Bavarians:                            (78)
                    ⎧ "Eu"    84 ⎫
70—80 Bastards      ⎨ "Mitt"  79 ⎬   81
                    ⎩ "Hott"  82 ⎭
8 Hottentots:                              72
```

Table XCI
Width of Hand
(Met. lat. — Met. med.)

Mm.	N	N(I)	NNW	NNW(I)	NW	NW(I)	NWW	NWW(I)
74	—	—	—	—	—	—	1	—
75	1	—	1	—	1	—	—	—
76	—	—	1	—	—	—	—	—
77	—	—	1	1	2	1	1	—
78	—	4	—	—	3	2	—	—
79	1	—	3	2	—	1	1	—
80	3	2	2	2	—	3	—	1
81	1	—	10	4	15	2	2	2
82	14	3	11	5	4	3	4	4
83	11	1	17	2	12	3	7	7
84	4	3	12	2	9	3	3	4
85	15	—	8	5	10	5	1	3
86	9	7	8	4	4	6	1	2
87	10	3	9	3	9	4	1	1
88	8	5	7	6	6	4	2	1
89	14	5	8	5	4	4	—	2
90	5	—	10	3	6	8	2	1
91	4	—	5	4	6	2	1	—
92	4	—	6	2	1	1	1	1
93	1	1	3	1	—	1	1	1
94	2	—	2	—	—	3	1	—
95	1	—	1	—	2	—	—	—
96	1	—	1	—	—	—	—	1
97	—	—	—	—	—	1	—	—
98	—	1	1	—	—	—	—	—
99	—	—	2	—	—	—	—	—
100	—	1	—	—	—	—	—	—

26. LENGTH OF MIDDLE FINGER, RIGHT HAND (Table XCII).

The comparisons which were made in Chapter III for this trait were in terms of proportion of finger length to the length of the body. The cadavera comparisons showed that the American Negro finger lengths were 2.7 mm. longer on the average than the White, while the table of proportionate lengths showed that the African populations had such variation among themselves that in some the ratios were smaller, in others larger than in the European populations for which these proportions were given. Therefore, in the following

Table XCII
Length of Middle Finger
(Phal. III-Dak. III)

Mm.	N	N(I)[1]	NNW	NNW(I)[2]	NW	NW(I)[3]	NNW[4]	NWW(I)
91	—	—	—	—	—	—	1	1
92	1	—	—	1	—	—	—	—
93	—	1	—	—	1	—	—	—
94	—	—	—	—	—	1	—	—
95	2	—	—	—	1	—	—	—
96	—	—	3	—	—	1	—	1
97	2	—	3	—	1	—	2	—
98	—	2	5	—	1	—	—	1
99	2	1	1	—	1	—	1	2
100	—	—	—	—	1	—	1	1
01	3	—	5	2	5	1	2	2
02	4	—	5	1	4	2	2	2
03	4	1	3	4	3	3	1	1
04	4	2	4	3	5	2	1	1
105	5	4	5	4	10	4	1	2
06	8	2	8	4	4	5	1	3
07	6	2	11	3	4	4	—	1
08	3	2	13	4	9	2	2	2
09	6	3	7	5	3	5	2	1
110	11	1	8	4	6	1	6	4
11	8	1	9	3	9	6	1	2
12	7	2	7	2	8	3	1	—
13	11	2	7	—	5	3	1	1
14	2	2	5	—	2	4	1	1
115	2	—	1	4	—	1	1	—
16	8	3	6	1	3	3	—	—
17	—	2	—	1	3	1	—	1
18	2	1	4	1	1	2	—	—
19	4	—	2	1	2	—	1	1
120	2	—	2	—	—	1	—	—
21	1	—	2	—	1	—	—	—
22	1	1	3	1	—	—	—	—
23	—	—	—	1	—	—	—	—
24	—	—	—	—	1	1	—	—

[1] Add. 125—1. [2] Add. 130—1. [3] Add. 126—1. [4] Add. 130—1.

list of means and variabilities for this trait, the respective relative finger lengths as well as the absolute lengths for the genealogical classes are given:

Class	Without Indian				With Indian			
	No.	Average, (mm.)	σ	% of Stature	No.	Average, (mm.)	σ	% of Stature
N	109	109.3	± 5.96	6.43				
N(I)					36	109.3	± 6.79	6.47
NNW	129	108.8	± 6.04	6.40				
NNW(I)					51	109.1	± 6.39	6.34
NW	94	108.2	± 5.69	6.29				
NW(I)					57	109.5	± 6.03	6.37
NWW	30	107.2	± 7.41	6.23				
NWW(I)					31	105.8	± 6.10	6.15

The measure decreases with the amount of white blood. The variability of the NW class is the smallest of the eight, the N(I) group being the most variable.

27. PIGMENTATION, BLACK (N) ELEMENT, UPPER OUTER ARM
(Table XCIII).

Pigmentation is the most markedly dissimilar trait when Negroes and Whites are compared as to physical characteristics, and this is also the case between Negroes and Indians, although the difference is not as emphatic between them as in the former case. Between Indians and Whites, although this trait has not been studied by the quantitative method employed in this research, the Indian skin would presumably have a higher value for the N element, although not nearly so much higher as the Negro. It will be remembered that in the discussion of this trait in Chapters II and III, it was brought out that there is a difference in the subjective element, which goes with differing judgements, as to when the blended colors of the top and the color of the skin are alike. At the same time, it was also shown that observations on different groups by the same observer should be very readily usable for comparative purposes, since the subjective error is a constant which can be determined by the computation of his mean observational error; and this error, in my own case, was shown to be quite small. The statistical constants for the N value of the color-top are:

Class	Without Indian			With Indian		
	No.	Average, (%)	σ	No.	Average, (%)	σ
N	109	75.5	± 10.34			
N(I)				36	74.9	± 9.51
NNW	127	68.2	± 11.58			
NNW(I)				50	70.3	± 10.39
NW	94	61.2	± 12.01			
NW(I)				56	59.4	± 11.20
NWW	30	48.7	± 13.67			
NWW(I)				31	56.9	± 14.39

The percentage of N grows smaller with larger proportions of White blood in the various classes.[1] In the groups without Indian mixture this holds without exception, and there are considerable differences manifest between the averages of any two of these classes. In those having partial Indian ancestry, the same phenomenon may be noticed. Except in two instances, this also holds when all the classes are grouped together; the NNW(I) has a greater percentage of N than the NNW, and the NWW(I) shows a larger amount of N than its corresponding paired group. The difference between the other two classes, with and without Indian, is also not as great as the difference between classes of different amounts of Negro ancestry. This would, therefore, tend to reinforce confidence in the validity of the genealogies, as we would expect the classes with Indian ancestry to be somewhat darker than the corresponding ones without it, except the unmixed Negro group, which should be darkest of all. This in the main is what appears to be the case. There is a decided massing toward the larger percentages in the distribution for the less mixed Negroes, while the other classes have a tendency that is much less noticeable toward a skewing off in the lower ranges.

We may consider the N group especially in the light of the results which Davenport claims to have obtained when using the color-top employed in this research; namely, that there is a bimodality in the frequency distribution of the N (black) value for an unmixed Negro series which argues a dimorphism of the black in pure Negro peoples. He arrived at this conclusion after using the color-top on a very small sample of Negroes (18 in number) whose statements as to the absence of mixture represented in their ancestry could not be verified. Further, Davenport failed to recognize the fact that the colors used on the top have been arbitrarily selected and do not resemble in any fashion (except perhaps the red, the color of which is "ox-blood") the actual colors which go into the composition of pigmentation. Finally, he did not make the correction which was necessary, due to the fact, as explained above, that the red disk is in reality 59 % black, and his tabulation is of these uncorrected readings for the N. There is, as has been said, a skewness to be noticed in the unmixed Negro series — one much larger than his, incidentally, — a massing at the higher percentages. But there is

---

[1] Barnes (I) who worked over the family (not Howard University) material of this study for skin-color, obtained means for the N which fully corroborate this statement. The average percentages of N for the members of the other series discussed in this work as computed by her are:

Genealogical class	No.	Average value of N	σ
N	492	72.74	± 8.93
NNW	1063	67.19	± 11.21
NW	445	58.73	± 11.12
NWW	391	52.73	± 12.35

The Validity of the Genealogies

no evidence at all of bimodality, the modal value being very clearly at 80 %. We may also use this unmixed Negro group for purposes of comparison with Todd and Van Gorder's sample discussed at some length in Chapter III, the mean and sigma of which were computed by me to be 82.79 % ± 6.11 %. This, although it is closer to the mean for the unmixed Negro class of this study than it is to that of the entire adult male sample utilized, is not sufficiently close to invalidate the remarks which were made as to the comparability of our results in the discussion in Chapter III, although it must be admitted that it heightens the probability that the difference

Table XCIII
Pigmentation, Upper Outer Arm, Black Element (N)

%	N	N(I)	NNW	NNW(I)	NW	NW(I)	NWW	NWW(I)
26—27	—	—	—	—	—	—	—	1
28—29	—	—	—	—	—	—	2	—
30—31	—	—	—	—	—	—	1	—
32—33	1	—	—	—	1	—	1	—
34—35	—	—	—	—	1	—	2	1
36—37	—	—	2	—	3	1	1	1
38—39	—	—	—	—	1	1	3	1
40—41	—	—	—	—	1	1	3	4
42—43	1	—	1	—	1	3	1	—
44—45	—	—	—	1	3	2	1	1
46—47	1	—	4	—	2	3	1	1
48—49	—	—	—	1	2	6	2	—
50—51	1	—	4	2	4	2	2	1
52—53	2	2	5	—	2	—	1	—
54—55	1	1	4	—	6	1	1	1
56—57	1	—	9	4	7	4	—	2
58—59	1	—	3	—	7	3	1	2
60—61	2	—	5	3	8	4	—	—
62—63	1	1	3	3	4	4	—	4
64—65	6	1	7	3	4	2	2	1
66—67	3	2	7	3	3	3	1	2
68—69	2	1	7	1	7	4	—	1
70—71	4	6	7	1	7	1	—	1
72—73	7	—	5	5	4	2	1	2
74—75	7	2	13	2	6	4	1	3
76—77	11	3	11	5	4	1	—	—
78—79	6	3	8	5	2	3	—	—
80—81	16	5	9	4	1	—	2	—
82—83	15	2	4	3	1	1	—	—
84—85	9	2	6	2	—	—	—	—
86—87	8	3	3	2	2	—	—	1
88—89	1	2	—	—	—	—	—	—
90—91	2	—	—	—	—	—	—	—

between the dead and the living enters as a factor, or that the
element of social selection might have entered into Todd's sample.
The former supposition, however, is contrary to the statement of
Todd and Van Gorder that there is no difference between the living
and the dead in respect to the percentage of N in the living skin
and in samples from cadavera.[1]

The lowest variability among the genealogical classes themselves
is that of the N(I) group, and the next lowest that of the N group.
The highest variability is that of the NWW(I), and it is followed in
this respect by the NWW class.

28. Pigmentation, Red (R) Element, Upper Outer Arm
(Table XCIV).

The averages for the entire male sample of this study and the
series of Todd and Van Gorder, for Negro cadavera, it will be
remembered, differed by 4.77 %, the sample of this study having
the larger mean of 12.38 %. There seems to be an amount of red
coloring in the pigmentation of Negroes somewhat smaller than in
the case of Whites. This may be due to greater thickness of skin
of the Negro, or to the greater ease with which the red in the White
skin can be seen in comparison with its visibility in the dark skin.
There are no comparative data with which the validity of the results
obtained below may be tested:

Class	No.	*Without Indian* Average, (%)	σ	No.	*With Indian* Average, (%)	σ
N	109	10.8	± 2.93			
N(I)				36	11.0	± 2.61
NNW	127	12.45	± 2.79			
NNW(I)				50	12.2	± 2.94
NW	94	13.2	± 2.33			
NW(I)				56	13.6	± 2.18
NWW	30	13.9	± 2.25			
NWW(I)				31	13.4	± 1.68

Here again there is seen to be, in the main, a steady change. The
trend is from the smallest percentage of R in the unmixed-Negro
class to the greatest in the NWW. If we consider, as before, those
groups in which there is no Indian admixture, the increase from
one class to the next with increasing amounts of White ancestry is
steady: in the case of the groups where there has been Indian
mixture, this holds except in the case of the last one, where there
is a slight lessening of the mean percentage of R. Similarly, when
we regard all eight of the averages, the NNW(I) has a lower mean

---

[1] See further discussion of this point in Todd, Blackwood, and Beecher, (I),
and in Todd and Lindala (I).

The Validity of the Genealogies

percentage of red than its corresponding NNW, and the NWW(I) has less than the NWW. Whether this is the effect of Indian mixture or not cannot be said, but in view of the fact that two of the groups mixed with Indian show greater percentages of R than the corresponding ones without Indian ancestry, and two exhibit lesser ones, this appears to be a question upon which the present series can shed no light. We find that there is slight evidence of skewness in the resulting curves, as would be expected from the fact that, since the factor of blood contributes so largely to this color, the distribution of it would be expected to follow the normal distribution curve. A survey of the mean square variabilities shows that the N group is next to highest in this instance, and only .01 % lower than the most variable of the eight groups, the NNW(I). The lowest variability is that of the NWW(I), and next to it in this respect comes the NW(I).

Table XCIV
Pigmentation, Upper Outer Arm, Red Element (R)

%	N	N(I)	NNW	NNW(I)	NW	NW(I)	NWW	NWW(I)
4	1	—	—	—	—	—	—	—
5	2	1	—	—	—	—	—	—
6	—	1	—	—	—	—	—	—
7	8	3	10	2	2	—	—	—
8	9	2	—	3	—	—	—	—
9	23	4	11	6	6	2	—	—
10	15	2	8	6	3	—	2	1
11	13	5	22	7	12	9	3	3
12	9	7	9	4	13	7	2	7
13	7	4	8	3	6	9	7	3
14	11	5	34	5	24	11	5	10
15	3	2	11	5	14	6	4	5
16	5	—	8	6	8	8	2	1
17	1	—	3	2	5	2	2	—
18	—	—	—	1	1	1	3	1
19	—	—	2	—	—	—	—	—
20	2	—	1	—	—	1	—	—

29. Pigmentation, Yellow (y) Element, Upper Outer Arm (Table XCV).

The difference between the adult male sample, on the average, in this color of the top, and the mean of the Western Reserve cadavera, was 5.83 %. There is again, no comparative material available for White populations, so that only conjecture may be made as to what should follow if the genealogies were valid. On the whole, however, yellow contributes to a greater lightness of the skin, and therefore something of an increase should be expected in the percentages of it in the readings of the color-top as groups of greater degree of White mixture are involved. The results actually found in the present genealogical classes are:

Class	Without Indian			With Indian		
	No.	Average, (%)	σ	No.	Average, (%)	σ
N	109	7.76	± 3.57			
N(I)				36	8.17	± 3.64
NNW	127	10.49	± 4.32			
NNW(I)				50	9.74	± 3.98
NW	94	13.98	± 4.38			
NW(I)				56	13.61	± 4.38
NWW	30	14.30	± 4.11			
NWW(I)				31	13.35	± 3.06

Table XCV

Pigmentation, Upper Outer Arm, Yellow Element (Y)

%	N	N(I)	NNW	NNW(I)	NW	NW(I)	NWW	NWW(I)
2	2	—	1	1	—	—	—	—
3	7	1	2	—	1	—	—	—
4	8	6	4	1	1	—	—	—
5	17	3	10	6	2	2	1	—
6	12	4	6	5	2	1	1	—
7	14	5	18	3	5	2	1	—
8	12	1	7	7	6	3	1	2
9	6	4	10	5	4	2	1	1
10	10	2	14	2	7	5	—	5
11	6	5	6	1	8	3	1	2
12	3	1	4	7	6	3	3	3
13	3	1	9	2	9	5	2	2
14	1	—	8	2	11	4	1	2
15	4	1	10	3	4	6	4	5
16	1	—	5	2	12	5	5	5
17	1	2	6	2	5	4	2	2
18	2	—	2	—	7	5	4	1
19	—	—	3	1	4	3	1	—
20	—	—	1	—	—	2	1	1
21	—	—	—	—	—	—	—	—
22	—	—	1	—	—	—	1	—
23	—	—	—	—	—	—	—	—
24	—	—	—	—	—	—	—	—
25	—	—	—	—	—	—	—	—
26	—	—	—	—	—	—	—	—
27	—	—	—	—	—	—	—	—
28	—	—	—	—	—	1	—	—

The Validity of the Genealogies

Here a general change from lesser to greater percentages of Y in the groups having larger amounts of White ancestry may be seen, as might be expected from an *a priori* consideration of the action of this color. It will be seen that there is a massing toward the lower ranges in the N, N(I), and NNW classes due to the high value of the variability as compared to that of the average. The NW group, on the other hand, seems to show a massing toward the upper ranges, while the remaining four groups follow more or less closely the normal type of distribution.

30. Pigmentation, White (W) Element, Upper Outer Arm (Table XCVI).

Here again, as in the case of the black, there need be no conjecture as to what should be expected from the genealogical classes when the unmixed Negro group is compared with the others possessing larger or smaller amounts of White blood. The difference in skin color of the two races is so obvious that it would demand greater percentages of W where larger amounts of White ancestry were present. And again, the effect of the Indian element cannot be foretold, due to a lack of comparative material taken on the Indian with the color top. The results for the genealogical classes are as follows:

Class	Without Indian			With Indian		
	No.	Average, %	σ	No.	Average, %	σ
N	109	6.00	± 5.24			
N(I)				36	5.97	± 4.02
NNW	127	8.68	± 5.80			
NNW(I)				50	7.66	± 4.69
NW	94	12.40	± 8.21			
NW(I)				56	13.48	± 7.33
NWW	30	23.00	± 10.77			
NWW(I)				31	16.97	± 10.79

Here also there is the change which would be expected. The change is steady and so great as to be decisive. The difference between the pairs claiming part Indian ancestry and their Negro and Negro-White counterparts seem to show, except in the case of the NW and the NW(I), that the classes mixed with Indian have the smaller percentages of White. Whether this is due to the darker skin of the Indian as compared with that of the White is difficult to state. Here we see, as may be understood from an inspection from the averages and mean square variabilities in the table above, that there is a large degree of skewness, — a heavy massing about the lower ranges, and a skewing off toward the upper, in every class. For when we compare the means and sigmas, we find that the latter are sometimes almost as great as the former. The difficulty of observing small differences between two fairly high percentages

Table XCVI
Pigmentation, Upper Outer Arm, White element (W)

%	N	N(I)	NNW	NNW(I)	NW	NW(I)	NWW	NWW(I)
1	1	—	—	—	—	—	—	—
2	5	1	1	—	—	—	—	—
3	31	10	13	6	4	2	1	—
4	18	8	18	10	5	2	—	—
5	18	4	19	6	11	5	1	5
6	6	1	11	3	4	2	1	1
7	10	4	9	5	8	2	—	—
8	4	1	7	3	5	4	2	3
9	3	3	9	5	4	2	—	—
10	1	1	2	2	5	3	1	3
11	1	—	8	—	6	3	1	2
12	2	—	1	1	3	4	—	2
13	1	—	6	1	5	3	1	—
14	—	—	2	2	2	3	—	2
15	2	—	3	2	4	1	—	1
16	2	1	4	1	5	4	—	—
17	1	1	5	—	5	2	3	1
18	—	—	2	2	1	1	1	—
19	—	1	—	—	1	2	—	1
20	1	—	1	—	2	1	—	—
21	—	—	—	—	1	1	1	—
22	—	—	2	—	1	—	—	—
23	1	—	2	1	—	3	2	—
24	—	—	—	—	2	—	1	1
25	—	—	—	—	2	—	—	—
26	—	—	—	—	1	2	—	—
27	—	—	—	—	1	1	—	1
28	—	—	—	—	—	—	3	1
29	—	—	—	—	—	1	—	2
30	—	—	—	—	1	1	4	2
31	—	—	1	—	—	1	—	—
32	—	—	—	—	—	—	1	—
33	—	—	—	—	2	—	—	—
34	—	—	—	—	—	—	1	—
35	—	—	1	—	1	—	—	1
36	—	—	—	—	1	—	1	—
37	—	—	—	—	—	—	—	—
38	—	—	—	—	—	—	1	—
39	—	—	—	—	—	—	2	—
40	—	—	—	—	—	—	—	1
41	—	—	—	—	1	—	—	—
42	—	—	—	—	—	—	—	—
43	1	—	—	—	—	—	—	—
44	—	—	—	—	—	—	1	1

The Validity of the Genealogies

of White, which has been remarked on in Chapter II, certainly accounts in considerable measure for this skewness, but the corresponding skewness of the N element mentioned before shows that this is not the entire reason. We may here only question the entire technique of this manner of determination of pigmentation, and assert the necessity for further research into the extent to which it can be generally used in studies of this kind.

The consideration of the traits as given above, for the various genealogical classes of this sample of American Negroes, brings us again to the two problems which are involved in their consideration: the validity of the Negro genealogies, and the extent to which we may regard an individual as of a definite amount of Negro-White ancestry through a consideration of his physical features. As to the former, I think it may be asserted, as far as the sample used in this chapter is concerned, that the genealogical information gathered here is as reliable as data of this kind are usually found to be. That the reliability of the genealogies of the Howard series argues a like reliability for the others of this study, and so perhaps of the American Negro population as a whole, is an inference which may be drawn from the results of Chapter IV. The question as to how well Negroes not of University training may know their ancestry is answered, I believe, by the manner in which both genealogies and physical traits of the non-University series check in their likeness to the Howard University group. I believe that the results given in this chapter demonstrate satisfactorily that Negro genealogies may be utilized, and, if proper care be taken in collecting them, that material thus obtained will well repay the effort involved.

As to the possibility of telling how much mixture is represented in an individual by a consideration of his physical characteristics, the results show that this is not possible. If any trait of the ones given above be considered, and particularly such a "key" trait as pigmentation, which is usually employed in estimating the racial background of a given individual, it will be seen that there is so much overlapping between the various classes of different genealogical composition that the chances of "placing" a person would be very slight. Of course, a very light Negro may be assumed to have a large percentage of White ancestry, and an excessively dark one little or none, but more than this cannot be stated, certainly as far as the finer shadings of percentage of racial ancestral composition is concerned. This is expecially true when the Indian element involved is considered, for, as was noted above, the Indian traits are so submerged in the larger streams of Negro and White blood that they cannot be segregated even for groups.

CHAPTER VII
CORRELATION OF TRAITS.

I have not correlated every trait measured with every other, for both the male and female series, for the results would obviously not repay the enormous amount of labor involved. It has been shown that some traits are not significant; others are closely related morphologically, as, for example, the thickness of the lips on the right side and at the center of the mouth. The various elements of skin color recorded in the study are artificially selected and their distributions are so asymmetrical that it does not seem advisable to utilize them for the study of correlations. Ten traits have been selected from which correlations might perhaps profitably be computed, and nine sets of coefficients of correlation, and eighteen sets of regression coefficients, have been determined for them. Only the Howard University series has been utilized, but the coefficients have been computed not alone for this Howard sample as a whole, but also for each of the eight genealogical classes composing it. The traits used in correlating are:

Length of Head
Width of Head
Height of Head
Width of Nose
Thickness of Lips
Height of Ear
Interpupillary Distance
Width of Face
Height Sitting
Length of Legs (Stature minus Sitting Height)

It will be seen that, except for the width of the head and the height of the head, which were correlated with the length of the head, since it is desirable to obtain the relationship of the head diameters in these groups for comparative purposes, the traits used in the correlations are such as have significance in Negro-White crossing. The correlations which were computed were as follows:

Length of Head	×	Width of Head
Length of Head	×	Height of Head
Width of Head	×	Height of Head
Width of Nostrils	×	Thickness of Lips
Width of Nostrils	×	Height of Ear
Thickness of Lips	×	Height of Ear
Width of Nostrils	×	Interpupillary Distance
Breadth of Head	×	Width of Face
Sitting Height	×	Length of Legs.

The computation of these coefficients of correlation was followed by the calculation of the coefficients of regression, first of trait x on trait y, in any given set of two, and then the opposite. All these results will be given below.

Before this presentation, however, it may be well to give in some detail the methods by which these coefficients of correlation, and from them the regression equations, were derived. There were three of these. The first was what may be termed the Coefficient of Variability method. It was developed by Pearson[1] and may be used when the means and standard deviations of the two characters to be correlated are known, and also the mean and standard deviation of the index of the two. If we let V stand for the coefficient of variability, it being derived from the formula

$$V = \frac{\sigma}{m}$$

where m is the absolute value of the measurement, then the formula from which the coefficient of correlation (r) may be obtained is

$$r_{xy} = \frac{V_x^2 + V_y^2 - V_i^2}{2 V_x V_y}$$

where V_x is the coefficient of variability of the first trait, V_y that of the second, and V_i that of the index between the two. This method was used in computing the first coefficient of correlation in the list above.

The next method, which was used for the second and third sets of coefficients of correlation in the table above, was the Pearson product-moment formula, which is

$$r = \frac{\Sigma_{xy}}{n \sigma_x \sigma_y}$$

in which x and y represent the deviations of the individuals in the population from the mean for each trait correlated, n the number of correlated pairs. This method was employed for the correlations between height of head and the other two traits because the unequal number of cases measured for length and breadth of head, on the one hand, and height of the head, on the other, made the use of the labor-saving formula which follows impossible. It will be remembered that height of head was measured only on the Howard University men, because of a change in instruments, and that therefore the number of cases for this trait is materially less than that for the other two traits with which it has been correlated.

The remaining sets of coefficients of correlation were computed by using the mean square deviation of the differences between the

---

[1] Karl Pearson, (I), p. 386.

absolute values of the traits to be correlated, and the standard deviations of these traits. It may be well to repeat here the development of this formula. If x represents the deviation of the first trait, and y that of the second, then the mean square deviation of their difference may be represented as

$$\sigma^2_{x-y} = [(x-y)^2]$$

the brackets representing averaging.

$$[(x-y)^2] = [x^2] + [y^2] - 2[xy],$$

or
$$\sigma^2_{x-y} = \sigma^2_x + \sigma^2_y - 2r\,\sigma_x\,\sigma_y$$

and
$$r = \frac{\sigma^2_x + \sigma^2_y - \sigma^2_{x-y}}{2\,\sigma_x\,\sigma_y}$$

Slight differences may be expected in the results obtained from the same material by these three methods due to roughness in the measurements and consequent rounding off in the results. Hooton, for example, has found a difference in the results obtained between the use of the Pearson product-moment formula and that which employs the coefficients of variability[1], and I have also had a similar experience.[2] Therefore, the coefficient of correlation for the N class was computed by each of the three methods described above for the correlation of length with breadth of head, with the following results:

Number of cases	109
r (Pearson formula)	.205
r (Coefficient of Var. formula)	.223
r (Difference formula)	.237

The differences, as may be seen, do not change the result sufficiently to deter us from using the short-cut formulae which have been employed, nor from comparing results obtained from them.

The usual formulae for computing the regression equations were employed, these being, for the regression of x on y,

$$q_{xy} = r\,\frac{\sigma_x}{\sigma_y}$$

and for the regression of y on x,

$$q_{yx} = r\,\frac{\sigma_y}{\sigma_x}.$$

In computing the coefficients of correlation and regression, the genealogical classes NWW and NWW(I), or those with the greatest amount of White ancestry, without and with Indian mixture, have

---

[1] Hooton, (I), p. 267, found that this short-cut method had the effect of reducing r, whereas my experience has been that it makes it slightly greater.
[2] Herskovits, (IV).

been combined, since each alone has too few cases to make the results significant.

The following series of tables contains the results for the various sets of correlations and regressions. It will be seen that there seems to be a disturbance in the correlations with various amounts of racial mixture, but the results are not decisive enough, nor is there sufficient consistency in the change from one genealogical class to another to make detailed discussion of the results for each set of correlations profitable. It was hoped that some insight into the results of crossing might be obtained from the computation of these coefficients, but whatever there is, is so slight as to be of doubtful value. The results are given, however, for what they may be worth:

1. Length of Head and Width of Head.

Class	Number of cases	r	q_{xy}	q_{yx}
Total series	539	.22	.26	.19
N	109	.223	.29	.18
N(I)	36	.346	.41	.29
NNW	129	.264	.29	.24
NNW(I)	51	—.021	—.03	—.02
NW	95	.071	.09	.05
NW(I)	57	.135	.15	.12
NWW and NWW(I)	61	.462	.48	.44

In the regression equations, x is length of head, y width of head.

2. Length of Head and Height of Head.

Class	Number of cases	r	q_{xy}	q_{yx}
Total series	473	.33	.51	.22
N	102	.37	.57	.24
N(I)	33	.29	.38	.22
NNW	112	.38	.55	.26
NNW(I)	44	.33	.64	.17
NW	87	.25	.39	.16
NW(I)	45	.52	.48	.55
NWW and NWW(I)	49	.48	.80	.29

In the regression equations, x is length of head, y height of head.

3. Width of Head and Height of Head.

Class	Number of cases	r	q_{xy}	q_{yx}
Total series	473	.23	.31	.17
N	102	.42	.55	.32
N(I)	33	.29	.34	.25
NNW	112	.28	.36	.23
NNW(I)	44	.02	.03	.01
NW	87	.26	.30	.22
NW(I)	45	.07	.08	.06
NWW and NWW(I)	49	.32	.50	.20

In the regression equations, x is width of head, y height of head.

4. Width of Nose and Thickness of Lips.

Class	Number of cases	r	q_{xy}	q_{yx}
Total series	539	.34	.28	.425
N	109	.22	.15	.33
N(I)	36	.37	.33	.42
NNW	129	.26	.21	.325
NNW(I)	51	.45	.58	.35
NW	95	.33	.25	.43
NW(I)	57	—.076	—.06	—.09
NWW and NWW(I)	61	.37	.43	.32

In the regression equations, x is width of nose, y thickness of lips.

5. Width of Nose and Height of Ear.

Class	Number of cases	r	q_{xy}	q_{yx}
Total series	536	.05	.0475	.0525
N	108	.16	.10	.26
N(I)	36	.14	.11	.18
NNW	129	.42	.36	.49
NNW(I)	51	.12	.14	.10
NW	94	—.097	—.08	—.12
NW(I)	57	.198	.20	.20
NWW and NWW(I)	61	.218	.26	.18

In the regression equations, x is width of nose, y height of ear.

6. Thickness of Lips and Height of Ear.

Class	Number of cases	r	q_{xy}	q_{yx}
Total series	536	—.06	—.065	—.055
N	108	.084	.076	.09
N(I)	36	.41	.36	.46
NNW	129	—.14	—.15	—.13
NNW(I)	51	.079	.076	.082
NW	94	—.02	—.022	—.02
NW(I)	57	.29	.34	.24
NWW and NWW(I)	61	.13	.13	.13

In the regression equations, x is thickness of lips, y height of ear.

7. Width of Nose and Interpupillary Distance.

Class	Number of cases	r	q_{xy}	q_{yx}
Total series	529	.39	.40	.38
N	108	.099	.09	.11
N(I)	36	.31	.325	.29
NNW	125	.37	.35	.40
NNW(I)	51	.46	.51	.41
NW	93	.31	.28	.35
NW(I)	56	.23	.22	.24
NWW and NWW(I)	60	.016	.02	.01

In the regression equations, x is width of nose, y interpupillary distance.

8. Width of Head and Width of Face.

Class	Number of cases	r	q_{xy}	q_{yx}
Total series	537	.57	.55	.64
N	108	.45	.44	.46
N(I)	36	.77	.59	1.01
NNW	129	.62	.58	.66
NNW(I)	51	.65	.73	.585
NW	95	.52	.42	.65
NW(I)	57	.70	.72	.78
NWW and NWW(I)	61	.51	.42	.62

In the regression equations, x is width of head, y, width of face.

9. Height Sitting and Length of Leg.

Class	Number of cases	r	q_{xy}	q_{yx}
Total series	475	.35	.25	.49
N	102	.255	.18	.35
N(I)	34	.385	.30	.49
NNW	115	.49	.35	.68
NNW(I)	46	.22	.11	.43
NW	87	.29	.24	.35
NW(I)	44	.18	.15	.22
NWW and NWW(I)	47	.61	.38	1.01

Length of leg was determined by subtracting sitting height from stature, after which these values were correlated. In the regression equations x is height sitting, y, length of leg.

It is obvious, from the presentation of the coefficients of correlation and regression given above, that there is little to be gained, either from a consideration of them for the sample as a whole, or from comparison of them for the genealogical classes within the total groups for a given set of correlations or regressions.

CHAPTER VIII
RESULTS OF THIS STUDY.

The data which have been presented in the preceding chapters are the results of four years' research on the physical form of the American Negro. I have attempted, in this presentation, to define the physical characteristics of this racially crossed group as they have developed through long continued mixture with the White population and the aboriginal American Indian types then living in the region to which the Negroes were taken. In summarizing these results and entering upon a final discussion, it may be well first to present, in tabular form, the averages and mean square variabilities for the traits which have been measured on the total adult male and female series, and, in the case of such traits as have not been measured on the entire group, the results for the adult male Howard University series. This material is contained in Table XCVII. From it may be obtained a general concept of the form which the various traits take in this sample of our racially mixed population, a sample which, as has been explained at length in Chapter I, is believed to be representative to a reasonable degree of the American Negro population at large.

With this table in mind as a general summary, we may first turn, in recapitulating the material of this study, to a general review of the manner in which this people are to be compared with other populations in these traits, and particularly how they compare with the types from which they have been derived.

1.

If we again take as representing the entire series, and, through this, the American Negro type, the adult male series which was utilized in Chapter III, we find the comparative position of the American Negroes, trait for trait, as follows: The sample of this study has longer heads than any of the other populations to which they might be genetically related, except the Old White Americans and the Scottish men; for width of head the mean of this sample is between those for African peoples and, with the exception of the Swedish series, those of the European populations. The average value of their cephalic index is slightly lower than any found among those European populations which may be related to the American

Negro, but considerably higher than the averages for the West African tribes represented. In nasal height, the average of the American Negro seems to lie between the means of the three racial types of African, European, and American Indian, and a similar result is had, on the whole, for the width of the nose. In nasal depth, the population living in West Africa is closely approx-

Table XCVII
Averages and Standard Deviations for Traits Measured in Male and Female American Negro Adults.

Trait	Males			Females		
	No.	Average	σ	No.	Average	σ
Stature (cm.)	887	170.5	± 6.40	916	158.65	—
Height Sitting (cm.)	840	87.7	± 3.50	808	82.2	± 3.39
Width of Shoulder (mm.)	476	402.45	± 20.45	—	—	—
Width of Hips (mm.)	476	185.1	± 18.30	—	—	—
Length of Head (mm.)	961	196.5	± 6.51	929	187.0	± 6.16
Width of Head (mm.)	961	151.4	± 5.74	928	145.4	± 4.99
Cephalic Index (%)	961	77.1	± 3.45	928	77.8	± 3.10
Height of Head (mm.)	839	134.0	± 4.64	758	129.9	± 5.25
Minimum Forehead Width (mm.)	539	106.65	± 5.65	—	—	—
Dist. between Inner Corners of Eyes (mm.)	538	33.1	± 2.99	—	—	—
Dist. between Outer Corners of Eyes (mm.)	535	102.45	± 5.02	—	—	—
Interpupillary Distance (mm.)	529	66.4	± 3.77	—	—	—
Height of Nose (mm.)	960	53.4	± 3.75	759	50.6	± 4.57
Width of Nose (mm.)	961	40.9	± 3.99	930	37.0	± 3.73
Depth of Nose, sn — tip (mm.)	535	21.3	± 2.04	—	—	—
Depth of Nose, cr — tip (mm.)	535	35.4	± 2.23	—	—	—
Upper Facial Height (mm.)	538	71.3	± 4.06	—	—	—
Total Facial Height (mm.)	534	122.6	± 6.31	—	—	—
Bizygomatic Width (mm.)	956	139.2	± 5.92	917	132.2	± 5.25
Width of Mouth (mm.)	534	53.15	± 4.01	—	—	—
Lip Thickness, center (mm.)	959	21.2	± 4.50	817	18.9	± 4.12
Lip Thickness, right (mm.)	535	23.6	± 4.22	—	—	—
Height of Ear (mm.)	959	60.7	± 4.32	752	58.3	± 4.31
Width of Ear (mm.)	960	33.8	± 2.68	756	32.3	± 2.54
Width of Hand (mm.)	538	85.75	± 4.25	—	—	—
Length of Middle Finger (mm.)	538	108.6	± 6.21	—	—	—
Pigmentation, Black (%)	593	66.65	± 13.98	192	68.4	± 12.03
Pigmentation, Red (%)	593	12.4	± 2.84	192	13.3	± 3.07
Pigmentation, Yellow (%)	593	10.8	± 4.66	192	11.2	± 4.90
Pigmentation, White (%)	593	10.0	± 8.44	192	7.3	± 6.23

imated by the present sample, while those for European populations (not those related to the American Negro, unfortunately), are somewhat higher. The few comparative data on lip thickness show the American Negro mean smaller than any of those for African peoples, and somewhat greater than that for the one White population available.

There is no considerable difference between the widths of mouth of Europeans and Africans, at least as far as is indicated by available data, and the mean for the sample of this study, although slightly lower than the European and American White averages, lies within the range of the more numerous African means. In upper facial height, for which no averages for European peoples are available, that for the American Negro sample seems to be greater than any except that of the East African Bahiru, who presumably represent a large element of Hamitic descent. Respecting total facial height, a large number of averages for other populations are available. While the mean for the present sample is much higher than the averages for the various African peoples represented, it is also, but to a lesser degree, higher than the means of the Old White Americans, the American Indians represented in the table, and the Bavarians. At the same time, for both upper and total facial height, the upper landmark is so unreliable that the comparison of different populations measured by different students is precarious.

Facial width is greater than all except one of the African samples, practically identical with the White American populations measured in this trait, and somewhat smaller than the European populations for which we have comparative data. The measurement of ear height of the American Negro may be compared with the mean for Negroes in general, computed by Karutz, and with his computation of the average ear height for Europeans in general. It lies almost exactly between them. It is higher than the averages for specific West African populations, but lower than that of the Old Americans measured by Hrdlička. There is no apparent difference between African and European ear widths, but the present sample has a surprisingly low average, smaller than that of any of the other peoples listed except the Marquesans, the Great Russians, and the Ainu.

The hand width of the sample is greater, on the average, than those for other Negro or White Americans, or for African peoples among whom this trait has been measured, while in relative hand width the present sample stands between the Africans and Europeans. The length of the middle finger is not as great as that of most peoples for which it has been recorded, European or African. Pigmentation cannot be discussed from a comparative point of view, both because there is an inherent methodological difficulty in the manner in which observations have been made, and because of the difficulty of comparing results of different observers in a trait which involves such a large element of subjective judgement, to say nothing of the fact that the color top used by us has been employed in so few other studies.

The average for forehead width of American Negroes is slightly larger than that for the Old Americans, and much greater than that for the Ashanti of West Africa. The head height comparisons are of slight significance since the difference in the instruments employed by other investigators when compared to the head-spanner we used, the few instances in which the latter was used in other studies, and the uncertainty of the measurement as taken without it, made comparison of no great value. The distance between the outer corners of the eyes of the sample used in this study is greater than that of the Europeans, but generally smaller than that of the Africans for whom data are available. The same holds true, in the main, regarding the distance between the inner corners of the eyes. The interpupillary distance is greater in these American Negroes than in the German soldiers who have been measured in this trait, but, other than these, there are few significant comparative data available.

In shoulder width, the present sample has a larger mean value than the African peoples measured, but smaller than the American Whites represented in the table. The absolute hip width is narrower in the American Negro than in the American White and, relative to stature, it is greater in the Europeans from whom the White ancestry of these American Negroes principally came, than in the present sample, and greater in the latter than in the Africans for whom observations of this trait are available. The height sitting of the present series of American Negroes is greater than that of the Africans, but absolutely smaller than those of the American White and Indian troops. Translated into proportions of stature, or relative height sitting, these values are smaller for the series of this study than for American Whites and Europeans, and generally greater than for the African peoples for whom these figures are available. Finally, as to stature, that of the American Negro is materially greater than that of the West Africans, but slightly smaller than that of the Europeans to whom the present sample would be expected to be related, and smaller than the American Indian populations who might have contributed to their ancestry.

Thus it appears that the American Negro, at least to the extent to which he is represented by the sample used in Chapter III, has combined the two principal racial stocks of which his ancestry is composed. There is one minor point which may be used to illustrate this. It will be remembered that the present American Negroes are much taller than the West Africans, and somewhat smaller than the European peoples to whom they are most likely related. During the Civil War, a large number of Negroes were measured for this trait, as they were in the last war, both averages being given in the table mentioned. The mean of the Civil War Negroes is much nearer the African than is the mean for the present sample, being slightly larger than these, but materially smaller than the European averages for height. This increase in stature may well be due to improved living conditions rather than to the increased amount of White blood introduced into the Negro population since the time when the Civil War Negroes were measured.

2.

In earlier studies made on the basis of measurements taken on New York City school children measured by me, and through correlations of length and width of head in these children and in the Howard University series, it was shown that the Negro is tending to establish in this country a relatively homogeneous physical type.[1] The phase of this research discussed in the section above places the inquiry one step further, by describing this type relative to other populations, particularly those from whom it is descended. Generally, as has been shown, it may be regarded as a composite of the principal racial stocks it represents. In a large majority of traits which have been measured, the means for the American Negro sample of this study fall somewhere between the averages for West African populations, and those of the Western Europeans (including in this term the English and Scottish). That the data from these regions, particularly from Africa, are as scanty as they are, is to be regretted, but we can only use such material for our comparisons as is available.

As to the extent to which the data of the present study may be considered as representative of the American Negro, we may call to mind the discussion in Chapter I, in which it was shown that compared with two entirely different samples of American Negroes, that of some 6,000 men in the army measured in Southern cantonments and that of 100 Negro pauper cadavera from Cleveland, Ohio, the closeness of the means and standard deviations demonstrates very clearly that we are dealing with a representative sample of the entire American Negro population. This is further assured by an analysis of the places of birth of the adult members of the series, which was given in Table III, and which showed that the geographical distribution of these birth places included practically all States where Negroes are found in any considerable numbers, and in addition a large series from the West Indian islands. There may be local types which differ in physical form from the present sample;

---

[1] Herskovits, (II), (IV), (V).

but it is more than doubtful whether such types may be thought of as representative of the American Negro, particularly in these days of extensive Negro migration.

In any event, the data presented in Chapter IV do not seem to allow of such an hypothesis. For there, it will be remembered, the differences between the averages and variabilities of the component series were compared, and a striking lack of difference was found in trait after trait for the several series. Now, it must again be emphasized that these series contained members who were of the most diverse geographical origin. Two of them comprised West Indian Negroes who had migrated to New York City, and two others were made up of American-born Negroes who, at the time of measurement, were living in that city. And few of these had been born in New York, for as was shown, their places of birth encompassed every part of the United States, and the large majority of them were born in the southern states. This was also seen to be true of the Howard University series, which was another one utilized. Then there were the West Virginians, representing such an inbred, sedentary group most likely to differ from the migratory and possibly selected populations of the cities, or of the colleges. Further, there was the Von Luschan series, measured throughout the south, and Miss Blackwood's female southern series.

But the differences which, I must confess, I myself looked for, at least between University and non-University Negroes, did not materialize. Nor were there any apparent differences arising from the fact that the rural West Virginia Negroes, whose ancestors for several generations had been living in the same few counties, marrying among others of the same restricted district, had not been in contact with other local types, as might be the case with the New York Negroes. The Tuskegee Institute females were like the American and West Indian New Yorkers, and the West Virginia females, and the West Virginia males were no different, — in those traits in which no methodological difficulties of measurement made impossible the comparison of results, — from the male series of all these localities, and from the Howard University series. In only one of the component groups were significant differences manifested, and that was the selected well-to-do and professional Harlem series. But in this case there was intentional selection, and a social condition that made it likely that the more Caucasoid traits found among this series should occur there.[1] Finally, the

---

[1] Why well-to-do and professional Negroes should be lighter in skin-color and generally present a non-Negroid appearance can be undoubtedly referred to the historical development of the Negro in the United States. Mulatto children of Whites were often sent north, freed, and given economic opportunities not available to their darker fellows; they thus obtained a

correspondences mentioned in Chapter I between the adult male sample of this study and the Negroes measured in the army by Davenport and Love (of southern birth, in the main), and between the Negro pauper sample measured in the northern city of Cleveland, may allow us to assume that the series of this study represents neither a selected group, nor any local type, but rather the American Negro.

For this American Negro type, which has been described in the course of the development of this work, is apparently so uniform that it may be tapped in any locality where there has not been intensive inbreeding, or social reasons for isolating the Negroes of that locality from the others, and the results will apparently be no different from those obtained from the series presented here. And we may conclude from this, extending our reasoning one step further, that the American Negro, through crossing with the Whites and American Indians with whom he has been brought into contact during the time of slavery and the period following its abolition, is consolidating the racial differences of his various types of ancestry into this definite type, one which is fairly uniform throughout the country, and is (although this is most tentatively put forward) perhaps to be found even in the islands of the Carribean Sea.

3.

If this be the case, there must be a mechanism accounting for the increasing uniformity of type which we have found characteristic of the American Negro. The genealogical data, it will be remembered, showed that only slightly over 20 % of the adults of the total series knew of no White or Indian admixture in their ancestry. There should be some way of accounting first, for the large percentage of individuals who have White and Indian blood, and then, for the selective influence, if there is any, which will explain this consolidation of type.

The answer to the first question is not difficult: while there are only a negligible number of those in the present sample who are primary crosses between Negro and White (using Negro here to mean American Negro), there are many who have White or Indian ancestry in the grandparental generation and before, and this fact, I believe, points to increasing inbreeding within the Negro population, rather than to a continued crossing with the Whites. The Indian mixture, for obvious reasons, must have practically ceased several generations ago, and this is shown by a study of the

---

position of advantage during the post-slavery period which has persisted to the present. I have discussed my reasons for not believing that the favorable social and economic condition in which the lighter colored Negroes are found has other than social reasons in Herskovits (XIV).

genealogical material, and also by the anthropometric analysis of the data, in which the Indian influence, as has been repeatedly remarked, is not to be seen. But the changes in the *mores* within the Negro population regarding inbreeding with Whites is a phenomenon that is not nearly so generally recognized, nor one which would be as readily admitted. However, the smallness of the amount of White parentage in the present sample, and the relative smallness even of White grandparentage, seems to demonstrate that primary crosses are becoming more and more rare. What seems to have happened, therefore, is that the pressure to mate within the Negro community, pressure which is operative almost as strongly within the Negro population, as is that which compels similar racial endogamy on the part of the Whites, has made the individuals, who already represent mixture with White and Indian, marry within the Negro community, thus tending to consolidate the type.

At the same time, are we able to discern a socially selective mechanism at work to produce this result? Light color and non-Negroid traits maintain a strongly invidious position among the Negroes. Can these be pointed to as the primary reason for such a selection, if it exists? I believe strongly, on the basis of the data which are to be given below, that there is such a social selective process at work among the American Negroes. Back of it all, probably, lies an economic motive, which, as I shall point out, is combined with the marriage pattern current in the larger population of which the Negroes form a part. That light color has this invidious character within the Negro community may be seen even when one has only casual contacts with American Negroes. I first noticed it in the Harlem district in New York City, but it is as prevalent in Washington as it is in New York, and those to whom I have mentioned it assert that it is not only true of the Negroes in all other parts of the country, but also of many portions of the West Indies. Certainly the figures as to the relative colors of the parents of the Howard University men measured, and of the husbands and wives who themselves were observed by us when they were measured in Harlem (which will be given below, and which represent couples who come from every part of the United States) would argue that this color selection is not confined to any particular section of this country.

I have been able to point out[1] many instances in which this is operative, and the fact that in a class at Howard University I have obtained from the students twenty-four different names for various degrees of skin color indicates the importance in which this trait is held by the Negroes. That other non-Negroid physical traits are prized may be seen from casual inspection of Negro periodicals[2],

---

[1] Herskovits (III).
[2] Guy B. Johnson (I).

where the percentage of advertisements of products which aim to lighten the color of the skin, straighten the hair, and the like, is at once observable. It has already been mentioned that the study of hair-form is impossible in the American Negro, because of the extensive use of ointments and hair-straightening devices by both men and women, while the terminology at present in use among Negroes as to different types of hair and facial features need only be mentioned to make the point. That is, there are two general types of hair, "good" hair, which is wavy or almost straight, and "stubborn" hair, which is tightly curled. Again, there are two types of facial traits, "broad" features, which are those comprising the wide nose and thick lips of the typical Negro, and "good" ones, which are the reverse. It would, of course, be strange if the Negro did not react to the prevalent behavior patterns and prize the traits which are those of the dominant class in the population of which he forms a part. And skin color, being the outstanding trait which marks the Negro most plainly as such, and distinguishes him most readily from his White neighbors, he reacts to this most strongly.

The prevalent American pattern with regard to marriage, for the entire population of this country whether Negro or White, can be stated as being that the part of the man is to care for his wife, while, on the other hand, he wishes to marry a woman who will bring him social prestige. That the first part of this pattern is reacted to strongly on the part of the Negro has already been shown,[1] for I found that the proportion of wives of men engaged in a given class of occupation is seen to grow smaller as there is a rise in the economic scale, since the income of the husband relieves is wife. The second takes this form: the dark man wishes to marry a wife whose color is lighter than his own, since she will bring him prestige within his own group through being lighter-colored. She, on the other hand, is the social superior in the arrangement, and feels economically more secure in it. As it seemed to those Negroes who discussed the matter with me, then, there is a tendency for light women to marry darker men, the dark women either marrying dark men or not marrying at all, while the light men, to an appreciable extent, "pass" over into the White community[2]. A simple test of this hypothesis was made, and the results show, if we regard them conservatively, a strong tendency in this direction.

---

[1] Herskovits (VII).
[2] Confirmation of this is seen in the analysis of the 1920 Census figures by Charles S. Johnson, given editorially in Opportunity (I), where it is noted that while among the "black" population there are 1,000 females to every 1,008 males, in the "mulatto" there are only 886 males to every 1,000 females. The earlier analysis by Hart (I) points to the same phenomenon, which can be accounted for most readily by the assumption which I have drawn above.

Of the men who were measured at Howard University, 380 were asked the question, "Who is the lighter, your father or your mother?" The possible answers are, of course, three: father lighter, mother lighter, or both parents about the same color. The actual results from the answers, in numbers, were

> Father lighter: 115
> About the same: 50
> Mother lighter: 215

or, to throw the gross figures into percentages of the total,

> Father lighter: 30.3%
> About the same: 13.2%
> Mother lighter: 56.5%

Certainly a percentage of this size, in a three-way possibility, is provocative, and seems to indicate, as I have said, that this strong tendency toward a mating of men with lighter women actually exists. And such a tendency, if continued, must even further affect the physical type of the American Negro.

As the research went on, a further opportunity presented itself to check, and in some measure obtain a control for the percentages which I have given for the parents of the Howard men. For these, after all, are only valid if the statements of the men as to the comparative color of their parents were correct. It will be remembered that the measuring done in New York City by Louis King and myself during the winter of 1925—1926 was for the purpose of obtaining measurements on family groups, in order that the genetic problems involved in this racially mixed population might be adequately studied. To obtain these data, we attempted in every case to measure each family as completely as possible, — and as a result our material contains 174 two-parent families, who, because of the color-top study of pigmentation, furnish the material necessary for such a control study, in quantitative fashion, of the manner in which this color selection operates among the American Negroes.

The proportions of the relative darkness of husband and wife as observed, check to a remarkable extent with the statements of the Howard University students, the proportions for the three classes given above for the Harlem couples being:

> Father lighter: 49   29.0%
> Same color: 25   14.5%
> Mother lighter: 100   56.5%

This shows that the tendency for light women to marry darker men observed through the statements of the Howard students is valid, but it is of interest to see the extent to which further analysis throws light on the manner in which the tendency operates. The average values for the black element of the color-top (in the terms we have used for it, i. e., percentage of the total surface of the top) and their variabilities are:

$$\begin{array}{lcc} \text{Husbands:} & 72.5\% & \pm\ 13.33 \\ \text{Wives:} & 67.7\% & \pm\ 13.56 \end{array}$$

and it is thus seen that the men who are party to the matings are darker than the women.

The possibility that a sex difference in color is involved here must always be considered, — that is, that pigmentation is a sex-linked characteristic, and that there is an innate tendency for women to be lighter than men. However, the data given in Chapter V demonstrate what whatever differences may exist as far as the various series of this study are concerned, are not due to inborn sex differences.[1] Because of their importance for the present argument, I give here once more the statistical constants for the value of the black in the color-top, for the total adult male and female series which I myself measured:

$$\begin{array}{lccc} \text{Males:} & 593 & 66.65 & \pm\ 13.98 \\ \text{Females:} & 192 & 68.36 & \pm\ 12.03 \end{array}$$

Or we may check again by considering a male and female series of the same age group, one which includes persons who are somewhat younger than the adult series just given. Taking the age for which there are the most adequate female data, that of 7 years, we have, for boys and girls of this age:

$$\begin{array}{lccc} \text{Males:} & 150 & 70.94 & \pm\ 11.43 \\ \text{Females:} & 62 & 70.70 & \pm\ 10.11 \end{array}$$

These results give forceful testimony that there is no sex-linked difference involved in the average skin color of American Negroes, and it may therefore be assumed that the lighter average value of the black color from color-top readings of the pigmentation of the wives of this Harlem series, when they are compared in this respect to their husbands, is actually the result of social selection.

It is of interest to consider in detail the color of each husband with respect to that of his wife, and we have the results which are given in Table XCVIII. As has been emphasized before, all the curves for the colors of the color-top tend more or less to skewness, and the black for both sexes masses heavily toward the upper ranges. Therefore, the calculation of the coefficient of correlation, which is

---

[1] This point was even more firmly established by the curves showing age-changes in pigmentation for the entire series worked out by Barnes(I), who, by introducing a corrective factor, was able to combine the measurements made by the different observers. Sex differences are shown in her work to be those of chance only.

Results of this Study

essentially applicable only to relationships between distributions which follow the Gaussian curve, has not been attempted. The average color (expressed in amounts of the percentage of black) of the wives for each color of husband is given in the same table. Because of the general character of slightly related correlation values, and the difference in the averages of the two series, the wives in the lower ranges are somewhat darker than the husbands. This is not strange, as the very light men would naturally have some difficulty in marrying women who are lighter than themselves. When we come to the darker men, however, and where the number of cases becomes somewhat larger, the wives appear to be lighter than their husbands. Graphic expression of these results are shown in Figure 21.

We may also consider the color of each wife with respect to that of her husband (Table XCVIII). Here, in thirteen of the classes, the

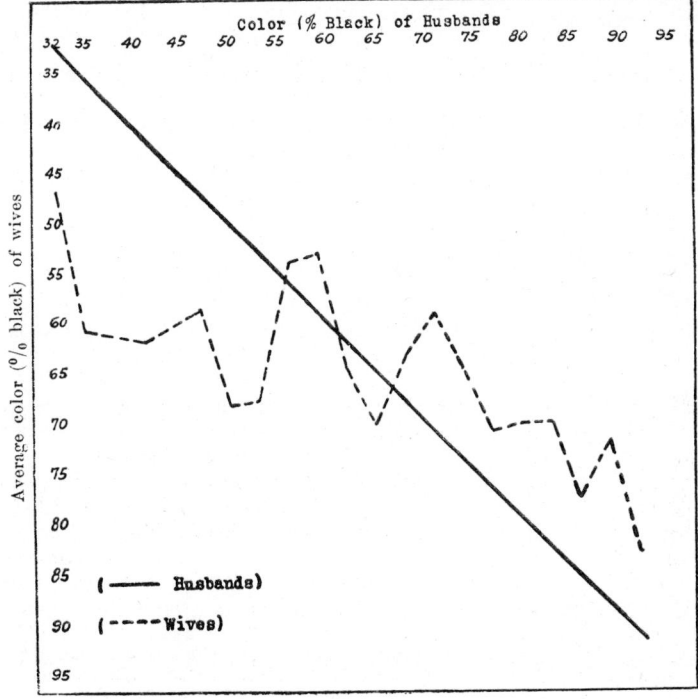

Fig. 21.

Average Skin-Color of Wives (% black) for Increasingly Dark Husbands.

husbands are darker than their wives; in two (including the darkest) they are of the same color; while in only six are they lighter. The relationship between the two series also comes out somewhat more clearly if the graph, Figure 22, be consulted, where it may be seen to be strongly curvilinear. The darkest women, again, as might be expected, seem to marry men of about their own or lighter color, but the lighter women, and those not pronouncedly dark, marry men decidedly darker than themselves.

An attempt was also made to see whether the selection among the Negroes is on the basis of color only, or is also made with regard to the extent to which other traits are Negroid or non-Negroid. Lip thickness and the width of the nose were correlated (there being no skewness to the curves for these traits), but the resulting correlations show practically nothing, being, for lip thickness,

Table
Skin Color of Husbands and

		31—33	34—36	37—39	40—42	43—45	46—48	49—51	52—54	55—57	58—60	61—63
Color of Wives (in % of Black)	31—33	—	—	—	—	—	—	—	—	—	—	—
	34—36	—	—	—	—	—	—	—	—	—	1	—
	37—39	—	—	—	—	—	—	—	—	—	—	—
	40—42	—	—	—	—	—	—	—	—	—	—	—
	43—45	—	—	—	—	—	—	—	—	1	—	—
	46—48	1	1	—	1	—	—	—	—	—	1	1
	49—51	—	—	—	—	—	—	—	—	1	1	—
	52—54	—	—	—	—	—	—	1	—	2	3	—
	55—57	—	—	—	1	—	—	—	—	1	—	1
	58—60	—	—	—	—	—	1	1	—	1	1	1
	61—63	—	1	—	—	—	—	—	—	—	—	2
	64—66	—	—	—	—	—	—	—	1	1	—	1
	67—69	—	—	—	—	—	—	2	—	—	—	—
	70—72	—	—	—	—	—	—	—	1	—	—	1
	73—75	—	1	—	—	—	—	2	—	—	—	2
	76—78	—	—	—	—	—	—	—	—	—	1	—
	79—81	—	—	—	—	—	—	—	—	—	—	1
	82—84	—	—	—	1	—	—	1	—	—	—	—
	85—87	—	—	—	—	—	—	—	—	—	—	—
	88—90	—	—	—	—	—	—	—	—	—	—	—
	91—93	—	—	—	—	—	—	—	—	—	—	—
	Totals	1	3	—	3	—	1	7	2	7	8	10
	Averages	47.0	61.0	—	62.0	—	59.0	68.4	68.2	54.3	53.4	65.0

	Average	σ
Husbands	72.5	± 13.11
Wives	76.7	± 13.56

+ 0.22, and for nose width, + 0.13. The averages for the wives are well below those for the husbands, but this is to be accounted for as being due to sex differences.

Thus it seems that a social selection among the Negroes of this country on the basis of skin color is occurring. What the effect on future generations will be depends largely on the continuing in force of the present *mores* regarding such selection. If they continue, however, the daughters of these matings will, in the main, be darker than their mothers, and, if they are selected in turn and choose still darker men, the effect will be that the American Negro population will become more like the Negroid type as far as skin color is concerned, since the relative amount of Negro blood in the Negro population will be increased. However, the genealogies presented in this study show conclusively that there is too much White and

XCVIII
Wives, New York Negroes
(in % of Black)

64–66	67–69	70–72	73–75	76–78	79–81	82–84	85–87	88–90	91–93	Total	Av.
—	—	—	—	—	—	1	—	—	—	1	83.0
—	—	—	—	—	—	—	—	—	—	1	59.0
—	—	1	—	—	—	—	—	—	—	1	71.0
—	—	1	1	—	—	—	—	1	—	3	78.0
—	—	1	—	—	1	—	—	—	—	3	69.0
—	—	—	—	—	—	2	1	—	—	8	60.1
—	1	—	1	1	—	1	—	—	—	6	69.5
1	—	—	1	1	1	—	—	1	—	11	65.8
—	—	—	3	—	1	—	—	—	—	7	65.9
—	6	1	1	1	2	1	1	—	—	18	68.3
—	2	2	1	—	2	2	—	—	—	12	69.7
1	1	—	—	1	1	—	—	1	1	9	71.3
—	2	1	1	—	1	—	—	—	—	7	65.9
—	—	1	1	2	1	1	2	1	—	11	74.4
1	1	1	1	2	1	1	3	—	—	16	69.5
1	2	—	—	1	5	2	1	1	—	14	77.0
—	—	1	2	2	3	4	—	2	—	15	79.0
1	—	—	1	1	2	4	1	1	—	13	74.9
—	—	—	1	—	—	2	5	1	1	10	85.1
—	—	—	—	1	1	—	3	1	—	6	85.0
—	—	—	—	—	—	—	—	—	2	2	92.0
5	15	10	15	13	22	21	17	10	4	174	
70.1	63.8	59.9	65.0	71.2	70.6	70.6	78.0	72.5	83.7		

American Indian blood in the American Negro population to permit of reversion to the pure Negro type. On the other hand, with this social selection in operation, and with the stoppage of crossing with the Whites to any appreciable extent, it seems reasonable to assume that there will not be change toward the White norm.

As for the aspect of the homogeneity of the American Negro type which is being established, this social selective mechanism is of the greatest significance. For, if it continues, and if the present *mores* concerning race crossing persist and continue — the isolation of the Negroes from the Whites in this country, on the one hand, and the feeling of the Negroes regarding the undesirability of crossing with the Whites on the other, — then an even greater homogeneity of type than exists at present may be expected.

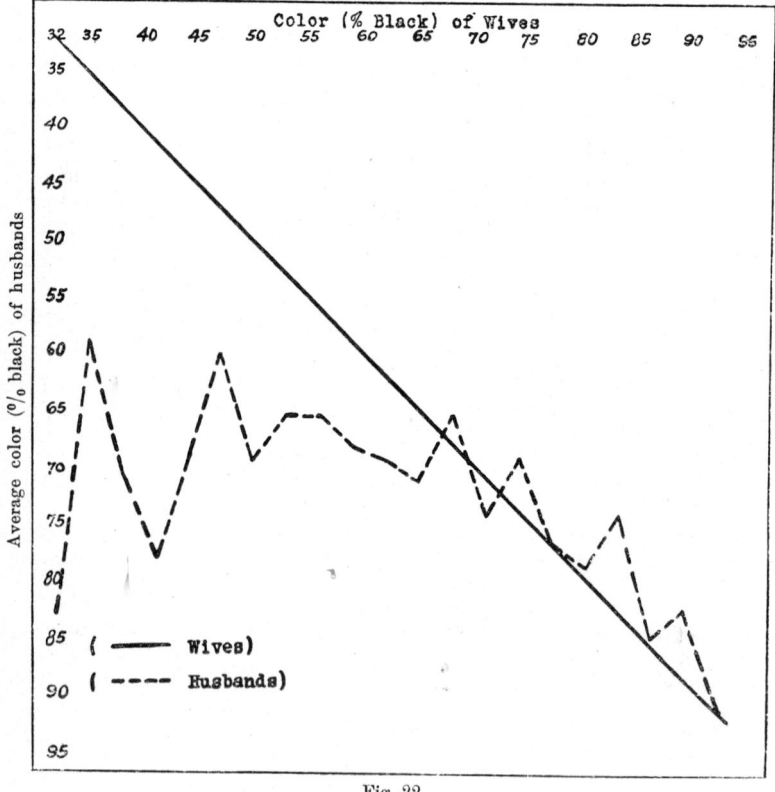

Fig. 22.

Average Skin-Color of Husbands (% black) for Increasingly Dark Wives.

4.

The earlier study of the homogeneity of American Negroes has been carried on, mainly, with sets of fraternities from one of the public schools in New York City. The calculations involved in analyzing this sample are suggestive. Low variability is an index of homogeneity[1], and if we compare the variability of the entire sample of this study with the variabilities of the peoples from which it has sprung, and, when possible, with available samples of White Americans selected at random, it should give us further material for consideration of this point. And if such a comparison is made, it will be found that the variability, as expressed by the standard deviation (sigma), is usually lower for a given trait in the American Negro population than it is for a corresponding one in the Whites, and that it is not much greater, if greater at all, than those of the European and British populations which may be regarded as having contributed materially to its ancestry.

If we take the traits which have been measured during this research *seriatim* with regard to their variabilities, we find that that for head length is much smaller than for Todd's White Americans, but materially larger than the variability of the Old White Americans (a selected group), the North European, and the West African populations for which standard deviations are available. For head width, it is the highest of all the populations recorded, except for the foreign-born Bohemians. The variability of the cephalic index of American Negroes is much smaller than that of Todd's Whites, but it is greater than the variabilities of the other populations represented in the comparative table for this trait in Chapter III, except that of the Delaware Indians, Swedes, Ekoi, and Akikuyu, in which case it is about the same.

With regard to nasal height, the mean square variability of the American Negroes is, generally speaking, of about an average amount, while in nasal depth they are less variable than the Ekoi, the only people for whom this value was available. The variability of lip thickness, when compared with that of American Whites and the West African Ekoi, is greater in the sample used in this study; in mouth width the American Negro is less variable than the Vai, but more so than the Ekoi. The variability of upper facial height of the American Negro is the smallest of all the populations listed in Chapter III, these all being African, and the standard deviation for total facial height is comparatively low. For bizygomatic width, the American Whites measured by Todd are materially more variable than the Negroes measured by him, or by myself, although

---

[1] It must be emphasized that variability is here employed as an index of homogeneity, and not, as is often the case, as one of racial purity, something which is obviously not a characteristic of the American Negro. For a somewhat extended discussion of this theoretical point, see Herskovits, (X).

these last are more variable in this respect than of other populations listed, including the Old White Americans, except Goring's series of English criminals.

As to height of the ear, the Marquesans, the English criminals, and the Old White Americans are more variable than the American Negro, while the Ekoi and the Swedes are less so; while for breadth of the ear, the present sample varies more than do the Swedes or Old White Americans, and less than the Ekoi. The hand width of the American Negroes is less variable than that of the Whites although it is more so than the West African Ekoi, while the sigma for the length of the middle finger of this sample is the largest of any population for which comparative material for this trait has been found. There are only a few populations for which variability of the minimum forehead width could be obtained, but of these this sample of American Negroes is the most variable, while in head height it exhibits the lowest variability of any population for which this measurement is available.

For the distance between the inner corners of the eyes, the present sample lies between the two African populations given; in the case of the distance between the outer corners, three peoples are less variable, and one more so. The variabilities of the Whites and Negroes measured in the army for shoulder width shows the Whites to be more variable than the Negroes, and they are also materially more variable than the present sample, which, in turn, varies more than the Sioux and the Ekoi. The same is true for hip width as regards the Americans, for the Negro troops are less variable than the White, while the sigma of the present sample is smaller than those of either of the above. The mean square deviation for sitting height of the sample used here, when compared with that of the other populations for which variability has been computed, is seen to be relatively in a median position. In stature, this sample is smaller in variability than most of the West African populations, the White troops measured during the late war, and most of the White populations to which it might be expected to be generically related, except the Old White Americans.

If the variability of the adult male series used in Chapter III to represent the sample as a whole, or, for that matter, the American Negro population in general, be roughly classed (as it must be in a comparison such as I am attempting here) as more or less variable than other populations, we find that in ten of the traits these adult male American Negroes are at about the top of the list, that in seven, they are about at the center, while in about six they are among the least variable. This would be surprising, had the relative homogeneity of the American Negro not been foreshadowed in several earlier short studies based on portions of these data or through the consideration of the comparative variability of Todd's cadavera material of Whites and Negroes. What is apparently happening, therefore, it may again be repeated, is that this group of Negro-Indian-White hybrids, so greatly mixed racially, are inbreeding to form a type, the general variability of which in numerous traits is not only less than that of an unselected sample of American Whites, but in many instances no greater than the unmixed European, African, and American Indian peoples who have contributed to its ancestry.

This would be a result sufficiently unexpected in itself, but when it is considered in the light of the commonly accepted generalization that the variability of a population is an index of its racial purity, it is even more surprising. When the data from the genealogical groups bearing on their relative variability are reviewed and conclusions are drawn from these data as they arrange themselves under statistical analysis, this theoretical problem will be discussed somewhat at greater length. But here it suffices to say that our finding that the American Negro-hybrid population has smaller, or about the same variability in a large portion of traits when compared with the "pure" populations from which it has come, gives one pause as to the tenability of the theory that variability is an index to racial purity. It must also cause us to reconsider the Mendelian mechanisms operative in a large number of crosses between individuals of racial groups as diverse in the traits measured, as are the ancestral races of the American Negro. If we disregard for the moment the Indian element, and consider only the Negro and White, we have a situation something like this: if we assume a variable trait in one population having a mean a and in a second having a mean b, the two means being as different as are some of those of Negroes and Whites, then, if there be any segregation of characteristics at all, the variability of this hybrid group must be increased in the F_2 and succeeding generations. If we add an Indian mean, c, then the increase in variability might be even greater. But we find that these hybrids, mixed, as we have seen, from all three stocks, have, as far as we know, in many traits a variability as low or lower than any of the parent populations, — a result certainly not consonant with the theory as it is generally set forth. In this connection it is worth remarking that lack of increase in variability of width of face of half-breeds of Indian and European ancestry, races which differ much in regard to this trait, has been shown by Boas (II) and Sullivan (II). The greater the number of assumed unit factors, the less will be the increase in variability, but without auxiliary hypotheses the decrease in variability cannot be explained.

Let us, however, leave this phase of the matter until later, when the variability of the genealogical classes in the traits measured will be discussed, for there one may compare variations of the mixed groups with that of one which has been shown to be in the main pure Negro. We may state at this point that as a result of comparing means and standard deviations for the traits measured in this sample and in other populations for which these are available, the conclusion must be reached that the American Negro is forming a type which lies somewhere between the European, African, and American Indian, ancestral types which have gone to make his physical form what it is, and further that in spite of this enormous amount of racial mixture which it represents, it has no unusually high variability, i. e. it is relatively homogeneous.

5.

The genealogical analysis of the Howard University sample showed that these men, as well as the other male and female adults comprising the other series of this study, could be classified into four principal groups on the basis of amounts of Negro ancestry, and that each of these four classes could again be divided into those with Indian ancestry, and those without it. This latter group, it will be remembered, comprised 72.7 % of the entire sample, while those with Indian mixture constituted the remaining 27.3 %. The Indian element in the ethnic composition of this group of American Negroes is the most uncertain of the three from which it is descended because of two reasons. In the first place, an invidious element is attached to Indian ancestry among the American Negroes, and, therefore, it may well be that statements as to the presence of this element in one's ancestry are something in the nature of family tradition without too secure basis in fact. The other reason why this ancestral element might fail to be accurately given is the fact that most crossing with the Indians seems to have occurred before the abolition of slavery or shortly thereafter, and that in consequence enough generations have passed so that the tradition of remote Indian mixture might well be inaccurate.

Certainly the genealogical analysis of the anthropometric data does not indicate any great influence of the Indian element upon the physical characteristics of the American Negro. For, as may be seen from the averages for the genealogical groups in the traits measured, there is ordinarily no appreciable difference between a class with a given amount of Negro and White ancestry but no Indian, and a corresponding one which has the same amounts of these racial elements, with Indian in addition. There is surely nothing like the very suggestive differences observable for classes having different amounts of White mixture. However, that there has been some influence is suggested by the average for the entire sample when this is compared with those of such Indian populations for which there are available data, and those of European and African peoples, since the American Negro averages for most of the traits fall between them. Pending the collection of more comparative material among those Indian tribes which have contributed most to the ancestry of the American Negro, this question must be regarded as one for further research.

Results of this Study

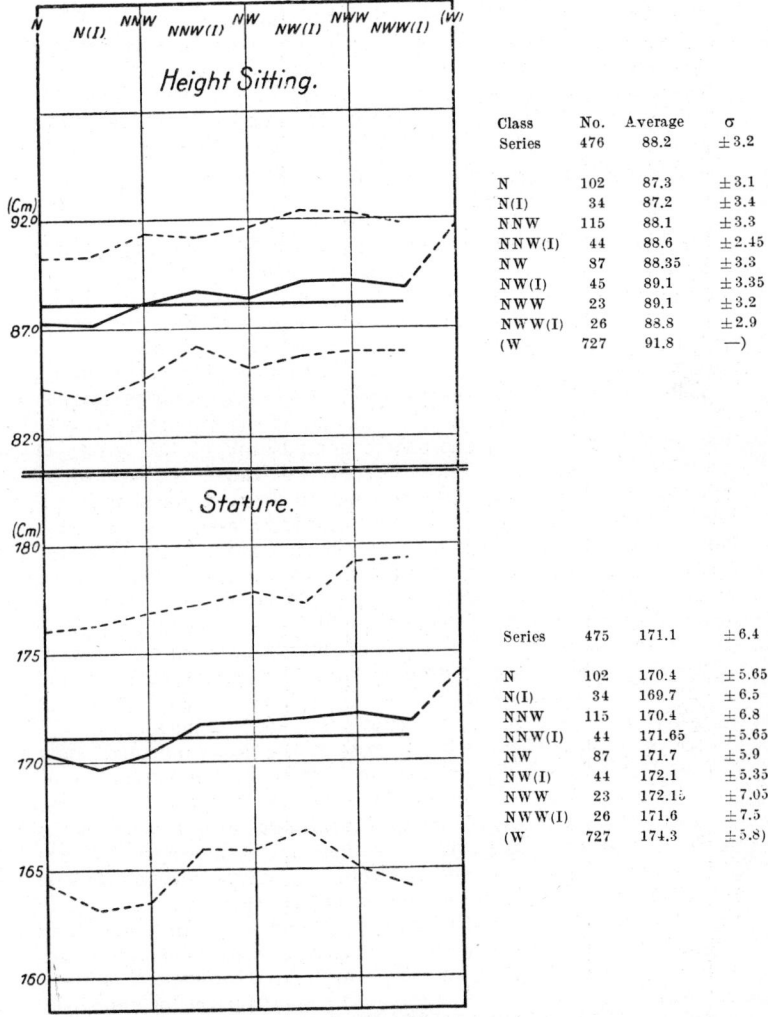

Class	No.	Average	σ
Series	476	88.2	±3.2
N	102	87.3	±3.1
N(I)	34	87.2	±3.4
NNW	115	88.1	±3.3
NNW(I)	44	88.6	±2.45
NW	87	88.35	±3.3
NW(I)	45	89.1	±3.35
NWW	23	89.1	±3.2
NWW(I)	26	88.8	±2.9
(W	727	91.8	—)

Series	475	171.1	±6.4
N	102	170.4	±5.65
N(I)	34	169.7	±6.5
NNW	115	170.4	±6.8
NNW(I)	44	171.65	±5.65
NW	87	171.7	±5.9
NW(I)	44	172.1	±5.35
NWW	23	172.15	±7.05
NWW(I)	26	171.6	±7.5
(W	727	174.3	±5.8)

Fig. 23.
Change in Average Values of Height Sitting and Stature, with Various Degrees of Mixed Negro-White Ancestry. Howard University Sample.

254   The Anthropometry of the American Negro

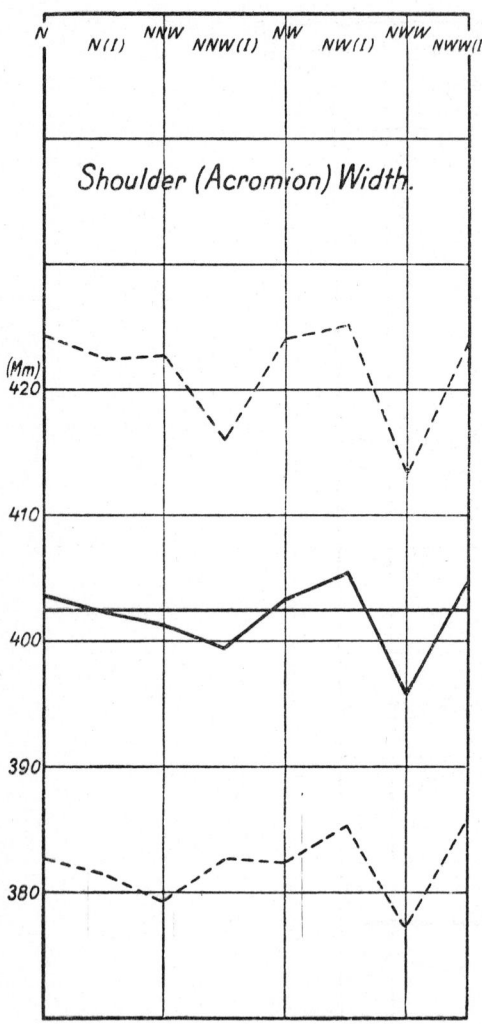

Class	No.	Average	σ
Series	476	402.45	±20.4
N	102	403.95	±20.8
N(I)	34	402.05	±20.55
NNW	115	401.35	±21.55
NNW(I)	44	399.45	±16.7
NW	87	403.1	±20.9
NW(I)	45	405.15	±20.05
NWW	23	395.75	±18.1
NWW(I)	26	405.0	±19.15

Fig. 24.
Change in Average Values in Acromion Width, with
Various Degrees of Mixed Negro-White Ancestry.
Howard University Sample.

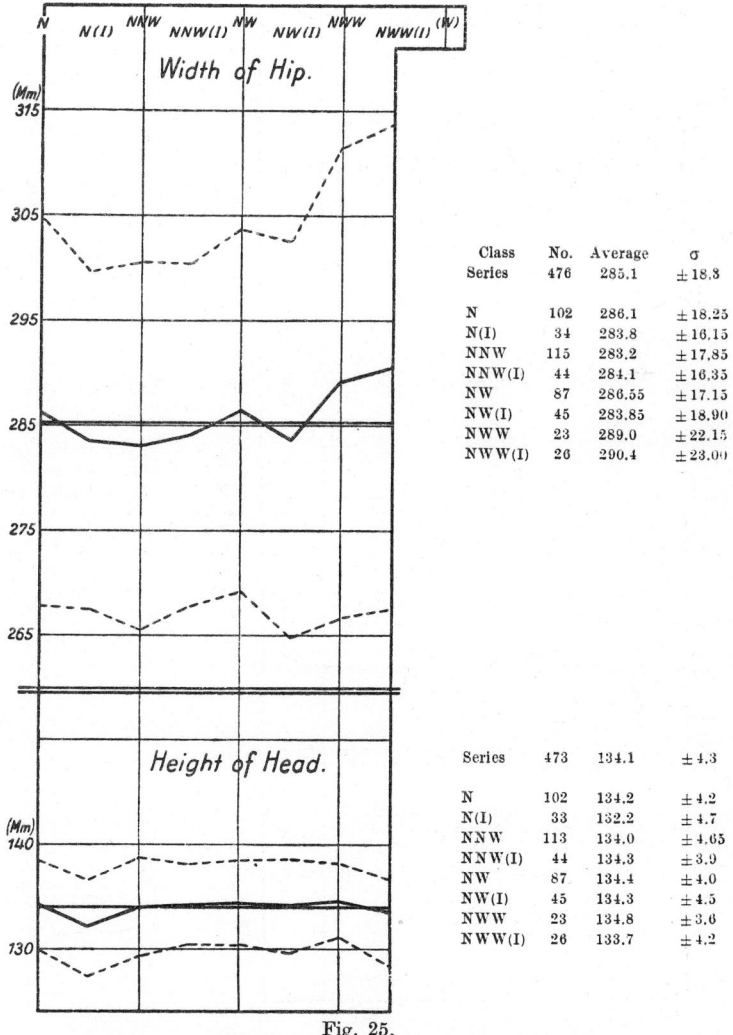

Fig. 25.
Change in Average Values of Width of Hip and Height of Head, with Various Degrees of Mixed Negro-White Ancestry. Howard University Sample.

256 The Anthropometry of the American Negro

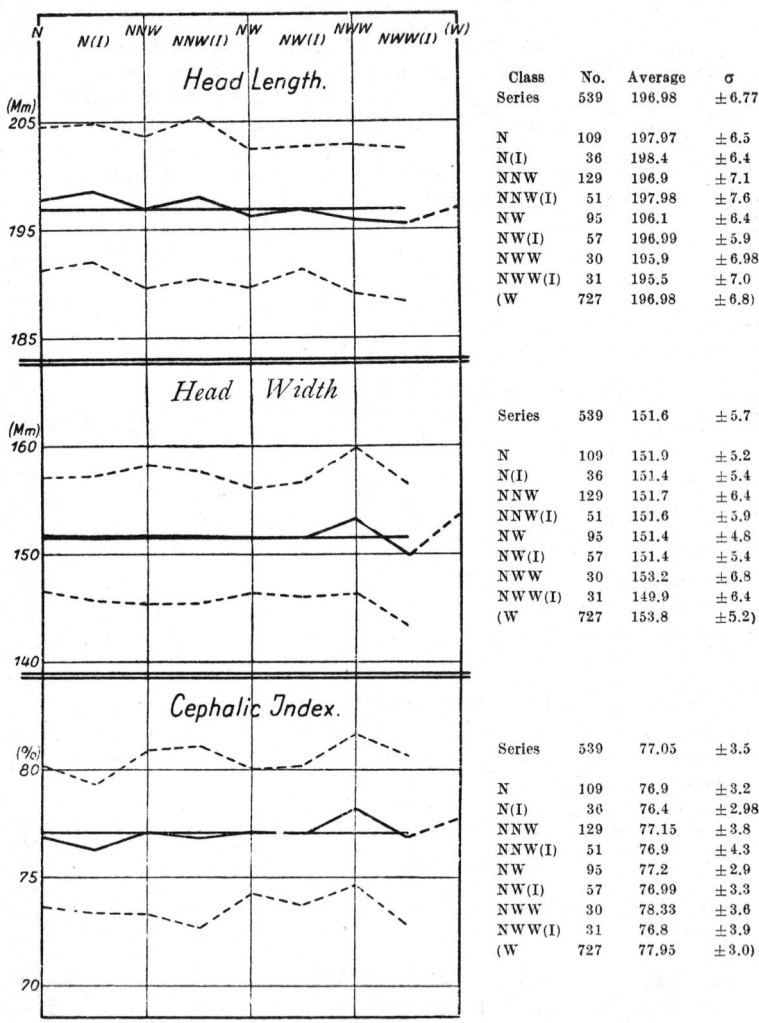

Fig. 26.
Change in Average Values of Head Length, Head Width, and Cephalic Index, with Various Degrees of Mixed Negro-White Ancestry. Howard University Sample.

Results of this Study

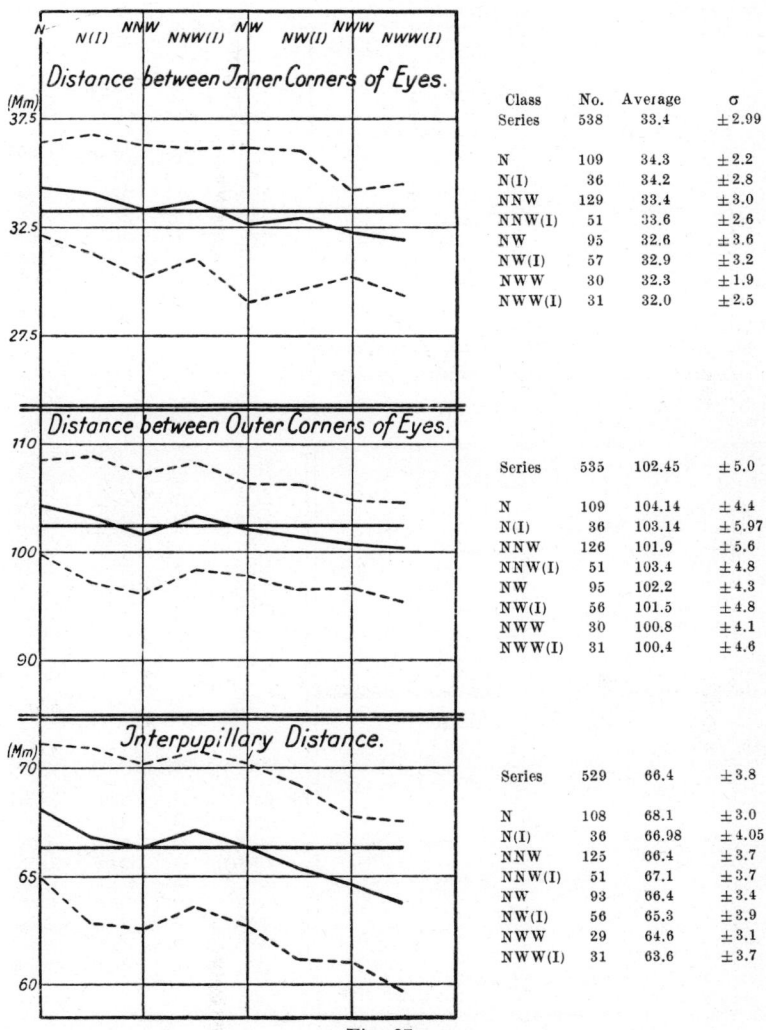

Fig. 27.
Change in Average Values of Distance between Inner and Outer Corners of Eyes and Interpupillary Distance, with Various Degrees of Mixed Negro-White Ancestry. Howard University Sample.

Distance between Inner Corners of Eyes

Class	No.	Average	σ
Series	538	33.4	±2.99
N	109	34.3	±2.2
N(I)	36	34.2	±2.8
NNW	129	33.4	±3.0
NNW(I)	51	33.6	±2.6
NW	95	32.6	±3.6
NW(I)	57	32.9	±3.2
NWW	30	32.3	±1.9
NWW(I)	31	32.0	±2.5

Distance between Outer Corners of Eyes

Class	No.	Average	σ
Series	535	102.45	±5.0
N	109	104.14	±4.4
N(I)	36	103.14	±5.97
NNW	126	101.9	±5.6
NNW(I)	51	103.4	±4.8
NW	95	102.2	±4.3
NW(I)	56	101.5	±4.8
NWW	30	100.8	±4.1
NWW(I)	31	100.4	±4.6

Interpupillary Distance

Class	No.	Average	σ
Series	529	66.4	±3.8
N	108	68.1	±3.0
N(I)	36	66.98	±4.05
NNW	125	66.4	±3.7
NNW(I)	51	67.1	±3.7
NW	93	66.4	±3.4
NW(I)	56	65.3	±3.9
NWW	29	64.6	±3.1
NWW(I)	31	63.6	±3.7

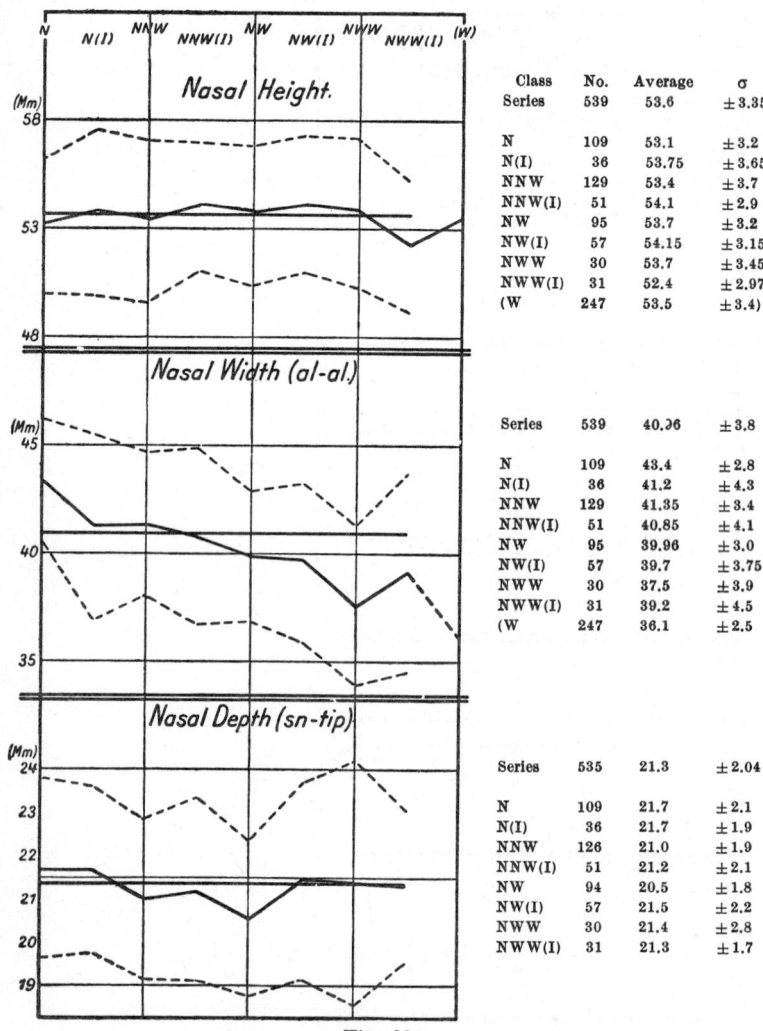

Fig. 28.
Change in Average Values of Nasal Height, Width and Depth (sn. — tip), with Various Degrees of Mixed Negro-White Ancestry. Howard University Sample.

Results of this Study 259

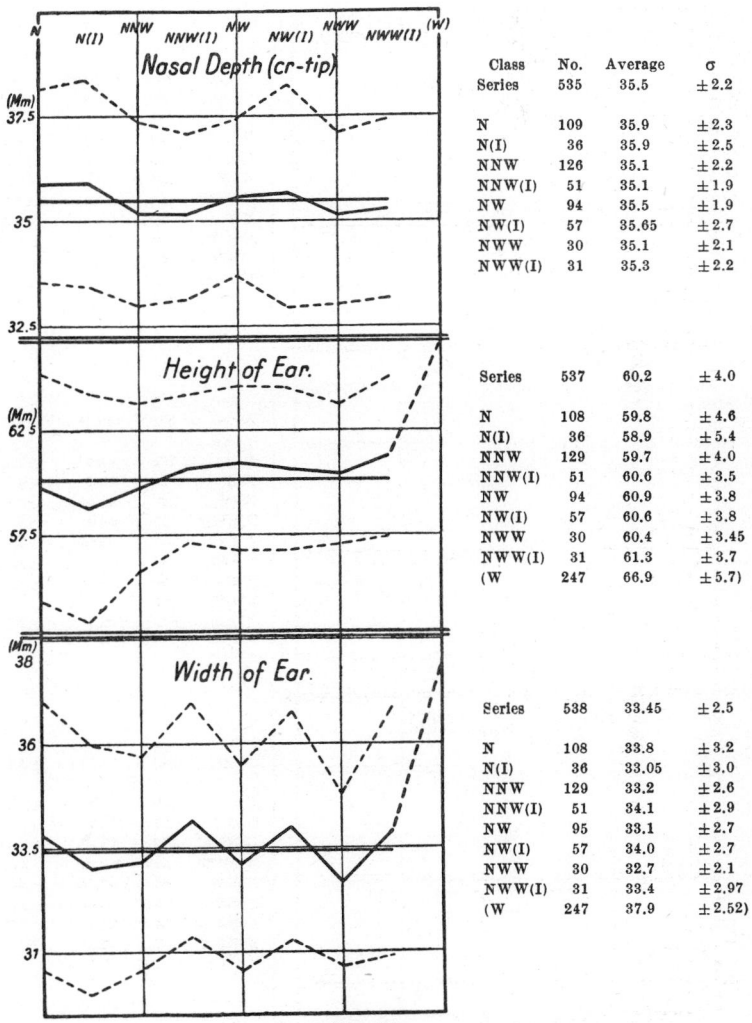

Class	No.	Average	σ
Series	535	35.5	±2.2
N	109	35.9	±2.3
N(I)	36	35.9	±2.5
NNW	126	35.1	±2.2
NNW(I)	51	35.1	±1.9
NW	94	35.5	±1.9
NW(I)	57	35.65	±2.7
NWW	30	35.1	±2.1
NWW(I)	31	35.3	±2.2
Series	537	60.2	±4.0
N	108	59.8	±4.6
N(I)	36	58.9	±5.4
NNW	129	59.7	±4.0
NNW(I)	51	60.6	±3.5
NW	94	60.9	±3.8
NW(I)	57	60.6	±3.8
NWW	30	60.4	±3.45
NWW(I)	31	61.3	±3.7
(W	247	66.9	±5.7)
Series	538	33.45	±2.5
N	108	33.8	±3.2
N(I)	36	33.05	±3.0
NNW	129	33.2	±2.6
NNW(I)	51	34.1	±2.9
NW	95	33.1	±2.7
NW(I)	57	34.0	±2.7
NWW	30	32.7	±2.1
NWW(I)	31	33.4	±2.97
(W	247	37.9	±2.52)

Fig. 29.
Change in Average Values of Nasal Depth (cr — tip), Height and Width of Ear, with Various Degrees of Mixed-Negro White Ancestry. Howard University Sample.

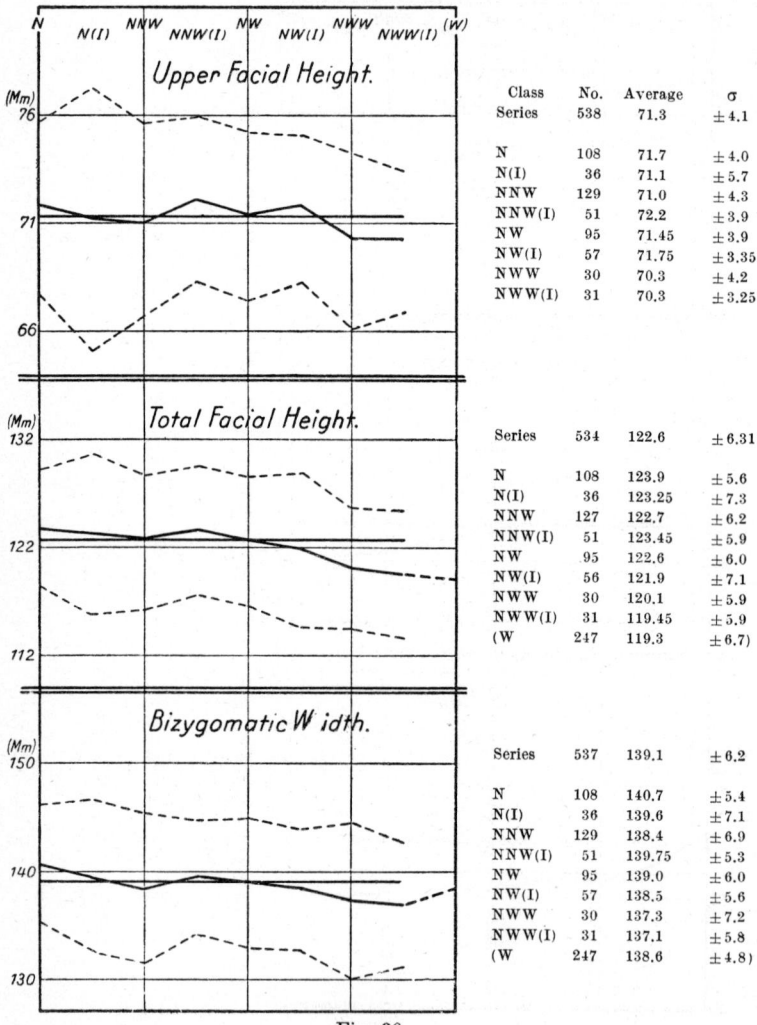

Fig. 30.
Change in Average Values of Upper and Total Facial Height and Bizygomatic Width, with Various Degrees of Mixed Negro-White Ancestry. Howard University Sample.

Results of this Study

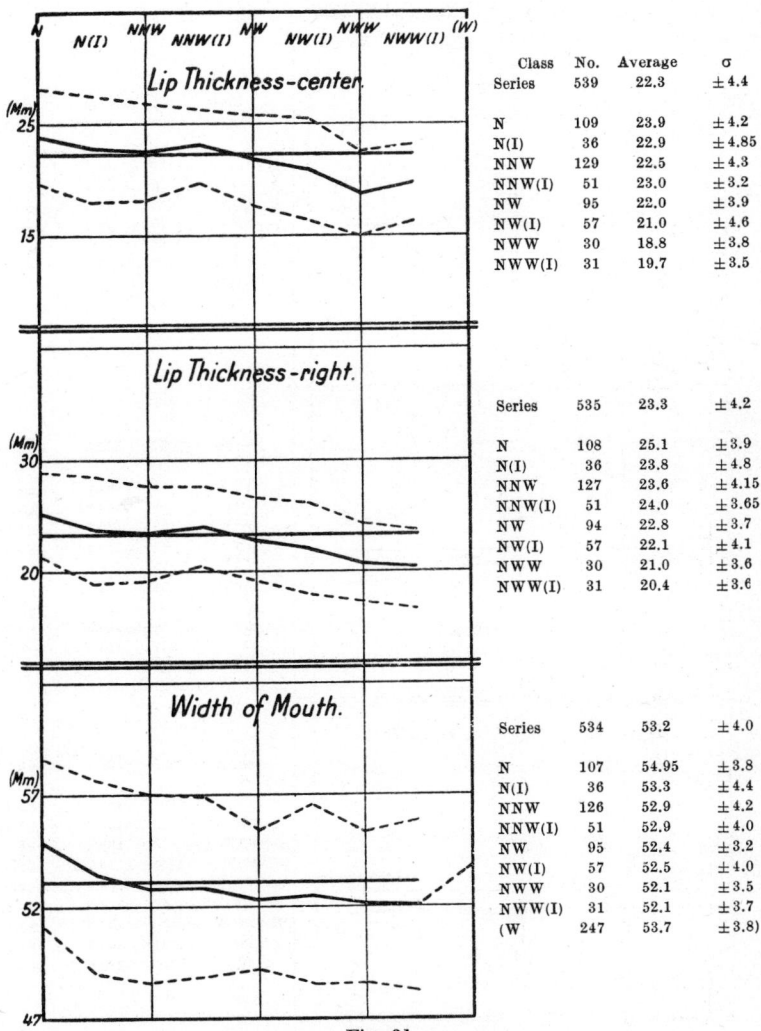

Fig. 31.
Change in Average Values of Lip Thickness, Center and Right, and Width of Mouth, with Various Degrees of Mixed Negro-White Ancestry. Howard University Sample.

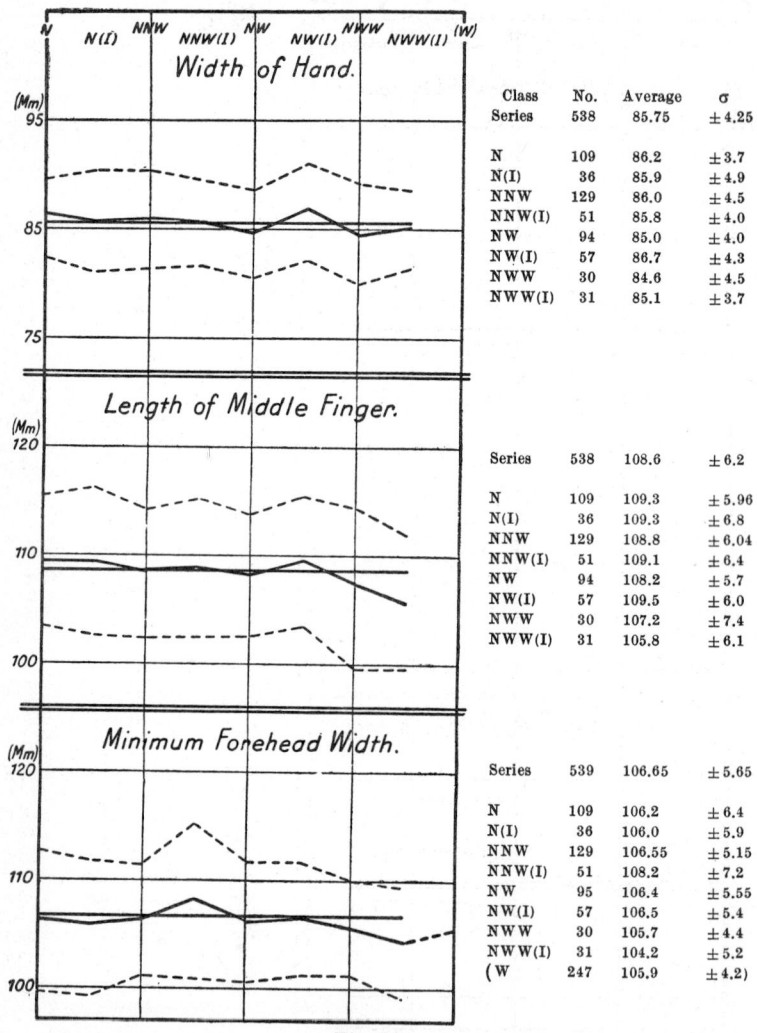

Fig. 32.
Change in Average Values of Width of Hand, Length of Middle Finger, and Minimum Forehead Width, with Various Degrees of Mixed Negro-White Ancestry.
Howard University Sample.

Results of this Study

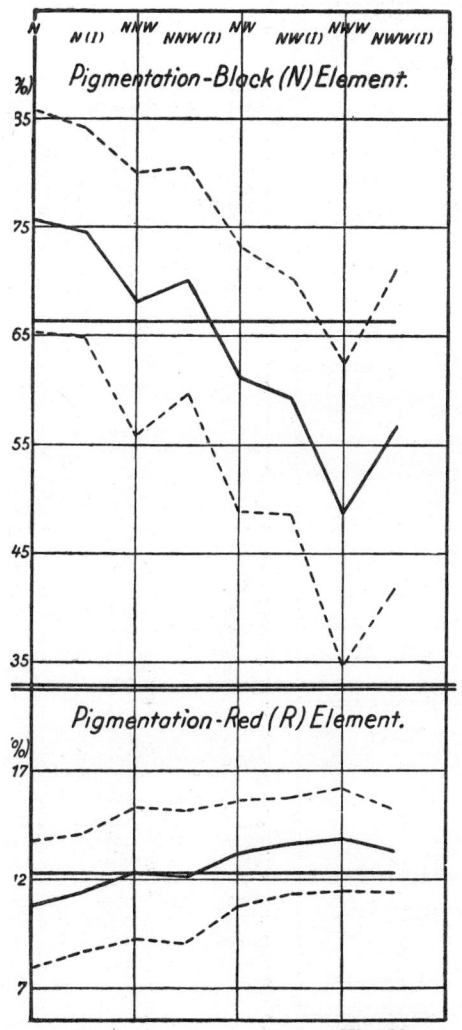

Class	No.	Average	σ
Series	534	66.4	±13.85
N	109	75.5	±10.3
N(I)	36	74.9	± 9.5
NNW	127	68.3	±11.6
NNW(I)	50	70.3	±10.4
NW	94	61.2	±12.0
NW(I)	56	59.4	±11.2
NWW	30	48.7	±13.7
NWW(I)	31	56.9	±14.4

Series	534	12.4	±2.8
N	109	10.8	±2.9
N(I)	36	11.0	±2.6
NNW	127	12.45	±2.8
NNW(I)	50	12.2	±2.9
NW	94	13.2	±2.3
NW(I)	56	13.6	±2.2
NWW	30	13.9	±2.25
NWW(I)	31	13.4	±1.7

Fig. 33.
Change in Average Values of Pigmentation, Black (N) and Red (R),
with Various Degrees of Mixed Negro-White Ancestry.
Howard University Sample.

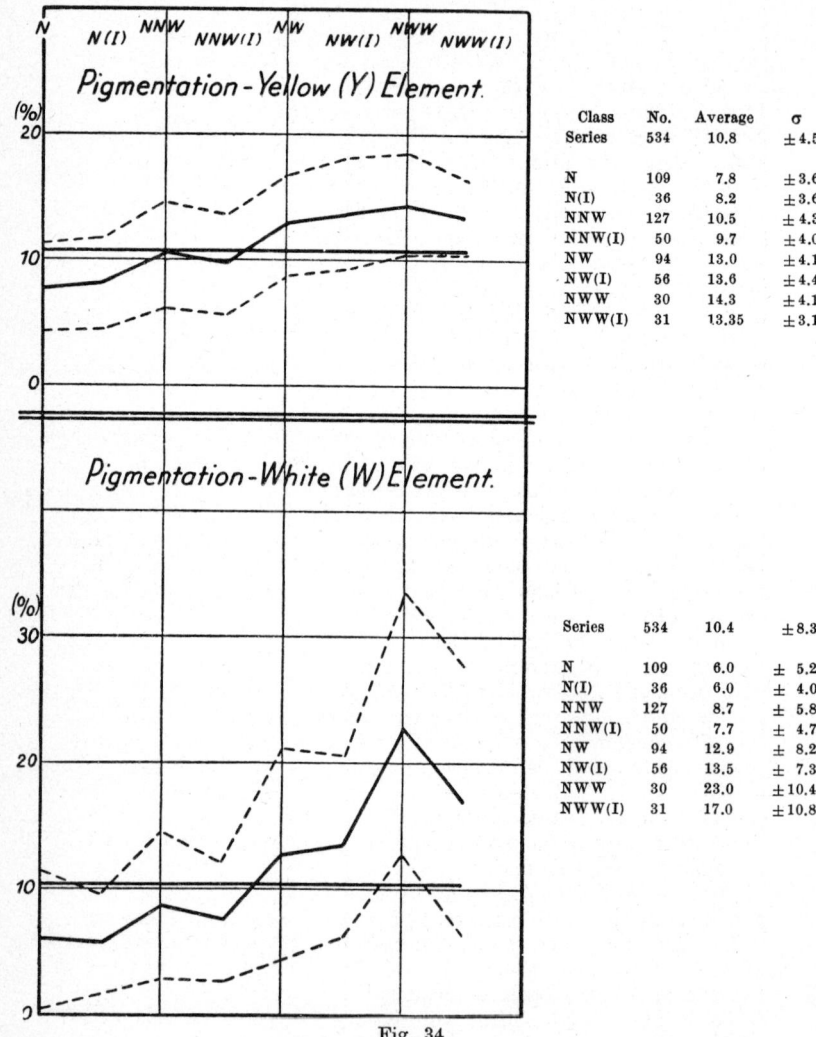

Fig. 34.
Change in Average Values of Pigmentation, Yellow (Y) and White (W), with Various Degrees of Mixed Negro-White Ancestry. Howard University Sample.

When the influence of the various amounts of White ancestry on the physical form of the American Negro is considered, there is no such question. In this case, crossing is a matter of common historical knowledge, the only point being the extent to which the mingling of these two racial types has occurred. The genealogical figures apparently show that the White element has mixed with the Negro to a much greater degree than has been generally recognized, since only 22.0 % of the total number of adults of the present sample who gave their genealogies claimed to be without either White or Indian ancestry. It is possible, of course, that isolated communities would exhibit greater proportions of unmixed Negroes, but I believe that the results which have been given before in the various discussions of this point are not of such a nature as to lead us to the position that this would make any great difference in the percentage of unmixed Negroes in the American Negro population as a whole.

In any event, the consideration of the genealogies brings us to the question of their validity. For convenience, the results which have been discussed in some detail in Chapter VI are again presented in the preceding diagrams, which have been constructed in order to give the differences between the averages in graphic as well as tabular form, so that they may be the more readily envisaged. In the graph for each trait, the heavy horizontal line represents the mean for the series as a whole, while the heavy broken line connects the averages for the eight genealogical classes, which are placed on the vertical lines running down the page. The dotted lines above and below the heavy irregular line represent respectively plus (above) and minus (below) once the mean square deviations of the respective means. A consideration of these average values shows us that in the traits of head length (and cephalic index), of nasal width, height of the ear, lip thickness, both at the center and at the right side of the mouth, width of the mouth, total facial height, bizygomatic width, length of the middle finger, all four colors of the color top for pigmentation, the distance between the inner and outer corners of the eyes and interpupillary distance, hip width, height sitting and stature, there are consistent differences between the averages.

The traits for which there seem merely to be chance distributions of the averages about the mean for the entire sample are head width, nasal height, both depth dimensions of the nose, ear width, upper facial height, hand width, minimum forehead width, acromion width and height of the head. It will be readily observed that the first list comprises, without exception, all the traits which differ strikingly in White and Negro types, while the others are such as were measured because it was felt that significant differences might be indicated by them. However, it will be seen that, in the main, those traits for which there are appreciable differences between the averages of the classes follow the change from Negroid to the White type with increasing amounts of White ancestry, while those which do not follow this line of change (the second list above), are those in which the differences between the unmixed parental stocks are indeterminate. There are some traits, indeed, which move in the opposite direction from that which would be expected. These are mouth width (although lip thickness goes very strongly from more to less Negroid with increasing White ancestry), total facial height, and bizygomatic width. Of course, these latter two are doubtful, since there are not sufficient data from White populations to allow us to draw conclusions. But, in the main, it may safely be said that the genealogical classes, selected on the basis of the statements of the persons measured, follow from Negroid to Caucasoid characteristics as the individuals group themselves as having lesser or greater amounts of White ancestry.

This is of particular methodological interest, for it indicates that more use can be made of Negro genealogical material than has hitherto been thought possible. It has been a commonplace that the Negro is unable to give genealogical information that can be at all relied upon. This is held to be due, in large part, to the historically attested looseness of family ties during slavery, and also to the widely accepted thesis of sexual irresponsibility of the Negro. I do not hold that the individual statements of the persons who have given these genealogies can be accepted at their face value, for I do not believe that genealogical information, no matter from whom obtained, gives anything but the roughest sort of instrument for the analysis of populations, especially where generations preceding the parental one are investigated. But I believe that the data gathered in this study demonstrate that the current idea that "the Negro does not know his father" is fallacious, and that, for a given group for which genealogies are taken, such use can be made of their statements as to ancestry as can be made of statements from any other element of our population that lacks written records of ancestry.

There are, of course, several important practical reservations which must always be kept in mind in the use of genealogies of Negroes; the element of suspicion which is present when these data are being obtained by a White student; the element of reluctance to admit White ancestry when there is any suggestion that these data may be made public or used in any fashion which might cast social discredit on the individuals from whom they have been obtained; the invidious nature of Indian ancestry in the *mores* of the Negro population of this country; and finally, perhaps most important of all, the necessity of making very clear just what is meant by the term "Negro" so that it will be understood in its biological rather than in its current sociological sense, — all these make it difficult to obtain data of this kind. In certain cases, there is also a tendency to claim White ancestry, where the claim of descent from distinguished historical White personages is thought to bring prestige. But when precautions against these obstacles are taken in the manner in which we have tried to take them, it is believed that the statements to be obtained are as reliable as any genealogical statement, and I believe that the anthropometric data prove the truth of this assertion.

6.

But not only are the genealogies substantiated as to their trustworthiness by the anthropometric data taken from those who gave them, but I believe that the classes themselves, in the differences between their means, point to the traits which are of the greatest importance in studying Negro-White differences.[1] This may be reasoning in a circle, and undoubtedly would be, if a preliminary study which I made,[2] using measurements taken on Negro school children of unknown ancestry, had not been undertaken with the object of surveying the data in hand in order to obtain possible clues for further procedure. In that study, the two outstanding traits which show racial differences, width of nose and thickness of the lips, were tabulated for a group of 116 American Negro boys of from 13 to 14 years of age. The nasal width was divided at the average, and also the lip thickness, four classes resulting: narrow lips and thin nose (NT), broad lips and thin nose (BT), narrow lips and wide nose (NW), and broad lips and wide nose (BW). Other traits were then allowed to vary within these four groups, although it might have been better had the second and third of them been consolidated, leaving three classes: most White, about the same amount of White and Negro, and most Negroid, as far as the two traits used as criteria were concerned. That they are the two which would logically be selected from those which can be measured objectively goes without saying, and that they vary together in reasonably satisfactory fashion to allow of their use appears from the correlation which I obtained between them when I correlated them for the Howard University sample as a whole, + 0.3. The results of this preliminary investigation may be given here again, although only the means are included in the presentation below:

Trait	NT	BT	NW	BW
Stature (cm.)	146.4	147.8	150.0	151.8
Head Length (mm.)	184.7	186.3	187.2	186.5
Upper Facial Height (mm.)	61.5	64.8	63.2	63.3
Total Facial Height (mm.)	106.4	111.2	110.9	111.7
Bizygomatic Width (mm.)	123.4	124.6	128.3	127.6

---

[1] See Todd and Lindala (I), for the traits which their work has shown to be important in this connection.
[2] Herskovits, (I).

Trait	NT	BT	NW	BW
Height of Nose (mm.)	44.3	45.75	47.0	47.1
Depth of Nose (mm.)	18.8	19.1	20.3	20.1
Height of Ear (mm.)	55.1	57.6	57.9	58.2
Width of Ear (mm.)	33.6	33.6	32.9	33.8
Width of Hand (mm.)	73.2	75.0	77.8	76.9
Length of Middle Finger (mm.)	90.9	94.4	96.0	94.9
Pigmentation, N (%)	75.7	73.0	75.8	77.8
R (%)	11.3	12.2	10.8	10.2
Y (%)	7.9	8.0	6.6	6.0
W (%)	7.1	6.8	6.6	6.9
Height Sitting (cm.)	73.1	74.0	74.7	76.0

It will be seen from this tabulation that the traits included vary within these groups of differing nose and lip measurements much as they would be expected to vary from the comparative tables in Chapter III, but not so closely as is the case with the genealogical classes.

It has been suggested that if a third trait were added to nose width and lip thickness, such as the black element in pigmentation, or ear height, the correspondence would be much closer, nor do I doubt that this would be the case. But from the general correspondence between this preliminary study of a small group, and that of the much larger genealogical classes in the Howard University adult male Negro sample, we may safely state that those traits which are of value in showing differences between Negroes and Whites, and in studying samples of our Negro population of differing amounts of crossing, are those in which the differences between the genealogical groups come out most clearly. This result could also be obtained from a study of the existing data on European and African populations, but these are only available in satisfactory number for a very few traits, and it is believed that the value of the present study with regard to this methodological point is to indicate such traits as should be included in future measurements of populations of both types.

7.

Let us now consider the variabilities of the several genealogical classes within the Howard sample, and the light which this may throw on the problem that has already been discussed. It will be remembered that the variability for the sample of this study is, for a majority of traits, smaller or no larger than those for other unmixed populations of the three parent stocks. In view of the opinion so largely held that the mean square variability is an index to racial purity, the present analysis should also prove of interest beause of the light it may throw upon heredity.

It must be remembered that the four genealogical classes into which the Howard University series has been divided do not represent persons whose complete ancestry is known, and therefore these classes are not to be regarded as genealogically homogeneous. Sample genealogies which show the manner in which the lacunae were treated have been presented in Chapter I (p. 14). However, it may be well to repeat that the genealogical classes were formed on the basis of the racial position of the known ancestors. This means that the actual composition of each of the four genealogical groups is more heterogeneous than the simplified nomenclature indicates, for the greater the number of unknown ancestors in a group, the greater the heterogeneity of descent that group may be assumed to have. Table XCIX shows that in all groups, the racial background of a considerable proportion of the grandparents was unknown.

Theoretically, the effect of this should be as follows: assuming that the classes represent definite combinations, each having four ancestors either racially pure or at least evenly mixed (something not by any means the case) the following classes would result:

$$N_4 \quad N_3W \quad N_2W_2 \quad NW_3 \quad [W_4]$$

In these the number subjoined to the letter indicates the number of grandparents belonging to each race which the members of each of the five classes would have. In the case of a person who failed to report one grandparent, then, it is obvious that this grandparent, if known, might cause the person to be classified in a group adjacent to that in which he has actually been placed; i. e., a member of the NNW class failing to report one grandparent might actually be N or NW. When we consider the cases of those who failed to report two grandparents the matter becomes more complicated, for the two unknown ancestors would represent the following classes, in the frequencies indicated by the parentheses following each grouping:

$$N_8(1) \quad N_7W_1(2) \quad N_6W_2(3) \quad N_5W_3(4) \quad N_4W_4(5) \quad N_3W_5(4)$$
$$N_2W_6(3) \quad N_1W_7(2) \quad [W_8(1)]$$

Of the present descendants of these twenty-five classes one group would be N, one NW, and 23 NNW. In the event that three ancestors are unreported, 125 possibilities present themselves.

Lacking historical data, it is impossible to calculate the proportion of those who belong to other classes because they did not give their complete ancestry in the second ascending generation, since the ratios of the classes in preceding generations are unknown. The ages of most persons represented in the Howard series range between 20 and 25 years. If we assume the average age of their parents at the time of the birth of these men to be 25 years, they would have been born from 45 to 50 years ago, and the grandparents from 70 to 75 years ago, or before the Civil War. It is quite possible, therefore, that any of those, of the unmixed Negro class who gave incomplete genealogies may actually represent some White admixture, and of the 14.7% of those in the unmixed Negro group who knew three grandparents, one set of individuals may be pure N, others varying degrees of NNW, while, among those who reported only one grandparent, 20 out of the 125 possible groupings mentioned above may actually belong in the NWW class.

At the same time, when we test our assumptions in this regard, we find that there is surprisingly little difference in variability between the members of each genealogical group who report four ancestors, and those who give incomplete reports. The differences

Table XCIX
Proportion of Persons in Howard University Series Reporting all or part of their Ancestry in the First and Second Ascending Generations

Genealogical Class	No. of Parents Reported as Known			No. of Grandparents Reported as Known				
	0	1	2	0	1	2	3	4
N								
No.	2	3	104	12	6	15	16	60
% of total H. U. series	1.8	2.75	95.4	11.0	5.5	13.8	14.7	55.05
N(I)								
No.	0	3	33	5	5	5	3	18
% of total H. U. series	0.0	8.3	91.7	13.9	13.9	13.9	8.3	50.0
NNW								
No.	1	3	125	10	7	18	17	79
% of total H. U. series	.8	2.3	96.9	7.8	5.5	14.1	13.3	59.7
NNW(I)								
No.	0	3	48	2	1	8	6	34
% of total H. U. series	0.0	5.9	94.1	3.8	1.9	15.1	11.3	66.7
NW								
No.	3	7	85	15	10	18	9	43
% of total H. U. series	3.2	7.4	89.5	15.8	10.5	18.95	9.5	45.3
NW(I)								
No.	0	1	56	0	4	7	12	34
% of total H. U. series	0.0	1.8	98.2	0.0	7.0	12.3	21.05	59.65
NWW								
No.	1	1	28	1	1	2	6	20
% of total H. U. series	3.3	3.3	93.3	3.3	3.3	6.6	20.7	66.7
NWW(I)								
No.	0	0	31	0	0	2	5	24
% of total H. U. series	0.0	0.0	100.0	0.0	0.0	6.7	16.7	77.6

may be seen in Table C, in which a number of traits in which Negroes and Whites are distinctly different have been utilized as a check on the conclusions that have been drawn from a consideration of the variabilities under discussion. The members of the four genealogical classes (without Indian) who reported all four grandparents and those whose reports are incomplete were sorted out from their groups and the averages and variabilities computed. The results show that in spite of the element of added knowledge of ancestry, there is little

Table C
Averages and Variabilities of Howard University Genealogical Groups for those of Completely and Incompletely Reported Grandparental Ancestry.

	Four Grandparent Series			Less-than-four-Grandparent Series		
	No.	Average		No.	Average	
Head Length (cm.)	59	197.6	±7.01	50	198.3	±5.32
	75	197.2	±7.52	49	196	±5.85
	46	195.1	±6.28	49	197.1	±6.36
	22	196.2	±6.96	8	195.1	—
Cephalic Index (%)	59	77.1	±3.44	50	76.6	±2.80
	75	77.2	±3.70	49	76.5	±3.53
	46	77.6	±2.73	49	76.9	±3.05
	22	78.2	±3.46	8	78.0	—
Nostril Width (mm.)	59	43.5	±2.69	50	43.4	±2.91
	75	41.6	±3.83	49	40.9	±2.82
	46	39.8	±2.95	49	40.1	±3.04
	22	36.9	±3.76	8	39.25	—
Lip Thickness	59	23.65	±3.90	50	24.6	±4.58
	75	22.1	±4.36	49	22.55	±4.14
	46	21.6	±4.43	49	22.6	±3.46
	22	17.6	±3.51	8	21.0	—
Ear Height (mm.)	59	59.4	±4.91	50	60.3	±4.19
	75	59.3	±3.88	49	60.3	±4.17
	46	61.7	±3.79	49	60.9	±3.77
	22	60.6	±3.61	8	61.0	—
Length of Middle Finger (mm.)	59	109.9	±5.71	50	108.6	±5.88
	75	108.4	±5.86	49	108.8	±6.42
	45	107.3	±6.07	49	109.05	±5.16
	22	105.8	±6.36	8	111.0	—
Height Sitting (cm.)	58	87.2	±3.11	44	87.4	±2.89
	70	88.4	±3.59	42	88.4	±2.92
	41	88.6	±3.31	46	88.1	±3.21
	18	89.6	±2.83	5	89.5	—
Pigmentation, (% N)	59	75.4	±10.31	50	75.5	±10.14
	75	67.5	±11.90	47	69.1	±11.03
	45	60.9	±11.81	49	61.4	±12.59
	22	45.9	±11.58	8	56.7	—

difference to be seen, so that the failure to report apparently does not affect conclusions which have been drawn from the consideration of the variabilities of the group as a whole. This may be in part due to lack of definite knowledge of the ancestry of grandparents, for it may be expected that definite information in regard to their position in the four classes is not available to the informants.

There is the added difficulty, previously mentioned, of the meaning of the term "Negro". As has been pointed out, the term as applied in the United States is, in the main, a sociological one, and indicates

Table
Variabilities of Traits Measured in Adult Male American Negroes, by
(The class lowest in variability

Trait [1]	N	N(I)
Stature (cm.)	5.65	6.49
Height Sitting (cm.)	3.07	3.36
Width of Shoulders	20.80	20.55
Width of Hips	18.25	*16.15*
Length of Head	6.54	6.40
Width of Head	5.23	5.43
Cephalic Index (%)	3.22	2.98
Height of Head	4.19	4.67
Width of Forehead	6.44	5.88
Inner Corners of Eyes	2.20	2.78
Outer Corners of Eyes	4.42	5.97
Interpupillary Distance	*3.03*	4.05
Nasal Height	3.16	3.65
Nasal Width	*2.81*	4.26
Nasal Depth (s.—t.)	2.14	1.91
Nasal Depth (c.—t.)	2.29	2.48
Upper Facial Height	4.01	5.69
Total Facial Height	*5.59*	7.34
Bizygomatic Width	5.40	7.07
Width of Mouth	3.77	4.40
Thickness of Lips, center	4.16	4.85
Thickness of Lips, right	3.91	4.79
Height of Ear	4.57	5.44
Width of Ear	3.21	3.01
Width of Hand	*3.71*	4.87
Length of Middle Finger	5.96	6.79
Pigmentation: N (%)	10.34	*9.51*
R (%)	2.93	2.61
Y (%)	3.57	3.64
W (%)	5.24	*4.02*
	159.85	171.04
Average	5.33	5.70
Number of traits for which variability is lowest	4	3

[1] The unit of measurement is millimeters, unless otherwise noted.

any person who has partial Negro ancestry. Individual Negroes react to this, and when asked if their ancestors were Negro will answer quite naturally in the affirmative unless it is made very plain to them just what is meant by the word. It has already been explained how this was guarded against. All these objections to the contrary notwithstanding, the fact does remain that the means of the unmixed Negro class, in by far the greater number of traits, approach the means for the West African populations more closely than do the averages for any of the groups of various degrees of mixture with White.

CI
Classes of Various Degrees of Mixture according to Genealogical Statements.
f or each trait is italicized).

NNW	NNW(I)	NW	NW(I)	NWW	NWW(I)
6.77	5.65	5.93	*5.29*	7.05	7.54
3.30	*2.45*	3.27	3.35	3.19	2.92
21.55	*16.70*	20.90	20.05	18.10	19.15
17.85	16.35	17.15	18.90	22.15	23.00
7.06	7.59	6.40	*5.86*	6.98	7.00
6.44	5.93	*4.78*	5.37	6.76	6.40
3.77	4.27	*2.88*	3.29	3.58	3.86
4.65	3.92	4.01	4.46	*3.56*	4.21
5.15	7.18	5.55	5.36	*4.40*	5.18
3.04	2.57	3.62	3.21	*1.90*	2.53
5.64	4.79	4.30	4.82	*4.10*	4.63
3.68	3.66	3.40	3.91	3.10	3.71
3.71	2.93	3.24	3.15	3.45	*2.97*
3.44	4.08	3.01	3.75	3.86	4.53
1.86	2.08	1.78	2.23	2.79	*1.73*
2.17	1.93	*1.90*	2.67	2.10	2.20
4.28	3.87	3.92	3.35	4.17	*3.25*
6.20	5.86	6.03	7.13	5.93	5.94
6.87	*5.32*	6.00	5.60	7.18	5.82
4.23	4.01	*3.21*	3.99	3.46	3.71
4.31	*3.20*	3.94	4.57	3.77	3.48
4.15	3.65	3.73	4.09	*3.56*	3.58
4.00	3.53	3.79	3.80	*3.45*	3.74
2.58	2.88	2.67	2.74	*2.06*	2.97
4.54	3.97	3.97	4.33	4.54	3.73
6.04	6.39	*5.69*	6.03	7.41	6.10
11.58	10.39	12.01	11.20	13.67	14.39
2.79	2.94	2.33	2.18	2.25	*1.68*
4.32	3.98	4.07	4.38	4.11	*3.06*
5.80	4.69	8.21	7.33	10.37	10.79
171.77	156.76	161.69	166.49	173.00	173.81
5.72	5.22	5.39	5.55	5.77	5.79
0	4	5	2	7	5

18

Table

Variabilities of Genealogical Classes in Traits Given in Table CI, Reduced to

Trait	N	N(I)
*Stature	.92	1.05
*Height Sitting	.98	1.08
Width of Shoulders	1.02	1.01
*Width of Hips	1.00	.89
*Length of Head	.97	.95
Width of Head	.92	.95
*Cephalic Index	.94	.87
Height of Head	.98	1.09
Width of Forehead	1.12	1.03
Inner Corners of Eyes	.78	.98
Outer Corners of Eyes	.92	1.19
Interpupillary Distance	.86	1.15
Nasal Height	.95	1.10
*Nasal Width	.81	1.23
Nasal Depth (s.—t.)	1.06	.95
Nasal Depth (c.—t.)	1.04	1.13
Upper Facial Height	.99	1.40
*Total Facial Height	.91	1.19
*Bizygomatic Width	.89	1.16
*Width of Mouth	.98	1.14
*Thickness of Lips (center)	1.02	1.18
Thickness of Lips (right)	.99	.96
*Height of Ear	1.14	1.36
Width of Ear	1.16	1.08
Width of Hand	.89	1.17
*Length of Middle Finger	.97	1.11
*Pigmentation N	.92	.84
*R	1.14	1.01
*Y	.90	.92
*W	.77	.59
Total	28.94	31.76
Mean Weighted Percentage of Variability	.965	1.06

The variabilities of the eight genealogical classes for each of the traits measured are summarized, for purposes of comparison, in Table CI. If this table be considered from the point of view of the number of traits in which each of the genealogical classes is lowest in variability, and with special reference to the unmixed Negro group, we find, contrary to what might be expected, that the latter is least variable in only four out of the thirty traits considered, the NWW being so in seven of them, the NW and NWW(I) in five each. The averages of the mean square deviations of all traits measured, for each class, are given on p. 276.

CII
Percentage of Average Weighted Variability of all Classes in each Trait.

NNW	NNW(I)	NW	NW(I)	NWW	NWW(I)
1.10	.92	.96	.86	1.14	1.22
1.06	.79	1.05	.98	1.02	.94
1.06	.82	1.03	.98	.89	.95
.98	.90	.94	1.04	1.22	1.26
1.05	1.13	.95	.87	1.04	1.04
1.13	1.04	.82	.94	1.18	1.12
1.10	1.24	.84	.96	1.04	1.10
1.09	.92	.94	1.04	.83	.99
.90	1.26	.97	.94	.77	.91
1.08	.91	1.28	1.14	.67	.89
1.16	.99	.88	.99	.84	.95
1.05	1.04	.97	1.11	.88	1.05
1.12	.88	.98	.95	1.04	.89
.99	1.18	.87	1.08	1.11	1.31
.93	1.03	.88	1.11	1.39	.86
.99	.88	.86	1.21	.95	1.00
1.06	.96	.97	.83	1.03	.80
1.01	.95	.98	1.16	.96	.96
1.12	.87	.98	.92	1.18	.95
1.10	1.04	.93	1.04	.90	.97
1.05	.78	.96	1.11	.92	.85
1.05	.92	.94	1.04	.90	.91
1.00	.88	.95	.95	.86	.93
.93	1.04	.96	.99	.74	1.01
1.09	.95	.95	1.04	1.09	.90
.98	1.04	.93	.99	1.21	1.00
1.03	.92	1.06	.99	1.21	1.27
1.08	1.14	.90	.85	.87	.65
1.09	1.01	1.03	1.10	1.04	.77
.86	.69	1.21	1.08	1.53	1.59
31.24	29.12	28.97	30.29	30.45	30.04
1.04	.97	.966	1.01	1.02	1.00

Testing our results in this fashion, we find again that the lowest summated average variability is not that of the unmixed Negro group, where it would be expected were low variability and lack of racial mixture as closely correlated as biologists have assumed, but rather in the group whose descent is more Negro than White, mixed with Indian. On the other hand, the greatest variability is not at the point of greatest mixture (the NW) but rather in that group which is composed of persons who are of preponderantely White ancestry with some Negro admixture.

Class	No.	Summated Average Variability
NNW(I)	51	5.22
N	109	5.33
NW	95	5.39
NW(I)	57	5.55
N(I)	36	5.70
NNW	129	5.72
NWW	30	5.77
NWW(I)	31	5.79

At this point, objection may very readily be raised to the above procedure on the ground that the values are unduly weighted; that if the unmixed Negro were most variable in such a trait as that of stature or width of shoulders, it would tend materially to raise the average of the raw variabilities. The expedient was therefore, tried of reducing the variability of each class in every trait to a percentage of the total weighted variability of all the classes for the trait being analyzed. These results are represented in Table CII. This, of course, does not change the number of traits for which the unmixed Negro group was least variable — four. But it does throw the averages of the summated weighted percental variability into somewhat different groupings for the several classes. The results are as follows:

Class	No.	Average Weighted Percental Variability
N	109	.965
NW	95	.966
NNW(I)	51	.97
NWW(I)	31	1.00
NW(I)	57	1.01
NWW	30	1.02
NNW	129	1.04
N(I)	36	1.06

If only the traits that show considerable differences between Whites and Negroes are considered, the values are as follows:

N	.931
NNW(I)	.966
NW	.983
NW(I)	1.01
N(I)	1.04
NWW	1.04
NWW(I)	1.04
NNW	1.05

Curiously enough, the groups comprising least and most crossing are seen to be practically identical in the first of the above tables, while the highest variability occurs in a group where the infusion of Indian blood must have taken place long ago and which, therefore, might be supposed to have been more or less submerged in the

Negro stream. In the second table only those traits which most decisively differentiate Negroes from Whites have been used. These have been marked with an asterisk in Table CII. It is worthy of further note that the greatest variability is not found in the group representing the greatest racial mixture, the NW, but that in both tables this class is near the N class in average variability.

The problem may be attacked in another way. A portion of the total series of this study comprised measurements of parents and children, taken with the object of making available data for the further study of human heredity. Not many of these data have been worked over as yet, but I have computed the variability of the fraternities in the series, utilizing formulae the derivation and significance of which have been developed by Boas[1] and employed by myself in an earlier study.[2] Briefly, the importance of consideration of statistical results of data of this nature are that granted a given population group composed of various descent lines, then the greater the inbreeding, the lower will be the variability of these strains. On the other hand, the more homogeneous the original stock in the trait being considered, the lower the fraternal variation in that population should be, it being an indication of an original homogeneity or heterogeneity of the ancestry of the population being studied in the trait under consideration. The values of the fraternal variability of cephalic index for the four genealogical classes (disregarding Indian), computed from the family data of this study, are as follows:

Class	Fraternal Variability
NWW	2.66
NNW	2.67
N	2.80
NW	2.88

While the group of greatest mixture shows the largest fraternal variability, that of least, the unmixed Negro, is second highest. An explanation may perhaps lie in the possible absence of decisive differences in head-index in the original populations; in a word, we would be dealing with a cross that, while racially very different in its component elements, would be, for the purposes of head form a mingling of groups which, taken together, might be regarded as relatively homogeneous. However, there is also the possible explanation that the children comprising the fraternities belong to families for many of which only one parent could be located for measurement. In such cases, the genealogical statement of the parent measured was taken as the criterion of the classification into which the children were placed, and it is therefore possible that, were the N group further divided into those families of which

---
[1] Boas, (VIII).
[2] Herskovits, (V).

both parents were measured, and those of which only one could be located, the results for the former group might be more in keeping with the demands of theory.[1]

This last assumption is rendered more plausible by the results obtained by Miss Barnes in her study of the heredity of pigmentation of the present series[2], in which the same procedure was followed. Her results for the N element in the color-top, were:

N	5.67
NNW	6.19
NW	6.99
NWW	7.31

Here we have a result somewhat closer to expectation, although the class of greatest mixture, the NW, does not exhibit the largest fraternal variability, as would be expected.

From this evidence it appears that in no case are we dealing with Mendelian inheritance determined by a single or a few unit characters. The point may be made that a very complex sort of multiple Mendelianism is operative, and that the results obtained in this study do not allow us to dispute this position. Whether blending, in the accepted use of the term, has occurred between the parent types which have gone into the formation of the American Negro or not, is again a point for dispute. Statistically, when we envisage the averages for the American Negro population in comparison with those for the corresponding traits in the African, European and American Negro peoples to whom it is related, and its homogeneity as evidenced by the variabilities of these traits, there can be no doubt but that this is a possible interpretation. But an apparent blend based on the consideration of statistical constants, and one that is a true blend in the genetic use of the term are vastly different. Miss Barnes' analysis of the heredity of pigmentation in the families of the series of this study, while it showed that simple Mendelian heredity, or even multiple Mendelian heredity with two or three factors is certainly not operative, also demonstrated that simple blending is also not the process by which the present form of pigmentation of the American Negro has developed. These results substantiate my own earlier analysis of the same data for cephalic index, one result of which has been given above.

It is not maintained that these data, and the results obtained from them, are sufficient to do anything more than furnish a

---

[1] The study of the heredity of pigmentation in the families of the series of this study made by Barnes (I), shows that neither blending nor simple Mendelian heredity, nor multiple Mendelian heredity working with two or three unit characters, is operative. Multiple factors may be assumed as a possible hypothesis. But if these are operative, there are so many factors at work that they cannot be discerned.

[2] Barnes, (I).

lead for further study of the mechanisms of heredity in human beings. This calls for much more family material than is available, and analysis of the measurements of parents and children in many more traits than the two referred to above. But, by and large, if Mendelian principles are operative to the degree to which it has been claimed, it is strange that findings as indecisive as those presented here have resulted from an intensive analysis of a mixed population.

8.

If the findings of this research be summarized, the following points may be said to represent the conclusions which have been drawn:
1. The study of Negroes by means of genealogical methods is feasible, and the idea that parentage among Negroes is so uncertain as to vitiate any findings made through the utilization of genealogical material is contrary to the evidence, since groups based on genealogical statements of the individuals measured show the differences between groups of unmixed Negro blood and various amounts of Negro-White crossing which would be expected if the statements were valid.
2. The genealogical information obtained in this study, as to the amount of racial mixture represented in the American Negro population as a whole, shows that the Census estimate of 85% pure Negro ("Black") is not correct.
3. The analysis of traits within the genealogical groupings shows that the traits vary from Negroid to Caucasoid with the amount of crossing which has occurred in the various classes; that the Indian element does not seem to make appreciable difference; and that it is difficult to discern segregation of genetic types in the genealogical groups.
4. Although the Indian element is not readily discernible in the analysis of traits within the genealogical classes, there is no reason to doubt the statement of 29% of the persons measured who claim to have partial Indian ancestry, partly because of known historical contacts between the Negroes and the Indians, and particularly because the statements as to the amounts of Negro-White ancestry check so satisfactorily with the results of anthropometric measurements.
5. The validity of the sample of this study as representative of the American Negro population in general is indicated. By the analysis of the places of birth of the individuals comprising it, by checking the component series from various localities one against the other, and by comparing the adult males of this study with other samples of male American Negroes, one much larger than this one, we obtain ample grounds for assuming all these series to be samples of the same larger population.

6. Skin color should be studied as an important index of differences between Negro and White racial groups, but until a method of studying it in more objective fashion, and with less arbitrary classification of elements is devised, it requires careful statistical manipulation to compare the results of different observers. Observations on different groups by a single observer with known observational error are directly comparable, and the amount of the black (N) segment of the color top is a valid indication of varying degrees of darkness of skin in such a case.
7. If the averages for the total adult male portion of the entire sample be compared with those for similar traits studied in populations of African Negro, European or American White, and American Indian composition, the values for the American Negro usually fall between those for the Negro groups, on the one hand, and the White--Indian peoples, on the other.
8. The type which the American Negro seems to be evolving in this country is a relatively homogeneous one, as shown by earlier studies made in the course of this research, and by the fact that the variability of the adult male section of the sample of this study (as well as of other samples of American Negroes available) has not been increased beyond the variabilities of the parental races, in which many local varieties exist that are much more variable than their mixed Negro descendants.
9. The current *mores* among the American Negro population bearing on the invidious nature of light color, makes for a strong tendency toward marriage between dark men and light women. This serves to set up a social mechanism which, if continued, will bring about more Negroid features for this type in the future.
10. The lesser variability of the American Negro sample, when it is compared to unmixed parent populations, shows that the physical types cannot be explained as being due to simple Mendelian inheritance. Rather does it seem that if Mendelian principles are to be said to apply, multiple factors must be assumed for each character.

REFERENCES.

Baxter, J. H. (I), Statistics, Medical and Anthropological, of the Provost-Marshall-General's Office. Washington, 1875.
Bean, R. B. (I), Some Ears and Types of Men. Amer. Anth., (n. s.), xvii (1915), pp. 529—632.
— (II), The Sitting Height. Amer. Jour. Phys. Anthropology, v, (1922), pp. 349—390.
— (III), review of "The American Negro", by M. J. Herskovits, Amer. Jour. Phys. Anthropology, xii, (1928), pp. 218—220.
Boas, Franz (I), The Half-Blood Indian, an Anthropometric Study. Popular Science Monthly, (1894).
— (II), Zur Anthropologie der Nordamerikanischen Indianer. Verh. d. Berliner anthrop. Gesellschaft, (1895), pp. 367—411.
— (III), Changes in Bodily Form of Descendants of Immigrants. Senate doc. 208, 61st Congress, 2nd Session. Washington, 1910.
— (IV), ibid., Final Report. Washington, 1911.
— (V), Report on an Anthropometric Investigation of the Population of the United States. Jour. Amer. Statistical Ass'n., (1922), pp. 181—208.
— (VI), Bemerkungen über die Anthropometrie der Armenier. Zeit. f. Ethnologie, (1924), pp. 74—82.
— (VII), The Cephalic Index. Amer. Anthropologist, (n. s.), i, (1899), pp. 438—446.
— (VIII), On the Variety of Lines of Descent represented in a Population. Amer. Anthrop. (n. s.), xviii; (1916), pp. 1—9.
— (IX), Data personally communicated.
— (X), Remarks on the Anthropological Study of Children. Trans. 15th Int. Cong. of Hygiene and Demography. Washington, 1912.
Czekanowski, J. (I), Wissenschaftliche Ergebnisse der Deutschen Zentral-Afrika Exped., (1907—8). Bd. I, (1922), pp. 143—473. Ethnographie, Anthropologie, IV.
Davenport, Charles B., (I), Heredity of Skin Color in Negro-White Crosses. Carnegie Institution of Washington. Washington, 1913.
— (II), Race Crossing in Jamaica. Scientific Monthly, xxvii, (1928), pp. 225 — 238.
Davenport, Charles B. and Steggerda, Morris (I), Nasal Breadth in Negro x White Crossing. Eugenical News, xiii (1928), pp. 36—37.
Davenport, Charles B. and Love, Albert G. (I), The Medical Department of United States Army in the World War. vol. xv, Statistics; part 1, Army Anthropology. Washington, 1921.
Department of Commerce, (I), Instructions to Enumerators (for the 14th Census of the United States). Washington, 1919.
Dowd, Jerome (I), The Negro in American Life. New York, 1926.
Fischer, Eugen (I), Die Rehobother Bastards. Jena, 1913.
Ferguson, George O., Jr. (I), The Psychology of the Negro, an Experimental Study. Archives of Philosophy, no. xxxvi. Columbia Univ. Contributions to Philosophy and Psychology, (xxv), no 1, 1910.
Goring, Charles (I), The English Criminal. London, 1913.
Gould, B. A. (I), Investigations into the Military and Anthropological Statistics of American Soldiers. Amer. Sanitary Commission. Sanitary Memoirs of the War of the Rebellion. New York, 1869.

Hallowell, A. I. (I), Unpublished measurements on the Montagnais-Naskapi.
Hart, Hornell (I), University of Iowa Studies in Child Welfare, vol. i, no. 7.
Herskovits, Melville J. (I), Preliminary Observations in a Study of Negro-White Crossing. Opportunity, iii (1925), pp. 69—74.
— (II), A Further Discussion of the Variability of Family Strains in the Negro-White Population of New York City. Jour. Amer. Statistical Ass'n., (n. s.), xx, (1925), pp. 380—389.
— (III), The Color Line. The American Mercury, vi, (1925) pp. 204—208.
— (IV), Correlation of Length and Breadth of Head of American Negroes. Amer. Jour. Phys. Anthropology, ix (1926), pp. 87—97.
— (V), On the Negro-White Population of New York City: The Use of the Variability of Family Strains as an Index of Heterogeneity or Homogeneity. Proceedings, xxi Congrès International des Américanistes. The Hague, (1926), pp. 5—12.
— (VI), Age-Changes in Skin Color of American Negroes. Amer. Jour. Phys. Anthropology, ix (1926), pp. 321—327.
— (VII), Social Pattern, a Methodological Study. Social Forces, iv (1925), pp. 57—69.
— (VIII), Some Observation on the Growth of Colored Boys, Amer. Jour. Phys. Anthropology, vii (1924), pp. 439—446.
— (IX), Growth of Interpupillary Distance in American Negroes. Amer. Jour. Phys. Anthropology, ix (1926), pp. 467—470.
— (X), Variability and Racial Mixture. The American Naturalist, lxi (1927), pp. 68—81.
— (XI), Some Physical Characteristics of the American Negro Population. Social Forces, vi (1927), pp. 93—98.
— (XII), The Physical Form and Growth of the American Negro. Anthropologischer Anzeiger, iv (1927), pp. 293—316.
— (XIII), The American Negro, A Study in Racial Crossing. New York, 1928.
Hooton, E. A. (I), The Ancient Inhabitants of the Canary Islands. Harvard African Studies, vol. vii, 1925.
Hrdlička, Aleš (I), The Old White Americans. Proc. xixth International Congress of Americanists, Washington, (1917). pp. 582—601.
— (II), The Stature of the Old Americans. Amer. Jour. Phys. Anthropology, v (1922), p. 210.
— (III), Bulletin 30 (Handbook of the American Indian), Bureau of American Ethnology, pp. 55—56.
— (IV), The Old Americans. Baltimore, 1925.
— (V), Anthropology of the American Negro. Historical Notes and Bibliography. Amer. Jour. Phys. Anthropology, x, (1927), pp. 205—235.
— (VI), The Full-blood American Negro. Amer. Jour. Phys. Anthropology, xii (1928), pp. 15—35.
Johnson, Guy B. (I), Newspaper Advertisements and Negro Culture. Jour. of Social Forces, iii, (1924—5), pp. 706—709.
Karutz, Dr. (I), Ein Beitrag zur Anthropologie des Ohres. Archiv f. Anthrop. Bd. (xxvi), p. 375.
Leys, N. M. and Joyce, T. A. (I), Notes on a Series of Physical Measurements from East Africa. Jour. Royal Anth. Institute, xliii (1913), pp. 195—267.
Lundborg, H., and Linders, G. (I), The Racial Characteristics of the Swedish Nation. Stockholm, 1927.
Macdonnc!!, ‾.7. R. (I), On Criminal Anthropometry and the Identification of Criminals. Biometrika, xi (1915—19), pp. 67ff.
Mansfeld, Alfred (I), Urwald Dokumente, Vier Jahre unter den Crossfluß-negern Kameruns. Berlin, 1908.
Martin, Rudolf (I), Lehrbuch der Anthropologie in Systematischer Darstellung. Jena, 1914.
"Opportunity" (I), Editorial, The Vanishing Mulatto. iii (1925), p. 291.
Orensteen, Meyer M. (I), Correlation of Anthropometrical Measurements in Cairo-born Natives. Biometrika, xi (1915—17), pp. 67ff.

Pearson, Karl (I), Phil. Trans. Royal Soc. clxxxvi, "A", p. 386.
— (II), The Chances of Death. vol. I, p. 295.
— (III), Note on the Skin-Color of the Crosses between Negro and White. Biometrika, vi (1908—9), pp. 348ff.
Pearson, Karl and Tippett, L. H. C. (I), On Stability of Cephalic Index within the Race. Biometrika, xvi (1924) pp. 118—138.
Puccioni, Dott. Nello (I), Richerche Antropometrichi sui Somali. Archivio per l'Antropologia e la Etnologia. xli (1911), pp. 295—306.
Rattray, Capt. R. S. (I), Ashanti. (especially appendix entitled "Notes on the Measurements of the Ashant", by L. Dudley Buxton, p. 335). Oxford, 1923.
Reuter, Edward B. (I), The Mulatto in the United States, Boston, 1908.
— (II), The American Race Problem. New York, 1927.
Sawtell, Ruth (I), Sex Differences in the Bone Growth of Young Children. Amer. Jour. Phys. Anthropology, xii (1928) pp. 293ff.
— (II), Studies in the Ossification and Growth of Children from One to Eight Years. Amer. Jour. of Diseases of Children (1929).
Schuster, E. (I), First Results from the Oxford Anthropometric Laboratory. Biometrika, v (1906—7), pp. 298ff.
Seligman, C. G. (I), Some Little-known Tribes of the Southern Sudan. Jour. Royal Anth. Institute, lv, (1925), pp. 13—37.
Sullivan, Louis R. (I), Marquesan Somatology, with Comparative Notes on Samoa and Tonga. Memoirs, Bernice P. Bishop Museum, ix, no. 2. Honolulu, 1923.
— (II), Anthropometry of the Siouan Tribes. Anthrop. Papers, Am. Museum Nat. Hist., xxiii, III (1920), pp. 81—174.
Struck, Bernhard (I), Versuch einer Karte des Kopfindex im mittleren Afrika. Zeit. f. Ethnologie, liv—lv (1922—3), pp. 51—113.
Todd, T. Wingate (I), Cranial Capacity and Linear Dimensions in White and Negro. Amer. Jour. Phys. Anthropology, vi (1923), pp. 97ff.
— (II) Entrenched Negro Physical Characteristics. Human Biology, i (1929), pp. 57—69.
Todd, T. W., and Kuenzel, Wilhelmina (I), The Thickness of the Scalp. Jour. of Anatomy, lviii (1924).
Todd, T. W., and van Gorder, Leona (I), The Quantitative Determination of Black Pigmentation in the Skin of the American Negro. Amer. Jour. Phys. Anthropology, iv (1921), pp. 239—260.
Todd, T. Wingate, Blackwood, Beatrice, and Beecher, Harry (I). The Color-top Method of Recording Skin Pigmentation. Amer. Jour. Phys. Anthropology, xi (1928), pp. 187—204.
Todd, T. Wingate, and Lindala, Anna (I). Dimensions of the Body; Whites and Negroes of Both Sexes. Amer. Jour. Phys. Anthropology, xii (1928), pp. 35—121.
Tocher, J. F. (I), The Anthropometric Characteristics of the Inmates of Asylums of Scotland. Biometrika, v (1906—7), pp. 298ff.
Tremearne, A. J. N. (I), Notes on the Kagoro and other Nigerian Head-hunters. Jour. Royal Anth. Institute, xlii (1912), pp. 136—199.
Virchow, Rudolf (I), Kopfmaße von 40 Wei- and 19 Kru- Negern. Verh. Zeit. f. Eth., xxi (1889), pp. 85—93.
Von Luschan, Felix, (I), Unpublished measurements on Hawaiian adult males.
West, G. M. (I), Anthropometrische Untersuchungen über die Schulkinder in Worcester, Mass. Archiv f. Anthropologie, xxii (1894) pp. 13—48.
Wissler, Clark (I), The American Indian, New York, 1917.
— (II), Distribution of Stature in the United States. Science Monthly, xviii (1924), pp. 129—143.
— (III), Sex Differences in Growth of the Head. School and Society, xxv (1927), no. 631.